EXTENT OF OLD PARABOLIC DUNE

N 060

EXTENT OF OLD PARABOLIC DUNE

N 040

E 040

E 040

E O60

N

EDGE OF PIPELINE TRENCH

N 020

N 040

E O60

E 000

DATUM

THE CASPER SITE

A HELL GAP BISON KILL
ON THE HIGH PLAINS

STUDIES IN ARCHEOLOGY

Consulting Editor: Stuart Struever

Department of Anthropology
Northwestern University
Evanston, Illinois

THE CASPER SITE

A HELL GAP BISON KILL ON THE HIGH PLAINS

Edited by

George C. Frison

Department of Anthropology
University of Wyoming

Academic Press, Inc.

New York   San Francisco   London
A Subsidiary of Harcourt Brace Jovanovich, Publishers

COPYRIGHT © 1974, BY ACADEMIC PRESS, INC.
ALL RIGHTS RESERVED.
NO PART OF THIS PUBLICATION MAY BE REPRODUCED OR
TRANSMITTED IN ANY FORM OR BY ANY MEANS, ELECTRONIC
OR MECHANICAL, INCLUDING PHOTOCOPY, RECORDING, OR ANY
INFORMATION STORAGE AND RETRIEVAL SYSTEM, WITHOUT
PERMISSION IN WRITING FROM THE PUBLISHER.

ACADEMIC PRESS, INC.
111 Fifth Avenue, New York, New York 10003

United Kingdom Edition published by
ACADEMIC PRESS, INC. (LONDON) LTD.
24/28 Oval Road, London NW1

LIBRARY OF CONGRESS CATALOG CARD NUMBER: 74-21592

ISBN 0–12–268550–4

PRINTED IN THE UNITED STATES OF AMERICA

Contents

List of Figures

List of Tables

Acknowledgments

The Casper Site was discovered by amateur archeologists and their wives, Mr. and Mrs. Roderick Laird and Mr. and Mrs. Egolf of Casper, Wyoming. Laird and Egolf dug into the deposit after finding artifacts and bone on the surface. They kept a record of what they found, and immediately reported their findings to the State Archeologist. They could have easily looted part of the site for artifacts, but they did not, and full credit must be accorded to them in recognition of their restraint and concern. Any other course of action on their part could have resulted in a serious loss to Paleo-Indian studies. Both Mr. Laird and Mr. Egolf have made the materials they found at the site available for study.

The site is in an exposed location beside U.S. Interstate 80. Protection was provided by the Wyoming Highway Patrol, the Casper Police Department, and members of the Wyoming Archeological Society living in Casper. The County Commissioners of Natrona County, and especially Mr. John Burke, provided power equipment and fencing to protect the site both before and during excavation.

Funds for excavation were provided by the Wyoming Recreation Commission and the University of Wyoming. A diesel tractor with front end loader and scraper was provided for the duration of the excavation by the late Mr. Bob Barber of Glenrock, Wyoming. Storage facilities were provided by Mr. Tex English and Mr. Travis Womack of Casper. Mr. Womack also provided a number of photographic supplies and services.

The regular crew at the Casper Site consisted of George Zeimens, Timothy Karnes, Charles Reher, Sandra Reher, Ross Hilman, Sandra Poe, Roger Garling and Gordon Taylor. The late Bob Barber and Florence Coates of Glenrock, worked nearly every day at the site. Others helped in their spare time, especially Evelyn Albanese, Robert Brown and Roderick Laird of Casper, Margaret Powers of Sheridan, Wyoming and Mr. and Mrs. William Barlow of Gillette, Wyoming. A contingent of students from Casper College spent two days working at the site. Members of the Wyoming Archeological Society came from all parts of the state to visit and work at the site. The first test excavations were done with the help of Mary Garling and Evelyn Albanese of Casper, and Charles Love and Joanne Mack, at that time both graduate students in Anthropology at the University of Wyoming.

An excellent spirit of cooperation and interest in the project was expressed by the citizenry of Casper. Especially I wish to thank the management of Control Data Corporation for allowing us to excavate the site, and for tolerating the inconveniences caused by the continual stream of visitors. I also especially with to thank Mr. and Mrs. Tex English for the many excellent meals and other refreshments they brought to the crew during the excavation. Many others, though too numerous to mention, also extended hospitality of many kinds to the crew. Their help is deeply appreciated. It should be mentioned that the period of excavation was a difficult one emotionally due to the location and number of visitors. Our intention was to receive everyone with courtesy and welcome. If we sometimes failed to make this sense of hospitality felt, I can only extend my apologies.

A number of individuals provided valuable professional expertise in the analysis of the Casper Site materials. B. Robert Butler of Idaho State University provided an excellent calf skull of *Bison antiquus* and was helpful in discussions of bison taxonomy. Fruitful discussions on various aspects of bison studies were held with Joe Ben Wheat of the University of Colorado, Larry Agenbroad and his students of Chadron State College, Dennis Stanford of the Smithsonian Institution, Dan Witter, graduate student at the University of New Mexico, and Paul O. McGrew of the University of Wyoming. Still others include C. S. Churcher, Stephen A. Hall, John M. Hillerud, Brian O. K. Reeves, and John E. Storer.

Many ideas on bison handling and butchering, along with valuable skeletal materials, came to us from the managers of present day Wyoming bison herds. These include the commercial herd of approximately 2700 head owned by the Durham Meat Company of Gillette, whose foreman Arthur Busskohl, cooperated with us at all times, as did Pete Gardner, who runs a commercial herd of about 500 near Wheatland and George Crouse, who until recently ran about the same number near Laramie.

Much of the nonbison faunal material was identified by Elaine Anderson, who at that time was at the Idaho State University Museum, Joseph R. Jehl of the San Diego Natural History Museum, and Hildegarde Howard, of the Los Angeles County Museum. Identification of snails was done by Aurele La Rocque at Ohio State University. The bone date from the Casper Site was enabled by a small grant from the Wyoming Geological Survey.

Of greatest value was the continual interaction and free association between individuals representing many different areas of interest and expertise.

Drawings of general views of the site and of bone tools were made by Abbie Current. Flaked stone tools were drawn by Connie Robinson. Teeth from the Casper Local Fauna were sketched by Michael Wilson.

June Frison and Diane J. Wilson contributed their services in the typing of final photo-ready copy, and deserve our sincere thanks.

C. Robert Swaim of the University of Wyoming, Department of Anthropology is responsible for the superb photographs of specimens from the site.

Chapter

1

ARCHEOLOGY of the CASPER SITE

GEORGE C. FRISON
University of Wyoming

The Casper archeological site was a bison trap operated by a Paleo-Indian group whose apparent cultural affiliations were to the Hell Gap complex. Hell Gap was formalized as a projectile point type by Agogino (1961) and was first recognized as a cultural complex at the Hell Gap Site in southeastern Wyoming (Irwin-Williams et al. 1973). The chronological position of Hell Gap in relation to other Paleo-Indian complexes was well defined also at the Hell Gap Site.

The Casper Site consisted of a steep-sided trap formed by the wings and leeward end of a parabolic sand dune, into which bison of a form now extinct were driven and killed. The animals were subsequently butchered and the parts saved were removed to another area for further processing. A parabolic dune is best described as U-shaped in transverse cross section with sides anchored by vegetation and its long axis extending to the windward. Such dunes occur as features in areas

of sand that are mostly stabilized by vegetation (Hack 1941). No evidence of cultural activity other than the kill site is presently known from the immediate area although it is assumed that a processing area for the meat and probably also a camp site must have been close by.

THE PRESENT ENVIRONMENT OF THE CASPER SITE AREA

Geography

The site is located about 3,000 feet north and 100 feet above the level of the North Platte River near the west edge of Casper, Wyoming (Fig. 1.1) and also at the north end of Casper Mountain, which forms the extreme northern extension of the Laramie Range (Fig. 1.2). The location is close to the southwestern edge of an area of sand dunes that are all presently covered with

FIGURE 1.1 *Aerial view of the Casper Site area before (top) and after earthmoving activities that revealed the site.*

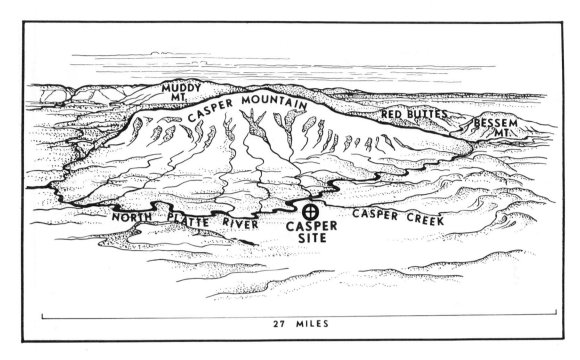

FIGURE 1.2 *Casper Site location along the North Platte River at the north end of the Laramie Range.*

vegetation with the exception of a few active but widely-separated parabolic dunes. The dunes along the North Platte River in the site vicinity have been disturbed recently by industrial building activity and highway construction. This activity has necessitated several attempts at re-stabilization to prevent the serious problems that are resulting from sand transport during periods of high winds so frequent to the area.

The sand dunes extend eastward along the north bank of the North Platte River for about 24 miles and to the north for about the same distance to form a dune area of several hundred square miles (Fig. 1.3). The dune in which the bison were trapped rests directly on the fourth terrace above the present level of the North Platte River. The deepest part of the trough of the old dune was either directly on, or a few inches above this gravel and cobble terrace. A profile cut to the gravel terrace at right angles to

the long axis of the old dune clearly defines its configuration because of pond deposits that formed after the bison kill (Fig. 1.4). In addition the contact between the horizontally-laid sand into which the old dune was formed and later sand deposits that filled the depression can be clearly observed in profile (Fig. 1.5). The main concentration of butchered bison was in the lowest part of the trough. The degree of articulation, the undisturbed nature, and the quality of preservation of the bones indicated that they were covered with sand shortly after they were left. Although the bones in places were covered by as much as 25 feet of sand, there is no evidence that any of the skeletal elements suffered distortion.

Wyoming is an area located at the origin of several major river drainages of the western United States. These include the Green River, one of the major tributaries of the Colorado River, which is west of the Continental Divide

4

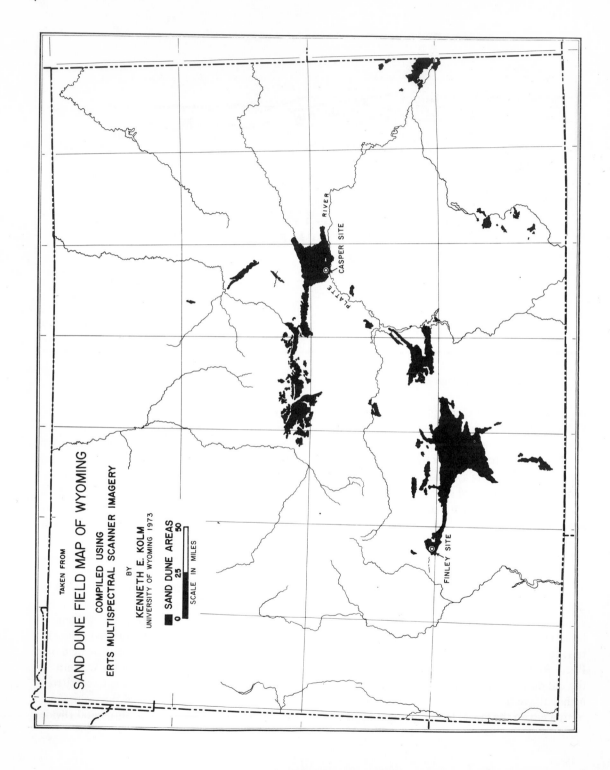

TAKEN FROM

SAND DUNE FIELD MAP OF WYOMING

COMPILED USING
ERTS MULTISPECTRAL SCANNER IMAGERY

BY

KENNETH E. KOLM
UNIVERSITY OF WYOMING 1973

SAND DUNE AREAS

0   25   50

SCALE IN MILES

CASPER SITE

FINLEY SITE

PLATTE RIVER

FIGURE 1.5 *Profile of the old sand dune at the Casper Site showing contact between two sand units.*

and flows south. The Snake River is also west of the Continental Divide, flows west and is a major tributary of the Columbia River. The Yellowstone River, The Wind River-Big Horn River and the Powder River are east of the Continental Divide, flow northeastward and are major tributaries of the Missouri River. The Belle Fourche River, the Cheyenne River and the North Platte River are also east of the Continental Divide, flow eastward to the Missouri River and drain most of eastern Wyoming.

The Rivers systems along with a number of mountain ranges, isolated erosional remnants and intermontane basins (Fig. 1.6) create an area of varied topographic relief and ecological zones. It is, however, the area of eastern Wyoming drained by the North Platte River that is of the greatest significance in this study of Paleo-Indian bison hunters.

The North Platte River drainage area in

FIGURE 1.3 *(Opposite page) Map of Wyoming showing major sand dune areas.*

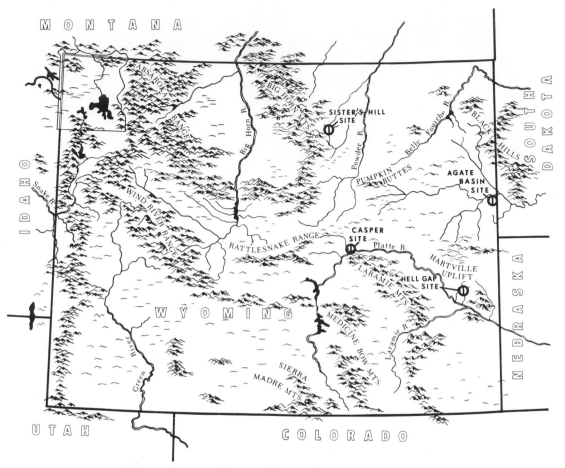

FIGURE 1.6 *Major rivers and topographic features of Wyoming.*

Wyoming and Nebraska is relatively rich in Paleo-Indian evidence. Surface finds are common. A number of sites have been professionally investigated including the James Allen Site (Mulloy 1959), the Scottsbluff Bison Quarry (Schultz 1935), and the Hell Gap Site (Irwin-Williams et al. 1973). The Lindenmeier Site is just over the divide in the South Platte River drainage in Colorado (Roberts 1935, 1936). Many other sites will undoubtedly be discovered in the future both by chance and by design as systematic investigations progress.

The North Platte, one of the major rivers in Wyoming, originates in the high mountain country of extreme northern Colorado and flows directly north into Wyoming through a broad, fertile valley between the Medicine Bow and Sierra Madre mountain ranges. Further north, just before the river flows through the Seminoe Mountains, a dam forms Seminoe Lake, the first of two major artifical reservoirs. The second, a few miles further on, is Pathfinder Lake. At both of these reservoirs, the flats exposed during periods of low water level have yielded quantities of both Paleo-Indian and later cultural materials.

Beyond Pathfinder and the smaller adjacent

Alcova Reservoir, the North Platte River begins to flow eastward around the north end of the Laramie Mountains. After it leaves the vicinity of the Casper Site, it meanders eastward as far as Douglas, Wyoming and then takes a southeasterly direction and follows this course to North Platte, Nebraska and its confluence with the South Platte River, which flows northeasterly out of Colorado. Paleo-Indian material is well known from surface collections gathered along the North Platte River area of Wyoming from Douglas to the Nebraska line. The flats exposed during low water at Glendo Reservoir near Glendo, Wyoming have been especially productive.

The Laramie Range originates near the Colorado-Wyoming line between Cheyenne and Laramie and trends northward for about 75 miles, then trends to the northwest for about the same distance and finally terminates a few miles south of the city of Casper. The Laramie Mountains are rough, and at their higher elevations, open parks alternate with timber-covered and boulder-strewn slopes. The highest point is Laramie Peak, a well-known landmark with an elevation of 10,274 feet. Its position is about 25 miles west and slightly north of Wheatland, Wyoming. The Laramie River, the largest major tributary of the North Platte, originates on the eastern slopes of the Medicine Bow Mountains, flows eastward through the Laramie Basin, then through the Laramie range just south of Laramie Peak, and on to its confluence with the North Platte River at Fort Laramie, Wyoming.

The Laramie Range is about 30 miles across at its maximum width just north of Laramie Peak. Along both flanks of the range in this area are extensive aboriginal stone quarries where weathered limestone formations have exposed deposits of cherts of various kinds and qualities. It seems almost certain that these quarries were used extensively during the Paleo-Indian period as well as later. It seems almost certain also that some of the stone recovered as artifacts at the Casper Site originated at these quarries.

About 30 miles east of Laramie Peak, the North Platte flows just to the south of the Hartville Uplift, a relatively low range of hills which extends northward about 25 miles from its origin near Guernsey, Wyoming. Paleo-Indian evidence in this area includes the Hell Gap Site, the well-known Spanish Diggings and numerous other aboriginal quartzite and chert quarries. Southwest of the Laramie Range lies the Laramie Basin and to the northwest the Shirley Basin. The two basins are separated from each other by a low divide. Both basins have produced a substantial amount of Paleo-Indian evidence, although usually in poor geological and archeologicaly contexts, with the possible exception of the James Allen Site near Laramie. Red quartzite quarries located in Shirley Basin seem almost certainly to be the source of some Casper Site raw materials.

Casper Mountain at an elevation of 8,130 feet is the northern terminus of the Laramie Range. The mountain measures about 20 miles east to west and four miles north to south and has a steep face that breaks off abruptly toward Casper and the North Platte River. From its summit on a clear day, the easternmost end of the Rattlesnake Range can be seen about 25 miles directly to the west, and the southernmost part of the Big Horn Mountains can be observed 60 miles to the northwest. The land between is an open plain dissected by meandering arroyos, both dry and intermittently flowing.

Less than 20 miles north of Casper is an almost imperceptible divide which drops down on its far side into the South Powder River and becomes the southernmost boundary of the Powder River Basin. Sixty-five miles north of Casper and slightly east are the well-known landmarks known as the Pumpkin Buttes. These are erosional remnants capped by the White River Formation and they form a divide between the Powder River Basin and the Belle Fourche River drainage.

Directly northeast of Casper about 30 miles is another low divide which separates the drainage of the Cheyenne River and the North Platte. Eighty miles further in the same direction is the southern terminus of the Black Hills in South Dakota.

Geomorphology

The Casper Site area demonstrates widely varied ecological conditions over short distances. Numerous mountains, smaller uplifts, faulted and deeply eroded areas result in a number of conditions that affect the ecosystem. Precipitation patterns are affected by air movements and changing elevations. Erosional patterns are different in different kinds of exposed geological formations. Different soil types result from different parent materials, erosional processes and conditions of deposition. Plant communities differ from north to south slopes and also as the result of varied temperatures and soil moisture.

To the north, east, and west of the Casper Site the country consists of open rolling hills except for the steep sandstone escarpments along the North Platte River. Much of this area is covered by presently vegetated sand dunes. The precipitation which goes into the sand dunes with little or no runoff raises the water table within the dune areas and causes occasional interdunal ponds that usually dry up in late summer, although some remain the year round. The sandy areas in general lack the arroyo drainage patterns characteristic of the remainder of the region. Exposed outcrops of sandstone are common in the sandy areas however, including some quite long escarpments and buttes where the bedrock has been especially resistant to erosion. Away from the sandy areas the soils are quite different and vary from areas of brown sandy loams to areas of tight clay loams commonly referred to as "gumbo" which make any kind of travel difficult during wet periods. Minor uplifts such as the Rattlesnake Range to the west of the site area

and the Hartville Uplift to the east, break up the monotony of the open, relatively flat country and provide for a variety of flora and fauna.

South of the Casper Site conditions change rapidly. The elevation changes from 5,200 feet at the site to 8,130 feet about 10 miles east on Casper Mountain. The steep mountain slopes are dissected by numerous deep, narrow canyons. The alternating hard and soft sedimentary strata result in alternating perpendicular scarps and steep talus slopes. Further south of Casper Mountain a few miles lie the extensive areas of exposed Precambrian granites that cap the Laramie Range and form yet another set of distinctive landform patterns.

Vegetational Patterns

The site area is on the extreme southwestern edge of a large, continuous area of vegetated sand dunes, with now only occasional areas of moving sand that typifies active parabolic dunes. It is believed, however, that present conditions are not too dissimilar from conditions at the time the Casper Site trap was utilized. Since the trap at the time of use was an active parabolic dune, and since the bison were driven into the sand dune, it seems reasonable to assume that the animals were present in quantities that would justify their regular exploitation through this communal procurement technique. It seems highly unlikely that a herd of bison was driven any great distance to the trap. More likely, the area itself was a favorable one for the animals and they tended to congregate there in large numbers. Successful communal bison procurement strategies almost certainly required a yearly concentration of a critical number of animals in an area, and if the concentration fell below such a critical number, the strategy was changed to one of individual or small-group hunting parties.

The area was then, as now, ideal bison habitat if present conditions are a reliable indicator. Grasses and forbs are plentiful both in and out of sandy areas. Water is available much of the year in interdunal ponds and year-round in the nearby North Platte River. The latter is attractive for other reasons also. Groves of trees and brush thickets provide summer shade and winter browse and shallow sand and mud bars provide places to wallow and fight flies during the summer.

The plant communities of the sand dunes differ from those of the nearby clay loam soils. Noticeable especially during the spring and summer months is the tall silver sagebrush *(Artemisia cana)* which is the dominant shrub in the sand dunes but is rarely found in the area of clay loam. Rabbit brush *(Chrysothamnus viscidiflorus)* is also common in the dune areas and largely absent in the areas of other soil types. The buckwheats *(Eriogonum* spp.*)*, yucca *(Yucca glauca)* and prickly pear *(Opuntia polyacantha)* are common to all of the area.

Away from the sandy areas, the clay loam soils support the big sagebrush *(Artemisia tridentata)* which is the dominant shrub. In areas of saline and alkaline soils along the terraces of meandering arroyos and the margins of playa lakes are extensive growths of greasewood *(Sarcobatus vermiculatus)* and salt bushes *(Atriplex* spp.*)*. The latter are excellent range feeds and prehistorically may have been a human food of considerable value.

Forbs are less choosy in their selection of soil type, but some including the wild onions *(Allium* spp.*)*, death camus *(Zigadenus venenosus)* and vetch *(Vicia* sp.*)* favor the sand dunes over the clay areas. Others including the loco weeds *(Astragalus* spp., *Oxytropis* spp.*)* sego lily *(Calochortus nuttalli)*, asters *(Aster* spp.*)*, and fleabanes *(Erigeron* spp.*)* are common all over.

The grasses undoubtedly formed the greatest attraction to the bison. The sand dunes favor a number of these including prairie sandgrass *(Calamovilfa longifolia)*, needle and thread grass *(Stipa comata)*, green needle grass *(Stipa viridula)*, blowout grass *(Redfieldia flexuosa)*, Indian ricegrass *(Oryzopsis hymenoides)*, and sand dropseed *(Sporobolus cryptandrus)*. Other grasses are found only outside the sandy areas; the most important include western wheat grass *(Agropyron smithii)*, sandberg bluegrass *(Poa secunda)*, and Junegrass *(Koeleria cristata)*. Several are common to all areas, including the blue grama *(Bouteloua gracilis)*, and a grass-like plant, the threadleaf sedge *(Carex filifolia)*. Buffalo grass *(Buchloe dactyloides)* is found close to but not in the site area although it does seem to favor somewhat sandy soils but not the actual dunes.

No trees are found in the sand dunes but the flood plain of the nearby North Platte River supports abundant cottonwoods *(Populus angustifolia* and *P. deltoides)*, boxelders *(Acer negundo)*, willows *(Salix* spp.*)* and a variety of trees, shrubs, and grasses of lesser importance. On the northern fringes of the sand dune area are exposed sandstone buttes and scarps that support an occasional stand of pine *(Pinus ponderosa)* and scattered junipers *(Juniperus* spp.*)*.

East of the Casper Site, the terrain rises sharply toward Casper Mountain. These slopes are dissected by deep arroyos, many of which contain small, year-round live streams. At lower elevations these water courses support groves of chokecherries *(Prunus virginiana)*, buffalo berries *(Shepherdia canadensis)*, currants and gooseberries *(Ribes* spp.*)*, wild roses *(Rosa* spp.*)* and other less important trees and shrubs. The drier slopes support skunkbrush *(Rhus trilobata)*, juniper *(Juniperus* spp.*)* and mountain mahogany *Cercocarpus* spp.*)*. As elevations increase, belts of juniper, ponderosa pine *(Pinus ponderosa)*, fir *(Pseudotsuga taxifolia)*, limber pine *(Pinus flexilis)*, quaking aspen *(Populus tremuloides)* and lodgepole pine *(Pinus latifolia)* successively overlap. Sagebrush *(Artemisia* spp.*)* is common at all altitudes. Plant food resources at the present are varied and abundant. A carefully scheduled pattern of intensive plant gathering would without doubt be significant in the diet of a human population of light density. We can probably assume much the same conditions in Hell Gap times.

Faunal Resources

The site area no longer supports any significant animal populations other than a few jackrabbits *(Lepus townsendii, L. californicus)*, cottontail rabbits *(Sylvilagus audubonii, S. nuttallii)*, ground squirrels *(Citellus tridecemlineatus, C. richardsonii)*, skunks *(Mephitis mephitis)*, pocket gophers *(Thomomys talpoides)*, and an occasional badger *(Taxidea taxus)* that successfully manages to negotiate interstate highway traffic. Mice *(Peromyscus* spp.*)* and voles *(Microtus* spp.*)* are also common. Prairie dogs *(Cynomys gunnisoni)* are found in open country close to the site area.

Towards the rough foothills of Casper Mountain a short distance away are found wood rats *(Neotoma cinerea)*, marmots *(Marmota flaviventris)* and porcupines *(Erethizon dorsatum)*. Along the North Platte River are beaver *(Castor canadensis)*, muskrats *(Ondatra zibethicus)*, and an occasional mink *(Mustela vision)*.

Just across Interstate 25, a few hundred feet to the northeast of the site, is fenced rangeland which is frequented by large herds of antelope *(Antilocapra americana)* as are most of the open plains areas of Wyoming. Some mule deer *(Odocoileus hemionus)* are found in the sand dunes along the North Platte River and in large numbers throughout the rough foothills of the Laramie Range. Coyotes *(Canis latrans)*, bobcats *(Lynx rufus)* and an occasional red fox *(Vulpes vulpes)* are frequently seen close to the site area.

Cattle, sheep and horses presently graze the area, which is regarded as good open range for livestock. In the recent past, mountain sheep *(Ovis canadensis)* were indigenous to all of the mountain ranges and rough, dissected areas of the intermontane basins of the region. Now newly transplanted herds are found in the Laramie and Big Horn Mountains, and some of the original herds are still found in the Wind River, Absaroka and northern Big Horn Mountains. Wolves *(Canis lupus)* were common until the early 1920's when the concentrated trapping and poisoning of the previous several decades finally brought about their local extinction. Elk *(Cervus canadensis)* are now common as they have been throughout the historic period in all of the area, while the Laramie, Medicine Bow, Ferris, Shirley, Big Horn, Bear Lodge, Seminoe, and Green Mountain ranges now support transplanted herds. Original herds reside in the Wind River and Absaroka areas. Elk have also been successfully transplanted into more remote lower elevation areas such as the Red Desert and into the Powder River Basin which was probably more comparable to their original habitat. The distribution of elk in the region during the earlier prehistoric period needs to be studied since their remains are quite rare in archeological sites older than a few hundred years. Black bear *(Ursus americanus)* were present throughout the area, but are now limited to the more inaccessible reaches of the mountain ranges. Grizzly bear *(Ursus arctos)* were present also, but the closest at present are limited to the northern Absaroka mountains and the area of Yellowstone National Park.

Important birds common in the area include the sage grouse *(Centrocercus urophasianus)*, golden eagles *(Aquila chrysaetos)*, various hawks *(Buteo* spp.*)*, crows *(Corvus brachyrhynchos)*, great horned owls *(Bubo virginianus)*, ravens *(Corvus corax)*, magpies *(Pica pica)*, and many small groundbirds. Various waterfowl appear in significant numbers at certain times of the year along the Platte River and on interdunal ponds. Recent bird counts in the Casper area resulted in the sighting of over sixty species but few other than the sage grouse and some waterfowl can be considered as of any significance in the economics of prehistoric human populations.

Climatic Considerations

The climate at the Casper Site is probably little changed from what it was 10,000 years ago. The presence of the parabolic dune which was used as the trap, and the later pond formation, suggest rainfall conditions similar to the present. The balance between vegetational stabilization of the dune field and extensive sand movement is critically dependent upon the amount and timing of precipitation. In an area with an average annual precipitation of approximately thirteen inches, a loss of a very few inches over a period of years can result in extensive sand movement. Such periods must have existed, as is evidenced by the hundreds of square miles of old parabolic dunes now stabilized by vegetation. The fact that the dunes presently active in the site area are in exact alignment with the fossil dunes would seem to indicate that the prevailing winds are now similar to those blowing when the site was in use.

A general increase in annual precipitation is noted east of the longitude of Casper. This can be documented from recording stations (Becker and Alyea 1964a) where long term precipitation records are available. These records demonstrate that precipitation west of Casper, excluding the higher mountains, is generally less than ten inches a year, while those areas east of Casper generally receive well over ten inches. This discrepancy is reflected in generally better grass conditions to the east.

The site area is one of cold winters and, with the exception of a few hot days, usually cool summers. July is the warmest month and the only month in which frosts have not been recorded in the city of Casper, although frosts do occur even in July at slightly higher elevations towards Casper Mountain. Highest maximum observed temperature is 105° F. in July while the mean monthly temperature for July is 73°F.

January is the coldest month with a minimum recorded low of -37° F. while the mean monthly temperature for January is 26° F. (Becker and Alyea 1964b). Winds are a regular occurrence in the area and chill factors are therefore usually much lower than actual temperature readings indicate. Some gauge of past wind velocities can be made by noting the large sand grains covering the bones in the trough of the old dune. Any disturbance of the vegetational cover on a stabilized dune can result in its reactivation, as evidenced by the recent industrial activity that has removed the vegetational cover and subsequently necessitated the construction of rows of snow fence in the site area to prevent drifting of the sand. Chinook-like winds are also common to the area and as a result heavy snow cover may disappear quite rapidly. Overall, the climate of the area is rather harsh, but vegetation is usually abundant and snow cover is generally light enough to allow good feed utilization by large herbivores throughout the winter months.

TOPOGRAPHIC FEATURES UTILIZED IN PALEO-INDIAN BISON PROCUREMENT

An uncertainty that always seems to frustrate precise analysis of kill sites is whether the site is the locus of the kill itself, or if it is the scene of an intermediate butchering and processing area to which animals, whole or in part, were removed after slaughter elsewhere.

The evidence is not always clear, but in kills of the later period it can often be resolved by the discovery of separate kill and butchering or processing areas (Frison 1967a, 1971a, 1973). In other sites, the location of one or the other often cannot be found; but from consideration of the site location itself in terms of suitability for the purpose intended from analysis of tool types and frequencies, bone frequencies, the size of butchered units, and the amount and kinds of treatment of bones, along with other more subtle kinds of evidence, a decision can usually be made as to the nature of the site and whether or not it is in fact a kill or butchering station. Wheat (1971:25-26) has already made these same kinds of observations. The topography of the site and the content and configuration of the bone bed should distinguish a kill from a butchering site, although we can usually presume in any case, that a certain amount of basic dismemberment must have taken place wherever the animals were killed. The topography itself undoubtedly affected the distance and amount of meat transported from the kill area.

Once the nature of the site and the topographical features involved are determined, it is usually possible to develop some hypotheses about the actual handling of the animals. If we know, for example, that the kill was made around a waterhole, in an arroyo, or a sand dune trap, in a corral or over a jump-off, then it is possible to hypothesize methods that might reasonably have been used to bring the animals to the area and confine them or otherwise control them while they were killed.

In some cases, the primary topographical feature can be quite positively identified. At Olsen-Chubbuck (Wheat 1972) the animals were stampeded into an arroyo. The old arroyo is present and the configuration of the animals in the bone bed even indicates the direction of the stampede. Plainview (Sellards et. al. 1947) is also regarded as a stampede site, but over a low steep bluff into a stream channel rather than into an arroyo. The Lipscomb Site (Schultz 1943) could have been a trap or drive over the bank of a stream. Unfortunately the actual number of animals is not given, but complete specimens were found. Bonfire Shelter was a stampede over a bluff (Dibble and Lorrain 1968), almost identical in topography to many Late Prehistoric Period jumps. The Casper Site was a trap in a parabolic sand dune. Reinvestigation of an area within a few hundred yards of the Finley Site (Moss et al.

1951) revealed a bone level which had been disturbed and then carefully covered over again. Enough of the area was still intact, however, to indicate that the animals here as at the Casper Site were killed in a parabolic sand dune. According to Wheat (1971:25) there is some evidence of the use of blowout traps at the Linger and Zapata Folsom sites. Although a wide variety of geomorphological features were utilized, it would appear from these examples that the sand dune trap was one of the most frequently and successfully used methods of obtaining the extinct bison.

A trap known as the Hawken Site that contains remains of extinct bison (Frison n.d.) in the fringes of the Wyoming Black Hills was investigated by the author in the summer of 1972. Interpretation indicates a trap in which the animals were driven into an increasingly narrow, steep-walled arroyo and finally corralled against a several-foot-high wall at its box canyon-like terminus. That it was used several times is shown by four distinct bone levels separated by sterile strata. The taxonomic position of the animal remains is not easily defined, but they were definitely much larger in horn core and in overall size than *Bison bison*. A population study of the skeletal remains indicates a fall-of-the-year operation. A radiocarbon date of 4520 $\pm$ 140 years was obtained on a charcoal sample. Cultural affiliations may be with the Logan Creek Complex (Kivett 1962). It is interesting to note that although this particular location was not suitable for use as a jump, later Late Prehistoric groups did operate a number of jumps nearby. In any case, this type of arroyo trap can still be demonstrated today to be an efficient corral.

At other sites, the procurement means are not as surely known. The Simonsen Site (Agogino and Frankforter 1960) is a kill site with no certain interpretation. The possibility of a terrace over which animals were driven is suggested.

The Fletcher Site (Forbis 1968) is another Paleo-Indian bison kill for which no secure evidence of the method of confining the animals could be determined. In this case the bones were exposed around a waterhole and no evidence for jumping or corraling was found. The site was not thoroughly investigated however.

A number of other sites are butchering stations that were probably in close proximity to kill areas which have not been found or may no longer exist. The Horner Site is an example. It was a fall-of-the-year operation (Jepsen 1953) but the actual method of killing the animals is not known. The surrounding terrain was favorable for stampeding animals over steep terraces or into arroyos, provided the topography then was similar to the present. The Horner Site has been claimed to be a kill by stampede over unfavorable terrain (Hester 1967:181) but this interpretation has to be considered hypothetical until much firmer evidence is found to support it. The James Allen Site (Mulloy 1959) is also a kill and butchering site with no good evidence to indicate the method of killing the animals. The possibility of a stampede into a shallow steep-sided arroyo seems probable however, if we assume conditions similar then to those at present.

A very puzzling site in terms of actual method of procurement is located in northwestern Nebraska. Known as the Hudson-Meng Site (Agenbroad 1973), it contains an extinct form of bison and is apparently of late Plano affiliation. An extensive bone level was found along the bank of an arroyo covered with varying amounts of overburden. The site is still under investigation and its magnitude and extent area-wise is as yet uncertain. A number of large butchering units are present suggesting that if this is not the actual kill site it cannot be far away. Complete analysis of this site will undoubtedly enhance the entire spectrum of Paleo-Indian bison studies.

The Agate Basin Site (Roberts 1943, Bass 1970) is quite extensive. Unfortunately, it underwent considerable destruction before any systematic investigations were made. It seems certain that the first known recovery of material from the site was from a kill area, but the records are not complete enough to even guess at the kind of topographic feature the kill involved. The writer remembers one account of a person who dug for artifacts at the site in the early 1930's who claimed to have found "four legs of an animal sticking into the dirt and broken off above the hocks" which, if reliable, suggests an animal bogged down in mud and subsequently killed and butchered. A major portion of the kill area of the site was destroyed before Roberts (1943) was able to do his first work. A large reservoir now covers the area of first excavation and makes further interpretation difficult. The area, judging from the present topography, would have presented possibilities for either a stampede and jump into a steep arroyo, or a drive into an arroyo trap. The presence of one animal that may have been mired in a swampy area is neither surprising nor of itself sufficient evidence to support a hypothesis that miring was the tactic used to confine the animals for killing. Certainly, there are a few areas that are true bogs in the sense that bison might have been driven into them so deeply as to have been unable to escape hunters. It is, however, almost impossible to drive animals into such bogs if they are disinclined, although it is not uncommon to see them up to their knees grazing in bogs where the feed is lush. Under such grazing conditions it is not unusual for an old or weak animal to become inextricably mired and eventually die, but a healthy animal can almost always remove itself from boggy areas with ease.

The Agate Basin Site requires further investigation before definitive statements can be made concerning the geomorphological feature that was utilized to confine or control the animals. Even if we accept the observation of an animal that appeared to have died with its feet in the mire, this does not necessarily mean that the killing tactic itself was one of bogging the animals. A crippled animal could easily have died in a sitting position in a wet boggy area of the site. It seems plausible also that only the upper parts of such an animal would be butchered. An analogy is the animal that was killed at the Casper Site that died sitting on its haunches. When excavated, its hind legs had the appearance of being deep in the sand.

A stampede of a herd of tightly-packed animals into a bog could have resulted in some temporary restraint and possibly even a few broken legs as the animals piled over one another and stumbled and fell. Another relevant consideration is that a swamp or bog makes an extremely unpleasant and difficult location to butcher and retrieve a dead animal as large as a bison. This will be readily confirmed by anyone who has had to remove cattle from bogs. The Paleo-Indians seemed to possess other and more sophisticated strategies for bison procurement than stampeding animals into bogs. A bog that would confine enough animals to make the operation worthwhile would have made a situation where retrieving the meat would have been extremely unpleasant and difficult. Some might argue that the condition of the meat when processed or eaten was not an important factor to the Paleo-Indians, but this is an assumption that can not be accepted at face value. An animal that has been stampeded into a bog, trampled by other animals, and then killed is not in the best of condition. It is wet and covered with mire which makes manipulation during the butchering process exceedingly difficult. It is almost impossible to dismember such an animal without impregnating the meat with the sand, clay and undesirable muck from the bog, thus rendering the meat unpalatable regardless of cultural preferences. The idea that the Paleo-Indian regarded bison as so difficult to obtain that it was food regardless

of location or condition, cannot be accepted.

It seems certain then, that the Paleo-Indians were using both the stampede over bluffs or low terraces and the drive into arroyo and sand dune traps. Whether or not they were building corrals is not yet known for certain. Evaluation of a landform for its worth as a trap or jump is not for the novice. It is knowledge that comes from observation and experience and is then passed from generation to generation. Trial and error had to figure into the final result. Animal behavior in a driving situation is predictable only within certain limits. A slight change in timing or the direction of approach to a trap or jump can often drastically affect the chances of success. There may have been fortuitous situations, of course, when animals just happened to be in favorable positions to be driven or stampeded, but for year in and year out subsistence the Paleo-Indians had to develop a thorough knowledge of reliable animal handling techniques. They certainly knew well enough how to maneuver herds of proper size through whatever movements were necessary to drive them into traps or stampede them over bluffs or into steep-sided arroyos.

BISON DRIVING AND HANDLING

Today there is a surge of interest in making bison ranching a profitable economic venture. Good breeding stock demand higher prices than cattle. Some of this is a kind of hobby of course, but bison do possess some very real advantages over cattle. They are better able to exist under natural range feed conditions and are less expensive to winter than cattle. One would expect this. They have had several thousand years to make a natural adaptation to the range grasses, topography and climate. They are also less susceptible to most ordinary diseases than cattle. As a result, the bison herds are increasing and more and better observations on their behavior are possible.

Ranch bison are becoming somewhat domesticated as a result of high fences, strong corrals, and the frequent trips through chutes and squeeze gates they have to make for various reasons, but they still maintain a wild pattern of behavior that is distinctive when contrasted with domestic range cattle. Some of the commercial bison breeders operate under open range conditions. They maintain a minimum amount of contact, and their animals are reminiscent of the Yellowstone Park herd, which lives almost completely free from the processes of domestication. In any case, bison are not easy to handle in corrals, so any close contact of this nature is understandably avoided if possible.

It is impossible to reconstruct the exact relationship that existed between modern bison and the pre-horse inhabitants of the New World. We are on even more dangerous ground yet where the extinct forms of *Bison* are concerned. Some general observations should hold true however. A predator-prey relationship between man and the bison undoubtedly existed in the past and its intensity must have depended on the number of persons in relationship to the number of animals, how much time was spent, and how it was distributed in pursuing the animals. Some analogy can be derived from observations made about the hunting of wild game under present conditions.

Today most hunting is controlled as a seasonal affair. During the hunting season the animals become extremely wild, difficult to find, and often impossible to approach. When the season ends and the animals cease to be molested they become continually less and less fearful of man. In the National Parks, where any disturbance of animals by man is forbidden, it is possible, though not wise, to approach within a few yards of animals such as deer, bear, moose, and bison. When hunting it is also noticeable that the further one goes into remote areas the less fearful of man the game animals are. With

increased hunting pressure, however, the animals rapidly become wild and a point is soon reached when it becomes more profitable for the hunter to move on to another area and let the animals rest awhile and lose their wariness of man.

In any livestock business, whether cattle, bison or whatever, it is occasionally necessary to drive the animals through chutes for purposes of vaccinations, branding, pregnancy tests, etc. The animals do not like much handling, but with sturdy enough facilities and the proper know-how they have no choice in the matter. After a session of this nature, they are understandably wild and suspicious of man for a period of time. Fortunately for man, however, animals seem to have short memories. This is exemplified clearly by those domestic range cattle whose calves are weaned at the same time and place every year. Whether a young cow or an old cow, the weaning away of the calf seems to come as a complete surprise every year, and brings on several days of the most traumatic behavior possible. Game animals are as regularly and reliably surprised. Every year they will predictably congregate in the same location, where the same annual slaughter takes place the first day of every hunting season. Both cattle and bison can be corraled or run through a chute for various purposes, and will be wild for a day or so, but if allowed to settle down for a few days they can be given the same treatment again.

Hypothesizing from this, continual pursuit of the same animals day after day could not have been as rewarding as intermittent pursuit. In the communal procurement situation there must have been a number of important considerations. Bison can be maneuvered or driven short distances even up to a mile or so without too much difficulty but the continued presence of someone forcing or pressuring them finally begins to affect their behavior, and if pursued too persistently they will break and run. Once this has happened, they are almost impossible to stop until they decide to do so of their own volition. On the other hand, a herd can be subjected to gentle influences which will bring their movements for a day within a favorable position relative to the selected trap or jump. Once a herd has been taken through a trap or over a jump and several of its members have been killed or crippled, it would have required a period of settling down, or else a new herd would have had to be found, before the process could be repeated successfully. Alternative kill locations must have been present to allow for the seemingly capricious nature of the animals being present in large numbers in one location and then suddenly moving to another. This pattern of unpredictable shifting and roaming also undoubtedly occurred from year to year, since grazing conditions can change rapidly over short distances on the plains from such various causes as short term moisture fluctuations, insect infestations, and intense hail storms. Successful communal kills, year after year, must have required complete familiarity with a hunting territory and knowledge of how the animals themselves exploited it.

During the Late Prehistoric Period on the Plains, bison jumping techniques became quite sophisticated, and there is evidence that the Indians were able to move herds several miles without horses (Frison 1967b: 64-106, 1970). Lines of stone piles leading to jump-offs may have had a variety of uses, both functional and otherwise, but the writer feels their placement was mainly to serve as an indicator of where the animals had to be contained in order to finally terminate the drive in a favorable location for a final stampede over the jump-off. They were, in a sense, simply traffic markers. The stone piles or drive lines in many locations are placed in such a way that someone familiar with bison can interpret them as a device for orienting the driver's position in relation to the herd. Lacking horses, the Indians had to maneuver the bison very carefully, and the stone piles probably served primarily to orient

the drivers. This seems so since the line of stone piles often follows a rise or the edge of an escarpment in such a way that a man could quickly approach and observe the drive lane ahead without revealing himself to the animals. Rapid movement of the drivers parallel to the herd was necessary since the drivers had to appear in the proper position to keep the herd headed in the right direction. The stone piles would have indicated very rapidly where to move in order to view the herd and establish a proper position in relation to it. If a driver's position was not exactly right, he could have ducked out of sight and moved either forward or back, whichever was necessary, and then oriented himself with another stone marker for proper position. Such a situation would have been very different than driving domestic cattle where the drivers on horseback are continually alongside the animals, urging them on. Much visible activity of the kind we now use to drive domestic animals, if employed around a normal bison herd, would ordinarily have caused a stampede at the wrong time.

There are, however, many close parallels between handling bison and domestic cattle. Early observers claimed range cattle and bison were similar as far as handling was concerned (Dodge 1877:123; Jones 1899:246). The behavior of range cattle a few decades ago was very different from what we are familiar with today and under certain circumstances they were as wild and intractable as any bison. The point is, that the behavior patterns of bison and cattle are quite similar in many respects, and a familiarity with one carries over to the other as far as handling is concerned. We have developed a methodology for handling cattle and bison with horses which is inapplicable when handling them on foot; however, foot methods with cattle should apply to bison. The sudden and unexpected loss of a horse while handling range cattle can, in fact, very dramatically point out the handicaps that existed in the pre-horse period as far as bison procurement was concerned.

Another idea that continually appears in hypothesizing on bison drives is the use of fire. Sauer (1944: 543) proposed the idea and suggested that fire alone was the means by which numbers of animals could have been taken. Prehistoric use of fire has also been used as an explanation for the extinction of Pleistocene fauna due to changing environments resulting from its widespread use (Stewart 1956, Sauer 1944). Eiseley (1946) very cogently pointed out the flaws in Sauer's hypothesis but some other thoughts can be added to the argument.

The archeological record has not produced evidence to support or disclaim use of fire as a means of actually driving bison and as Hester (1967: 187) points out there is not even satisfactory evidence for widespread fires in the past. The problem here is bison driving rather than extinctions and it would appear that fire could not have been used in any situation that required control over the animals such as driving them into a trap or over a jump. Anyone who has fought range fires over the years is well aware of the unpredictability of fire of this nature. Driving bison under about any set of circumstances requires split-second timing and fast reactions. Large range fires could have produced stampedes and any stampede of a large herd would likely have killed animals but this is not the kind of controlled procurement that is suggested from the evidence in known kill sites. In order to have realized a stampede into a given trap or over a bluff by the use of fire, a number of conditions would have had to be met. The animals would have had to be in exactly the right position, the wind direction and velocity correct, and the condition of the grass and terrain exactly right. To have gotten the animals headed in the proper direction and to have kept them headed that way is entirely too much to expect from the use of fire.

Most topographic features used in traps and jumps require an approach pattern that is very critical and a few degrees of change in the angle of approach or a few yards deviation from the steepest and highest part of a river channel or bluff could often have resulted in the herd going on its way with no casualties. Bison, although they may appear awkward, are extremely agile and unless crowded and forced by other animals, can easily avoid dangerous obstacles. This is why a stampede of a large number of animals was required for a successful jump. It is practically impossible to force a small number of animals over a jump-off since it is the pressure of a mass of animals that forces some over the edge. The same is true of an arroyo. A large mass of animals traveling at high speed gives the leaders little choice but to pile into the arroyo and this is especially true if the animals are tightly-packed together. A single animal or a small group can avoid the arroyo easily by stopping or turning to one side or the other. Whatever the effects that prehistoric use of fire may have had on the plains environment, it is not possible to regard it as having been a reliable means of driving or stampeding bison into traps or over jumps.

Decoying of animals was probably a common practice although a combination of both decoying and driving a herd was probably the best method at least under most circumstances. The ease with which bison may be approached using a buffalo hide as a disguise and the subsequent behavior of the animals is well-described (McHugh 1972:66-67) and leaves little doubt of the possibilities of decoying the animals.

This brings up one more point which is to mention that there is a difference between handling a small group of bison compared to a large herd, and a difference also between driving and stampeding a herd. Driving without horses required careful manipulation of a herd to prevent an uncontrolled stampede while a controlled stampede such as one over a jump-off required human action such as running, shouting, and waving a hide or some other object in order to frighten the animals into running blindly at full speed; but at the same time their direction of flight had to be controlled. The Paleo-Indian was apparently well aware of the size require-ments and methods of driving needed for the topographic feature that was utilized.

AGE, SEX, AND TIME OF YEAR DETERMINATIONS

Another aid in the interpretive process of bison procurement is age and sex determination and time of year of the operations. Animals of dif-ferent ages and sexes demonstrate different be-havior patterns and the time of year affects the methods of handling and the probabilities of success of a given procedure. Age structures of large population samples will also indicate whether the operation was restricted to short periods of time or extended over more than one season of the year. Age structures can be deter-mined from tooth eruption and wear schedules and are based on known-age specimens from modern herds (Frison and Reher 1970) which is assuming that these age structures will be valid also for the extinct varieties of *Bison* found in communal Paleo-Indian procurement sites. Other age determiners such as ossification schedules may be used but the mandibles are usually quite well preserved, seldom utilized and generally re-main in the sites. The ages of the older animals can be determined by tooth wear provided an adequate sample of the population is present.

A decade ago, the methodology for determining time of year was not developed to a point where it was considered meaningful (Wendorf and Hester 1962: 167). The method presently used has been applied successfully to fossil populations (Voorhies 1969) and to Late Prehistoric Period bison populations to indicate time of year (Reher 1970, 1973). It was applied with good results to an antelope *(Antilocapra americana)* population found in a Late Prehistoric Period Shoshonean site that was apparently obtained through some

sort of a trapping situation (Nimmo 1971). It is used in the Casper Site analysis (see Chapter 2) and appears to be valid and also sensitive enough to reliably indicate the time of year of a kill pro-vided a large number of animals were involved and a valid sample can be recovered. We were, for example, immediately able in a Late Prehis-toric Period stratified buffalo jump to pick out one kill level as one that occurred in mid-summer in contrast to the remaining levels that contained animals killed in the fall.

During the last two years a sample of 90 man-dibles and third molars was obtained from a kill area that had been dug at the Finley Site but one that the original investigators (Moss et al. 1951) had been unaware of. The age structure of the animals indicates the Finley Site was a fall-of-the-year operation. I feel also that the Olsen-Chubbuck Site was a late summer or early fall operation. The animals there fall into age groups of approximately .35, 1.35, 2.35 year-old etc. age groups and assuming the calves were born in April and May, the procurement operation had to occur in the late summer or early fall. The juven-ile class specimen pictured in Wheat (1972: 30a) is a calf in the .3 to .4 year-old age group. A very rough age determination can even be made from the picture of the mandible based on the erupt-ion of the first molar but a more precise age determination requires actual observation of the specimen. The entire collection has not yet been analyzed but at least 11 calves are in the .3 to .4 year-old age range. There seems little doubt that the Olsen-Chubbuck kill occurred as much as three months earlier in the year than the Casper kill.

A good sample of mandibles and third molars was obtained from the extinct bison kill at the Hawken Site (Frison n. d.) dated at around 4,500 B. C. and this population contains calves in the .5 to .6 year-old age range indicating another fall-of-the-year kill. It would appear to be es-pecially significant in this case because it was a kill site that was operated for at least four different years during the same season of the year and suggests a pattern repeated from year to year.

The Horner Site contained remains of an estimated 200 animals and according to the investigator they were killed in "autumn or early winter" (Jepsen 1953: 11). Nothing of the time of year of operation is known for the Agate Basin Site, the Simonsen Site, or the Scottsbluff Bison Quarry Site although this kind of determination should be possible provided large enough samples of skeletal material were recovered and saved.

At the Plainview Site the animals were killed in the spring of the year based on the presence of "several fetal skeletons which, judging from their size, must have been nearing the time of birth." (Sellards et al. 1947: 934-935). It would be well to do an entire population study of the Plainview Site specimens because some fetal material turns up in almost all bison kill sites from Paleo-Indian to historic times. It is known that although the great majority of bison calves are born within a period of a few weeks during the regular calving season, there are always some that are born at odd times. At the Casper Site, there were recovered 19 calves that were born in the normal calving period along with three fetal specimens. Two of the latter were evidently close to full term and one was still some time away. Judging from a recently-obtained modern *Bison* fetus, it may have been about a seven month specimen or just slightly over two months away from full term. This phenomenon of late calves occurs in all known bison herds today.

There is no attempt in any of the commercial bison operations at present in Wyoming to regulate breeding and the males have free access to the females at all times. In this situation it is common to observe as many as five or six percent of late calves. These calves, if they are born too late in the year, usually survive only if the cow and calf are given special winter care. Otherwise a calf born in late summer or early fall stands a poor chance of survival unless an unusually mild winter follows. Conditions such as this probably existed also in prehistoric periods. It is not uncommon to observe game animals that have offspring late in the summer or early fall and these seldom survive a bad winter.

There are other mechanisms as well that seem to eliminate bison not born during the normal calving period from the population. An early-born female calf for example may survive and be larger and more mature than others of the same generation. This calf may also breed during its second summer or at an age of about 1.2 to 1.3 years rather than the following year which is normal. Early breeders such as this usually have trouble calving and death loss is high because the fetus is too large for normal birth and the cow is so wild and difficult to handle that usually the cow or calf or both are lost. Every buffalo breeder is fearful that an unusually large and healthy female calf will breed a year early and thus be in danger of losing a valuable animal. In the wild conditions, much the same conditions probably existed.

The late female calf that survives will not affect the population structure to any extent. Instead of breeding at the 2.2 to 2.3 year-old age period it will be delayed until the next year and her first offspring will consequently be born during the normal calving period only a year later than the ones of her generation that were born during the normal spring calving period.

The time of year had to affect the kind of procurement methods used. A buffalo cow in the spring with a newborn calf is more difficult to drive than at any other time of the year with the possible exception of when she is in rut. Animals change behavior in the spring also when the new grass first appears. They are usually weak from the long winter, but once the new grass appears in quantity their condition improves. The young animals are now quite wild while the females usually separate from the herd for several days while calving. Cows with young calves are best left alone for several days. Young calves often tend to bolt from the herd when frightened and the mother usually follows, which is extremely disruptive for any attempt at driving. Shortly after the regular calving season the rutting season begins and for all practical purposes, a systematic driving of the animals is impossible until it is over.

After the rut, the older mature males separate from the herd and remain so singly or in groups of up to as many as a dozen. This is the most favorable period for driving the animals. The meat is best because the grass is dry and the back and intestinal fat is the thickest. The meat will not spoil as fast as with an animal on green feed where intestinal gasses spread rapidly throughout the carcass after death and cause rapid spoilage. The older males which are difficult to drive are mostly off to themselves leaving the more desirable cows, calves and young adult animals in large groups. Weather conditions are more favorable with cooler nights but still with hot, dry days favorable for drying meat.

The time of year can also affect the topographical features utilized. An arroyo is usually wet and muddy in the spring but dry and hard in the fall. The area used for gathering a herd may be a bog in the spring but perfectly dry by late summer. The distribution of animals in an area is largely dependent upon the location of feed, water and cover. In the spring, water holes may be everywhere but are often scarce by fall. Bison can easily travel several miles to and from water but as water becomes scarce, grazing patterns change and this can affect the workability of a given procurement location. The nature of the site and the area around it at the time of the kill can often tell something of the nature of the procurement techniques used.

Comparative studies of large bone samples in kill sites should within limits distinguish the sex of the animals involved (see Chapter 6). Male bison in general are much larger than females but a large female may be as large as a young male. It is important to know age and sex of the animals killed so that for one reason, differences in butchering techniques between different classes of animals can be studied. It is known also that the extinct variants were larger than the modern one. Identification of species has been based largely on horn core structure and relative size of certain bones, especially the astragali, metatarsals and metacarpals, largely because these three bones are usually the best preserved in kill sites while skulls often deteriorate. Bone measurements must be better controlled. The average size of a sample of a given bone from one site compared to a similar sample from another site is not valid unless animals of the same age and sex are being compared. An example is the Casper Site from which only three known males are represented. The Finley Site sample contained apparently many more males and a simple average of the volumes of the astragali from both sites suggests the Finley Site animals were larger than those from the Casper Site, which is not the case.

Different sex ratios in different kills remain unexplained and whether or not this is significant needs to be resolved. In a trapping situation, small groups of animals of varying composition with regard to age and sex could have been taken, which might explain some of the discrepancies found. It is common for a cow and calf and her calf from the year before to remain together. A small group of bison totaling 25 or so in the late summer or fall could have contained cows, calves, yearlings and two-year-olds of both sexes while a group of the same size could also have contained a small group of immature bulls and even a mature one or two. Although the mature males do tend to range by themselves after the rut, they have to move back and forth to water and will occasionally intermingle with the other animals. It is extremely difficult, however, to drive or otherwise do anything with a bull beyond his prime since they usually remain apart from the herd and will drop out when any attempt at driving is made. Male animals of extreme age are rare in herds today because they are usually removed from the herd and disposed of in deference to younger animals. This is one reason why most people regard bison meat as tough and strong-tasting. Until recently, the only animal that was commonly butchered was an old bull that became unmanageable or was too old for breeding purposes and above all was not ideal for eating.

It would appear that before the cultural systems of the Paleo-Indian can be understood, the seasonality of communal bison procurement must be better understood. If the communal activities were confined largely to a certain period of the year as is now being suggested by the evidence from known kill sites, economic activities for the remainder of the year must be accounted for. To hypothesize further, if the now extinct variants of bison handled the way the modern form does, it was not likely that the Paleo-Indian was able to go out at any time during the year and successfully obtain a large number of animals in a trap or stampede over a bluff although individual or small-group hunting could have been done at about any time of the year. Evidence to support these hypotheses has been found through animal population studies of animal remains recovered in communal bison kills but more such studies need to be made. Some of this kind of information can still be obtained from a number of the old classic Paleo-Indian kill sites and this should be done before further destruction of these sites occurs.

THE BISON PROCUREMENT AT THE CASPER SITE

The bison at the Casper Site were trapped in a parabolic sand dune. This geomorphological feature is described (Hack 1941) as occurring in areas of sand anchored by vegetation. The open end or wings of the dune extend windward and this feature is common to the area today. It is possible to stand in one spot in the large dunefield northeast of the Casper Site and observe a

half-dozen or more active parabolic dunes within a radius of several miles. In addition there are hundreds of these same features that are presently stabilized with vegetation but have been active at some time in the past.

Dunes that are active today in the dunefield close to the Casper Site are variable. Some would make good bison traps while most would not. The most desirable one observed in terms of a bison trap is long and narrow with steep sides and leeward end (Fig. 1.7). The maximum slope on the sides is about 35 degrees. At any time and especially after extended dry periods the steep, sandy slopes are extremely difficult to negotiate by large, heavy, split-hoofed animals. Even a horse is at a distinct disadvantage if forced to climb out of this dune and it is not at all easy for a man. There is a tendency also for the last few feet of the slope to be nearly perpendicular as the result of grass roots holding the sand. In this situation, an animal cannot possibly escape over the sides of the dune and is in an extremely vulnerable condition when attempting to do so.

The dunes migrate to the leeward. Some fences and roads have been moved several times within the past few decades as a result of the continual wind action that loosens the sand and transports it up over the leeward end. Water tends to collect to the windward of the active front of some dunes depending upon the factors affecting the height of the water table. In some instances, these ponds retain water the year round and it is not unusual to observe an active dune with a clear pond ringed with lush vegetation a few yards to the windward of the active dune area (Fig. 1.8). The water and vegetation certainly constituted a major attraction for bison then as they do for livestock today. Dunes in which the troughs are cut to a stable surface such as the gravel terraces of the North Platte River present a level approach between the wings. In other dunes suspended high in the sand, however, the wind may etch out a perpendicular drop-off as much as

FIGURE 1.7 *Looking leeward into a parabolic sand dune near the Casper Site.*

eight feet in height on the windward end. One dune of this nature was observed in which the windward end as well as the leeward end would have sufficed as a trap (Fig. 1.9).

As already mentioned, the parabolic sand dune in which the animals at the Casper Site were trapped, lies directly on the uppermost gravel terrace of the North Platte River about 100 feet above the present stream level. The gravel terrace provided a base to which the sand was removed. Only a small remnant of the original dune trap remains. Some of the old dune was removed by wind action subsequent to its use as a trap. Most, however, was removed recently with heavy industrial equipment. Enough remains, however, to leave no doubt of its identification as a parabolic dune with evidence of pond formation

afterward (Fig. 1.4).

A total of 121 partial and complete mandibles and teeth from 19 more represent a minimum of 74 animals and in addition , three fetal animals were represented. There is a possibility of about half this many more originally killed since approximately 15% of the kill area was removed by a pipeline trench and another 10% of the site is still intact. It seems highly improbable that this represents a single drive but probably a series of drives over a single season with little possibility of more than one season. The state of articulation and difference in bone preservation from one end of the site to the other might suggest the possibility of site use for more than a single drive season although this could more reasonably be explained as the result of one part of the bone level being

FIGURE 1.8 *Active parabolic dune with a year-round pond to the windward.*

exposed more than another part. The state of almost perfect preservation and articulation of some butchered units does suggest that sand must have covered the units very soon after they were butchered; otherwise they would demonstrate more disarticulation, breakage, and chewing from carnivores. The strongest evidence for use during a single drive season is found in the population study (see Chapter 2). The lack of animals in the 1.6 year-old age category can possibly be explained by some catastrophic event such as a selective human kill or a spring blizzard that removed the calves the year before. The probability of such an event happening two years in a row is quite low. It does not seem likely that only a single year's age gap could appear in the age structure of the Casper Site bison population if the kill represented more than a single year's operation.

A sidelight on the possibility of extremely bad weather conditions killing the young calves should be mentioned. The winter and spring of 1972-1773 was probably one of the most disastrous for livestock on record for Wyoming. A severe spring blizzard began on the 18th of April, 1973 at the height of the calving season. A large percentage of spring calves of the domestic cattle was lost along with a surprising number of mature animals. The buffalo herd at the Durham Meat Company operating with about 2,500 head 35 miles south of Gillette, Wyoming in the center of the storm did not lose a single buffalo calf or mature animal. There seems little doubt that buffalo can withstand much more adverse weather than domestic cattle.

Trapping and killing buffalo was much more than merely driving the animals into the trap and everyone concerned randomly throwing spears or darts into the herd until the animals lay dead. Every person experienced in hunting has learned

FIGURE 1.9 *Looking windward into a parabolic sand dune near the Casper Site.*

the futility of shooting into a bunch of animals or birds. A single animal or bird has to be chosen in the group and in the case of a bison, the proper spot on the animal selected to drive in the projectile. In rare kills where carcasses are somewhat intact, projectile points are usually concentrated in the rib cages and the vertebral column. This can be done only by selecting out a single animal and driving the projectile point into the lethal spot. The inevitable results of bunch-shooting are wounded animals and wasted effort.

At the Casper Site, it is postulated that the animals were driven into the dune through the opening between the wings. Some animals were probably speared while still in the wings of the dune. Once the animals were far enough into the dune that the leeward end began to steepen there

was undoubtedly some confusion on the part of the animals. At this moment each hunter selected an animal or possibly there were prearranged teams of two or more hunters formed to kill a single animal. It may have been possible for each person or team to kill more than one animal before the herd escaped if a large number of animals were involved or to kill the entire group if only a few animals were present. If either a cow or calf were killed the chances of obtaining the other one of the pair were good. This is especially true if a cow were killed in which case the calf would usually stay close to the mother. This has been observed in other large traps where cow and calf often appeared together and the chances are high that biological pairs are represented. In addition, a cow's calf from the year before often tends to stay close to the mother and the situation of a cow, calf, and yearling together has been observed in traps; and very likely this represents female and offspring. A bison calf in the fall of the year and also the yearling from the same female will often remain close to the mother during periods of handling in corrals.

It is not at all likely that a trap of this nature would have contained the animals for very long. The sand was soft and the walls were steep but there would have been only a short period of confusion when the animals were at a great disadvantage. If extinct bison behaved at all like the modern form, it would have required an extremely sophisticated fence in conjunction with the natural form of the dune to hold the animals any length of time. A fence of this nature, however, seems a very unlikely possibility. Loose sand is an extremely difficult medium in which to construct a fence. More likely the animals were herded into the dune and a number of them killed or disabled during a short period of confusion. Nearly all of the animals would have naturally ended up in the trough of the parabolic dune when they died and that is where they were butchered.

ASPECTS OF BONE PRESERVATION

There are many different aspects of carcass preservation to consider. Some depend upon the time of year involved. For example, a large animal such as a cow or horse that dies on the open range in warm spring or summer weather becomes putrid within a few hours. Unless carnivores find it almost immediately, it very soon approaches a stage of decomposition so bad that no carnivore will touch it. Birds such as magpies, ravens, and vultures are unable to do much more than pick out the eyes due to the heavy hide. Within a week or so, the carcass is an unapproachable mass of decayed meat and maggots. In a month or so the flesh is gone, the heavy hide

is dried in the form of a stiff armor over the articulated bones, and if not disturbed, the carcass will remain this way for a year or more with perfect preservation and good articulation of the bones.

Winter time is another and different proposition for the animal that dies. Carnivores and scavengers are much more alert for food and the carcass is usually torn apart, disarticulated and scattered over a large area within a few days or even hours. The softer parts of bones, the muscle attachments such as the tubers ischii, tubers coxae, various trochanters, and tuberosities are usually chewed away.

If, however, the animal dies in winter and freezes solid, the meat may still be edible when it thaws in the spring or during warmer weather, but by then, more desirable food may be available. Chances are then good that the animal will putrify and stand a good chance of not being disturbed. A number of large animals that winter-kill together are often quite well preserved, usually because they die in inaccessible locations such as the bottoms of steep arroyos, swamps, heavy underbrush, or the like and carnivores and scavengers are unable to gain access to them especially if they cover with snow. An animal that dies in the bottom of an arroyo may collect mud and debris from the first spring runoff and thus stands an excellent chance of complete bone preservation and good articulation.

Animals killed by carnivores at any time of the year must be considered separately. In this case the carcass is immediately opened up and torn apart. Access to any part is then possible and scavengers are able to utilize what the carnivores leave. Even in summer, the chances of meat rapidly becoming putrid is lessened with the intestinal cavity opened.

All of this needs to be considered in analyzing bone conditions in many different kinds of bison kills. In several jumps, traps and corrals investigated by the writer (see e.g. Frison 1970, 1971a,

1973) the operations were carried out in the late summer or early fall. Nights are then cool but days are hot and a pile of butchered bones with very little meat remaining along with the contents of the intestines would have soon created a putrid mass that would attract carnivores and scavengers but not provide them with much food. Spring runoff and later storms might have begun to cover the bones and consequently there was a good chance of bone preservation without extensive damage by carnivores and scavengers. Every site, however, that was preserved was unique. The site may have been in a meander of an arroyo that was aggrading or the bones may have created an obstacle in the bottom of an arroyo of sufficient magnitude that enough debris collected around them so that the course of the arroyo was changed. In the case of the Casper Site many of the butchered units and individual bones were stacked in piles. Judging from present conditions the wind could have begun drifting sand over the remains within a few hours although a period of several days may pass without high winds. The site profile indicates there was pond formation over the top of the bones as indicated by pond sediments above the bone level. It is strongly indicated, however, that regardless of subsequent events, the bones must have been covered with sand quite rapidly after the kill and were never again exposed until the recent excavation. Otherwise there would have been no chance for the kind of preservation and articulation that was present at the site.

This is further substantiated by observations on present-day carcasses. Bones of a cow or horse may lay exposed at the top of the ground for a year without serious deterioration but they do tend to become disarticulated unless as mentioned, they are protected by an armor-like hide.

After two years of exposure, the bone surfaces show deterioration and exposure beyond this results in bone that is extremely difficult to interpret much in terms of butchering marks.

Another problem of exposed bones is that carnivores and scavengers continue to carry away and gnaw on bones as long as they are extant.

BUTCHERING CONSIDERATIONS

Butchering represents a large increment of the economic activities for a hunting group and one of considerable importance. Every animal or bird utilized by man as food must have some manner of preparation to maximize its value as food. Certain parts of the organism are favored over others as being tastier, more palatable, or easier to prepare. Some parts of the organism are unpalatatable and some may be harmful while any part may be both of these if not properly handled. Most human groups at the lower levels of culture regard some part or parts of the animal as somehow connected with the supernatural and proper allowance is made thereof.

The kind of animal procurement, butchering, and utilization of the animal that is the life style of a hunting and gathering society is difficult if not impossible to generalize to our modern society. Few of us hunt for the expressed purpose of filling an empty stomach. In fact, hunting has become a status pastime in which the effect of a certain style of bullet at a given velocity and distance is discussed with a good deal more interest than the quantity and quality of the meat. Very few of us have experienced the unique feeling of knowing that an empty stomach can only be relieved by applying every bit of personal expertise toward obtaining game animals. There is a profound difference between having to outwit an animal in order to survive and to outwit an animal while carrying a supply of concentrated food that may be eaten at any time. Prehistoric butchering was undoubtedly affected by some things that we are not and cannot be aware of simply because it is not possible to put ourselves into the cultural system similar to that within which the Casper Site bison were taken and utilized.

Prehistoric butchering in the New World was accomplished without metal tools with few exceptions and these can be ignored. Some descriptions of bison butchering by Plains Indians using both native and introduced tools and methods are known. An exhaustive review of these sources has been done by Wheat (1972) and they need not be considered further here. The main problem in gleaning reliable butchering data from these kinds of sources is that the informants were neither butchers nor anatomists and their descriptions are so general they serve very poorly in an attempt to approach any strictly empirical study of butchering. A detailed analysis of butchered bison bone from a number of kill sites covering nearly 10,000 years of time suggests that many subtle details of aboriginal butchering changed from one site to another. Different tool assemblages appear. One group may rely more on chipped stone cutting tools while another relies more on heavy chopping or crushing tools. One group may have favored bone tools and another stone tools. Some of these variations may be cultural and some may be the result of availability of raw materials. At this point in time, however, there seems little chance of establishing a butchering typology that will serve as a reliable chronological or cultural indicator for archeological sites.

Beyond this, there is always a considerable amount of intrasite variation that may have resulted from individual preferences or from many intangibles. The first animals butchered may have been more carefully butchered and processed than those later in the day. The number of animals obtained in a drive may have been insufficient which would have brought about better utilization of the carcasses than if a surplus had occurred. Even the weather could have affected the butchering processs in the same site. Wind, precipitation, heat and cold all affect the total overall process. Even butchering in a sand dune trap could have required some differences in technique from butchering the same animals in a steep-walled arroyo trap. Distances the butchered units had to be moved as well as the terrain probably affected the size of the units. All of these and others could easily add up to the butchering variations observed from site to site.

There are a number of considerations affecting the analysis of butchering in a site. It is assumed that the communal kill offers a maximum opportunity to analyze butchering techniques and tool usage. This is because it is further assumed that these kinds of economic operations were planned, predictable events and that it was realized beforehand that considerable effort would have to be expended to process the animals to avoid loss through spoilage. In this type of situation, it is expected that efforts would have been maximized to extract the most from human effort. Stylized butchering techniques, tools and tool usage should appear.

Several things should reveal something of butchering techniques. Relative frequencies of different bones might reveal something of preferences for certain parts of the carcass, but this must be considered along with the methods employed. The lack of certain bones may represent nothing more than a convenient way to prepare the carcass for removal to a processing area rather than a preference for the meat on that particular bone or unit. This could also indicate that certain bones were being collected for marrow or else used as tools. Distributions of bones in sites might reveal something of the sequence of events in the butchering process. This method was employed with some success in the analysis of the Olsen-Chubbuck site (Wheat 1972). There is a strong feeling after analyzing the bones from the Casper Site, however, that stacking of many bones may have been done after butchering and as such, a true picture of the units after completion of the actual butchering process was not present.

Some evidence of the butchering process can be expected on the bones themselves provided preservation of the original bone surfaces is adequate. Knives, hammerstones, and choppers leave distinctive marks on bone. Some marks are the direct results of a butchering technique such as the direct removal of a trochanter or tuberosity which was a muscle insertion or origin. Other marks are the by-products of butchering techniques, for example, the marks left on a bone as the result of cutting through the hide with a sharp tool.

It is significant that muscle insertions and origins, except for patellae, removed in the butchering processes are almost completely lacking from the bone deposits at the Casper Site. It is interpreted from this that they were used as handholds to strip muscles and possibly also as an aid in transport of the meat. Handholds such as these do make carrying a large, stripped-out muscle weighing several pounds or more much easier. Exceptions are, for example, the ends of dorsal spines and ventral branches of cervical vertebrae which were chopped or broken off because it was much easier to do this rather than attempt to cut around them. They should be found where the meat was processed but unfortunately at the Casper Site, no processing or other area was found. Conversely, it is regarded as significant in support of these ideas that the fragments of the trochlear ridges that were removed as a by-product of removing the patellae (and are not muscle attachments) were often recovered at the site.

A word of caution should be injected at this point also. Carnivores can and do chew off muscle attachments on a carcass and it is necessary to be able to recognize the difference between ones that were removed as the result of a butchering process and those removed by carnivores. Present-day carcasses such as deer, elk, or moose may have the tubers ischii or tubers coxae, for example, gnawed or chewed off but if bone preservation is adequate, it appears much different from those removed with a bone or stone chopper. Patterns appear different in the case of a carnivore as compared to those resulting from human activity. A case in point is that the distinctive marks on the trochlea of the butchered femur do not appear on the carnivore-chewed example; nor in the case of the front leg is the bone destruction limited to the proximal end of the humerus, but will extend to the distal end of the scapula as well. Once a familiarity is gained in butchering with prehistoric methods it is possible to distinguish between carnivore-chewed bones and those butchered by humans provided bone preservation is adequate.

A word of caution in butchering interpretations is attempting to generalize butchering with metal tools to that done with stone or bone tools. It is interesting to see the difference in techniques, for example, in opening a skull with a metal axe and knife compared to accomplishing the same task with a bone or stone chopper and stone knife. The differences in operations are obvious although both processes accomplish the desired end. The differences can be observed also from the marks left on the bones from the tools (Frison 1973: 15-16).

Actual butchering of animals in all bison kill sites investigated was accomplished by means of a relatively simple but functional tool kit. It was not realized until late in the excavation of the Casper Site that bone tools played an important role in the butchering process. It was at this time also that the actual nature of bone tools at several Late Prehistoric Period kill sites was being recognized. They were first considered to be some sort of scraping or polishing tool because of the polish on the working edges. Once they were recognized as chopping tools, butchering processes became better understood. The total tool kit at the Casper Site consisted of tools made from long bones of bison, hammerstones selected locally from cobble terraces, uniface flake and blade cutting tools, and possibly some use of projectile points as cutting tools although evidence for the latter is not at all conclusive.

A general discussion of the butchering tool assemblage is necessary to better understand general butchering processes. The bone tool assemblage was of importance at the Casper Site and at many other sites as well. Bone tool use was first postulated because of a lack of stone choppers and also because of abundant evidence for chopping loose of several major muscle attachments in order to strip out the muscles. In addition, some of the marks on bones resulting from chopping did not resemble marks left by stone choppers.

Ideas on bone chopper tool use were tested experimentally on modern bison. The tibia was the bone most often utilized as a chopper tool in all contexts studied and preparation of the tool for use was done in a stylized manner. There was apparently no preference for a right or left tibia. This bone was used most for chopping probably because it is shaped most properly and for the punishing use during chopping, it is apparently the strongest structurally of all the long bones. Either end of the tibia could and did serve as the handle and varying amounts of adjacent articulated bone were retained depending largely on weight requirements necessary for providing proper balance in chopping. The distal end of the femur was sometimes left articulated and on one specimen the entire femur was still articulated. The distal end of the tibia is much lighter than the proximal end and a chopper was sometimes formed by using the distal end of the tibia articulated to several of the tarsal units. The fibular tarsal may have sometimes served as a handle with the metatarsal removed or in some cases, varying amounts of the metatarsal were retained. It is strongly suggested also that the metatarsal may have been used as the handle in some cases. Weight is an important factor with a bone

chopper and retention of these adjacent articulated bones gives the necessary balance of weight and often provides a better handhold during use.

Preparation of the tibia for use as a chopper was stylized and repeated on a number of specimens. A hammerstone blow was usually directed to the lateral concave side of the tibia (Fig. 1.10a). This usually broke the tibia diagonally and produced a usable chopping edge on either one (Fig. 1.10b) and occasionally both sides of the break. Occasionally also, it shattered the bone in such a way that it was useless as a tool and in this case it was discarded. In some cases the broken edges needed some modification to render it usable.

The working edges of bone choppers of this nature may break during use. This may render a tool unusable but usually another working edge could be formed back of the original one. Broken points of bone choppers were found scattered throughout the butchered bone at the Casper Site. Some of these were in positions that strengthen considerably the claim for their use. This will be examined further under use of bone tools at the Casper Site.

Another bone less commonly used for chopping purposes at the Casper Site was the femur. usually a diagonal break was made close to the center of the diaphysis and the head of the femur was used as the handle. Several of these demonstrate evidence of use in the form of smoothed working edges and bone flakes removed as a result of impact during use. Several tools can be matched so that partial reconstructions of the entire original bones can be made. This clearly demonstrates the difference between the worn working edge of a tool and its matching surface on the unused portion of the bone on the opposite side of the break. At Late Prehistoric Period bison kill sites, many other bones were modified into tools including the pelves, large male horn cores, and metatarsals.

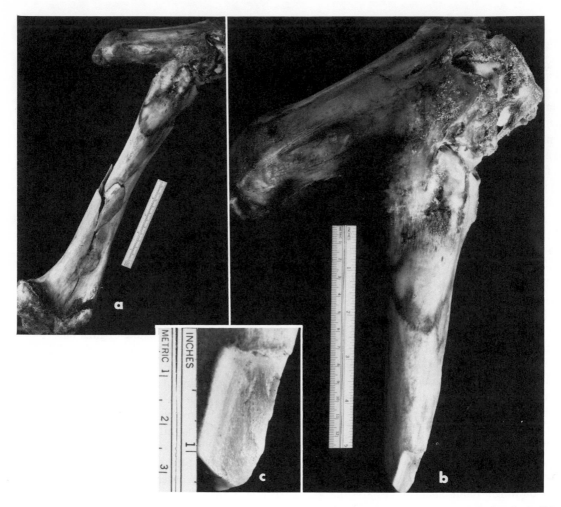

FIGURE 1.10 *Bison tibia broken with a hammerstone (a), to form a chopper (b). Chopping use produced a polish on the working edge (c).*

Another bone butchering tool type is one made from the humerus. This tool was used extensively at the Casper Site and at nearly all other bison butchering sites investigated. To prepare the tool, the proximal end of a humerus was removed just below the articular surface. The remaining portion of the bone expands its diameter continually from the distal end toward the break and the bone itself becomes quite thin adjacent to the proximal articular end. The interior cancellous bone is removed and the broken edge of the bone is scalloped around its entire diameter to form a number of sharp points. This tool was probably used in skinning and fleshing. The distal end is used as a handle and the sharp prongs are forced into the hide and provide a secure contact. By pushing on the tool, the hide is easily removed. Another probable use for this tool was to separate the muscles from bone surfaces. The thin, sharp scalloped edge cuts the flesh from the bones easily. In rare cases at some sites the distal end of a tibia, radius, or small femur was scalloped in similar manner and used as a tool. Another bone that was used only rarely as a tool at the Casper Site but commonly at many Late Prehistoric Period sites was the metatarsal.

Bones from a freshly-killed animal are extremely tough and superior in strength to bone that has been allowed to dry. Bone tools have been found in other bison kills (see e.g. Frison 1970) but the actual nature of their use was not well understood until recently. Smoothed and rounded working edges were interpreted as the result of scraping or polishing use until actual experiments were made using a *Bison bison* tibia chopper to chop loose the tuber ischii and tuber coxae on a cow pelvis. The tool stood up surprisingly well and the working edge became rounded and acquired what can best be described as a polish (Fig. 1.10c). Bone choppers are of little value in breaking heavy long bone but are every bit as functional as a stone chopper for removing muscle attachments and chopping into thin-walled bones such as dorsal spines and ribs.

The use of the scalloped edge humerus tool was first detected in a Late Prehistoric Period bison kill (Frison 1970) where unusually good bone preservation demonstrated a polish on the points of several of these tools. Much of the butchering process was stripping muscles from bones which can be done with a stone knife but for separating, for example, the flesh from an os coxae or removing the longissimus muscles or the flesh from the ribs, the scalloped edge of the humerus tool is unquestionably superior. For skinning, the same tool functions in a manner that is in many ways superior to the stone blade except of course for cutting. A major problem in skinning a large animal such as a bison that is lying on the ground, is to gain a handhold on the hide to pull it loose. The sharp prongs of the humerus tool eliminate this problem and it can also be used in conjunction with a stone knife for cutting.

Late Prehistoric Period bison kills where bone preservation was unusually good, demonstrate usage of a number of smaller bone tools made, for example, from pieces of ribs and dorsal spines. Preservation of bone was not good enough at the Casper Site to preserve this kind of evidence except in one instance where the medial side of a broken rib demonstrated an unmistakable wear pattern on a transverse break. Unfortunately this particular rib was not treated soon enough after exposure and most of the working edge disintegrated into a fine powder. The same was true of some other untreated bone at the site.

Other than bone tools, the butchering tool assemblage at the Casper Site consisted of hammerstones, flake knives, and possibly some of the projectile points. The hammerstones (20 of these were recovered) cluster around two weights of about 20 oz. (.57 kg.) and 42 oz (1.19 kg) and are generally elongate in form, some with a blunt but pointed end in order to concentrate the force in a small area and break heavy long bone (Fig. 1.11a-e) while others demonstrate rounded ends (Fig. 1.11f). Those with the more rounded ends were most likely used in breaking bone projections such as, for example, dorsal spines, ribs, ventral branches of transverse processes of cervical vertebrae, and transverse processes of lumbar vertebrae. Two of the hammerstones have what may be deliberate flakes removed to form crude choppers but it may have also been accidental or through use. These cobbles are available in gravel and cobble terraces of the nearby North Platte River and are usually of quartzite or granite. Similar hammerstones appeared in other kill sites although stone choppers in most other known kill sites were more carefully prepared than those at the Casper Site.

The next category of butchering tools is that of chipped stone. Three large flake tools and a single blade tool were recovered in the bone bed at the Casper Site. These represent a functional

FIGURE 1.11 *Hammerstones with pointed ends (a-e), and one with rounded ends (f) recovered from the bone bed at the Casper Site.*

class of bison butchering tools that was used in the Paleo-Indian period and was maintained in many contexts until they were replaced by metal tools in the historic period (see e.g. Frison 1967a, 1970, 1971a). They are almost certainly cutting tools.

There are many things to consider in the use of chipped stone tools in bison butchering sites. Some of these ideas are largely philosophical but even so, are based on observation and experiment. First, there is an urgency in butchering a large animal, especially in warm weather and days are quite warm in late summer and fall. An animal that does not have the intestines removed and the body heat allowed to escape will result in the meat becoming putrid or "sour". The ideal way to prevent this is to strip the meat from the carcass as soon as possible after the animal is killed and get it on a drying rack. In this way, the body heat is dissipated rapidly and if the sun is shining, the meat will form a hard outside glaze that flies cannot lay their eggs in (or "blow" the meat) and have them hatch. This can be satisfactorily proven quite easily. A thin strip of meat can be hung in the sun and although flies may cover it completely, they will not lay eggs in it. Flies were plentiful judging from the preserved layers of maggot cases that often appear in bison kill sites.

Another aspect of butchering has to do with economy of work and maximizing of effort. Butchering an animal the size of a mature bison is hard, difficult work. The task becomes harder the longer the animal is allowed to lay. The hide is removed easier from an animal that still retains the natural animal heat and the muscles can also be stripped easier. It would appear that the saving in effort alone would have speeded the butchering process in a communal kill.

Animal size is an important consideration in all butchering and one aspect of size is the tool used. An antelope can be butchered much easier than a mature bison. This can be demonstrated at present in the field and also from the archeological record (see e.g. Frison 1971b: 261-266). An antelope can be butchered with a small, thin, sharp flake. The hide of the antelope is thin and the small size of the animal allows easy manipulation of the carcass. The same flake will not hold up against a bison hide, although a bison can be butchered with small, sharp flakes. It is, however, a longer and more difficult task to do so. A small flake knife will simply not stand the hard pressure needed to rapidly cut the bison hide. In terms of maximizing effort, it is much better to obtain a large blade or flake that will withstand the necessary pressure, can be resharpened quickly and easily, and will withstand a number of resharpenings before it must be discarded.

Hafting a tool should be considered also. Adding a handle to a tool is a great advantage provided the handle can be added in such a way that it will withstand the necessary pressure over the period of usefulness of the tool. One experiment, for example, involved a medium-sized flake knife hafted with sinew and pitch to a wooden handle. The resulting tool functioned very well in slitting and skinning the hide of an antelope. The same tool was entirely ineffectual in rapidly slitting a bison hide. It would, however, have slit the bison hide if it had been done slowly and carefully, and always being aware of the limitations of the tool. It was found, however, that it was much easier to use a large flake tool that could easily be held in the hand and one which would withstand the necessary pressure.

Sharpening is another consideration. The small hafted flake tool will slit a thin antelope hide without serious dulling of the edge. The same does not hold true of the same tool in slitting a bison hide. In the latter case the tool soon becomes dull or perhaps it should be stated that it loses the keen cutting edge. As the keen edge is lost, more pressure is required and the limitations of the haft are continually tested. A decision is soon necessary to either sharpen the tool or risk destruction of the hafting. A small flake will not withstand much sharpening before the effective working edge of the tool is used up.

It would be desirous to have a functional haft on a large flake tool but it is still reasonably functional without it. There are methods by which a large flake tool can be hafted and withstand the necessary pressures but there are considerations. In order to attach a functional haft to a large cutting tool, a large part of the tool itself must be securely held in contact with the haft which in turn requires a large amount of haft binding. From experiment, a large hafted tool that is really effective in skinning a bison should have at least half and preferably more of the actual surface of the tool covered with haft and haft binding. The most effective method of hafting tried was to use a bison rib or a piece of wood of similar shape, and cut a long, deep slot in one side of the haft so that the tool will fit edgewise into the slot. The slot should be deep enough and long enough so that its sides extend well up both faces of the tool and from the base of the tool to at least half its length. Haft binding of sinew must then be applied over both haft and tool for at least a third and again, preferably more of the distance from the base to the point of the tool. To allow the tool to be better seated in the haft, a piece of thin tanned hide, shredded plant fibers or preferably pitch or bitumen may be placed between the tool haft and its contact surface with the tool. A stone tool hafted in this manner will withstand considerable pressure and enough working edge of the tool is exposed to allow for a number of sharpening and use sequences.

There are, of course, alternative hafting methods. During use of the tool, however, it is well to remember that continued contact between the sinew bindings and warm blood and other body fluids will cause the sinew bindings to become elastic. The result, of course, is that once a tool loosens in any way the haft is useless.

Pitch may be used to cover the haft binding which is some protection from body fluids.

Pitch may also be used as the sole binding but unless the stone is deeply seated in the haft, it is not too suitable for the heavy, intensive use encountered during bison butchering. Some fiber bindings which will contract somewhat upon becoming damp are not too successful, lacking the strength of sinew and thereby creating a bulkiness of the tool and making it difficult to manipulate. These and other reasons as well may be why the choice of a cutting tool in communal bison butchering sites was mainly a large percussion flake tool that could be held securely in the hand, sharpened easily with a hard or soft hammer, and discarded when no longer functional. There was a minimum of effort in manufacture and preparation which left fewer regrets when it had to be discarded.

Tool use in these kinds of situations was intense and attrition was high due to frequent resharpenings. There was little chance to develop the emotional feelings toward a tool similar to that a hunter feels for a favorite knife or a carpenter a favorite saw and for which much time and effort is expended to keep them in perfect condition and not use them for tasks that would unnecessarily hasten the demise of their period of usefulness. To state it another way, the hunter probably had a knife that was a carefully-chosen piece of stone and carefully prepared to produce an optimum cutting edge. It would last a long time under ordinary day to day use, but would last only a short time while subjected to intense use comparable to butchering in a communal bison kill. It was preferable to utilize tools that were nearly equally functional, less esthetic and upon which there was little investment in time and effort.

It must be admitted, however, that with any hypothesis there are data that do not fit. At the Wardell Buffalo Trap, a Late Prehistoric Period bison trap , for example, (Frison 1973) the animals were butchered with small, pressure-flaked cutting tools used in conjunction with stone choppers. There is no indication that any of the cutting tools were hafted and they were apparently able to accomplish the butchering with comparatively delicate chipped stone cutting tools.

THE POSTULATED BUTCHERING PROCESS AT THE CASPER SITE

The reconstruction of butchering at the Casper Site was made by considering evidence from a number of sources including tool assemblages, tool marks on bones, bone distributions in activity areas, composition of butchered units, and experimental butchering on modern *Bison bison*. A large share of the butchering interpretations here in general was derived from Late Prehistoric Period bison kills where bone preservation was much better than at the Casper Site. No evidence suggests wastage of meat at the Casper Site although not all of the prime marrow bones were taken. All in all, the butchering process was quite stylized although some variation can be detected.

Many of the individual bones and butchered units at the Casper Site demonstrated reasonably good preservation and apparently remained almost completely undisturbed from the time they were butchered. The combination of these two conditions allows a good basis for reconstruction of butchering processes. There is evidence to suggest deliberate stacking of various butchering units once the desired muscles were stripped. It is difficult to evaluate the effects of this when using the configuration of the butchered units as a means of establishing a sequence of events in the butchering process.

The first consideration in butchering is usually removal of the intestines to prevent spoilage. It is possible to leave the insides for a long as two or three hours if the animal is eating dry feed but if the animal is eating green or succulent feed the intestines should be removed as soon as possible. Otherwise the gasses from the digestive tract cause rapid bloating and spoilage. Temperature makes a difference also. Bloating occurs more rapidly on a hot day than a cool one. It would appear that with a large number of animals that would require a day's butchering, it would have been the practice to at least open the stomach cavity on all the animals before the butchers began the actual cutting-up of the separate carcasses. If only a few animals were killed, it would have been possible to first skin and strip the meat from a carcass and then open the animal and take whatever internal organs were wanted.

There are historic accounts of spread-eagling a dead buffalo and slitting the hide down the back. This method works perfectly well if only the choice parts of the animal are to be taken such as the hump and the loins. If the animal is to be completely butchered, however, it is a difficult method that does not fit in well with complete stripping of muscles. It is much easier to lay the animal on its side, slit the hide down the belly, remove the muscles from one side and then turn the animal and strip the muscles from the opposite side. To this point there is no irrefutable evidence to satisfactorily demonstrate that one method was preferred over the other at the Casper Site. The overall suggested process, however, leans toward having the animal on its side, slitting the hide down the belly and butchering one side at a time. The hide probably also served as a platform to protect the meat from sand since the butchering at the kill was performed in an area of loose sand which is one of the most disagreeable spots possible in which to butcher a large animal.

Some evidence is suggestive of the skinning process. Significant numbers of metatarsals and metacarpals demonstrate diagonal or transverse cutting marks on the diaphyses. These could be explained as marks resulting from cutting an initial hole in the hide for skinning. This is the easiest spot to make the initial cut. The hair is short, the hide is thin and is in direct contact with bone so that a few strokes with a sharp stone blade will make the desired opening in the hide. Once a hole large enough to insert a finger is present, it is relatively simple to hold the hide taut and continue the cut as desired.

Another location for similar-appearing marks is on the ventral edge of the mandibles directly below the diastema and most Casper Site mandibles demonstrate transverse sawing marks in this vicinity. It is postulated that these marks were the by-product of cutting a hole in the hide to begin a slit from the throat down the belly. Similar cutting marks on metatarsals, metacarpals and mandibles appeared in Late Prehistoric Period bison butchering contexts (Frison 1970, 1973). With a stone knife, the slit is easier from anterior to posterior following the natural direction in which the hair lies. With a steel knife, the sharp point of the knife can be inserted under the hide and pushed from anterior to posterior or vice versa. The stone knife works best when used with a sawing motion while held tightly against a taut hide and this is more difficult when going from posterior to anterior against the direction of the hair.

Another bit of evidence that may have resulted from skinning is that of 34 butchered units consisting of articulated pelvis, sacrum and two or more vertebrae, only two had the caudal vertebrae articulated. The units lacking caudal vertebrae without exception have part of one or one or two of the last sacral vertebrae broken off. The broken sacral vertebrae were not found in the bone deposits and it is believed they and the caudal vertebrae were removed with the hide.

Once the hide was removed from one side of the animal, the muscle stripping process began with the front leg. The radius-ulna was usually not disarticulated from the humerus nor was there separation of ulna from radius except what

occurred on a few specimens that were obviously broken for marrow collection. If they were stripping out the triceps muscle it was apparently done by first cutting it off at its insertion to the olecranon rather than chopping off the latter as was commonly done at some Late Prehistoric Period sites. Not one of 77 ulnae demonstrate evidence of chopping into, breaking or crushing part of the olecranon as was commonly done at the Glenrock Buffalo Jump (Frison 1970:14).

At the Casper Site the scapulae with one exception were always separated from the humeri. The single exception was a butchered unit from a large but immature male which consisted of the first five thoracics with the ribs attached and the articulated right scapula and humerus. Separation of humerus and scapula was usually done by chopping off the entire proximal end of the humerus just distal to the articular surface. In some cases the lateral and medial tuberosities on the proximal end of the humerus were chopped loose rather than the entire proximal end. Nearly all of the scapulae were complete and separation from the humeri was accomplished with little or no damage to the distal ends of the scapulae. Many scapulae demonstrate striations of various length especially in the areas of the supraspinous and infraspinous fossae, probably the marks left from tools used in removing flesh. Nothing suggests any use of the scapulae as tools at the site. Many scapulae were stacked in piles, one of which contained 16, another 12 and some contained two, three and four.

It is postulated that the proximal end of the humerus or the tuberosities, whichever was removed, was used as a handhold for stripping a number of muscles on the anterior part of the animal. Rarely were any of these parts of humeri recovered in the site deposits but all of those found demonstrate chopping marks from a sharp-pointed tool used in their removal (Fig. 1.12).

In many cases, the entire front leg was

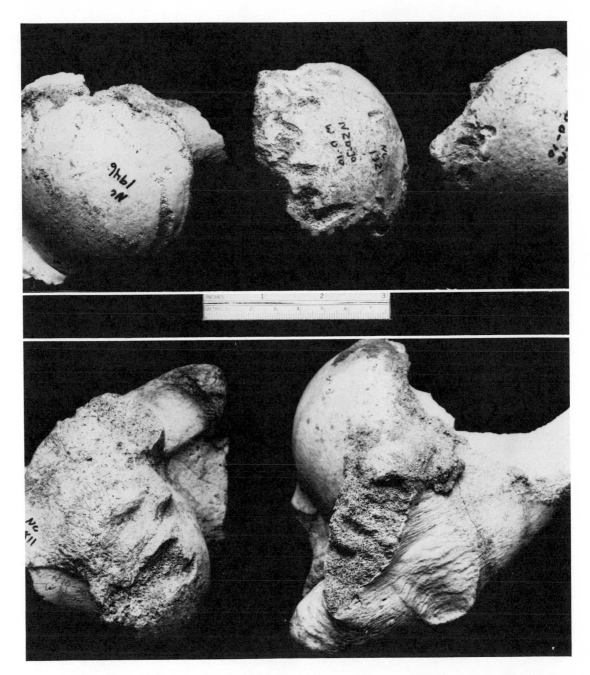

FIGURE 1.12 *Chopping tool marks on proximal ends of bison humeri from the Casper Site.*

discarded after the flesh was stripped but often also the humerus and radius were smashed open to gain entrance to the marrow cavity. Those that were opened (Fig. 1.13b) demonstrate clearly the fractures from the tools used in the process. A common butchered unit recovered was the distal humerus and proximal radius-ulna, probably the result of smashing the bones for marrow retrieval. The humerus was often utilized as a special tool probably for fleshing or skinning or both and when so used, the proximal end was scalloped to form a number of sharp prongs (Fig. 1.14b) and some of these demonstrate wear patterns presumably from use.

In only one instance was there positive evidence of removing a front foot by cutting the ligaments. The evidence for this is from cut marks on radial and ulnar carpals to sever the ligaments and separate the front foot at the distal end of the radius which was a common practice at a Late Prehistoric Period butchering site (Frison 1970: 11). No evidence of any utilization of metacarpals or the front phalanges could be determined. Usually the third phalanges or hoof cores were articulated but badly deteriorated.

After removal of the front leg, attention was then turned to the rear leg. Muscle stripping here was stylized and usually began with chopping into the trochlea on the femur to gain access to the patella. Evidence for this appears on nearly all femora as pieces of bone chopped out of the trochlea (Fig. 1.13c) and these pieces were occasionally found in the bone deposits. Tool marks appear on the trochles, the pieces removed, and on several patellae. The patella was removed in rare cases without chopping into the trochlea as for example on the the one butchering unit consisting of pelvis, lumbars, and both hind legs (Fig. 1.15) which was completely articulated but with the patellae missing.

With the patella as a handhold, the lateral muscles of the rear leg were stripped out to the

trochanter major which was chopped loose and again there is evidence of the use of a sharp-pointed tool (e.g. Fig. 1.13c). Muscle stripping now continued in an anterior direction until the tuber coxae was reached. This was then chopped loose (e.g. Fig. 1.13d) and the muscles lying between the ribs and dorsal spines were stripped out as far as the base of the skull if desired. This resulted in a long strip of meat beginning with the patella and reaching to the base of the skull that may be seven or more feet long depending on the size of the animal. It includes a good share of the choice meat on one side of the carcass and on a mature *Bison bison* cow, it may weigh over 50 pounds depending upon the various muscles included and the size of the animal.

Cutting marks from chipped stone knives often appear on the dorsal spines and lateral sides of the ribs as a result of cutting the muscles loose as they are stripped. Chopping tool marks appear on all except one ilium resulting from the removal of the tuber coxae. The sublumbar muscles appear to have been removed separately. In some butchering sites it was common to break the ends of the transverse processes of the lumbar vertebrae presumably to include the sublumbar muscles with the longissimus dorsii and other longitudinal muscles between the ribs and dorsal spines. This was apparently not the case at the Casper Site since the transverse processes of the lumbar vertebrae were usually not broken and it is quite difficult to include the sublumbar muscles without doing so.

The next step in the proposed butchering sequence was to chop loose the tuber ischii in order to gain a handhold for stripping out the posterior leg muscles (e.g. Fig. 1.13d). Of the 34 recovered units with complete pelves, only one still retained the tuber ischii and tuber coxae intact. Small depressed fractures strongly suggest this was accomplished with sharp-pointed choppers, probably of bone. Removal of all of these key muscle attachments was a standard process in a

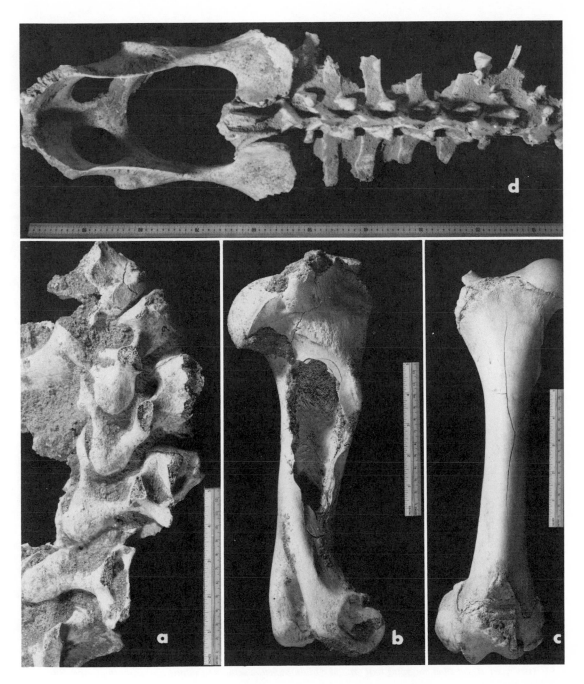

FIGURE 1.13 *Butchering marks on cervical vertebrae (a), humerus (b), femur (c), and a pelvis-lumbar-distal thoracic unit (d) from the Casper Site.*

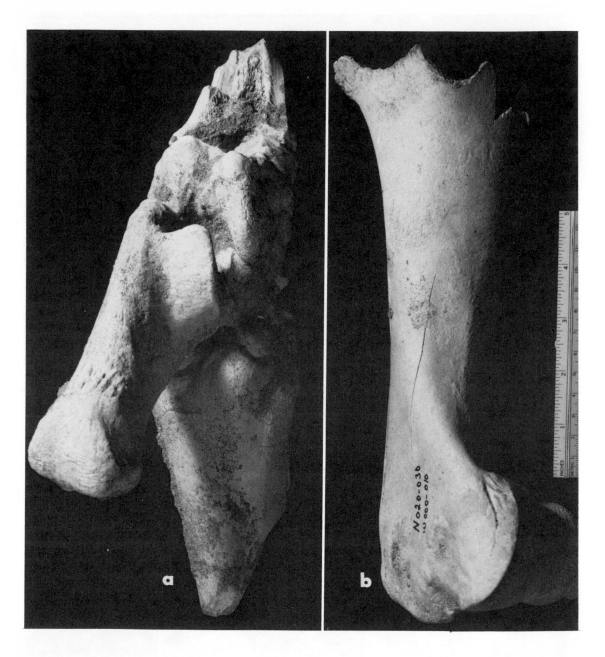

FIGURE 1.14 *Bison tibia chopping tool (a) and a bison humerus skinning-fleshing tool from the Casper Site.*

FIGURE 1.15 *Part of the bone bed with most single bones removed to show articulated units. At bottom left is the posterior end and a front leg unit of an animal in sitting positon. Above and to the right of this unit is a complete pelvis-vertebral column unit.*

number of other bison butchering contexts (Frison 1970, 1973).

There is no evidence at the Casper Site of breaking off or crushing the tuber calcis as was common in a Late Prehistoric Period site (Frison 1970) so that whether or not they were stripping out the gastrocnemius muscle is uncertain. It could have been accomplished by cutting its attachment to the tuber calcis and no evidence of this would have remained.

With only two exceptions, the head of the femur was removed from the acetabulum. This is not too difficult with the flesh stripped away. The leg need only to be given a sharp jerk using the hump formed by the chopped-off trochanter major as a fulcrum to lever the head of the femur

from the acetabulum socket. There is no evidence of cutting of ligaments around the acetabulum as was observed in a Late Prehistoric context (Frison 1970: 12) nor were they breaking off the head of the femur as in another (Frison 1967a: 33).

Some femora were broken for marrow. Depressed fractures appear on the diaphyses both proximally and distally. Several proximal ends of femora were utilized as bone choppers. Usable breaks across the diaphyses formed working edges and the heads were used as handles (Fig. 1.16). Only one example demonstrates a femur chopper utilizing the distal end as a handle and a diagonal break as the working edge. In this case, however, the working edge bears unmistakable polish and

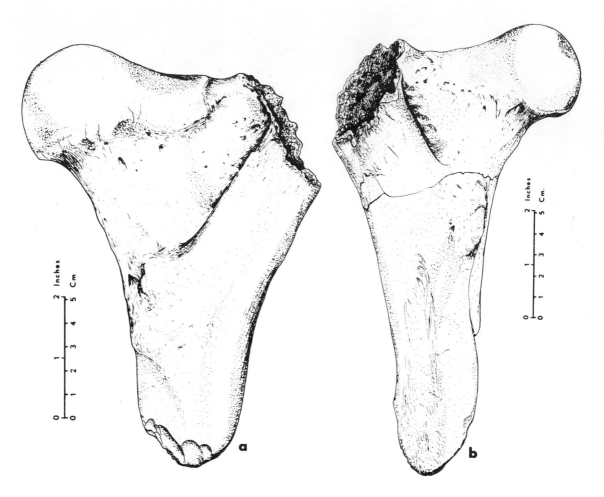

FIGURE 1.16 *Bison femur choppers from the Casper Site. Note the deliberate removal of the trochanter major on both examples.*

longitudinal striations from use. Several pieces of femora recovered from the bone bed are undoubtedly working edges broken from choppers.

Tibiae were often broken for marrow. As on femora, they were crushed to expose the marrow cavity. Tibiae were also the most important bones for use as bone choppers. Both proximal ends (Fig. 1.17) and distal ends (Fig. 1.18) were used as handles. Parts of femora on one end (Fig. 1.19) and metatarsals on the other end (Fig.

1.14a) were often left to form a better handle and probably also to add the necessary weight and balance to properly perform the necessary chopping tasks. On one tibia which was reconstructed from fragments in the bone debris, there is a strong suggestion of smashing purely for marrow removal. On others it appears the smashing was purposeful in attempts to break the tibia in order to form suitable chopping edges. In smashing for marrow, the blows are usually

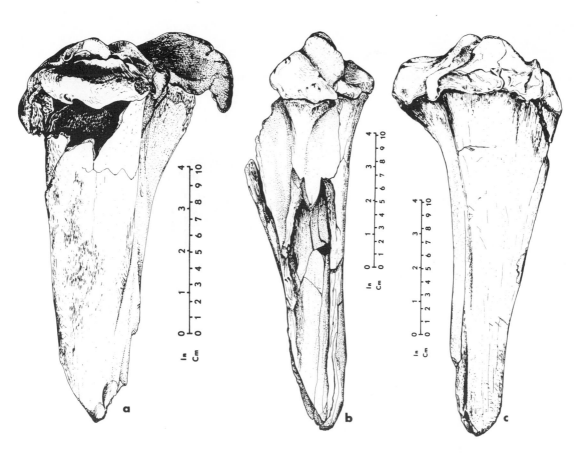

FIGURE 1.17 *Bison tibia choppers from the Casper Site.*

distributed the full length of the diaphysis leaving the marrow cavity exposed. As already mentioned, in order to manufacture a chopping tool from a bison tibia, the hammerstone blow is directed to the concave lateral surface distal to the proximal articular end and this usually results in a suitable chopping point (Fig. 1.10).

Another form of tibia chopper utilized the distal end articulated to the astragalus and calcaneus (Fig. 1.14a) which in some cases may have been used as a handle. If so used, it is functionally the same kind of tool as the experimental one (Fig. 1.10). Part of the metatarsal was left in Fig. 14a

probably to add the necessary weight. The working edge was formed by a suitable break on the diaphysis of the tibia a short distance from the distal end.

Several metatarsals were broken presumably for marrow retrieval although the yield for these is low. Wear striations on the broken edges of two of these suggest possible use as bone tools but for what purpose is as yet unclear. A common butchering unit was the distal tibia and remaining elements still articulated. In several cases the separation was made at the distal end of the tibia by holding the leg in the extreme extended

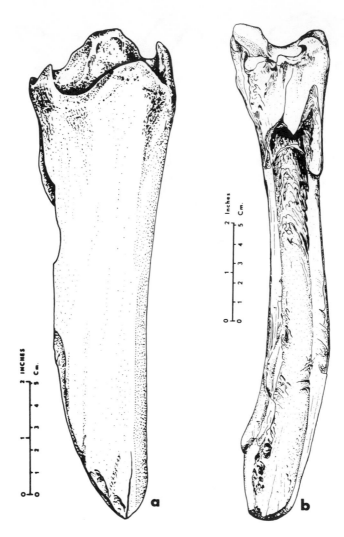

FIGURE 1.18 *Bison tibia choppers from the Casper Site.*

position and severing the ligaments by cutting around the posterior and medial sides of the astragalus and around over the calcaneus, and cutting tool marks are present on the bones in these locations. With the ligaments cut, the foot can be snapped off from the tibia. This method of removing the hind foot was common to Late Prehistoric Period sites (see e.g. Frison 1970:

12-13). It is possible also that this was a means of stripping the gastrocnemius muscle by using the tarsals and the remainder of the foot as a handle and cutting the muscle loose at the tuber calcis after it was stripped out. In modern butchering, a similar cut is made only more distally so that the foot is snapped off at the proximal end of the metatarsal. By doing this, the opening between

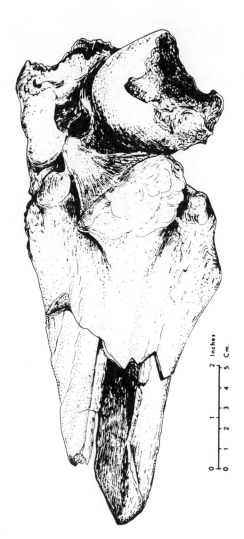

cartilage. Method of brisket removal was to chop off the distal ends of the ribs and presumably remove the brisket section as a unit. This same method is common to later sites. Most ribs were missing also and presumably were removed as units. No. 1 ribs, however, were usually ignored and often number 2 and 3 also. Almost without exception, the ribs were broken near the rib head and many of these remained articulated to the vertebrae. Only rarely were the ribs broken distally very far from the articular end. It was discovered in experimental butchering that instead of chopping or breaking with tools, the ribs were often broken by grasping the end of the rib already separated from the costal cartilage and giving it a sharp upward lift. This breaks the rib with little effort and in a distinctive manner and is quite different from the breaks made with a chopper. A bison foot can also be used to break ribs effectively but whether or not this method was employed at the Casper Site is purely conjectural.

With one exception on a single butchering unit, the dorsal spines were chopped or broken off all thoracics and the last cervical vertebra. This was usually done about half way between the base and distal end and was presumably for removal of the hump meat. The few distal ends of spines recovered and bases that remain suggest they were broken off with a sideways blow from a hammerstone or club, or in some cases, chopped off with a bone chopper (e.g. Fig. 1.20). The almost total absence of the distal ends of dorsal spines at the site suggests they were removed with the hump meat to a processing or camp area.

At this point, butchering of one side of the animal was completed and it was turned over and the process repeated for the other side. The vertebral column was separated usually in the vicinity of the last 1-4 thoracics (Fig. 1.13d, Fig. 1.21). A common method was to chop into the vertebra from the top or to chop into the body of the vertebra from the bottom. In most cases

FIGURE 1.19 *Tibia chopper from the Casper Site with part of the femur left articulated.*

the tibia and calcaneus is used to insert a gambrel for suspending the animal by the hind legs.

There is strong evidence to suggest the brisket was an especially desired cut of meat in most prehistoric bison utilization contexts. At the Casper Site, sternal bones were limited to a single well-preserved xiphoid and a single costal

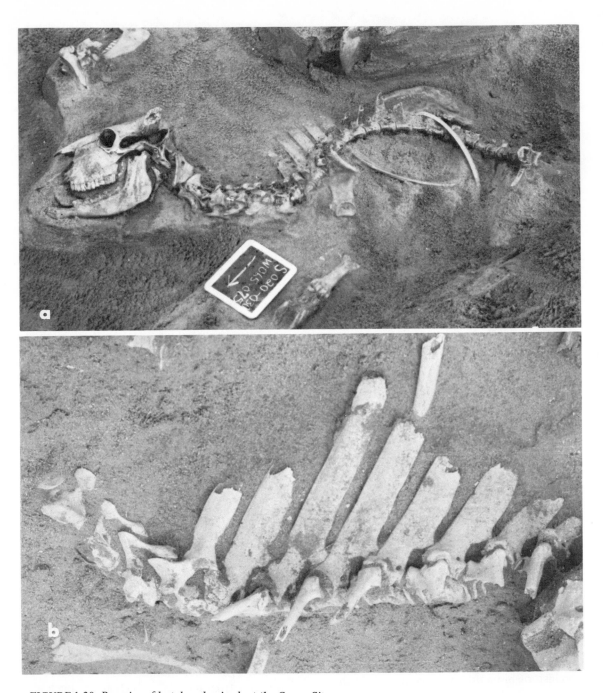

FIGURE 1.20 *Remains of butchered animals at the Casper Site.*

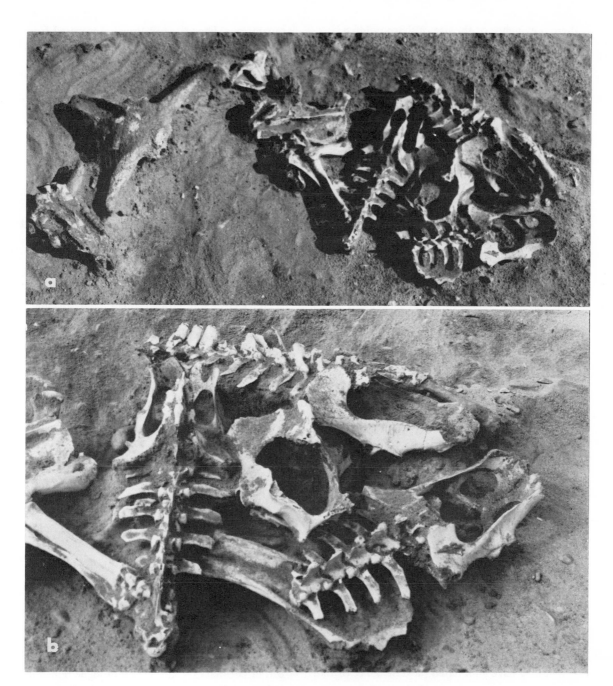

FIGURE 1.21 *Stacked units in a butchering activity area at the Casper Site.*

there is evidence of the use of sharp-pointed chopping tools. Several thoracics, usually the ones from 7-12 were often missing and it may have been common to remove several thoracics with one rib unit. In one case it is suggested that the entire "saddle" consisting of thoracics and ribs from 8-12 were chopped out and removed as a unit. This was the unit (Fig. 1.15) in which the posterior part of the animal was in a sitting position and the gap in the thoracics is clearly visible while the remainder of the anterior thoracics and ribs are still in position. Whether or not this was a common occurrence could not be determined. If not, however, it is difficult to understand why they continually made this separation of the vertebral column since it is easy to strip the meat from the entire carcass without doing so.

The vertebral column was also commonly separated in the vicinity of the first 1-2 thoracics leaving a unit that was discarded. It usually consisted of the cervicals minus the atlas and one or two thoracics (e.g. Fig. 1.13a). The atlas was usually separated from both skull and the other cervicals. Two exceptions are an articulated unit consisting of the skull and the entire vertebral column excepting the last two lumbars (Fig. 1. 20a) and another skull articulated with the cervicals and 1st thoracic vertebrae. In three other cases the atlas was articulated with a few cervicals and in one of these two thoracics also.

There were no butchering marks to suggest the exact means of removing the skull except that several atlas vertebrae have depressed fractures on the dorsal side of one or both wings and toward the posterior part. This might explain the means of separation from the axis although no cutting or chopping marks appeared on any of the latter. Unfortunately, most cervicals seem to have been stacked toward the top of the bone level and preservation was generally poor which may have eliminated most evidence of tool use.

The same is true of the skull and atlas separation. The atlas was usually separated from the skull but satisfactory evidence as to how this was accomplished was not present. No crushing of bone is evident and must have been done by cutting some ligaments after the muscles were stripped from the neck. Bone preservation was usually bad in the occipital area of the skulls and this would have erased any evidence of cutting.

The flesh on the neck was stripped. Evidence for this is that with only one exception, the large ventral branches of the transverse processes of the 6th cervical vertebra were chopped loose. Less commonly the same branches of the 3rd, 4th and 5th cervicals were also removed (Fig. 1.13a). This greatly facilitates removal of the neck muscles and by experiment on modern bison, the neck can be stripped clean of flesh by this method and is much easier and efficient than to cut around the ventral branches.

There is no evidence of utilization of the brains or breakage of any area surrounding the brain cavity except for one skull on which the occipital area was broken. Lacking entirely are the central holes in the frontal bones so common to Late Prehistoric Period bison kills. There is good evidence, however, that the tongue was taken. Sawing marks appear along the medial side of most mandibles suggesting they were cutting the mylohyoideus muscle holding the tongue. Proximal ends of hyoid bones were still articulated to the skulls while the distal ends were missing. Experiment shows these are marks commonly remaining when the tongue is removed with a stone knife. Mandibles were usually but not always separated from the skull subsequent to removal of the tongue. This was accomplished without damage to the skull or mandibles in many cases while with about equal frequency one mandible was broken across the diastema probably to facilitate the removal. This latter breakage cuts across earlier cut marks resulting from tongue removal indicating the sequence of events. A number of skulls were crushed or split in the vicinity of the palate to the extent that the maxillaries were broken out and this may have had to do with recovery of contents of cavities in the anterior part of the skull. A number of skulls also had the nasal bones removed probably for similar purposes. As a last gesture the skulls in many cases were placed on top of bone piles. As a result they do demonstrate considerable weathering compared to those bones and units closer to the bottom of the piles. Skulls and other units as well toward the northeast end of the parabolic dune were especially weathered (Fig. 1.22) but there were no discernible differences in the degree of articulation between these and the ones on the southwest end.

As already mentioned, several units at the Casper Site indicate deliberate stacking. This is best indicated from scapulae where as many as 16 were in one pile underneath other units and individual bones (see Endpiece). Pelvis-lumbar-distal thoracic units were deliberately stacked in at least one instance (Fig. 1.21) and the feeling was present that the skulls had been placed on top of this pile and had subsequently fallen off. At first it was felt that this stacking may have indicated a sequence of events and procedures in the butchering process. It is now believed, however, that the stacking was done after the butchering was completed. Whether it represents some cultural practice or merely capricious behavior cannot at this time be determined.

This then is the suggested butchering procedure for the Casper Site bison. There are some places where the sequence could have been changed. The neck and skull could have been removed early in the process but there is no real gain by doing this. It seems very likely from a considerable amount of butchering experience with stone and bone tools, that the animals were butchered by groups of two or three or even four persons working on a single carcass. It is much more efficient for one person to hold the animal or parts of the animal in proper position while others perform the actual operations. More than four persons working on a single carcass, however, results in decreased efficiency.

The evidence at the Casper Site does not suggest that any considerable amount of the usable parts of the animals was wasted. Several long bones including femora, tibiae, humeri, and radii that are prime sources of marrow were not taken. The brain was not utilized at all but this could have been related to cultural ideas. Very few of the mandibles demonstrated breakage of the ventral borders as is common in many known Late Prehistoric Period sites and was done to retrieve the contents of the pulp cavity at the base of the molar tooth row. Only four butchered units demonstrate any unusual amount of articulation and only two of these suggest that any significant amount of meat may have remained on it. The two in question are from a nearly mature male and even here, most of the muscles may have been stripped even though key muscle attachments such as the patella, tubers coxae, tubers ischii, torchanter major, and lateral and medial tuberosities on the humerus remained intact. This humerus was also the only one articulated to a scapula. The dorsal spines were also intact on the thoracics recovered from this particular animal. It is possible that the flesh on a large bull was not considered as desirable as that on females and younger animals but still the other older males in the site were utilized in the same manner as females and younger animals. It is possible also that for some reason this large male presented problems in butchering or, being a large male, it was left until last and part of it simply spoiled. It is easy to understand why a large male would have been left until last. The meat is not as good as that from the females and younger animals and it is much more difficult to butcher a male that weighs close to a ton than a female that weighs from 900-1200 pounds.

One other fairly complete unit already mentioned several times was a mature female on

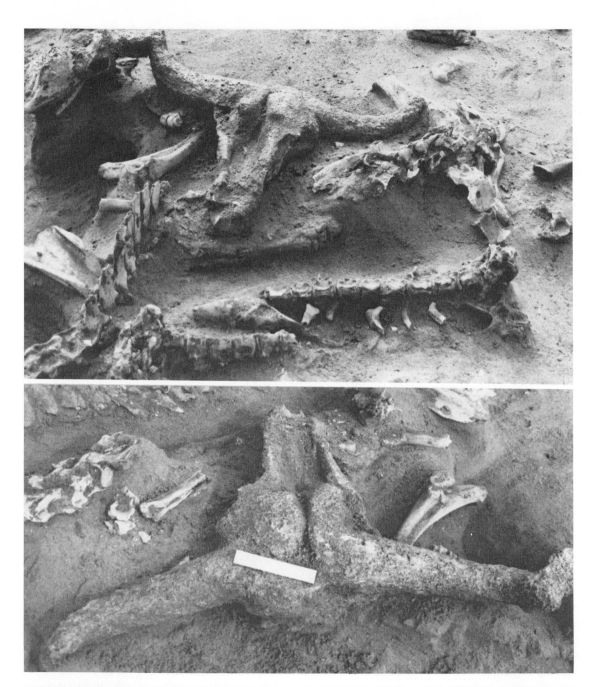

FIGURE 1.22 *Butchered units toward the northeast end of the old parabolic dune demonstrating poor bone preservation at the Casper Site.*

which all of the bones posterior to the 12th thoracic were present except for a few caudals and the patellae (Fig. 1.15). The animal was actually quite completely butchered. The left femur had the trochanter major intact and neither trochlea on the femora had been chopped into to gain access to the patellae. The tuber coxae and tuber ischii, however, were both chopped off. Some meat may have been left on this carcass but probably not a large percentage of the total amont.

The other more complete unit was another mature female (Fig. 1.20a). This unit included the skull and the entire vertebral column except for the last two lumbars. The tongue had been removed since the mandibles bear cut marks from cutting the mylohyoideus muscle and the hyoid bones are broken off. The dorsal spines were chopped off and one scapula remained in an articulated positon suggesting that the sub-scapular muscles on one side had not been taken. The ribs had all been removed except the 14th on one side and the 7th on the other side. Several rib heads were still in the articulated position. All in all, there is very little suggestion that any significant amount of meat remained on this unit.

The population study on the Casper Site bison demonstrates that animals in the long yearling (approximately 1.6 years) age group are lacking entirely (see Chapter 2). It is not believed that this is the result of removal of these animals from the site or of different butchering techniques applied to them. Not only are mandibles in this age category lacking but none of the long bones demonstrate the proper ossification found in long yearlings. The reason for their absence may be ecological or it may be the result of a human kill the year before. With this category of animals lacking, however, it is not possible to say whether or not they were butchered differently from the more mature animals. There is evidence that the calves were handled somewhat in a different manner. A number of appendicular units of calves remain but very few elements of the axial skeletons remain. A number of calf skulls were left behind, one with mandibles intact. It would appear that in most cases except for the skulls the calves were removed entirely In a minority of cases, however, the parts of the calves connected with the axial skeleton were removed but a number of appendicular units were stripped and left.

There can be no doubt that the calves at the Casper Site were clustering around an age of six to seven months and tooth eruption schedules bear this out. The first lower molar is well erupted with wear showing on both cusps. The first cusp of the second molar is just visible or very close to being visible. This compares well with *Bison bison* calves of about six months of age from modern herds. A conservative estimate is that a *Bison bison* calf of this age should weigh 400 pounds. A *Bison antiquus* calf was somewhat larger but in terms of butchering there is a great difference between handling an animal of this size and a mature female of perhaps 1,200-1,500 pounds.

It is difficult to tell much about the treatment of the three fetal specimens from the site. Two were close to full term and one was probably about two months earlier. Several parts of one of these were concentrated in a small area and included were parts of the vertebral column, ribs and scapulae. It is suggested the appendicular parts were removed, the opposite procedure to that of the calves. Other fetal material was not found in any interpretive context with respect to butchering.

THE CASE FOR THE USE OF BONE BUTCHERING TOOLS AT THE CASPER SITE

There has been hesitation in making strong, positive claims for bone butchering tool assemblages such as those at the Casper Site. Some of this is probably the result of Raymond Dart (1957) and his claims of early bone tools and the opposition and even ridicule that greeted his ideas. Use of bone tools of this nature is difficult to demonstrate indisputably in contrast to the stone tools for which, even though their actual use may be difficult to demonstrate, their use is accepted because of context. Bone tool use in butchering seems indisputable from several bits of concrete evidence and from several interpretive approaches to the evidence. Bone tools were not utilized in all communal bison kill contexts but when they were used, their use can often be detected.

A good deal of chopping is evident on certain parts of bones remaining at the Casper Site. By experiment, most of these chopping marks are not the product of any heavy stone tool left at the site. An unlikely possibility exists that a class of stone chopping tools was removed from the site after use. Experiment however, demonstrates that stone choppers with points sharp enough to leave the marks on the Casper Site bone will also regularly undergo breakage of the sharp points. The latter if they were extant, would have had to appear along with the rest of the assemblage. Lacking both the proper tools and the evidence of their presence and use, the case for another and different class of chopping tool is strengthened.

The tool marks in question cluster around articular surfaces and muscle insertions and origins where the bones are relatively soft compared to the diaphyses of long bones. One example is the proximal articular end of the humerus which was almost always removed (Fig. 1.12). Very few of the latter elements remained at the site but the ones present demonstrate chopping tool marks which were made with sharp-pointed tools that were swung with considerable velocity. Experiments on modern bison humeri demonstrated that between 12 and 27 strokes from a 3.2 pound bone chopper were required to accomplish this

although with more practice it would undoubtedly become much simpler. Much of the difference depends on the age of the animal and the consequent progress of ossification of the epiphyses. The same articular end can be removed with a sharp stone chopper but it is very difficult to remove with a blunt one. Lacking the proper kind of stone choppers or evidence for their use at the site, the bone chopper is the best candidate for having done the job.

The same general ideas are true of several other bone projections that were removed in butchering bison. The tuber coxae and tuber ischii are good examples. At the Casper Site they were removed by means of a number of blows from a sharp-pointed tool. The evidence for this is a number of depressed fractures and tool marks across the face of the fractured bones. The same bone projections can be removed with a stone chopper and the tuber ischii can be broken off with a hammerstone but both of the latter tools leave different tool marks.

The distribution of complete and broken tools is strong evidence for the nature of their use at the Casper Site. Broken points of bone tools turned up in bones where they were apparently broken during use. One was embedded in the cancellous bone on the proximal end of a humerus (Fig. 1.23 left) while another was found in the distal end of a femur in the cancellous bone under the trochlea (Fig. 1.23 right). The former had apparently broken off in an attempt to remove the proximal articular end of the humerus while the latter had broken off while chopping into the trochlea in order to remove the patella. A tibia chopper was recovered where it had been used presumably to chop off the ventral branches of cervical vertebrae and a humerus fleshing tool lay alongside the vertrebral column where it may have been used to remove longitudinal muscles along the back. Perhaps most convincing is a 12th thoracic vertebra that was chopped into dorsally to separate the vertebral column. One stroke

FIGURE 1.23 *Broken ends of bison tibia choppers in the proximal end of a humerus (left) and the distal end of a femur (right) from the Casper Site.*

of the chopper was about an inch high or glanced off and penetrated the thin outer bone but left the sharp point of the chopper embedded in the vertebra. There are many other instances of suggested tool use that were observed but these are representative.

A number of points broken from bone tools were also recovered. All demonstrate some evidence of use in the form of a polish on the chopping edge. Sometimes the polish covers flake scars broken out from use. Some of the bone tools can be matched with the other parts

of the bones from which they were originally broken. The working edges of the tools demonstrate a very noticable difference between the side of the breaks which were not used as tools and the sides that were used. One excellent example of this is a bone chopper which utilized a break close to the distal end of a tibia as the chopping edge and the remainder of the foot as the handle. When matched to the bone from which it was broken, the difference between the worn chopping edge and the unaltered bone opposite is easily demonstrated (Fig. 1.24).

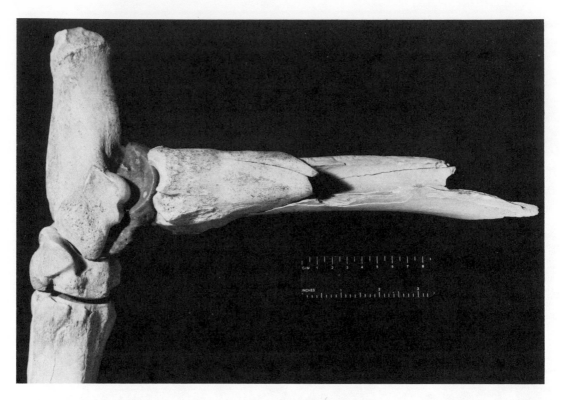

FIGURE 1.24 *Bison tibia chopper with part of bone replaced that was broken to manufacture the tool. Difference between the tool edge on one side of the break and unmodified bone on the opposite side is evident.*

Another bison tibia chopper retained the articulated femur as part of the handle. One chopping point broke, presumably from use, but left another point that was subsequently used. The point broken first was found and replaced and both points demonstrate unmistakable evidence of use (Fig. 1.25).

Specimens from the Casper Site regarded as bone tools have already been mentioned several times but need fuller description. The most common is the tibia chopper and the larger and heavier bones were selected with no apparent preference for right or left. Of 24 recognizable complete and broken specimens, 11 are lefts and 13 are rights. Experimentation indicates no proven superiority of a tool whether it is made from a right or left tibia.

Preparation was simple and usually predictable. The tibia was placed on a solid base and a hammerstone blow was delivered to the concave surface near the proximal end. The result was usually a pointed or transverse break across the thick, convex side of the tibia. Depending upon which side of the break provided the proper edge, either the proximal or distal end was then the handle and if the break was too far toward the proximal end, part of the femur was retained in order to have the proper mass for efficient chopping. On the other hand, if the desirable edge or point was formed on the distal side of the break and close to the distal end, part of the metatarsal or even the entire foot was retained

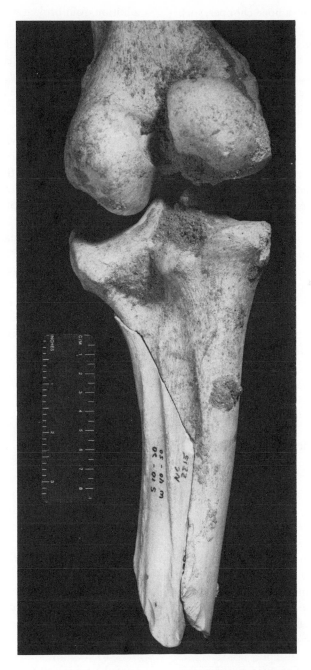

FIGURE 1.25 *Bison tibia chopper with two stages of use resulting from breakage of the original chopping point and subsequent use of another.*

as a handle. In actual use, a bone chopper, such as for example, a broken tibia with the metatarsal as a handle presents problems during use until the ligaments have dried sufficiently to form a rigid bond between the articulated bones. It is relatively easy, however, to make the metatarsal rigid enough for a handle by wrapping and tying it into the proper position with a strip of green hide.

Two types of wear appear on bone choppers. Small flakes of bone were often driven off and sharp edges were rounded and smoothed almost to a polish. At least nine broken pieces from working edges or points of tibia choppers were recovered throughout the bone deposits and two of these were matched to tools from which they were broken. There may have been some deliberate preparation of chopping edges but only to the extent of breaking the bone and not by cutting or grinding.

Seven specimens demonstrate that the distal end was used as the handle and a break across the diaphysis was utilized as the working edge. It is strongly suggested from the site specimens (e.g. 1. 14a) and from experiments using actual bone tools (Fig. 1. 10) that the calcaneus was occasionally used as a handle. Further evidence suggests also that in some cases the entire foot or at least the metatarsal was retained and used as a handle (e.g. Fig. 1.24).

Two of these distal tibia choppers retained enough of the bone so that they were of sufficient mass for light chopping without retention of any of the tarsal units. The proximal end of the tibia was found and matched to one of these (Fig. 1.18b) and the wear on the working edge can be demonstrated clearly by comparison with the opposite side of the break which remains unchanged. The size of this tool might suggest use as a scraper since it does seem extremely light for most chopping tasks.

Four proximal ends of femora, two rights and two lefts, were utilized as choppers and in addition, four broken working ends of femur choppers were recovered. The head of the femur was utilized as the handle (Fig. 1.16). One of these (Fig. 1.16a) was matched to the bone from which it was broken and, as in the case of tibia choppers, the difference between the working edge and its counterpart on the opposite side of the break leaves little doubt as to its use as a tool. Only one specimen provides convincing evidence of the distal end of a femur being used as a handle and in this case part of the working edge was broken off but was not recovered. Provenience data on tibia and femur choppers are given in Fig. 1.26.

Eighteen left and a single right humerus were given distinctive preparation on the proximal end. The articular surfaces were removed, the cancellous bone gouged out and the circumference of the bone around the break given a scalloped effect (Fig. 1.14b). They were presumably used in both skinning and fleshing and where bone preservation allowed, wear in the form of a polish appears on the sharp points. They are especially recognizable in Late Prehistoric Period sites where bone preservation is better than at the Casper Site. From experiment, the left humerus is more properly shaped for use by a right-handed person and the most functionsl tool is from a small to and the most functional tool is from a small to for humerus tools appear in Fig. 1.27).

All of this evidence provides what to the writer seems to be overwhelming and irrefutable evidence for the use of simple bone tools for butchering the Casper Site bison. The bone tools are there in context while the stone tool counterparts are lacking; evidence for bone tool use appears on butchered bone and this evidence is different from the marks produced by stone choppers; broken bone tools appeared in the bone deposits and broken points of tools appeared embedded in the bone where they were broken during use; differences between the part of the bone utilized as a tool and the part discarded can be demonstrated;

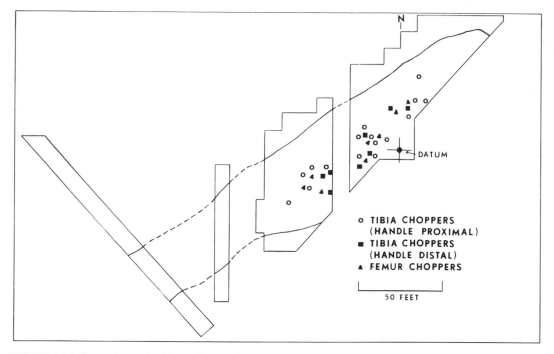

FIGURE 1.26 *Proveniences for bison tibia and femur choppers at the Casper Site.*

experimentation with bone tools demonstrates the same kinds of wear patterns on tools and the same kinds of marks on the butchered bones as those from the site.

Many other butchering contexts over a wide range of time demonstrate use of similar tools. Evidence is especially good in the Late Prehistoric Period kills where bone preservation is good and the evidence for chopping use can be seen without any doubt on the bone tools. From present evidence, it appears that many bone butchering tool types have at least 10,000 years of time depth on the Plains.

METHOD OF INVESTIGATION OF THE CASPER SITE

Discovery of the Casper Site occurred April 2, 1971. It resulted from two amateur archeologists investigating an area recently disturbed by heavy earthmoving equipment. They found Paleo-Indian artifacts and fragments of bone on the surface and just below the surface they found a large amount of bone, some articulated and apparently in place. They immediately notified the University of Wyoming and a crew under the direction of the writer tested the site the next day. It was confirmed as being a bison kill with probable cultural affiliations with the Hell Gap complex although the nature of the kill in terms of procurement method was obscure. There was also the question of the significance of a Clovis projectile point found by one of the discoverers of the site.

An area of 10 ft. by 20 ft. was tested initially. The bone although it appeared stable when first uncovered, soon deteriorated rapidly after exposure. It was obvious from the testing that special techniques of preservation would be needed if the bone was to be recovered in proper

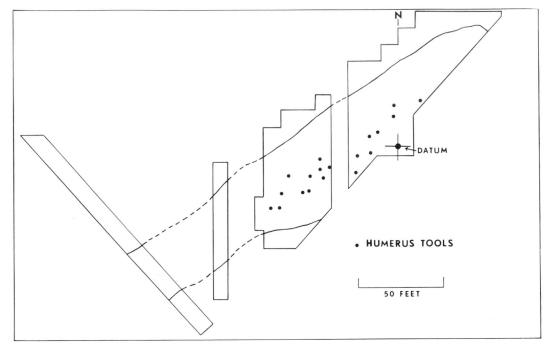

FIGURE 1.27 *Provenience for bison humerus tools at the Casper Site.*

condition for analysis. The site was sealed for nearly two months until proper help and facilities could be obtained. Several experiments were made to determine a chemical mixture that would stabilize the bones in the field.

Excavation of the site began on May 21, 1971 and was completed on June 25, 1971. Between the time of discovery and beginning excavation, details of industrial activity in the site area were investigated and the owners of the land, Control Data Corporation, offered complete cooperation in the investigation. It was known only at this time that earthmoving equipment had removed about 20 feet of sand and had ceased operations, purely by accident, a few inches above a large bison bone concentration which was later discovered to be lying in the trough of an old parabolic sand dune.

Some damage had been done to several skulls that for some reason were higher in the sand than the remainder of the bones and also some artifacts and bones that were higher up on the slopes of the dune trough were removed. The exact amount and nature of these will never be known since the material was used for fill in a parking lot. The landowner, Control Data Corporation, was able to provide a topographic map of the area before construction of their industrial complex (Fig. 1.28).

The surface formed by removal of overburden at the site sloped to the south so that the undisturbed sand deposits containing the Casper Site remained in the form of a wedge in north to south profile on top of a gravel and cobble terrace. A few feet south of the site datum, the heavy equipment cut into the gravel terrace while just north of datum a few feet, the remaining undisturbed sand is five to six feet in depth. Further north a few more feet is the trough of another parabolic sand dune that is presently stabilized

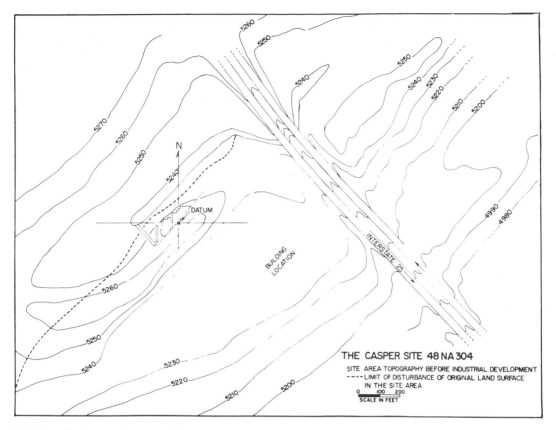

FIGURE 1.28 *Topographic map of the Casper Site area before land disturbance.*

by vegetation and is inactive. Removal of the sand for industrial purposes did create an area of renewed, active sand transport which threatens the remainder of the site although the installation of several rows of snow fence at 100 feet intervals at right angles to the prevailing wind has helped. Efforts to establish a new growth of vegetation have to date not been successful.

An arbitrary datum was established which later turned out to be directly over an old pipeline trench that cut diagonally through the old parabolic dune (Fig. 1.1). The site was excavated by ten foot squares with all bone and artifact material recorded in place both horizontally and vertically. The matrix was all put through eighth-inch mesh screens and part through sixteenth-

inch mesh screen. This was relatively easy since it was all clean, windblown sand.

The matrix surrounding the bone was all damp, windblown sand and in most parts of the site it was impossible to maintain perpendicular walls when dry. As a result, walls had to be maintained at about 75 degrees to prevent continual sloughing of the sand surface as it dried. The only other solution seemed to be to keep the walls damp which was not practical under the circumstances. The sloped walls did note create a serious problem since none of the deposits were over three feet in depth except for the profile trench. In some areas of the site, old root casts penetrated into the bone level and here the sand was partially cemented and quite stable. Some of the bone in these same areas was also coated with this carbonate material which aided greatly in their preservation.

The site was excavated to the bottom of the old parabolic dune trough which was the top of a gravel terrace and could easily be determined. The sand outside the trough of the old dune was horizontally-laid with distinctive light and dark laminations which contrasted sharply in color and texture with the sand in the trough of the old parabolic dune. Contact between the two was quite obvious (see Chapter 4).

The bones were extremely delicate when exposed and although some of the heavier long bones, for example, would dry to hardness in the sun, most required treatment with a solution of Elmer's glue and water while still damp. Otherwise they would disintegrate to a fine powder. Skulls were particularly difficult to retrieve. In about half of the site, however, preservation of bone surfaces was excellent provided special care was employed to prevent deterioration to a fine powder upon exposure. Several compounds were tried but Elmer's Glue seemed to be the most satisfactory in the field although all bone had to treated later in the laboratory.

Bone recovery did present some interesting problems. It was impossible to use metal tools of any kind because of damage to the bones. Most sand was removed by hand or with plastic or bamboo strips. It was often possible to slice a long bone in two with a trowel and not realize it while at the same time, if the bone was treated with Elmer's Glue and exposed to the sun, it would usually cure to a point that it could easily be removed intact and the original bone surface would be perfectly preserved.

In contrast to most of the bone at the site, several bone fragments at the bottom of the bone level were preserved to almost rock hardness. At first this was thought to represent different kills but many of the hard fragments were matched to the spot where they were broken from bones that

were extremely soft. It is believed that pond formation after the bone level was laid down had much to do with preservation of the bones and that some fragments were buried in the deposits deep enough so that they had a chance to mineralize slightly from elements in solution in the water. There were carbonate root casts extending into the bone level and some bones were cemented together slightly in the areas of these casts. The presence of the carbonates probably aided also in bone preservation throughout.

All bone including fragments was removed from the site and taken to the laboratory for study. Part of the site remains intact for future excavation and study although expanding industrial development may require that the remainder be excavated at any time.

Power equipment was donated for use at the site and was used to dispose of backdirt. It also was of indispensable value in digging two profile trenches that were necessary in studying the geology of the site.

THE BONE LEVEL AT THE CASPER SITE

The bone level laid in the trough of the old parabolic dune that trends in a southwest to northeast direction (Fig. 1.29). From the west edge of the profile trench to the easternmost remnant of the old dune is 245 feet (Fig. 1.30) and bone was recorded for the entire distance except for the areas that were not excavated (see Endpiece). Only a few small fragments and a radius were found in the west profile trench and a single rib was found at the easternmost end of the old parabolic dune. It is believed that the main concentrations of bone were in the areas excavated and except for an untouched strip from W 030 to W 040 and possibly a few bones between W 085 and W 100, little remains in the way of bison bone at the site. Bone preservation was quite good on the southwest end of the excavation (Fig. 1.31) and poor toward the

FIGURE 1.29 *Looking into the northeast and leeward end of part of the trough of the old parabolic sand dune containing the Casper Site bison.*

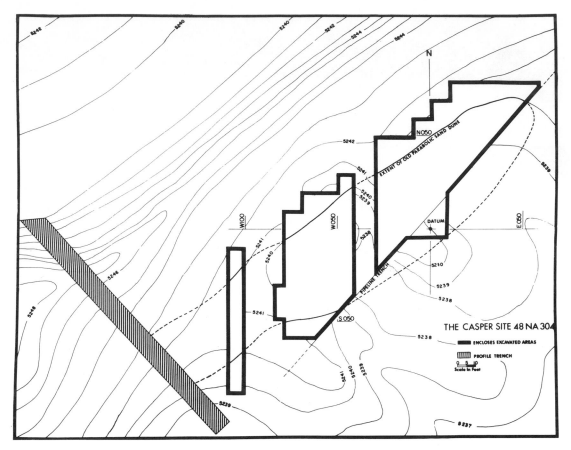

FIGURE 1.30 *Topographic map showing the excavated areas at the Casper Site.*

northeast end. The width of the bone bed varied from about 20 to 25 feet although an occasional bone fragment was found on the slopes on both sides of the trough of the dune.

There were six concentrations of bones although boundaries between are dim. All of the areas of bone concentration suggest some deliberate piling or stacking of the bones and some later scattering is suggested. The first pile from about W 065 to W 085 is separated several feet from the next adjacent pile and the bone was well preserved except from W 080 to W 085 where the bones rested on a slight rise of sand. The largest pile, from W 040 to W 060, demon-

strated the best bone preservation in the entire site. This one contained two deliberate piles of scapulae, one containing sixteen and the other six. The pile of bones between W 015 to W 030 and N 012 to S 010 contained at least four skulls. Adjacent to this in the pile between W 005 to W 025 and N 003 to N 015 were six skulls that may have been scattered and a pile of four pelvic-lumbar-distal thoracic units tightly packed together (Fig. 1.21). The second largest concentration of units was between E 002 to W 010 and N 015 to N 038 and contained a badly-scattered pile of 12 and another undisturbed pile of four scapulae. Four skulls were present with four

FIGURE 1.31 *Articulated butchered units at the Casper Site. Most unarticulated bones were removed for clarity.*

more that were almost completely deteriorated except for the upper teeth. The last concentration of bone appears badly scattered from E 002 to E 029 although this may have been two small piles.

The scapulae did tend to be at the lowest part of the bone concentrations. The largest pile of 16 rested directly on the gravel at the base of the dune trough and the other units were piled on top. As already mentioned, the skulls give the impression of having been piled on top of everything which may account for their relatively poor preservation and damage by power equipment. There is a question as to whether the bones were piled during or after butchering. The writer at this point tends to believe they were piled after butchering and the significance of this kind of cultural behavior is entirely speculative. If it were done during butchering, it could reveal something of the sequence of the butchering processes. The situation is quite different from that at the Olsen-Chubbuck Site (Wheat 1972) where the stratification of the bone bed in a deep, narrow arroyo can be profitably analyzed with the idea of determining butchering sequences.

A total of 5,385 readily-identified bones were taken from the Casper Site. This does not represent the total number of individual bones since some of those identified are undoubtedly parts of the same bones. Besides these there are several thousand bone fragments, most of which are identifiable if the need arises. It is possible to reconstruct many broken bones such as those that were broken to recover marrow or to manufacture tools. It was found that with enough patience, nearly any broken bone at the site could be put back together. The bone total includes 83 fetal bones representing three animals, two close to full term and one lacking about two months from full term.

Of the total bone, 2,319 bones represent 231 separate articulated units. Some of these units are small and include, for example, a thoracic vertebra and a single articulated rib. The largest includes a complete skull with mandibles, the vertebral column except for the last two lumbars, several proximal ends of ribs and one scapula (Fig. 1.20a). This number also includes six skulls with mandibles attached but not 11 sets of paired mandibles that were removed from the skulls but remained intact.

Of these 231 units, 132 (Fig. 1.32) are from the axial skeleton and 99 (Fig. 1.33) are from the appendicular skeleton. Only six of the total contain elements of both axial and appendicular skeleton. Seventy of the axial units contain skeletal elements posterior to the 8th thoracic and 62 units contain skeletal elements anterior to the 7th thoracic. Several units contain elements of both posterior and anterior ends while 40 units contain only thoracic vertebrae. Seven of the axial units do have the skulls with mandibles attached. One unit consists of the pelvis with all vertebrae except the atlas (Fig. 1.15 top left).

As mentioned, only six of the axial units have any of the appendicular skeleton attached. One has both rear legs articulated (Fig. 1.15 bottom left). Another unit had a complete left femur articulated while two others had a broken right and a complete left femur respectively articulated. One unit had an articulated right scapula and humerus while one other unit had a right

scapula only in articulated position.

Butchered units of the appendicular skeleton include 52 front leg units and 47 rear leg units and, as mentioned, six of these are attached to axial units. Variance in location of separation is noted and some of these were undoubtedly disarticulated after butchering and possibly also from a number of causes. Both the carpal and tarsal bones were sometimes scattered as well as the phalanges. It is difficult to explain why articulation of phalanges, carpals and tarsals was perfect on many specimens and badly scattered on others. It does suggest strongly that some of the units were exposed for some time while others were covered with sand almost immediately. The articulated units are described somewhat schematically in Fig. 1.32, Fig. 1.33 and in the endpiece. For the sake of clarity, individual non-articulated bones were not included in the endpiece except for scapulae and skulls. Non-articulated bones are enumerated in Tables 1, 2 and 3.

Twenty three skulls were in reasonably good condition while another 35 were recognizable only by teeth and petrous bones. Three of the better skulls were calves and one of these had the mandibles articulated.

A total of 62 left and 59 right mandibles plus teeth from 12 lefts and seven rights were recovered. In addition there were three fetal mandibles. These were all regarded as extremely valuable for aging and population determinations and special care was taken in their recovery and preservation. The best method found was to expose one side, give it several treatments of Elmer's Glue and water with a spray gun while still in place and damp from the moisture in the sand. After complete penetration of the mixture of glue and water, they were allowed to dry for a day or two. They were then stable enough to turn over and repeat the treatment on the opposite side.

From the evidence in the bone bed, the

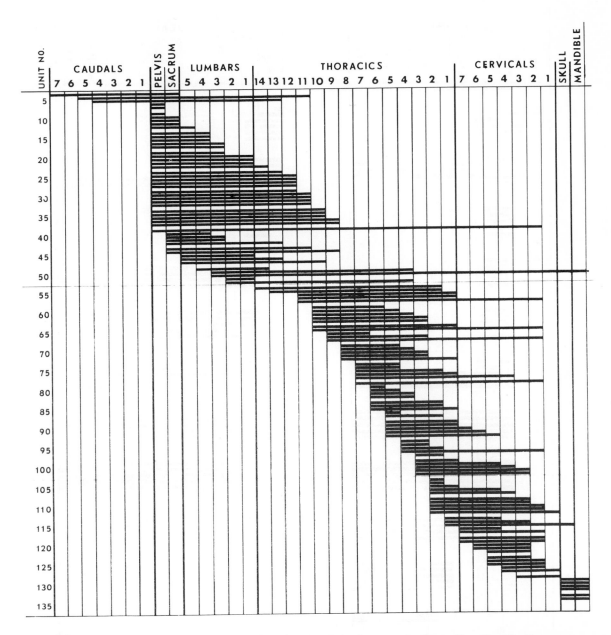

FIGURE 1.32 *Schematic representation of articulated axial skeletal units at the Casper Site. Note the absence of caudal and atlas vertebrae.*

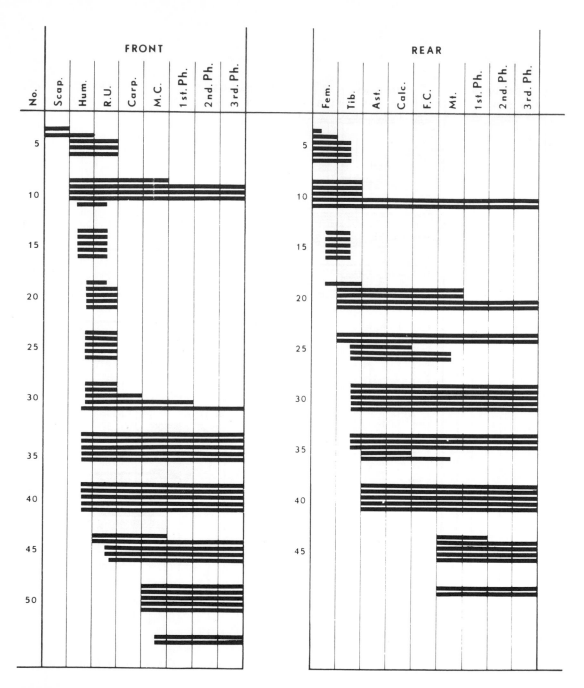

FIGURE 1.33 *Schematic representation of articulated appendicular skeletal units at the Casper Site.*

TABLE 1.1 *Non-articulated Appendicular Skeletal Bone from the Casper Site.*

Bone	Complete Left	Complete Right	Left Distal	Right Distal	Left Proximal	Right Proximal	Medial Fragments	Distal Epiphyses	Proximal Epiphyses	No Right or Left Identification	Total
Scapula	41	42			2	3	9				97
Humerus	12	13	20	11	3	4	25	1	8		97
Radius	10	7	3	13	6	4	19	4			66
Ulna	10	3		4	7	5	8				37
Radial Carpal	19	19									38
Ulnar Carpal	23	23									46
Fourth Carpal	18	15									33
Intermediate Carpal	12	22									34
Accessory Carpal	30	16									46
Fused 2nd & 3rd Carpal	12	24									36
Metacarpal	28	27				1	3				59
Femur	8	11	12	7	15	7	62		9		131
Patella	19	15									34
Tibia	2	14	5	5	15	11	142	6	1		201
Astragalus	9	12									21
Calcaneus	15	14									29
First Tarsal	7	5									12
Lateral Malleolus	16	10									26
Fused 2nd & 3rd Tarsal	11	17									28
Fused Cen. & 4th Tarsal	9	7									16
Metatarsal	8	14	3	4	3	3	13				48
Metapodial Fragments								8			8
Proximal Phalange	77	61									138
Medial Phalange	79	60									139
Distal Phalange	55	41									96
Second Metatarsal										13	13
Fifth Metacarpal										18	18
Proximal Sesamoid										312	312
Distal Sesamoid										99	99
Fetal Bones										83	83
Total											2041

sequence of events following the butchering of the bison at the Casper Site is believed to be as follows. The bones were first covered with sand and the "U" or nose of the parabolic dune mig-rated to the northeast or the direction of the pre-vailing winds. The bones themselves probably formed a barrier that trapped sand and aided in covering them. Some scattering of the bones may

TABLE 1.2 *Non-articulated Axial Skeletal Bone From the Casper Site Identified by Right and Left.*

Bone	Complete Left	Complete Right	Left Distal	Right Distal	Left Proximal	Right Proximal	Medial Fragments	Distal Epiphyses	Proximal Epiphyses	Total
Occipital	1	2								3
Maxilla	4	7								11
Premaxilla	1	3								4
Petrous	9	14								23
Paramastoid	2	3								5
Zygomatic Arch	8	5								13
Nasal	3	4								7
Hyoid			1		14	20	17			52
Coronoid Process					5	7				12
Mandibles	62	59								121
Mandible Fragments			3	6			2			11
No. 1 Rib	6	11			31	24	16			88
No. 2 Rib		1			21	10	1			33
No. 3 Rib	1				12	14				27
No. 4 Rib	2	2			9	17				30
No. 5 Rib	2	2			10	11	1			26
No. 6 Rib	1	1			3	9				14
No. 7 Rib		1			7	11				19
No. 8 Rib	1	1			5	9				16
No. 9 Rib		1					4			5
No. 10 Rib	2	1			3	4	2			12
No. 11 Rib	1			1	2	2	10			16
No. 12 Rib	1	1	1	3	3	2	19			30
No. 13 Rib	1				5	8	10			24
No. 14 Rib	2				4	10	5			21
Group Nos. 1-3 Ribs					1					1
Group Nos. 4-5 Ribs					2		12			14
Group Nos. 6-8 Ribs		1			1	1	24			27
Group Nos. 9-12 Ribs		2			1	1	33			37
Group Nos. 13-14 Ribs					2					2
Os Coxae	8	11								19
Acetabulum		4								4
Ilium					4	6	3			13
Ischium					5	8	4			17
Pubis					3	8				11
Total										768

have occurred although the usual chewing by carnivores is lacking. Bones highest in the deposits undoubtedly suffered more deterioration than lower ones. The bones in the leeward or northeast part of the kill area were slightly higher and demonstrated greater deterioration than those in the southwest part of the kill area.

An unusual and as yet unexplained feature

TABLE 1.3 *Non-articulated Axial Skeletal Bone from the Casper Site not Identified by Right and Left.*

Bone	Total
Skull Parts	38
Atlas	40
Axis	19
No. 3 Cervical	2
No. 4 Cervical	2
No. 5 Cervical	1
No. 6 Cervical	5
No. 7 Cervical	8
No. 1 Thoracic	7
No. 2 Thoracic	10
No. 3 Thoracic	2
No. 4 Thoracic	2
No. 5 Thoracic	1
No. 6 Thoracic	2
No. 7 Thoracic	-
No. 8 Thoracic	-
No. 9 Thoracic	1
No. 10 Thoracic	2
No. 11 Thoracic	3
No. 12 Thoracic	10
No. 13 Thoracic	5
No. 14 Thoracic	1
No. 1 Lumbar	-
No. 2 Lumbar	1
No. 3 Lumbar	-
No. 4 Lumbar	3
No. 5 Lumbar	3
Sacrum	11
No. 1 Caudal	9
No. 2 Caudal	7
Other Caudals	61
Sternebrae	1
Total	257

throughout the lowest part of the trough of the old parabolic dune in areas between bones was a number of circular-shaped stains. Eleven of these were recorded and they could be traced to depths of as much as two inches. They tended to decrease in diameter as the sand was peeled down-

ward. They did not appear to have been filled depressions and were manifest only as grains of sand stained a dark brown (Fig. 1.34). Whether the stains were organic or mineral was not determined.

At some date after the bones were covered with sand and the nose of the dune had migrated a short distance to the northeast, a pond formed over the top of the bones. Evidence for this is in the form of pond sediments that rest on wind-blown sand covering the bone level. The extent of the pond is not known since part of the old pond bottom was removed by the recent earth-moving activity. The pond may not have covered all of the bone level since, as mentioned, the bone level is slightly higher on the northeast end and also was in a more serious stage of deterioration. At a still later date, sand filled the trough of the old dune to an unknown depth. There is evidence of later scouring that cut partway into both the sand that contained the old parabolic dune and the subsequent fill. It did not, however, scour deep enough to disturb the bone bed. The bone level was never uncovered subsequent to pond formation until the site was excavated.

The remnant of the sand dune in which the site was contained lay upon the highest gravel and cobble terrace about 100 feet above the present level of the North Platte River. The terrace provided a base for excavation and no evidence of human activity was found below the gravel. Some bone and artifact material rested directly on the gravel in places in the lowest part of the trough of the old parabolic dune.

THE STONE ARTIFACT ASSEMBLAGE FROM THE CASPER SITE

The stone artifact assemblage recovered consists of three commonly recognized functional types which include projectile points, uniface cutting tools, and hammerstones. Two specimens might be classified as stone choppers but only a

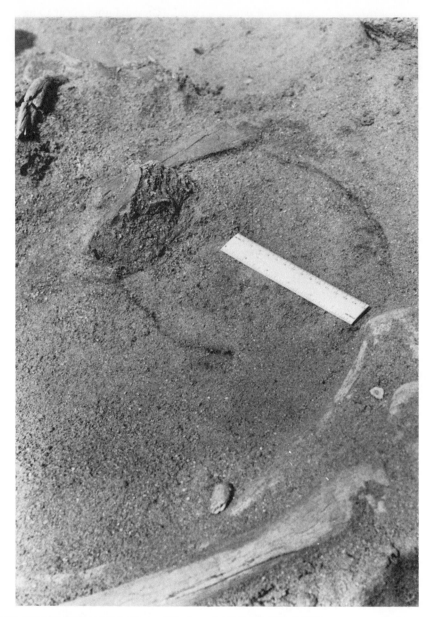

FIGURE 1.34 *Circular stain at the bottom of the bone level at the Casper Site.*

single large flake was removed in each case to form a barely functional chopping edge and this may have been entirely fortuitous or the result of use. The assemblage is sufficient for what was accomplished at the site although other tools may have been used and were not present at the site. Most of the debitage consists of tool-sharpening flakes and the remaining are impact flakes removed from projectile points. No evidence of core or biface reduction or tool or projectile point manufacture was present.

Projectile Points

Eighty one chipped stone items are considered as complete or parts of projectile points. Many of these are broken parts of the same artifacts that can be matched together so that a total of 60 separate projectile points are represented. Of this total, 27 are essentially complete of which 16 were found in one piece and 11 were found in two pieces at separate locations in the site. Seventeen others still retain enough of the projectile point to determine its general configuration and of these, four consist of two pieces found separately and one consists of three separate pieces. In addition to these there are seven bases and nine points or fragments of the distal ends (see Figs. 1.35-1.43). This does not include a number of small impact flake fragments some of which can be matched to flake scars on projectile points.

The projectile points and fragments all form a homogeneous group with one exception which is a typical Clovis projectile point (Fig. 1.37a) found at the site but not during the excavations. The Clovis projectile point was picked up by the discoverers of the site on the recently-disturbed surface of the dune and was the impetus for digging a few inches into the deposits and finding the buried bison kill site. Being found under these circumstances, it can only provide endless speculation. Its relationship to the site which is undoubtedly of Hell Gap cultural affiliations can not be known. The projectile point in question seems unmistakably of Clovis affiliation and at least a thousand or more years older than the Hell Gap material, and whether it was brought to the site by the Hell Gap cultural group or was left by a Clovis group is not known. The sand deposit in which the old parabolic dune was formed is necessarily older than the trough of the parabolic

dune into which the bison were driven and killed but how much older is another unknown factor. The Clovis projectile point is fluted on both sides and a heavy grinding extends for a distance of 30 mm. and 29.5 mm. from the base. The point itself does not appear to have a wind and sand polish indicating little if any previous exposure at the surface.

Technological aspects of manufacture of the Casper Site Hell Gap points are discussed elsewhere (see Chapter 5) and the metrical data are given in Table 4. There is, however, a suggestion that the projectile points were in different stages of manufacture. On some (e.g. Fig. 1.36a, b) the preform flake scars are very much in evidence with only a retouch on the edges to gain the desired outline form. On others (e.g. Fig. 1.37b) the preform flake scars are nearly obliterated while still others (e.g. Fig. 1.35a) demonstrate the preform flake scars completely gone.

In general, the range of variation in length and width is quite large. Differences in length and width ratios appear in many cases to be a function of the amount of reworking. The longest projectile point (Fig. 1.35a) appears quite different from some of the shorter ones but some of the latter have obviously been reworked to form new distal ends and the part of the original artifact that remains fits closely to the configuration of the basal part of an unmodified specimen (e.g. Fig. 1.39c). Flaking patterns on the reworked areas are always noticably different than the original pattern. This might possibly suggest resharpening while still in the haft.

It is believed by the writer that most of the reworking demonstrated on the projectile points was for the purpose of making them functional as projectile points and not as cutting tools. A number of things suggest this. First, the reworking done in all cases resulted in a symmetrical product, with a sharp point, one that experimentally at least is not the optimum shape for a cutting tool. Second, with one or two possible

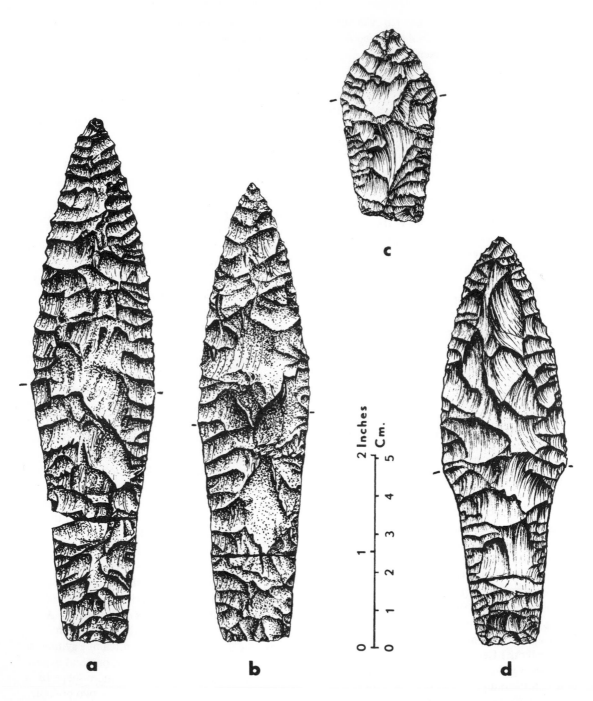

a

b

c

d

2 Inches

Cm.

FIGURE 1.35 *Hell Gap projectile points recovered from the Casper Site.*

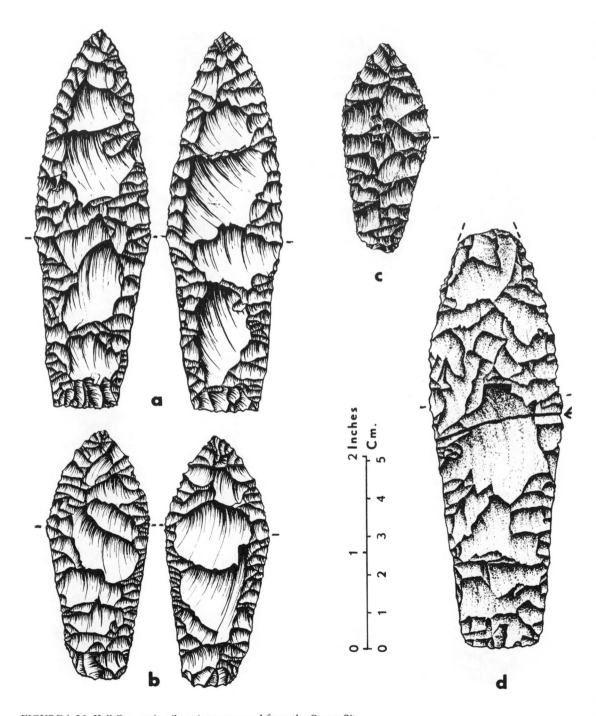

FIGURE 1.36 *Hell Gap projectile points recovered from the Casper Site.*

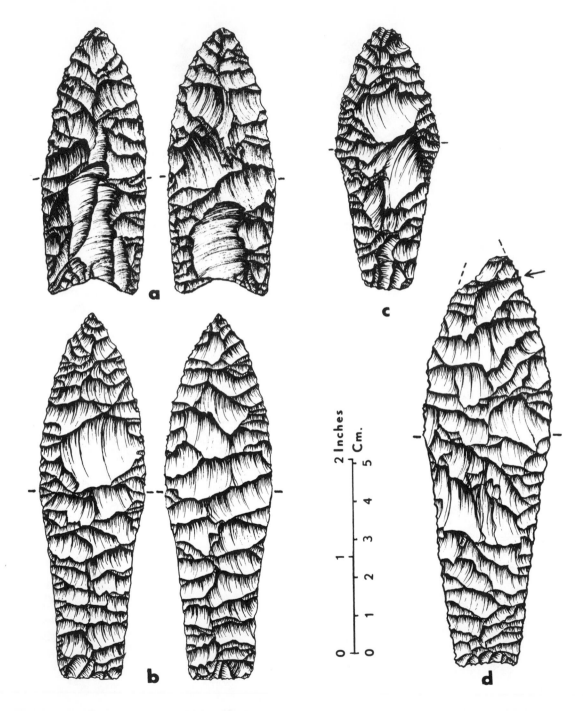

FIGURE 1.37 *Clovis projectile point (a) and Hell Gap projectile points (b-d) from the Casper Site.*

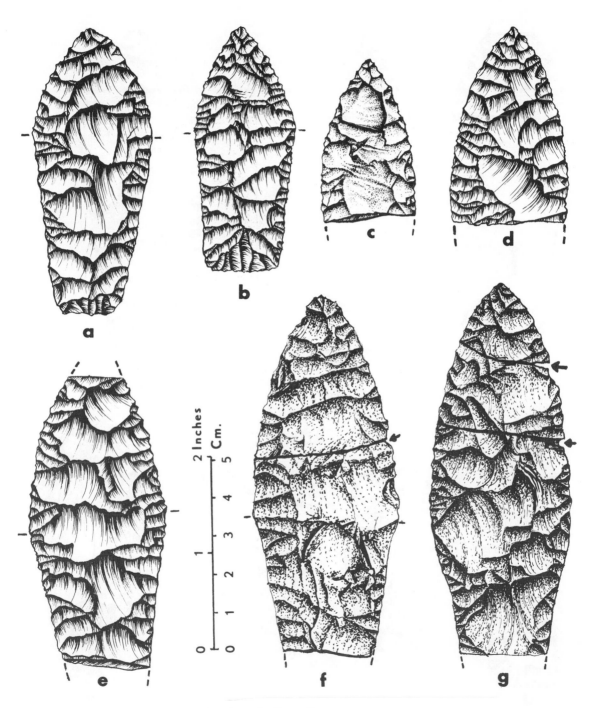

FIGURE 1.38 *Hell Gap projectile points from the Casper Site.*

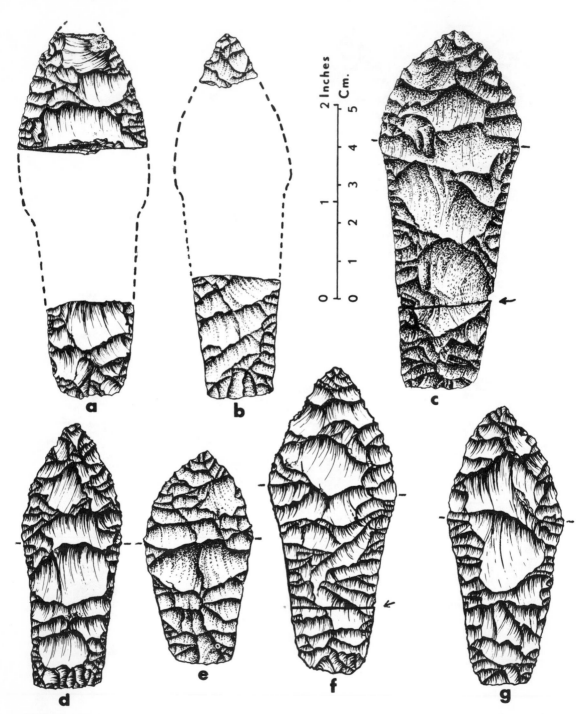

FIGURE 1.39 *Hell Gap projectile points from the Casper Site.*

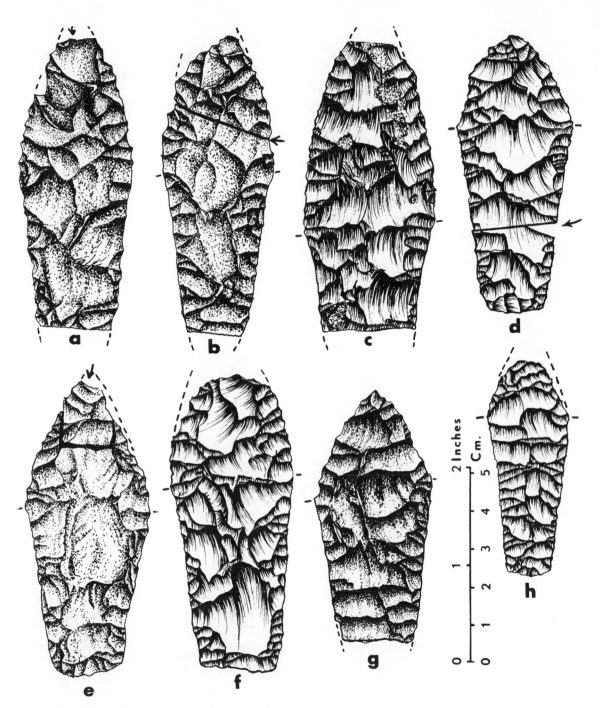

FIGURE 1.40 *Hell Gap projectile points from the Casper Site.*

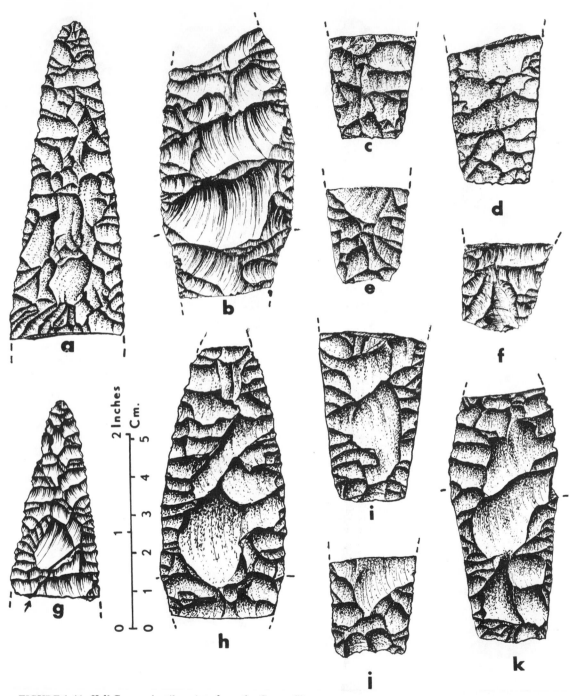

FIGURE 1.41 *Hell Gap projectile points from the Casper Site.*

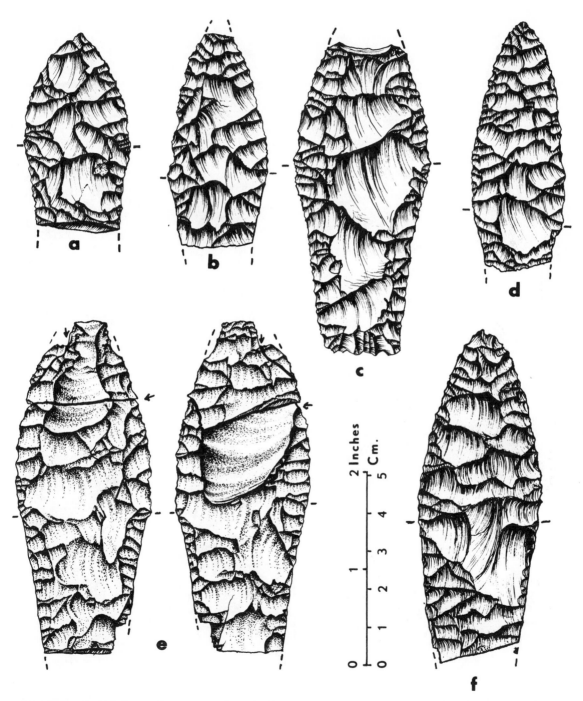

FIGURE 1.42 *Hell Gap projectile points from the Casper Site.*

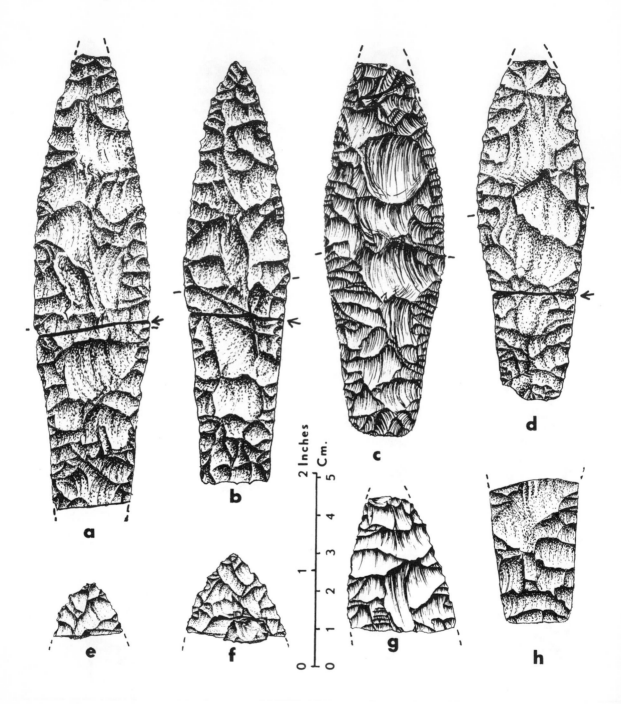

FIGURE 1.43 *Hell Gap projectile points from the Casper Site.*

TABLE 1.4 *Casper Site Projectile Point Measurements in Millimeters (see Fig. 5.2).*

Catalog Number	Length	Width	Thickness	Max. Stem Width	Min. Stem Width	Stem Length	Stem Angle (Degrees)	Fig. No.	Material
27000-27064	137.0	33.0	8.0	29.8	17.0	52.8	14	1.35a	Quartzite
27001	65.0	26.0	6.5	25.4	19.7	34.0	10	1.38b	Jasper
27002-27063		39.0	8.0	33.0			18	1.38f	Quartzite
27003-27011	93.0	37.8	7.8	33.9	20.0	59.4	13	1.39c	Quartzite
27004		36.5	7.9	28.0				1.41b	Jasper
27005-27018		29.5	7.0	26.2	15.7	40.1	13	1.43d	Metamorphosed Shale
27006			6.5		18.0		11	1.43h	Quartzite
27008			6.2		18.5		10	1.41j	Quartzite
27009		31.5	7.0	29.3				1.38d	Jasper
27010-27067	72.9	30.2	6.9	27.4	17.2	41.2	16	1.40d	Chert
27017		21.0	6.5	18.3	12.0	29.2	12	1.40h	Jasper
27019-27020	111.0	27.0	7.8	27.0	18.0	52.0	11	1.43b	Quartzite
27023		33.2	8.4	27.5				1.41h	Quartzite
27024		36.0	7.1	31.0			18	1.38e	Jasper
27025			7.8		17.4		12	1.39b	Quartzite
27027-27041		31.0	8.2	25.7			9	1.43a	Quartzite
27028		33.0	8.0	28.5	18.5		20	1.40e	Quartzite
27030-27087		34.5	7.9	34.5	20.0	63.0	13	1.36d	Jasper
27031		36.0	8.2	29.4	20.7	36.3	16	1.42c	Jasper
27032		27.5	7.0	22.5				1.42a	Jasper
27033		26.0	5.5	21.0				1.42b	Jasper
27034			7.3		17.0		15	1.41e	Quartzite
27035		32.0	6.2	29.0	20.0	41.5	11	1.40f	Chert
27040-27072		35.5	8.0	31.0			16	1.42e	Quartzite
27042	65.0	27.0	6.0	27.0	14.0	40.6	19	1.36b	Jasper
27043		24.0	6.8	18.3				1.42d	Knife River Flint
27044	75.2	31.0	7.0	28.9	18.0	40.3	17	1.38a	Jasper
27045	56.0	28.3	8.0	28.5	16.0	32.8	23	1.39e	Quartzite
27046	73.0	31.0	7.0	25.4	14.6	36.0	18	1.39g	Jasper
27047	68.0	27.1	7.0	22.5	13.0	29.4	20	1.37c	Knife River Flint
27048		32.5	6.5	28.2	18.0	37.0	17	1.43c	Jasper
27049		34.0	8.5	30.8	17.0	55.9	15	1.37d	Jasper
27051	70.0	27.8	7.5	23.9	18.0	31.8	10	1.39d	Jasper
27053-27054-27055		38.0	7.5	26.6			18	1.38g	Quartzite
27056-27057	120.0	29.0	9.0	26.1	18.8	50.8	8	1.35b	Quartzite
27058-27059	80.8	33.0	8.0	26.3	17.5	38.1	15	1.39f	Jasper
27060		32.3	7.9	28.3			11	1.42f	Jasper
27061-27062		30.0	8.0	26.8	17.1	36.0	13	1.40b	Quartzite
27065		32.0	7.5	29.2			13	1.40g	Quartzite
27066			6.9		18.0		15	1.41c	Quartzite
27069		29.9	7.5	26.0			14	1.40a	Quartzite
27073			6.9		17.8		11	1.39a	Jasper
27074			8.0		18.4		14	1.41i	Quartzite
27075		28.3	8.5	26.5	18.8		11	1.41k	Quartzite
27076	55.0	23.2	7.0	24.2	12.2	29.9	25	1.36c	Jasper
27077-27084	107.0	33.9	7.1	24.5	16.3	37.0	13	1.35d	Jasper
27080		34.8	8.4	29.8			16	1.40c	Jasper
27083 Clovis	70.5	28.0	8.3	27.9	24.2	29.6	9	1.37a	Jasper
27085	96.0	28.1	6.9	22.9	17.1	34.8	11	1.37b	Jasper
27086	100.0	31.0	6.0	27.0	17.8	38.3	12	1.36a	Knife River Flint
27089	49.9	26.0	6.8	25.0	16.7	32.6	19	1.35c	Jasper
27090			6.0		18.1		16	1.41f	Jasper
27091			7.9		17.8			1.41d	Quartzite

exceptions, a microscopic analysis of the blade edges does not yield satisfactory evidence of wear patterns commonly found on knives or other cutting tools that have been used in any kind of intensive butchering use. A third bit of evidence is that a total of 308 flakes were recovered from the site, most of which are believed to be the result of tool sharpening and of this total, not one was removed from any projectile point recovered at the site. This is exclusive of impact flakes which are quite different in both origin and appearance than sharpening flakes. Had there been a common practice of sharpening the projectile points for butchering purposes, we would expect to have found some of the sharpening flakes in the deposits. It is possible, however, that some use as cutting tools occurred on projectile points without sharpening. From experiments using stone knives in butchering, it takes only a small amount of use before a projectile point needs to be sharpened. All things considered it is difficult to interpret much butchering use from the Casper Site projectile points.

Of 43 specimens, 19 demonstrate unmistakable evidence of reworking of the distal end. In addition, on four of these (Fig. 1.35c, Fig. 1.39e, Fig. 1.40b, Fig. 1.40g) the bases were broken close to the proximal end and the resulting sharp corners were ground smooth without any flaking applied, presumably for purposes of reuse as projectile points. On another specimen, the base was broken and a steep retouch was applied to both sides (Fig. 1.42c) but it fails to obliterate the transverse break. At least two others suggest strongly that the bases were broken and treated in this same manner although no evidence of the actual break remains. It is postulated that the reworking of the projectile points was not done at the kill area nor was it done to make cutting tools for butchering the animals. The impression that emerges from the analysis of the entire projectile point assemblage is that any point that

could be reused was retrieved for that purpose.

Two of the specimens mentioned above demonstrate the extremes of the entire assemblage in terms of reworking. On one (Fig. 1.39e) the distal end was broken as well as the base and reworking was applied resulting in an abrupt but sharp point. The other (Fig. 1.35c) was treated almost identically except that the base was broken at a slight angle and no attempt was made to restore basal symmetry. Two other specimens demonstrate a similar abrupt retouch on the distal end. On one (Fig. 1.39c) the point is extremely dull and rounded but closer inspection reveals a small impact fracture that removed the extreme tip. The base of this specimen was broken but recovered and if it followed the general configuration of the other projectile points, it was probably the largest one of the entire collection before it was broken and subsequently modified. One other specimen (Fig. 1.38c) is a distal end with tip intact and reworking of the point is evident but does not quite obliterate the end of a long flake scar which appears to be an old impact fracture.

Widths vary from one specimen 21 mm. wide to another 39 mm. wide although the clustering is from 28 mm. to 36 mm. (see Table 4). The result is a projectile point ranging from a long, almost lanceolate in some cases (Fig. 1.35b) to a broad, bifacial blade-like appearance (Fig. 1.38f, g) with a smooth transition from one to the other. All are lenticular in cross section but the significance of this seemingly wide range in projectile point width is not clear.

The proximal or hafted ends of the projectile points as determined by the distance the edge grinding extends, must be considered from a number of perspectives. First, the length of the hafted part or rather the length of the hafted part in relation to to the length of the remainder of the point is large. This ratio changes by the amount of reworking of the distal end which must be considered also. Eight specimens that are complete and apparently not reworked have a ratio of hafting element to length of from .38 to .52 while ten others that are complete and obviously reworked have a ratio of the same measurements of from .55 to .67. Even the lowest of these values indicates that a large share of the Hell Gap projectile point was covered by the haft bindings and as the point was reworked the ratio increased.

Secondly, if this amount of the projectile points was hafted, it should indicate something of the nature of their use. Admittedly other evidence will undoubtedly figure into this kind of analysis. Twenty six of the distal end of projectile points demonstrate impact fractures. Some of these resulted from impacts of sufficient intensity to drive flakes for considerable distance down both sides of the point (e.g. Fig. 1.40a,e) while others were different and produced more of a crushing of the distal end (e.g. Fig. 1.37d, Fig. 1.40f). These kinds of impact must reflect extremely heavy use and a well-executed bonding between projectile point and shaft.

Third, the hafted or proximal ends of the Casper Site projectile points are distinctive when the entire range of the Paleo-Indian array of projectile points is considered. The proximal ends are heavily ground on the edges and it is assumed that this grinding in all cases is connected with the binding that holds the stone point securely on a wooden shaft or foreshaft. The ground edges of the Hell Gap points all taper inward toward the base. As the taper approaches the widest part of the point, the rate of expansion of the width increases so that a definite shouldering is seen on most specimens. On some the shouldering is quite evident (e.g. Fig. 1.35d). On others the shouldering is evident but less pronounced (e.g. Fig. 1.35a) while on some the reworking of the distal end has extended far enough toward the base to completely remove the shoulder (e.g. Fig. 1.36b). Grinding of the edges always extends from the base to the end of the shoulder. If lines are extended distally and parallel to the straight part of each ground edge, the lines will eventually intersect to form an angle. Of 46 measurable bases recovered, the angle of taper formed by the intersection of the two lines is quite variable and ranges from 8 to 25 degrees (see Table 4). At this point no significance has been attributed to this seemingly wide range of tapering angles. On one specimen (Fig. 1.43b) there is a slight expansion of the stem at the base but this is an exception. Bases are generally straight to slightly convex and only rarely concave.

Fourth, experimentation will soon reveal that there are advantages and disadvantages in terms of hafting a projectile point with a tapering tang as compared to a straight or parallel-sided tang. A straight tang can be bound with sinew to a split shaft quite efficiently and a small amount of movement forward or back will not greatly affect the rigidity with which the point is held. Upon impact, however, the force is imported to the wooden shaft mostly through the base of the point. Wrapping the shaft carefully with sinew and the addition of some vegetable or mineral bonding substance such as pitch or asphalt was probably universal and increased the efficiency of the binding by providing a better contact between point and shaft and also keeping out moisture which was a main source of failure for any sinew binding.

It would appear that a tapered tang would functionally and necessarily employ a different concept in hafting as compared to a parallel-sided tang. It is difficult to employ the idea of a split or nocked shaft to a tapering tang as being the most efficient. The binding is difficult to apply and the point itself is difficult to place in proper alignment and keep there until secured by the binding and difficult also to hold secure after it is bound in place although the application of pitch or asphalt or similar compound is of great value in bonding the point to the shaft.

Another problem of a tapered tang such as those at the Casper Site, is that the impact force is transmitted to the shaft through a relatively small base if a simple split shaft is used. In the context of the Casper Site projectile points there is also a noticeable lack of concern of basal preparation compared to the concern with the shaping and grinding of the sides. Another consideration is that with a tapered tang, almost any amount of movement frees the point and unless the split shaft and associated binding provide a substantial socket for the point, the bond between shaft and point is weakened.

This leads to the suggestion that the most functional way of hafting projectile points with tapered tangs such as those from the Casper Site would have been in some sort of a socket. There are advantages to a tapered haft when a stone projectile point is socketed in a wooden haft. The area of contact between wood and stone is increased, the heavy grinding equalizes the area of contact and upon impact the taper transmits the force evenly to a large area of the wooden haft. Upon impact also, the point is forced tighter into the socket and the chances of its turning sideways is lessened.

The chances of finding a hafted Hell Gap projectile point seem small and it will very likely never be known for certain how the task was accomplished. Experimentation has proven of value for interpretations concerning the handling of animals and butchering of animals. It might suggest something concerning the use of the projectile points in killing the animals as well.

There are many things we would like to know regarding the use of the Casper Site projectile points for killing the animals. Part of the problem is that there are a number of possible alternatives and all may have been employed. The first consideration to explore is whether the projectile points were used as thrusting spears, spears thrown by hand or as a dart with a throwing stick. In the case of killing the animals in a para-

bolic sand dune, I would argue for the points being socketed in a foreshaft which was in turn socketed in a long, heavy shaft that was used as a thrusting spear or in some cases thrown. The hunters were close enough to the animals for effective thrusting and the soft sand gave the man the advantage in out-maneuvering the animals. The projectile points do have sharp tips but distally from the points they expand rapidly and are relatively thick in cross section. This kind of projectile point design functions best in the end of a long, heavy shaft that contains sufficient mass to open a hole in the hide and follow through with the broad blade that cuts a large hole. The projectile points from the Casper Site will withstand the shock of a large man thrusting with all possible force provided they are properly hafted and are thrown or thrust so that the trajectory of the spear and shaft is close to a right angle with the surface of the animal at the point of impact. If the spear hits at much less than a right angle, the hide begins to slip and "bunch up" causing sideways pressure on the projectile point and the result is uaually snapping off the end of the point.

The hide of the animal is one of many limiting factors to the effectiveness of the projectile point. Buffalo hide is much thinner than cow hide upon which most of the experimental data were obtained. By actual measurement, the hide along the top part of the rib cage of a mature female *Bos taurus* averaged 3.5 mm. in thickness while hides from *Bison bison* of the same age and sex were 2.3 mm. on one and 2.1 mm. on another. Whether these figures can be generalized to include extinct forms of 10,000 years ago remains a question but from the close similarities of the skeletons other than size, it seems doubtful that the extinct forms were sheathed in hides that were too different from the present form. The hide of *Bison bison* is known to be much more delicate than that of *Bos taurus*. It is difficult to burn a brand into a *Bison bison* without blotching as a result of burning too deep and special care must be taken to avoid serious injury to *Bison bison* calves during branding. *Bison bison* are also subject to much more damage in shipping or handling than domestic cattle and much of this is due to the relative thinness and delicate nature of the hide.

Experiments With Hell Gap Projectile Points

With these thoughts in mind a number of alternatives were tried in an attempt to gain some information as to the relative effectiveness of the Casper Site projectile points. The experiments were done using *Bos taurus* carcasses that had just died lacking *Bison bison* material at that time. With regard to hafting, an attempt to use a conventional nocked shaft was not too successful. Even with the use of pitch and a sinew binding, the point was not well enough bonded to the wooden haft to withstand enough thrust to drive it into a mature female *Bos taurus* without splitting out although it was thrust successfully into a three month old calf. A heavier foreshaft and binding would probably have made a more serviceable mount but this involves a more bulky mass that tends to dwarf the projectile point and inhibits penetration.

Socketing the projectile point was then tried. The problem of socketing has relatively simple technological solutions. A shaft can be split for whatever distance is necessary and a wedge inserted to hold the split open while making the slot for the point. The projectile point may be socketed with the blade edges either at a right angle to or parallel to the split. It is relatively easy to carve out a receptacle for the tang either way using simple stone tools. Probably the easiest is with the blade edges parallel to the split in the shaft but the most effective is with blade edges at right angles. Once the desired slot for the projectile point is made, the shaft can be tapered to conform to the shape of the point. Pitch was applied to effect a solid contact between point and shaft and a sinew binding was

applied to prevent splitting. In this case, the projectile point was socketed directly to the shaft and not into a foreshaft. Foreshafts were tried later.

For actual experiments on domestic cow carcasses, a typical Hell Gap type, surface find projectile point was utilized that was made from a hard, basalt-like stone. Weight of the point was 40.3 grams. It was hafted so that of 123 mm. total length of the point, 64 mm. was covered by the haft which did not quite reach to the end of the shoulder which was 66 mm. from the base. The projectile point used was one that had been reworked on the distal end. The haft binding began 13.3 mm. from the extreme end of the shaft. At this location the minimum diameter of the shaft was 19.8 mm. while the projectile point was 7.7 mm. thick. Maximum width of the shaft with the applied sinew binding at the same point is 33.5 mm. compared to 33.0 mm. for the maximum width of the projectile point (Fig. 1.44, picture taken after point was used and broken). About seven grams of pitch, gathered from a scarred limber pine *(Pinus flexilis)* were used although about three grams of this amount were wasted by allowing the shaft to get too hot so that some of the pitch became too thin and was lost in the fire. Application of the pitch was extremely simple. The end of the shaft was held over a fire until the proper temperature was reached to melt the pitch and allow it to run into the split made on the shaft in order to form the socket. The pitch bonded tightly to both the wood and stone.

Several kinds of shafts were tried. Few hardwoods are available locally that are at all straight and it is difficult to obtain willow that is straight enough without some artificial straightening. The final choice determined largely by availability was between lodgepole pine *(Pinus contorta)* and quaking aspen *(Populus tremuloides)*. Lodgepole pine was finally chosen because of superior strength qualities. In addition they are easily

FIGURE 1.44 *Experimental hafting of a Hell Gap projectile point.*

obtainable on timbered north slopes above 8,000 feet elevation where competition results in slow-growing trees that are small in diameter, tall and straight. Strightness is important in order to deliver force to the projectile point in the proper way.

Different lengths and diameter sizes were tried for balance, strength and other aspects of functional utility. The one chosen as probably the best was 11 feet (3.35 meters) long, with a maximum diameter of 42 mm. and a minimum diameter of 38 mm. at the large end and was 22.3 mm. in diameter at the small end. Total weight including the projectile point was 1,654.5 grams or about 3.64 pounds. Every person would undoubtedly have an individual preference in length and weight that would result in a wide variance from these figures. The weight of the experimental model, however, is sufficient for thrusting or throwing. The shaft is strong enough to serve as some protection in keeping an animal away or keeping away from an animal if the projectile point is broken which would have been an important consideration in handling large animals confined in a corral or trap, a fact that can easily be confirmed in practice.

The tip of the projectile point was sharp and penetration of the rib cage was accomplished but on the first try, only the distance from the tip to the widest part of the blade, a distance of about 36 mm. or 1.5 inches. The next try, penetration was double this. On the third try, however, the sharp point was crushed in several small fragments but only for a distance of about 1.5 mm. Loss of the sharp point was critical and it was not possible to thrust it through the hide until it was reworked to a sharp point. After this, the point and haft were buried to a depth of about 15 cm. (6 inches) into the rib cage and it actually cut into the heart. It would have been a lethal wound to a live animal within a very short time. The next attempt was to pierce the neck but the angle was such that the hide slipped and "bunched up" so that penetration was impossible and the sideways pressure snapped the point just distal to the end of the wooden haft. The nature of the break is identical to several from the Casper Site assemnlage suggesting that something like this situation may have occurred more than once during the actual killing operation.

In order to pierce the hide and penetrate the rib cavity required an extremely hard thrust. There was, however, no damage to the socket or the haft binding nor was the tang loosened. Continued practice would undoubtedly improve both the techniques of preparation and use of the artifact. Whether or not this represents the manner in which actual preparation and use was accomplished, it demonstrates one possible effective solution. It can be accomplished using the recovered part of the material culture at the Casper Site and adding to this, items readily available in the natural environment and assembled in a reasonably short time with a simple tool kit.

The shaft with the broken point is not beyond use. About 70 mm. of the point still remains with the tang secure in the haft. It could be repointed in a matter of minutes and still be effective as a projectile point. It could also be used as a cutting tool with a minimum of modification. If necessary also, the wooden socket could be cut back in order to expose more of the projectile point. Several projectile points recovered at the Casper Site indicate breakage and subsequent resharpening. Certainly the quality of the flaking expressed in the resharpening of the Casper Site specimens is definitely inferior to that done in the original manufacture. Certainly also the possibility that the reworking of the Casper Site points was done to those broken but still hafted needs to be considered. It does not seem likely, however, that in a situation such as the Casper Site that any of the animals would have remained in the sand dune trap long enough to allow any of the hunters to repoint any broken projectile points. More likely the reworking was done afterward.

Another set of experiments concerned the use of sharpened wooden spears. Neither the lodgepole nor the quaking aspen could be made to penetrate a mature *Bos taurus* carcass although they did penetrate the carcass of a two month old calf. No amount of heating or fire-hardening was of any aid to their penetration. Harder woods may be more effective but these are difficult to obtain in proper size and straightness in this part of the country.

Further experimentation on the subject of the effectiveness of artifacts of this nature in killing large animals should involve the use of live animals although there are many limiting factors to consider before attempting this kind of activity. Expertise in the use of weaponry of this nature comes only with long practice and it is difficult to justify what might be a difficult situation for the animal purely as a result of a lack of expertise on the part of the experimenter. It could, however, be no worse than the average untrained bow hunter crippling or wounding an animal such as an elk or deer.

Even lacking this final part of the experimentive process, however, we do know the technological aspects of providing a proper weapon can readily be solved. We know what the weapon will do in terms of penetration and we can predict what the behavior of bison will be when moving them into a trap, pound or jump. At this point, the real gap in our knowledge is how close the behavior of the extinct forms of bison conformed to that of the modern bison. Other than the extinct forms being somewhat larger than the present form, the evidence of the kinds of terrain utilized over the past 10,000 years in communal kills strongly suggests similar behavior between the two forms.

Further exploration into the use of a thrusting spear is necessary however. It seems highly unlikely that a hunter would have limited himself to a single spear in the context of killing large bison in a temporary restraining situation such as a sand dune trap. There would also have been difficulty in carrying an extra spear while using another and a low probability of having been able to place extra ones nearby that would have been available where needed. Considering the evidence at the Casper Site for various kinds of impact damage that rendered a large number of the total projectile points non-functional, some means for replacement must have been allowed for.

There were technological solutions to the problem. One possibility might have been to manufacture a spear with a socket designed so that a broken or damaged projectile point could have been removed and replaced with a new one. This would have required that the projectile point was mounted only friction-tight in its socket and it would also have eliminated the use of any hardening adhesive such as pitch or asphalt. The wide variation in length, width and stem angle on projectile points would argue against this method of hafting. Another argument against this method of hafting is that any movement of the projectile point in its socket would have usually resulted in destruction of the socket, binding or both upon heavy impact. It would have been best to bond the projectile point as rigidly as possible in its socket. Even so, the possibility of having socketed a new projectile point in a friction-tight socket after discarding a broken base cannot be ruled out entirely.

Another possibility is that projectile points were hafted directly to the main shafts and both were discarded after the kill which was extremely unlikely considering the abundant evidence for reuse of projectile points. It seems even more unlikely that the main shafts would have been discarded considering that the technological problems of manufacturing a main shaft was considerably more than the manufacture of a projectile point. A number of main shafts may have been broken and were subsequently discarded although broken shafts with reusable projectile points would probably have been saved.

The foreshaft concept is another and better technological solution or at least seemingly so. A heavy foreshaft with a conical socketed joint between the foreshaft and the main spear shaft is argued for considering that it is easier to make a dependable, friction-type connection between two pieces of wood than between wood and stone. The large number of projectile point bases that match points would have to suggest the use of foreshafts that separated from the main shafts, retained the bases of the projectile points and were not recovered. The foreshaft idea seems the best answer considering also that if a projectile point mounted directly to the main shaft were driven into an animal, the hunter would have had to either pull it back out or let it go with the animal and be without a weapon. A foreshaft would have separated from the main shaft and remained in the animal. It might be worthwhile to consider the added killing power a large projectile point mounted on a foreshaft could have accomplished if it were penetrated into a rib cage and subsequent movements of the animal would have caused the projectile point to literally slice into the internal organs and further insure a quick death for the animal.

The same experimental spear with a projectile point mounted directly to the main shaft (Fig. 1.44) can be quite easily changed into one with a socketed foreshaft (Fig. 1.45). It appears every bit as functional as when it was mounted directly to the main shaft. Depending upon the degree of refinement that one wishes to add to such a weapon, it is relatively simple with stone tools to fabricate either a simple conical socket or a conical shouldered socket. The latter may possibly be superior in situations of extreme thrusting force since the rim of the socket on the main shaft would have transmitted force directly to the shoulder of the foreshaft instead of having the force directed toward the bottom of the socket which would have caused the shaft to split if the bindings around the outside of the socket failed.

Although the resharpening of projectile points at the Casper Site for use as knives is questioned for lack of evidence, it is obvious from observation and from experimentation that a projectile point mounted in a foreshaft such as the one pictured (Fig. 1.45) does make a useful cutting tool. As already mentioned, however, satisfactory evidence of knife or similar use wear is lacking on the Casper Site specimens. Wear pattern analysis is as yet inconclusive and while some blade edges suggest a small amount of use, this could have been the result of projectile point use

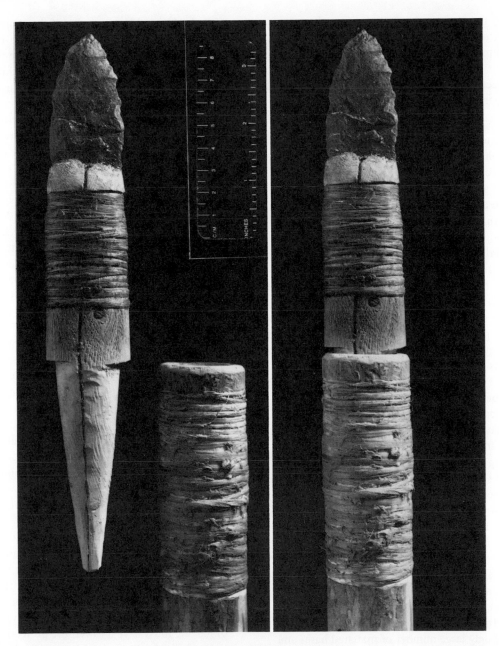

FIGURE 1.45 *Experimental socketing of a Hell Gap projectile point and foreshaft. This is the same experimental specimen that was hafted directly to the main shaft in Figure 1.44.*

also. Driving a projectile point into the ground or into a large animal often creates a certain amount of observable wear on the blade edges.

Projectile Point Distribution And Use At The Casper Site.

The distribution of the projectile points within the site should also be mentioned. The length of the old parabolic dune known to exist is about 245 feet (75 meters) and probably a few feet more are present since the site profile showed some of the dune still remaining. It is assumed the animals were being driven to the leeward through the open end of the dune in a northeasterly direction. Several projectile point bases were recovered at considerable distances away from their distal ends (Fig. 1.46). One interpretation of this could be that some animals were being speared as they were being driven into the main part of the trap while others were speared as they were milling around inside. This certainly seems like a logical sequence of events.

The distribution of projectile point bases that can be matched to points brings up other possibilities for consideration. First, during the actual operation of the trap, the animals were undoubtedly in a state of confusion and moving about trying to escape. Second, unless the animals were speared in such a way that the spinal chord was severed causing immediate loss of control, a lethal wound such as one into the rib cage, will allow an animal to travel some distance before it falls. Third, an object dropped in an area of deep blow sand is easily lost and subsequent activity such as butchering is not likely to move the object any significant distance from where it was originally dropped.

With these ideas in mind and considering the seemingly large number of matched bases and points (16) these might constitute a strong argument for the use of foreshafts as opposed to projectile points hafted directly to main shafts. The distance separating base and point in many cases

(Fig. 1.46) would suggest that if the projectile point were hafted directly to a main shaft, the hunter must have speared an animal, the point broke off and remained in the animal which ran a short distance and fell while the base must have somehow became detached or was discarded from the main shaft. This seems like a highly unlikely occurrence if the hafting was at all secure. It is hard to believe that such a large number of projectile point bases would have been left at the Casper Site assuming they were recovering main shafts unless there was a high incidence of breakage of the latter which seems unlikely. A last thought is that if a running animal were speared broadside, it would have been difficult to retrieve the main shaft unless a foreshaft was used. The animal was moving at or near to a right angle to the direction the spear was traveling and a sideways pressure would have been exerted if the hunter held on to the spear shaft. The best explanation appears to be that they were using foreshafts; there was considerable projectile point breakage from use; there was a relatively large loss of these broken elements due to the sand; and the lost items were not subsequently moved but a short distance and only accidentally as a result of site activity subsequent to the kill. It may very well be that the sand is the reason for the seemingly large number of projectile points at the site. They were simply not able to recover as many as they could have under different conditions.

Another thought to ponder is that a total of 17 projectile points were recovered with bases broken transversely across the tapered tang from 17 mm. to 45 mm. distance from the base. If they were socketing the point to the shoulder, which is assumed from the grinding present, the method of hafting must have allowed the projectile point to break inside the socket between the base and shoulder. This could have been the result of sideways pressure as would have been produced, for example, in spearing a moving animal and holding

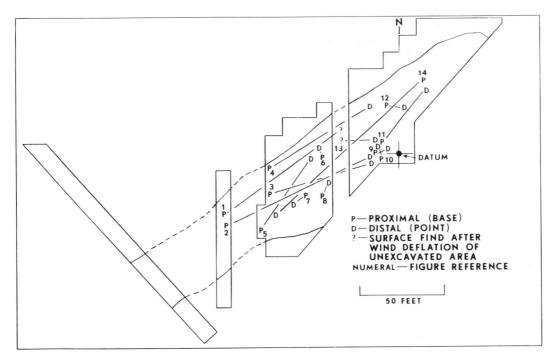

FIGURE 1.46 *Provenience of matched projectile points and bases at the Casper Site. No. 1-Fig. 1.35d, No. 2-Fig. 1.38f, No. 3-Fig. 1.35a, No.4-Fig. 1.39a, No.5-Fig. 1.39f, No. 6-Fig. 1.43a, No. 7-Fig. 1.35b, No. 8-Fig. 1.43b, No. 9-Fig. 1.43d, No. 10-Fig. 1. 39c, No. 11-Fig. 1.39b, No. 12-Fig. 1.40d, No. 13-Fig. 1.36d, No. 14-Fig. 1.38g.*

on to the spear shaft. Another possibility is that the projectile points were hafted with only part of the tapered tang in the socket but this would have negated the advantages provided by the shoulder. Further experimentation may clarify these aspects of projectile point hafting, use and breakage.

In summary, a number of things happened to the projectile points at the Casper Site. These include impact fractures that are present in the form of crushing of the point tip and also long flake scars extending down one or both sides. Impact flakes are discussed below under debitage. Blades were snapped both forward and behind the the widest part of the point with two exceptions, both of which were snapped almost directly across the widest part (Fig. 1.36d. Fig. 1.38c).

Distal ends were often reworked and occasional reworking of the proximal ends by both grinding and flaking was done presumably for reuse as projectile points. Another feature that should be mentioned is what appears to be either a deliberate or accidental form of burination on broken bases of several projectile points. The spalls were removed with the broken base as the striking platform (e.g. Fig. 1.42e, f). They could be regarded as accidental if it were not for the fact that on one (Fig. 1.42e) four spalls were removed in sequence. This may have been a means to prea broken base for reuse also rather than to prepare it for use as a tool.

None of the projectile points were found embedded in their original place in the carcasses which might have given a clue to the actual places they were attempting to hit. In bison kills of later periods where such determinations can be made, the rib cage, vertebral column and throat were favorite targets and ones into which they were regularly able to place the projectile points. This suggests good control over the animals, singling out a certain animal and selecting the proper spot to place the projectile point rather than everyone randomly throwing spears into the herd.

Functionally then, the projectile points were adequate for the indicated purpose at the Casper Site and can be interpreted into the whole communal bison procurement pattern. At this time, too few *in situ* Hell Gap cultural assemblages have been recovered and those that have been have not produced large quantities of interpretive material. At the Hell Gap Site itself, a few projectile points have been described (Agogino 1961: 558-560, Irwin-Williams et al. 1973: 46-48). Three fragmentary Hell Gap projectile points were found at the Sister's Hill Site in north-central Wyoming (Agogino and Galloway 1965). Hell Gap projectile points occurred at the Agate Basin type site in northeastern Wyoming but their stratigraphic relationship to the Agate Basin level is not known (Agogino and Galloway 1965: 190-191). Hell Gap points are known from surface finds over the entire Northwestern Plains and similar-appearing specimens are even more widespread (see e.g. Pettipas 1970, Agogino 1961, for a discussion of known occurrences). In terms of the type site specimen that most are familiar with (Wormington and Forbis 1965: 19, Fig. 5a, Agogino 1961: 559, Fig. 1a) the Casper Site projectile points are atypical. It would appear that the Casper Site specimens probably represent more the true nature of Hell Gap projectile points.

Chipped Stone Tools

Five chipped stone tools were recovered from the Casper Site although the flake debitage offers evidence for the use of a great many more as will be discussed later. Three are cutting or combination cutting and scraping tools made on large percussion flakes. One is similar to the first three except that it is a blade tool while the last one is a large, broken flake of bifacial retouch with a deliberate or use retouch on one section of an edge and it also appears to have had a burin spall removed from the original break. All, with the exception of the possible burin, are similar both functionally and in appearance to chipped stone tools found in a number of communal bison kill and butchering sites over a period of several thousand years.

The largest (Fig. 1.47) is a quadrilateral-shaped tool with the original flat face of the flake preserved. The original striking platform of the flake is preserved and demonstrates considerable grinding presumably in preparation for removal from the core. Two slightly convex working edges and two slighty concave working edges are present. One of the latter was formed fortuitously by the initial removal of the flake from the core and was not modified except for some use flake scars. The only modification of the flake was to prepare the working edges and other than this, both the face and the back of the flake are unchanged.

There are a number of working edges on this tool as mentioned. It was apparently the practice to utilize only small areas of the working edge during use, especially projections and areas around corners, and from experimentation this is a common pattern that develops in actual practice. As a result, a good deal of sharpening of a tool is done to prepare a relatively small part of the working edge. The tool in question here demonstrates this principle. A sharp cutting edge was formed around the corners while less attention was paid to the remainder of the working edge. The working edge angles vary from as low as 29 degrees to one as high as 57 degrees but mostly below 47 degrees which is suggested in

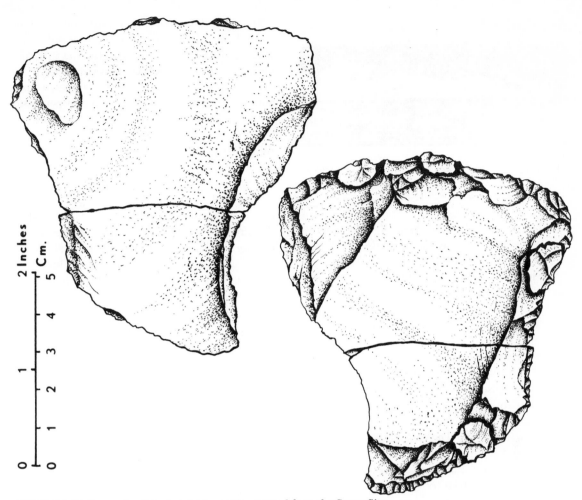

FIGURE 1.47 *Percussion flake butchering tool recovered from the Casper Site.*

another context (Frison 1970: 36-38) as within the range of variation of angles of angles used for cutting tools in bison butchering contexts.

This tool was also broken with the two pieces recovered nearly eight feet apart. A group of 10 flakes were in the same area with the smallest piece of the tool. Two of these can be fit into their original flake scars on the tool leaving no doubt as to their origin. Evidence of subsequent use of the tool appears as a gap of approximately 1 mm. between the face of the retouch flake re-in resharpening and its flake scar in the vicinity

of the working edge and for a short distance behind it (Fig. 1.48 left). Subsequent resharpening of the tool after breakage is indicated by flake removal performed on the largest piece that left a discrepancy of about 2.5 mm. between the two working edges when the broken edges are matched. Evidence for subsequent use of the tool after breakage is present also. Another group of eight flakes was recovered two feet from the largest piece of the tool and two of these fit into their flake scars on the tool. There is very little if any gap between the faces of these flakes and

FIGURE 1.48 *Photograph of working edge of uniface tool (Fig. 1.47) with sharpening flakes replaced.*

and their scars on the tool (Fig. 1.48 right). A sharp edge on the tool is also present suggesting little wear and also little use of the tool before it was lost or discarded. The flakes removed from this tool can readily be identified as a class described as side-scraper retouch flakes in another context (Frison 1968: 150).

From all of this, some history of the use of the tool in the site can be suggested. First, it was used in one area of the site and sharpened there where it was also broken. The smaller piece was apparently discarded but the larger piece was used and was resharpened several feet away from where it was broken. The tool was lost or discarded about two feet from this last sharpening after a small amount of use.

The next largest flake tool (Fig. 1.49a) is functionally similar to the first. Exceptionally rough use of the working edge is suggested by a scalar or step retouch presumably from use and this probably explains the lack of sharpening flakes recovered in the deposits that are from this tool since the flakes removed during use would have been extremely small. There is, however, underneath the use retouch a flaking pattern that appears to be a percussion retouch to form the original cutting edge. The working edge is convex in outline form and the edge angle varies from about 40 degrees to 46 degrees again suggestive of a cutting rather than a scraping edge.

The third flake tool (Fig. 1.49b) would be considered an end scraper except for a carefully prepared convex cutting edge opposite the striking platform end with a working edge angle of 35 degrees to 45 degrees. The tool is vaguely trapezoidal in outline form with the bulb of percussion missing. A second prepared cutting edge meets the first at an angle of about 90 degrees while a third cutting edge demonstrates use retouch but no deliberate preparation. Two sharpening flakes from the site can be matched to their flake scars on this tool. Working edge angles again indicate deliberate formation of cutting edges although in the butchering process, the two functions of cutting and scraping are closely interrelated. The tool is unquestionably of Knife River Flint.

The last flake tool is a thin (3 mm.) flake of bifacial retouch with a broad striking platform that demonstrates grinding preparation (Fig. 1.50). Adjacent to the striking platform is a convex cutting edge and demonstrating what appears to be a fine, deliberate unilateral retouch. In addition, this tool was either deliberately or fortuitously a burin. A burin spall was driven at right angles to a transverse break to form a burin point 1.3 mm. wide and demonstrating a number of microscopic flakes extending back from the working point and suggesting use in standard burin fashion. It is possible also that other burin spalls could have preceeded the present one.

A single blade tool is so designated because its length is more than twice it width (Fig. 1.51). It demonstrates a long, nearly straight working edge with a deliberately dulled edge opposite. No sharpening flakes for this tool were recovered but wear appears as a step retouch and crushing suggesting hard usage similar to that of Figure 1.48a and it was probably not sharpened at the site. A thick bulb of percussion provides a much more efficient handhold than is expected from merely observing its outline form.

The groups of sharpening flakes for the tools and their position in relation to the tools are

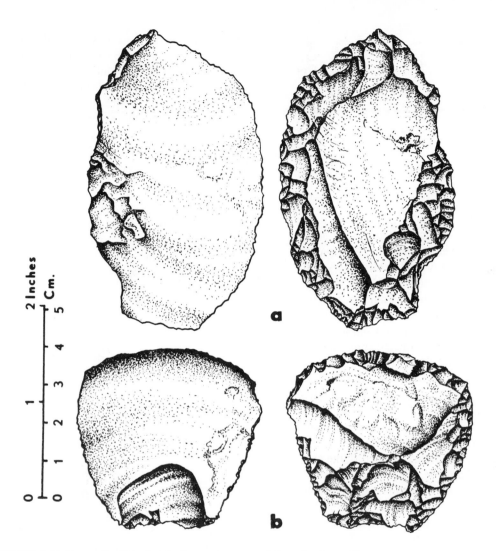

2 Inches

Cm.

FIGURE 1.49 *Percussion flake butchering tools recovered from the Casper Site.*

shown (Fig. 1.52). The presence of large numbers of similar butchering tools are indicated from analysis of the flake debitage. A great variety of flaking materials was exploited that demonstrates a number of distinctive colors and textures and within limits it can be shown that sharpening flakes were present in the bone deposits that were removed from tools not found at the site. This will be discussed under debitage.

Flake Debitage

A total of 308 flakes were recovered from the kill area of the Casper Site. Of these 48 were identified as flakes resulting from projectile point impact. They are distinctive and can usually be separated from the tool sharpening flakes. Positive identification was possible in some cases by replacing flakes in their flake scars on

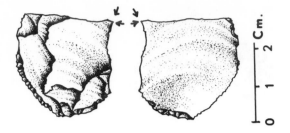

FIGURE 1.50 *Small flake tool and possible burin from the Casper Site.*

projectile points.

Several kinds of flakes resulted from impact. One kind is a flake extending from the tip in the direction of the base on one or both faces of the projectile point. Sometimes the force was sufficient and directed in such a manner that it produced something reminiscent of a channel flake (Fig. 1.42e left, Fig. 1.53a) and left a smooth flake scar. One projectile point demonstrates a long impact flake scar that was almost completely obliterated by reworking (Fig. 1.38c) while in other cases the flake scar demonstrates a series of ripples (Fig. 1.39a). In several instances the flake hinged out but in other cases it broke of squarely but left the distal end partially loosened but still attached to the projectile point (Fig. 1.40e, Fig. 1.53b). Striking platforms were usually destroyed and often the entire flake was badly shattered. In one instance it was possible to match five small slivers into part of an impact flake that fit into the flake scar on Fig. 1.42e left. Sometimes the impact flakes were driven off the blade edges rather than the face (e.g. Fig. 1.42e, Fig. 1.53c).

Impact resulted also in crushing of the tip. There were many variations of this and one noticeable thing is that the sharp tip was usually destroyed and at the same time a small part of the tip snapped off squarely. The part that was snapped of sometimes remained intact (Fig. 1.53 d) but usually it shattered (Fig. 1.37d, Fig. 1.53 e). Four of these extreme distal ends were re-

covered and each demonstrates loss of the extreme sharp tip as well as breaking off a short distance proximal to the point.

Distinctive flakes resulted also from snapping of the projectile point such as happened when the animal was hit at enough angle so that the hide slipped and "bunched up" causing sideways pressure. This often drove off flakes on the face of the projectile point on one or both sides of the

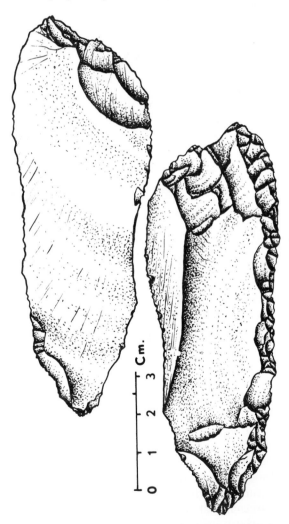

FIGURE 1.51 *Blade butchering tool recovered from the Casper Site.*

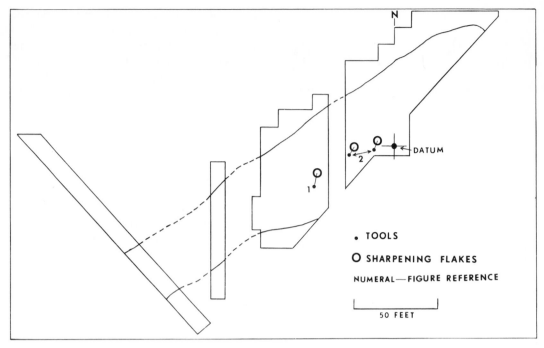

FIGURE 1.52 *Sharpening flakes and tools that match from the Casper Site. No. 1-Fig. 1.49b, No. 2-Fig. 1.47.*

break. These flakes uaually hinged out rather suddenly but some left large flake scars (Fig. 1. 42e right, Fig. 1.53f, g). Another distal end that was snapped produced an impact flake that was driven off toward the distal end of the projectile point and part of the impact flake was recovered (Fig. 1.43f). These kinds of impact flakes are all shown schematically (Fig. 1.53). Impact flakes were matched to projectile points in seven instances (Fig. 1.54).

The bulk of the debitage, however, consists of tool sharpening flakes which are quite distinctive. One hundred and five of these can be identified as coming from uniface butchering tools such as those described above. What remains of the striking platforms of these flakes are flat and are part of the original flake face of the tool. They usually expand quite rapidly and terminate on the back of the flake that formed the tool. On the backs of most of most of the complete flakes

and adjacent to the striking platforms can be seen part of the working edges of tools before they were sharpened. Beyond this can often be seen part of the unmodified back of the tool. Viewed from the side they are as Bordes describes (1961: 6) as "claw shaped", fairly thick in the vicinity of the striking platforms and curving smoothly to a sharp point. Occasionally a flake was not driven properly and it hinged out before reaching the back of the tool but these are the exception. Several flakes in this category lack striking platforms but from shape, color and texture most can be assigned to the identifiable groups of sharpening flakes. As already mentioned, not one flake in this category was recovered that was removed from projectile points at the site.

Twenty one groups of flakes besides those that were removed from the two tools were clustered in discrete areas of the site and are assumed to represent tool-sharpening events. These groups

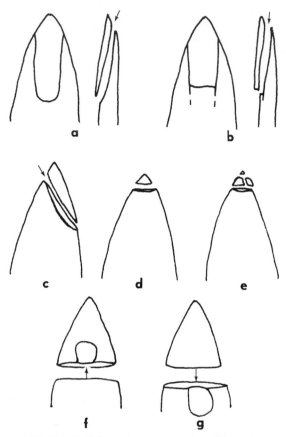

FIGURE 1.53 *Schematic representation of impact flakes from the Casper Site.*

were determined by color, texture and stone type. The groups contain as few as three and as many as 21 flakes but with most from six to eleven. There are in addition 12 tool-sharpening flakes that do not match any tool or fit in any of the groups but are unquestionably of different flaking materials.

Eight of the discrete groups of flakes were removed from four separate tools, two groups to each tool (Fig. 1.55). This is assumed for six of the eight groups on the basis of color, texture and stone type but it can be positively demonstrated for the other two groups. Three flakes

from one group totaling eight can be matched from overlapping flake scars and these will match the flake scars from two flakes from the other group that contains twelve. There is a gap of about 1 mm. between the two matched sets (Fig. 1.56) indicating sharpening of a tool and subsequent use that dulled the edge and then resharpening of the same tool. The tool itself, however, was not recovered. The two groups of flakes were about nine feet apart and each group was contained within an area of less than 50 sq. ft. This a sequence reminiscent to that demonstrated for one of the tools above (Fig. 1.47).

Two others of the eight groups containing seven flakes each are both of a distinctive light-colored, grainy quartzite with black intrusions and these two groups were about 18 feet apart. The four remaining groups are of dark grey quartzite with a light cortex and there is a strong likelihood that the four groups represent two tools since there are minute variations in the texture of the stone. Flakes within the groups can be matched to overlapping flake scars but none can be matched across groups. This is understandable and does not negate the possibility that they were removed from the same tool since they were not always resharpening the entire working edge of a tool at any one time. In this manner, the flakes from one part of a tool could be in one group while the flakes from another part could be in another group but both groups would still be from the same tool.

The remaining 13 groups of sharpening flakes were distributed throughout the bone bed and it is likely that many of the individual groups represent more than one sharpening event since several of the groups were scattered over areas of as much as 50 sq. ft. (Fig. 1.57). From experience, it is not unusual to sharpen a tool regularly and doing so often requires nothing more than the removal of a few flakes to rejuvenate a small area of the working edge. Some sharpening can be done also by merely abrading

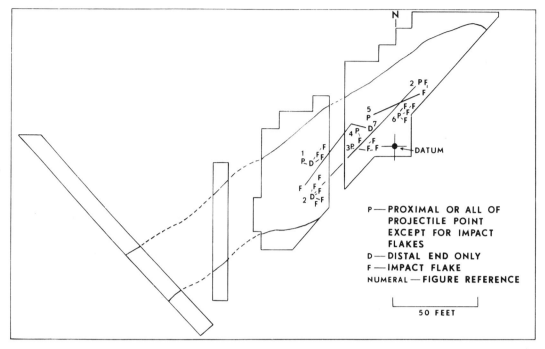

FIGURE 1.54 *Provenience of impact flakes and projectile points that match from the Casper Site. No. 1-Fig. 1-40b, No. 2-Fig. 1.42e, No. 3-Fig. 1.43c, No. 4-Fig. 1.37d, No. 5-Fig. 1.40e, No. 6-Fig. 1.40a, No. 7-1.43f.*

which is analogous to sharpening the edge of a steel knife on a whetstone.

In summary, the sharpening flake assemblage indicates that in addition to the five cutting tools recovered from the site, there were at least an additional 25 and possibly more tools sharpened and presumably used at the site. This number seems commensurate with the activities indicated in the butchering processes at the site. Why more of the tools were not left among the bone deposits at the site remains a question but it is felt that there must have been a meat processing area nearby and the missing tools may have been used there. It is also difficult to explain why if projectile points were lost in rather large numbers then why did they not lose more cutting tools.

Stone Flaking Materials

Four main types of stone materials are represented in the Casper Site projectile point assemblage. The only exotic material present is Knife River Flint of which three projectile points (Fig. 1.36a, Fig. 1.37c, Fig. 1.42d) were made. There seems little doubt that this is material from the source in North Dakota. A single projectile point (Fig. 1.43d) was made from a light-colored metamorphosed shale that is common in an area beginning about 100 miles north of the Casper Site and extending well into southern Montana. It occurs as the result of extensive coal beds that are believed to have burned in late Pliocene or early Pleistocene times. There are so many sources of this material that were exploited that it would be impossible at this time to determine the exact source.

For the remaining projectile points, preference was divided about equally between the chert and

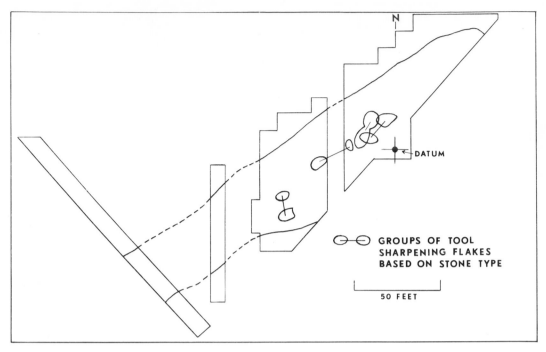

FIGURE 1.55 *Provenience of groups of sharpening flakes at the Casper Site.   Connected groups are believed to be from the same tool.*

jasper category and the quartzites. Most of the jaspers and cherts are probably derived from the almost unlimited quantities of materials found on both sides of the Laramie Range 50 to 100 miles southeast of the Casper Site. There are literally hundreds of areas that have been quarried and the range of colors and textures are so varied that even from the same quarry there is enough difference to make it extremely difficult if not impossible to trace materials from site back to quarry.

The same is true for the quartzites. Quite likely some of the red quartzites used were from quarries in the Shirley Basin about 50 miles south and slightly east of the Casper Site. Some of the quartzites may also have come from the so-called Spanish Diggings area about 100 miles east and slightly south of the Casper Site. There are hundreds of quartzite boulder fields and bedrock

outcroppings that have been quarried and, as for the other materials, the exact source of any given specimen of quartzite in the Spanish Diggings area is impossible to pinpoint.

The tools and sharpening flakes are divided almost equally between the chert-jasper and quartzite categories and appear to represent the same

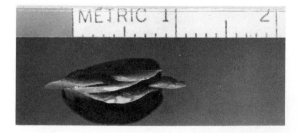

FIGURE 1.56 *Two overlapping groups of sharpening flakes demonstrating two separate tool-sharpening events at the Casper Site.*

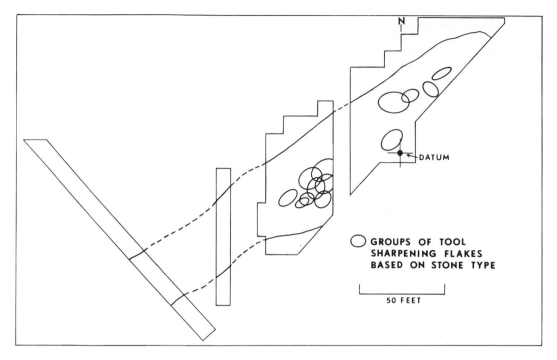

FIGURE 1.57 *Distribution of groups of tool sharpening flakes from the Casper Site.*

sources as the projectile points and tools. One tool (Fig. 1.49b) and two of its recovered sharpening flakes are of Knife River Flint.

Hammerstones

Twenty river cobbles were recovered in context with the bison bones at the Casper Site and they are believed to have been hammerstones for use in butchering (Fig. 1.11). Of this number, only four demonstrated good evidence of use and might have been recognized as actual tools out of context. They are generally elongate in shape and the butchers were apparently choosing cobbles with pointed ends in order to concentrate the force of blows in a small area. Two exceptions have rounded ends (e.g. Fig. 1.11f). From actual experience, these hammerstones are quite functional in duplicating the bone crushing and breaking observed at the Casper Site. It was found through experimentation that these

hammerstones will crush large amounts of fresh bone and not leave but very little evidence of use on the working ends. They are of quartzite, granite and chert and all available close to the site.

The hammerstones demonstrate a range in weight from 359 grams to 1,324 grams (Table 5). The two smallest ones have parts broken and missing and as a result were originally slightly larger. The weights cluster around two values. One is around 1,200 grams and the other is at around 500 grams. The broken point of one hammerstone (Table 5, no. 17) was found in the bone deposits. It appears to have been broken from use since it is of chert and a striking platform and bulb of percussion are lacking such as one would expect if it were a flake removed with a hammer. Two other pieces are probably similarly-broken points but no not match either of the other two broken specimens. It is strongly

TABLE 1.5 *Casper Site Hammerstones.*

Number	Weight in Grams
1	1324
2	1252
3	1230
4	1208
5	1173
6	1163
7	1140
8	763
9	640
10	601
11	540
12	538
13	536
14	531
15	501
16	483
17	418 (Broken)
18	377
19	362 (Broken)
20	359 (Broken)

suggested that these hammerstones were used mainly in smashing long bones and breaking off certain muscle attachments.

AMOUNTS AND UTILIZATION OF THE CASPER SITE MEAT PRODUCTS

Wheat (1972) has done an exhaustive study of the literature on the amounts of meat obtained, preservation, and consumption of bison in historic times and there is no reason to repeat his excellent work here. A figure generally accepted is that a mature female buffalo in good condition will produce about 400 pounds of usable meat and a mature male about 900 pounds. These figures are probably close. A mature female *Bison bison* killed in March, 1972 in fair condition stripped out 369 pounds of meat and this included the bones of the brisket and the distal ends of the dorsal spines of the hump. There were very few pounds of meat left on the car-

cass, certainly not more than 10. Another extremely old cow in poor condition with sucking calf was killed in December 1971 and produced just over 300 pounds of meat. The same cows in prime condition in the fall would have produced more. On the first animal the tongue weighed just slightly over three pounds, the liver eleven pounds, and the heart six pounds. No attempt was made to retrieve the bone marrow, brains or other contents of the skull cavity such as the soft gristle of the nose.

Seventy four animals were known for certain to have been killed at the Casper Site and there were undoubtedly more. There seems no reason to accept a total figure of less than 100 head. Wheat (1972: 114) allows 25% increase in size for the larger, extinct animals which is probably a reasonable figure. Of the 74 animals recovered, 19 or about 29% were calves which at the age of six to seven months should have very conservatively weighed around 350 to 400 pounds judging from *Bison bison* calves of about the same age. There were no long yearlings and only a few two year olds so the remainder of the animals butchered can be considered as adults. There were apparently only three mature males.

For easy computation we can use the hypothetical figure of 100 head of animals. If the observed percentage figures are valid, we could expect 29 calves out of the 100 head. Each calf should have produced at least 175 pounds of meat. The same percentage figures would allow another mature male or a total of four out of the 100 head. The total then would have been 29 calves, four mature males and 67 mature or nearly mature females and young males. Using Wheat's (1972: 14) figures and complete butchering of all animals, there might have been a total of about 42,000 pounds of meat taken at the Casper Site. This is exclusive of the tongues, hearts, livers and other items such as the spleen, brain, and soft gristle of the nose which, if utilized, would have totaled another 25 pounds of usable products from the mature animals. Bone marrow was also utilized from well over half of the adult animals judging from the fact that less than half of the long bones were present at the site and many of the ones that were present were broken in a manner strongly suggesting marrow retrieval. Brains were apparently not utilized at the Casper Site although there is some suggestion they were taking the soft gristle of the nose. The fact that they were not taking the brains raises some questions as to the treatment of hides. In Late Prehistoric Period times there was utilization of brains and much of this may have been for hide tanning purposes rather than for food.

Wheat (1972: 121) used a figure of ten pounds of fresh meat per person per day as an average figure for the fresh meat consumption for all members of a human group. This figure is based on a number of historical observations. The number of persons involved in the Casper Site kill is hypothetical. At one Late Prehistoric Period buffalo jump an estimate of 120 persons was made based on the presence of 20 stone circles or tipi rings representing lodges and assuming six persons per lodge. Wheat (1972: 120-124) considers several hypothetical situations with regard to the Olsen-Chubbuck Site. One hypothesis is that the group may have had dogs although no actual remains of dogs were found at Olsen-Chubbuck nor was any evidence found of dogs at the Casper Site. In contrast, however, dogs are common in bison kills of the later periods. If dogs were present, Wheat argues that they were consuming a good share of the meat. Wheat also argues that if the group did not have dogs, that between 150 to 200 persons were involved to have utilized the products of the kill considering that it was a single event with all of the animals being killed at one time which required more rapid meat processing and utilization than if the kill was divided into several smaller events over a period of several weeks. With dogs, a smaller

group of persons could have utilized the products of the kill in a shorter period of time than if dogs were not present. Wheat also feels that a number between 75 and 100 persons would better satisfy the cultural conditions required for a group of hunters in this time period.

With regard to the Casper Site, a group of 15 to 20 males seems reasonable for carrying out the trapping and butchering operations indicated. A few more would not have hindered the operation but neither would they have improved its efficiency. A suggested figure is that the human group assembled at the Casper Site consisted of between 75 and 100 persons which would allow for from 15 to 20 grown males to carry out the trapping operation. This is, provided of course, that hunting was strictly male-centered activity as it was during the Late Prehistoric Period.

The length of the communal procurement season at the Casper Site is somewhat speculative unlike at the Olsen-Chubbuck Site which was a single instantaneous event. It is not believed that the Casper Site represents a single kill but several, perhaps five or six over a period of possibly two to three weeks. There is a suggestion also that the trap may have been used earlier in the fall since six of the calf mandibles seem to cluster around an age of possibly four to six weeks younger than the remainder (see Chapter 2 concerning age determination).

It seems highly unlikely in this kind of trapping situation that each person could have relied on obtaining more than one animal in each drive and if a large herd were present, the remainder would have managed to escape. If a cow were killed or crippled, however, the calf would probably have remained close by and could have easily been killed. In one Late Archaic bison kill it was noted that a cow and calf pair would often be found together and the same behavior is true of most large game animals. If the mother is killed, the calf will usually remain close by and can usually be killed easily. This is especially true if the mother is wounded and is still on her feet or is even in a sitting position.

Meat killed in a situation such as the Casper Site had to be processed or eaten within a short period. If the hypothetical group of 75 to 100 persons consumed an average of ten pounds of meat per day for three weeks this would account for less than half of the total exclusive of internal organs. If the group had dogs, this might have accounted for the use of some of the animal products but there is no evidence to indicate dogs were present. It seems likely that some of the meat was being dried. Most of the long bones were missing presumably for the purpose of extracting marrow and some sort of pemmican or similar product could have been made. Whether or not the processed meat was stored or carried for future use is speculative.

According to reliable observers of hunters and gatherers (Lee and DeVore 1968: 12) "food surplusses are not a prominent feature of the small scale society." The problem of surplusses and storage needs to be explored in the Paleo-Indian case on the Northwestern Plains. The communal kill may have had sociological implications that were every bit as important as the economic. There is, however, a strong indication of effective utilization of the meat products in communal kills. The writer argues that some kind of minimal storage at least was necessary for an area of severe winters where it would be difficult for small human groups to survive on a day to day hunting and gathering basis. There are short periods of time during severe winters on the Plains when hunting and gathering is impossible. During periods such as these, some sort of food storage was necessary for survival.

At this point we have no direct archeological evidence for the methods of storage that might have been utilized. Drying of meat reduces weight by a ratio of about five to one and the bulk is similarly reduced. Further processing of the meat into some sort of pemmican by mixing powdered dried meat, bone grease and backfat as was common in historic times creates a compact, concentrated and extremely nourishing food. Considering that a full grown female bison can be reduced to about 50 pounds in this manner, this could have been an important food supply for short periods of time and one that was relatively easy to transport. The concept of processing relatively small amounts of food for use during short periods of food scarcity seems more reasonable than attempting to store large quantities to last the entire winter. Had they been storing these kinds of quantites, we would have expected by now to have found some evidence of the storage or an archeological site that represents the campsite where a group of people this large lived on these products.

The problem of storing large amounts of dried meat for any length of time on the Plains would appear to have been great. Several possible alternatives exist but all would have required almost constant attention to prevent loss. Perhaps it was more expedient to rely on a small amount of transportable storage than a large quantity of stored products that would have had to be consumed in one spot and cut down on the mobility of the human group. No known site at any prehistoric time period in the region suggests a location where a large group of people such as a communal bison hunting group spent the winter or any long period of time consuming a quantity of stored meat products. The best evidence at present suggests fragmentation of the band after the communal kill and whether or not they tried to store or carry their processed food products from the kill with them is entirely speculative at this time.

CULTURAL AND ECOLOGICAL RELATIONSHIPS OF THE CASPER SITE

Probably the most complete stratigraphic record of the Paleo-Indian occupation presently known for the High Plains is the Hell Gap Site in southeastern Wyoming (Irwin-Williams et al. 1973). According to the investigators, the cultural entity known as Hell Gap is estimated to have existed in a period roughly estimated at around 8,000 to 7,500 B. C. From this and the distribution of surface materials that appear to be of Hell Gap affiliation, it would appear that for a period of possibly 500 years the Northwestern Plains was occupied by this Hell Gap cultural manifestation. The relationship of Hell Gap to other areas has been speculated upon briefly (Agogino 1961) based on similarities between projectile points.

Representing this 500 year span of time are only three excavated sites which include the type site at Hell Gap, the Sister's Hill Site near Buffalo, Wyoming, and the Casper Site. Another large Hell Gap site is presently being excavated near Laird, Colorado and from the indications at this time it is apparently a butchering or processing area for a bison kill. There is also what appears to be Hell Gap material at the Agate Basin Site (Agogino and Galloway 1965: 190-191) but the context in which it was recovered was not good enough to determine the nature of its relationship with other cultural materials. Further investigation of the Agate Basin Site under carefully controlled conditions should clarify the relationships between the Hell Gap, Agate Basin and Folsom materials there.

This amount of archeological data are not yet sufficient for anything other than extremely speculative reconstructions of the cultural systems involved. Both the Hell Gap occupations at the Hell Gap Site and the Sister's Hill Site are camp sites. The Casper Site is a bison kill and the Laird, Colorado site is somehow related to a bison kill but for the latter, a more complete interpretation must await complete investigation and analysis by the investigators. These amounts of data are small for meaningful reconstructions of Hell Gap cultural systems.

Assuming that Hell Gap existed as a cultural entity for several hundred years, there had to be many more sites. At what point the idea of "archeological visibility" operates in a situation such as this is not known (Deetz 1968: 285). Certainly it seems like a concept that needs to be explored. If we consider the four Wyoming sites mentioned; Casper, Hell Gap, Sister's Hill, and Agate Basin; and connect them together, they enclose a trapezoidal area of about 9,500 square miles. All four sites are in or are close to an area of topographic diversity. The Casper Site is at the northernmost extension of the Laramie Range; the Hell Gap Site is in a small valley extending into the Hartville Uplift; the Agate Basin Site is on the western side of the southernmost extension of the South Dakota-Wyoming Black Hills; and the Sister's Hill Site is at the base of the eastern slope of the Big Horn Mountains.

The entire area is in many ways similar with rainfall averaging about 12 to 14 inches per year. It is dissected with numerous arroyos and in general has a good grass cover. Running water is available in seeps, springs and streams that flow from higher elevations through the area and there are occasional playa lakes and ponds that contain water at various times throughout the year. Large areas at higher elevations are near to all the sites.

The postglacial geology of the area is even less known than the prehistory. One major study was made of the postglacial chronology of stream terraces (Leopold and Miller 1951) and this was certainly not definitive nor was it intended to be so. Two later geological studies were made of local Paleo-Indian sites (Haynes and Grey 1965, Irwin-Williams et al. 1973). The details of the Altithermal Period from about 4,500 B. C. to 2,500 B. C. are poorly known as yet. In general, the area is known to be one of considerable erosion and deposition during post-Altithermal times (Mann 1968, Albanese 1970, 1971) but the details are as yet in the data-gathering stage.

Undoubtedly, arroyo cutting and filling has destroyed many Paleo-Indian sites and also covered many others. The situation at the Ruby Site (Frison 1971a) in the Pumpkin Buttes area south of Gillette, Wyoming and north of Casper is not an isolated example. Here the earlier alluvial deposits in a dry tributary of the Powder River were removed and a Late Archaic bison kill was in operation over a period of several years while the deposits were once again aggrading. After this, much of the deposits was once again removed by arroyo downcutting which destroyed much of the site (Albanese 1971). How much arroyo cutting and deposition occurred during the Altithermal Period and for a period of about 4,000 years before this has not been studied but all of these geological events have taken a toll of archeological sites.

The kind of "archeological visibility" that Deetz refers to concerns the amount of occupation or activity needed to produce evidence that can be recognized later by the investigator. Here, of course, the parameters affecting the amount of this kind of evidence and the preservation of it are numerous and diverse. Nomadic groups, even modern ones, may camp in an area for several days and unless conditions are right there is little evidence to be found within a few years except possibly for garbage pits provided they bothered to bury their garbage. The remains from surface fires soon blow away unless a pit was dug and surrounded by stones. A number of hunting camps in the mountains used for a period of two weeks or more by the same outfitting groups year after year for several decades leave almost no interpretive materials after a lapse of a few years.

In terms of "archeological visibility" it appears that the known Hell Gap sites represent high values. This is understandable at the Casper Site which must represent the intense activity of a larger than usual number of people for a short period of time. The high value is enhanced by the bison bone without which the site would have been much more difficult to recognize, especially considering there was no discolored occupation level commonly found in camp and processing areas.

The high visibility of the Hell Gap Site was apparently due to intensive occupation although the Hell Gap cultural level is described by the investigators (Irwin-Williams et al. 1973) as being of low concentration compared to other cultural units and possibly represents brief hunting camps.

The Sister's Hill Site was of fairly high visibility due to a dark stratum exposed in the perpendicular face of an arroyo cut that contained also artifact material. The site contained antelope, mule deer, porcupine, ground squirrel and other small mammal bones but no bison. Three projectile point bases were recovered along with a tool assemblage which included an oval knife, two spokeshave gravers, three side scrapers and four small endscrapers. Two preforms were recovered but no mention was made of debitage. No mention was made as to estimates of the size of the site or the relative amount investigated. It is an important site in gaining some concept of the nature of Hell Gap economic orientations since it is apparently not related to a bison kill or a related procurement situation.

As mentioned, the Agate Basin Site did produce some cultural material that seems unmistakably Hell Gap. The site to date has unfortunately never received the proper kind of investigation until a good share of it was lost. At present a good share of the recovered cultural material is in private collections. It is a site of high archeological visibility because the Paleo-Indian cultural levels are thick and exposed for considerable distances in arroyo banks. The stratigraphy may yet be resolved to determine the nature of the Agate Basin-Hell Gap relationships there.

The known sites in Wyoming that have produced Hell Gap material embrace a homogeneous area and include a variety of microenvironments that make of the macroenvironment in the same sense that the terms are used by Flannery (1968). The major part of the area is open grassland dissected by several large running streams such as the North Platte, the Powder, the Belle Fourche and the Cheyenne Rivers. There are a number of smaller streams that feed these larger ones and depending on their sources, whether in the mountains or the plains, they may be running or intermittent. The only major area of sand dunes in the area is that in which the Casper Site is located although some smaller areas are present. The open grasslands themselves represent a separate microenvironment and comprise the natural environment for bison and antelope. Floodplains and the breaks along the major watercourses along with a few scattered areas of extremely dissected hills represent the natural environment for deer and various small animals. Foothills and steeper mountain slopes present at least two microenvironments depending upon elevation and direction of the slope. North slopes are usually covered with more lush vegetation than the south slopes which usually support only sagebrush, sparse grass and some shrubs. Mountain sheep and deer along with some animals of lesser importance occupied the rough, deeply dissected mountain slopes.

Another microenvironment that was apparently attractive to some Paleo-Indian and later groups as well was the high mountain meadow or open high country at elevations around 7,500 to 8,500 feet. The only area of this nature that has received any systematic survey is in the Big Horn Mountain area. The Big Horns demonstrate rather steep and deeply dissected slopes and then flatten to large areas of thick timber and open parks at elevations of about 7,500 to 8,500 feet. Human occupation was of course limited to the late spring-summer-early fall periods if present conditions are an indication of the past. Surface surveys have indicated considerable amounts of Paleo-Indian cultural material including Hell Gap

but to date none of this material has been found in satisfactory context. As yet the economic orientations of Paleo-Indian groups utilizing the mountain meadow areas have not been well studied. It is known that *Bison bison* were common to the higher elevations and were hunted there in the post-Altithermal period by Archaic and Late Prehistoric Period groups but it is not yet known if the extinct bison were conducting any kind of seasonal movements from the open plains to the higher altitude mountain meadows.

Whether or not the Paleo-Indian was utilizing the areas around timberline and above in the area under study is not known. Areas of around 9,500 feet and above have not yet been properly surveyed archeologically and what has been done has indicated some Archaic and Late Prehistoric Period material but nothing conclusive of the Paleo-Indian.

It is suggested from the above that the Hell Gap cultural groups were exploiting a resource area that extended from the major river valleys and plains to at least the high mountain meadow areas. The one bison kill is not an adequate sample but it does indicate in this one case a fall-of-the-year operation. If this holds true in more sites, a strong case for scheduling of communal bison kills to a limited period of the year can be hypothesized. From the evidence at present it is suggested that there was a consolidation of persons for the communal kill in the fall and then fragmentation of the group for the remainder of the year and this pattern lasted from the Paleo-Indian period until the introduction of the horse. There has to be a large number of Hell Gap sites yet to be found and most of these are undoubtedly of low archeological visibility. Many others are no longer extant due to geological processes that have occurred in the last 10,000 years. It will probably be some time before enough of these sites are found, excavated and interpreted to make more meaningful statements regarding the Hell Gap cultural complex.

DATING THE CASPER SITE

The bone level at the Casper Site did not contain any burned bone or evidence of fire pits or hearths but small bits of charcoal were scattered throughout. This amount increased to the west of the site and was most concentrated between W 070 and W 080. An extension of the excavation was made from W 080 to W 085 in the hopes of finding a fire hearth but the effort was not successful. The total charcoal collected amounted to just under five grams. The source of the charcoal is not known. It is possible that a small fire hearth or other feature exists in the unexcavated area between W 085 and W 100 since the amount and size of the pieces of charcoal increases toward the west end but none was found in the north-south test trench from W 100 to W 110. There is no known reason to regard the charcoal as anything but contemporaneous with the bone deposit since it was in the same level and none was found above or below it. The charcoal pieces were angular suggesting they had not been moved any distance and the possibility of it being derived from a source that predates the bone deposits is remote. The date derived from the charcoal sample is 7880 B. C. $\pm$ 350 years (RL-125).

A bone sample was submitted for dating the following year. This sample consisted of a complete metatarsal and the result obtained from this was 8110 B. C. $\pm$ 170 years (RL-208). The dates seem very much in line with other dates on Hell Gap cultural levels from the Hell Gap Site and the Sister's Hill Site.

CONCLUSIONS

The amount of Hell Gap cultural material recovered to date in good contexts is small and actually consists of two camp sites, one bison kill and a bison butchering or processing area that is presently being investigated. Dates from the three excavated sites fall in the area of about 8,000 B. C. The best stratigraphic record of Paleo-Indian occupation for the area is at the Hell Gap Site near Guernsey, Wyoming and here it is suggested that the Hell Gap cultural manifestation lasted from approximately 8,000 to 7,500 B. C. Suggested also is the Hell Gap complex was somehow derived from the Agate Basin cultural complex and that it later developed into the Alberta cultural complex. Obviously these kinds of cultural reconstructions based on projectile point typologies need to be further studied and refined. The Paleo-Indian stratigraphic record today suggests discrete cultural groups and periods separated by sterile periods. The nature of and the kind of cultural continuity that had to be present needs to be better understood.

The Casper Site represents only one small increment of the total yearly round of activity. The evidence is present to indicate the time of year which was in the late fall. Considering what can be taken as fact and speculation from the results of the Casper Site investigations, a number of hypotheses need to be further tested regarding bison procurement and its relationships to the Paleo-Indian cultural systems involved.

(1) *In the pre-horse period, communal bison procurement was mostly limited to the late summer and fall.* Too few sites at this point in time have been investigated with this particular problem in mind. Most sites in the region including the Casper Site and other Paleo-Indian bison kill sites along with many more of the post-Altithermal Period indicate they were accomplished during this time of the year. Historically during the horse period on the Plains there was a spring kill. This was necessary and due to the larger human groups that had exhausted the winter meat supply. With horses there was no problem in obtaining bison at any time if the animals were in the vicinity, weather conditions were favorable and the animals could be found.

The time of year of pre-horse communal bison procurement needs to be further investigated before more definitive statements can be made.

(2) *Late summer or fall communal bison kills were so limited due to the behavioral characteristics of the animals.* This is a problem that may not be resolved satisfactorily since we must assume rightfully or otherwise that the extinct varieties behaved as do the present day ones that are in various stages of domestication. Also it must be remembered that in the present day the animals are handled on horseback and also with motor vehicles of various types. From a very generalized behavior pattern demonstrated by all of the present members of the *Bos* and *Bison* genera, it is suggested strongly that the predictability of success in bison driving was much higher in late summer or fall than in the spring or early summer. Further work in this area must necessarily involve the expertise of wildlife behavioralists as well as many other specialists. It will involve many other species as well as bison also.

(3) *The sociological implication of the communal drive were probably as important as the economic.* It was important to the well-being and continuity of the human band to have a well-defined period when they came together for various sociological reasons. Ethnological evidence suggests this is true among known hunting and gathering societies presently operating at the band level. The communal kill provided a predictable situation where temporary meat surplusses were possible. The effectiveness of the communal kill as compared to individual or small group hunting needs to be further investigated. The short time interval of killing represented at the Casper Site suggests that more meat was killed than could have been eaten at the time yet the remains of the animals at the site are in a condition that suggests good utilization of the animals with minimal waste. Some meat preservation is suggested but whether for immediate use to prevent spoilage or to save for periods when food was scarce is not known for certain. It may have been that the communal kill provided as much a means for the society to consolidate in larger than usual groups for social reasons as it provided economic benefits.

(4) *The communal kill was for the purpose of food storage to be used during unfavorable food procurement periods in the winter months.* This is closely connected with Hypothesis No. 3. Lee and DeVore (1968: 12) emphasize that "food surplusses are not a prominent feature" of hunting and gathering societies and the environment is the storehouse. The Eskimo, however, certainly is dependent on stored food and there must be a gradient of the tendency for food storage depending on the nature of the environment. The Eskimo environment is hostile enough for long periods of time to demand considerable food storage in order to survive. The High Plains environment, although not comparable in severity to that of the Eskimo, can be extremely hostile for short periods of time. This may have required some storage of surplus food.

The nature of this storage if it existed during the Paleo-Indian period is entirely conjectural. Whether or not they were making a form of pemmican is not known but if so, a hide container such as the historic parfleche or something similar would have sufficed. Since 50 pounds of dried meat would equal approximately an entire grown female bison, this amount could tide a family over a bad period of several days. Fifty pounds does not seem like an amount too large to transport from camp to camp for two or three months. Any sort of storage that required leaving it in or above the ground and unattended for long periods of time would seem to have been too precarious to take chances with considering the possible consequences.

(5) *The cultural group involved at the Casper Site and other Paleo-Indian communal bison kill sites was small, probably less than 100 persons,*

and they were fragmenting into smaller groups for most of the year. The size of Paleo-Indian bison kill operations, or at least that at the Casper Site, suggests that a group of 20 or slightly less grown males is about the optimum size. Ethnographic evidence for present day hunters and gatherers indicates they operate at about this level (Lee and DeVore 1968). For most of the year the societies fragment into smaller groups for various economic pursuits. There were many plant and animal resources that required careful scheduling of collecting activities in order to achieve the maximum economic benefits. Other than at the bison kills, no known sites suggest the groups maintained their maximum size during the entire year.

(6) *Although the communal bison kills appear large and impressive, small animal hunting and plant gathering was as important as large animal hunting to the total economy of the Paleo-Indian.* In the known hunting and gathering societies, the greatest share of food come from gathering efforts by the females. The amount of year-round dependence on bison or other large fauna by the Paleo-Indian is conjectural at this time. If a campsite is one associated with a bison kill, the evidence will suggest a strong dependence on the bison. Better means of determining seasonality of economic events must be explored and better means of determining economic use of food resources other than large mammals needs to be developed. Perhaps the greatest problem in the making these kinds of determinations is the one of differential preservation of archeological materials in sites. Bison bones are quite obvious and preserve relatively well but the remains of smaller animals are less well preserved while the remains of plants are extremely difficult to recover.

Although the hunting and gathering of small animals and plants is important to known cultural groups today, we have been warned and are we₁ aware of the dangers of ethnographic analogy in reconstructions of past cultural systems. At this point, however, we are largely dependent upon analogy of this sort for forming hypotheses to be tested.

(7) *The Paleo-Indian and later groups as well were able to devise means of communal procurement in any area where sufficient numbers of the animals were present regardless of the topography.* The limitations of the topography on communal procurement needs to be investigated. The use of corrals, traps and jumps suggests communal hunting was limited to areas favorable for these kinds of features. This may possibly be due to a lack of preservation of bone and the difficulty of locating artifact material resulting from a surround on the open, grassy prairie. Apparently the appropriate natural feature was utilized where present but this is not sufficient evidence to satisfactorily prove that other methods were not feasible also. We have been conditioned into believing that a large quantity of butchered bison bone has to be interpreted within a rather narrow range of procurement practices but all of the procurement possibilities have not yet been properly tested.

(8) *There was a critical number of bison within a given area below which communal procurement practices would not have been worthwhile in terms of diminishing returns.* Communal bison procurement was based on a large number of animals within an area so that if one effort failed it was possible to go back out, gather up another herd and try again. A herd of bison that was unsuccessfully driven might not stop running for several miles and it would have been useless to try and bring them back. When the density of bison dropped below a critical value in an area, hunting was limited to single and small group efforts.

(9) *Some means of distribution of exotic materials for stone flaking purposes existed during the Paleo-Indian period on the Plains.* A last consideration that needs to be understood

in terms of the Casper Site and the Paleo-Indian
in general is the nature of the distribution of
exotic stone flaking materials. There is a strong
probability that a number of chipped stone items
from the Casper Site are Knife River Flint and
their ultimate source is the quarry locality in
North Dakota. The nature of the distribution
of this and other exotic materials would undoubtedly aid in understanding Paleo-Indian
cultural systems in general.

All of these hypotheses are testable and some
of the testing can be done with evidence already
extant. A good starting point is to reevaluate
the known data from Paleo-Indian kill and
butchering sites such as Agate Basin, Horner and
Finley. In addition, the same sites still contain
worthwhile data yet to be gathered and more of
this is lost every year due to natural and human
destruction. A systematic reinvestigation of
these sites to gather data relative to testing some
of the above hypotheses is possible and should
have high priority in terms of Paleo-Indian
studies.

Chapter

2

POPULATION STUDY of the CASPER SITE BISON

CHARLES A. REHER
University of New Mexico

INTRODUCTION

On the prehistoric Plains the distribution and density of bison populations was one of the chief determinants of the distribution and density of human populations. The aggregation and dispersion of aboriginal social units was often a direct response to a seasonal variation in the size and composition of the bison herds. Processes in such subsistence strategies have been outlined both in an archeological sense (Frison 1967a: 28-37, 1970: 38-42) and in an ethnographic sense (Oliver 1962).

Evidence from almost every site on the Plains demonstrates that buffalo constituted the single most important food resource. The stored meat products obtained from large, seasonal kills, espedially during the fall of the year, were a critical resource in every sense of the word. During a bad winter or a series of bad winters,

stored meat could represent the difference between starvation and survival. As such, the buffalo killed at seasonal kills were a main "limiting" factor (Odum 1971: 106) for the levels of human population that were attained on the Plains.

It is assumed that changes in bison populations of sufficient magnitude would direct concomitant responses in the behavior of human populations. Reductions of buffalo on local or regional levels would cause shifts in subsistence strategies, such as utilization of alternate resources, or efficiency increases in exploiting remaining buffalo populations. More drastic or widespread reductions could result in direct reduction of human populations, from either migration or mortality. Similarly, increases and shifts in human population could be a function of increases in buffalo population. Gunnerson (1972) relates such shifts on the protohistoric Plains to possible buffalo increases. Further sesearch is needed to specify what degree of cultural change can be related to what degree of buffalo fluctuations.

Widespread population shifts are accompanied in the archeological record by technological and stylistic changes. It becomes clear than any movement towards explication of Plains prehistory demands that we first understand and secondly measure the parameters involved in the ecosystematic interrelationships of man and bison. As Frison has noted: "Understanding past cultural systems on the Northwestern Plains requires detailed knowledge of all phases of bison procurement" (1973: 3).

An attempt is made in this paper to examine the nature of some of these parameters which governed the interplay of human and bison populations. In the strictest sense it may be true that "At this time the numerical fluctuations of prehistoric *Bison* sp. herds and consequent effects on human populations cannot be known" (Frison 1973: 5). It is argued here that we can hypothesize these "consequent effects" and test their validity as data on *Bison* populations are recovered.

Accordingly, we must operationalize to monitor the expression of these ecosystematic parameters in the archeological record. This paper also presents techniques which have been utilized to study the size, composition and dynamics of bison populations from archeological contexts. It is the seasonal trap or jump which provides the necessary large samples and restricted context. The methodology outlined below was gained through study of *Bison bison* populations from two Late Prehistoric Period kill sites (Reher 1970, Frison and Reher 1970, Reher 1973), but was found to apply equally well to the *Bison antiquus* at the Casper Site.

THE CASPER SITE BISON POPULATION

The data for this section were obtained from 121 complete or partial mandibles and loose teeth from 19 other mandibles. These 140 mandibles represent a minimum of 74 animals, most of which were cows, juveniles and calves. This sample comes from approximately 75% of the total site area, so about 100 animals may have been killed at the site.

Determination of Individual Age

The determination of individual age is a critical process in study of bison populations. Schemes which include several years of age in one category (e.g. Skinner and Kaisen 1947) are less than satisfactory at this point, if the sample permits more accurate aging.

Almost all communal kill sites excavated are found to have been operated during the fall of the year. Since bison also have a seasonally restricted calving season, the animals in kill site samples break down into discrete age groups. That is, there will will be calves about .5 year old, born the spring of the same year, animals about 1.5 years old, born the spring of the previous year, 2.5 years old, and so on. The Casper Site population does in fact break into such discrete age groups.

Using tooth eruption schedules derived at the Glenrock Buffalo Jump (Frison and Reher 1970) most of the Casper Site calves are about .6 year or seven months old. This places the Casper Site operations around November. Three fetal mandibles were also recovered which, in the light of the above evidence, must be abnormal pregnacies.

The key to aging the younger animals is the state of eruption of the molar teeth (Fig. 2.1). At six months, the first molar is usually erupted to about the level of the other teeth, but wear is restricted to its first cusp. At the Casper Site there is usually slight wear on the second cusp, indicating an animal about 1 to 2 months older (Fig. 2.1i). Most calves cluster around this pattern but six of the 34 calf first molars seem to cluster at an earlier age, with slight wear on the first cusp

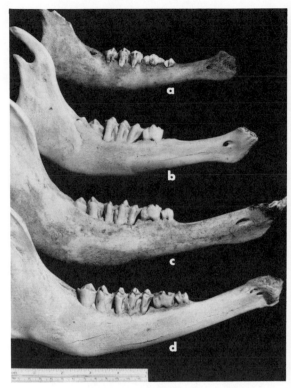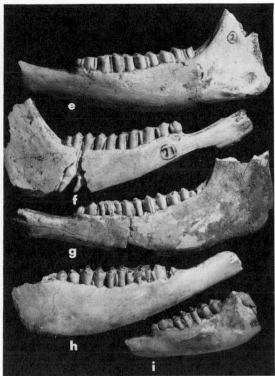

FIGURE 2.1 *Mandibles of newborn (a), two month old (b), four month old (c), and six month old (d) bison from modern local herds. Mandibles of .6 year old (i), 2.6 years old (h), 3.6 years old (g), 4.6 years old (f), and fully mature (e) bison from the Casper Site.*

and none on the second. This may be only a function of birth spacing in this area, but it also is suggestive of a use of the Casper Site trap earlier in the fall.

The age groupings of the Casper Site mandibles can be described as follows:

Group 1 (.6 year) DP 2, 3, and 4 in place and in wear on all cusps; M 1 erupted to level of other teeth, usually moderate wear on first cusp, slight wear on anterior side of second cusp; M 1 of some specimens has only slight wear on first cusp; tip of first cusp of M 2 can be seen in jaw behind M 1, occasionally this protrudes 1-2 mm. above jaw (Fig. 2.1i).

Group 2 (1.6 years) No specimens of this age were recovered at the Casper Site. We can infer

that animals of this age would have had the second molar erupted to the level of the other teeth with slight wear on the second cusp.

Group 3 (2.6 years) DP 2 and 3 still in place or P 2 and 3 erupted to varying extents. It should be stressed that the premolars in bison can vary almost two years in their eruption and are not useful indicators of age. DP 4 is usually still in place and well worn; M 1 and M 2 are in regular wear, cusps on both still quite pointed; first two cusps only of M 3 are erupted above jaw line, but not to level of other teeth and show no wear (Fig. 2.1h).

Group 4 (3.6 years) P 2 and 3 usually erupted to level of other teeth and showing slight wear; DP 4 still in place but being pushed out by P 4

and the roots are exposed, fossettes in DP 4
usually obliterated; M 1 and M 2 in regular wear;
all cusps of M 3 above jaw line but tooth is not
yet completely erupted, first cusp of M 3 moderately worn, second cusp unworn or with slight
wear, third cusp is never worn (Fig. 2.1g).

Group 5 (4.6 years) P 2, 3, and 4 fully erupted
and in moderate to regular wear; M 1 and M2 in
regular wear; first two cusps of M 3 in regular
wear, third cusp worn on anterior side; earlier-in-
the-fall wear on the third cusp is surrounded by
continuous enamel, but at the Casper site a thin
band of wear may continue across to join wear
pattern on second cusp (Fig. 2.1f).

Group 6 (5.6 to 11.6 years) This age group contains all animals with a fully-erupted, mature
mouth (e.g. Fig. 2.1e) which must be aged by
other techniques (see below).

The first five age groups are discrete, with no
intermediate forms. The same discrete age groups
exist in Group 6, but are not so easily separated.
Visual comparison of wear, even to known-age
specimens, is known to be unreliable (Keiss 1969,
Zawasky 1971). Analysis of annual cementum
bands is accurate (Scheffer 1950, Laws 1952,
Low and McT. Cowan 1963) but in dealing with
samples of this size, labor and equipment ex-
penditures are prohibitive.

Kurtén (1953, 1964) has used fossil populations to demonstrate that discrete age
groupings in a large, seasonally-restricted sample
can be monitored by measurements of tooth
wear. In such samples each discrete age group
will tend to cluster, giving a multimodal series of
approximate normal curves (Fig. 2.2a). The M 1
metaconid has been found to be the most accessible to measurements with the least damage to
the mandibles. Previous analysis by the writer
has shown measurements of M 2 and M 3 to
essentially duplicate the information gained from
M 1. The M 1 measurements for the Casper Site
specimens are given (Fig. 2.2d). Data from the
Glenrock Buffalo Jump and the Wardell Bison
Trap are included throughout this section to aid

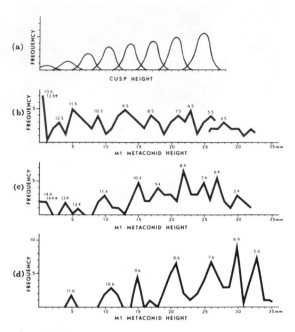

FIGURE 2.2 *Measurements of metaconid heights for*
determining age in seasonally restricted
samples. Hypothetical example (a), The
Glenrock Buffalo Jump (b), The Wardell
Buffalo Trap (c), and the Casper Site (c).

in comparative discussion. Ten M 1 metaconids
from the Casper Site sample were damaged to
varying extents during the butchering process and
were included in their approximate age groups via
less reliable estimations of wear. The final age
group tabulation for the Casper Site population
is given in Table 2.1.

Determination of Sex

Bison mandibles can be sexed by using
measurements from the bottom of the tooth row
to the ventral border of the mandibles. The more
rugged musculature and larger size of the male
buffalo are best reflected in this area of the mandible. The width of the mandible below the
center of M 3 (between first and second cusps)

TABLE 2.1 *Age groups and tooth wear measurements at the Casper Site.*

Age group	Age in years	Number of measureable specimens	Average enamel height	Number of animals in each group
1	.6	-	-	18
2	1.6	-	-	0
3	2.6	-	-	5
4	3.6	-	-	4
5	4.6	-	-	4
6	5.6	14	32.2 mm	8
	6.6	11	29.8 mm	7
	7.6	21	26.1 mm	11
	8.6	15	20.5 mm	9
	9.6	5	15.4 mm	3
	10.6	6	11.2 mm	4
	11.6	2	5.0 mm	1

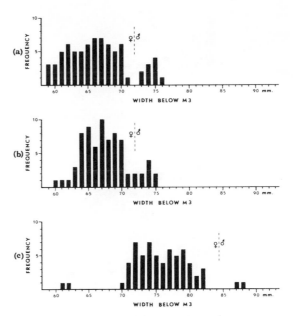

FIGURE 2.3 *Mandible widths below M3 for the Glenrock sample (a), the Wardell sample (b), and the Casper Site sample (c).*

on the interior side is the index used in these studies of bison populations. The frequency distributions for the Glenrock, Wardell, and Casper sites are given in Fig. 2.3.

After the rutting season in the fall, most bulls tend to congregate off by themselves (see McHugh 1958: 14) and this lack of large, mature males is seen in the kill site samples. As can be seen in Fig. 2.3, only two mandibles or 3% of the measureable specimens are definitely male. Two other mandibles which fall in the extreme upper range of the female mode appear to have the blocky, rugged shape of the mature bull. Analysis of skulls reveal a maximum of three bulls at the Casper Site (see Chapter 3).

Population Structure

Attritional mortality, the normal dying-off of the members of a population, will be reflected in a death assemblage by a preponderance of young and old individuals (Deevey 1947: 289) (see Fig. 2.4a). An example is a sample of 1,322 *Bison* sp. mandibles aged by Skinner and Kaisen (1947: 138) (Fig. 2.4b).

Catastrophic mortality will tend to freeze the

population as it existed at some moment in time and will contain more viable adult members (Fig. 2.4c). Populations from kill sites such as the Casper Site should reflect the catastrophic mortality of a "cow-calf" herd during the fall or early winter. If the missing bulls were added, the age-group distribution should resemble that for generalized catastrophic mortality. In fact they do not, for juvenile animals and especially calves are almost universally underrepresented in kill sites. Examples are Glenrock (Fig. 2.5a), Wardell (Fig. 2.5b), Casper (Fig. 2.5c), the Roberts Buffalo Kill (Witkind n. d., Zawasky 1971), Olsen-Chubbuck (Wheat 1972: 115), the Itasca Site (Shay 1971: 1), Bonfire Shelter (Dibble and Lorrain 1968: 90), and there are a number of others. Possible causes for this widespread divergence from the expected are discussed below.

Data from McHugh (1958: 31-32) indicate a

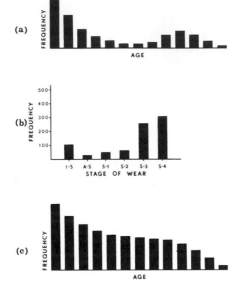

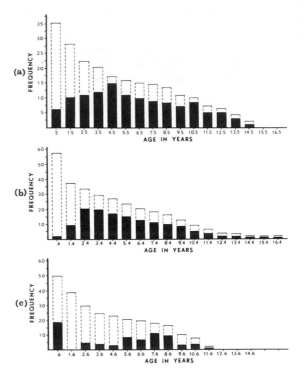

FIGURE 2.4 *Generalized age group distribution for attritional mortality (a). Age group distribution for Alaskan fossil bison (from Skinner and Kaisen 1947) (b), and generalized age group distribution for catastrophic mortality (c).*

FIGURE 2.5 *Age group structure recorded for Glenrock (a), Wardell (b), and Casper (c) (solid lines). Additions needed to approximate normal populations (dashed lines).*

possible pregnancy rate of 85-95% and a calf survival rate into the fall of 65-75%. From this the Casper Site population should have included about 32 calves instead of the eighteen recovered. The one and a half year-old age group at Casper was missing completely (Fig. 2.5c) but at least 25 were expected. Including estimations of missing juveniles and calves, the Casper Site population of 74 animals could represent up to 120 animals. Since these came from an estimated 75% of the total site area, as many as 160 animals may have been killed at the site. The additions necessary to approximate the catastrophic mortality of a normal population are represented by the dashed lines in Fig. 2.5. The data from both the Glenrock Buffalo Jump (Fig. 2.5a) and the Wardell Buffalo Trap (Fig. 2.5b) are Late Prehistoric Period in age.

Population Dynamics

Life tables, survivorship curves and other such media are a convenient way of summarizing the dynamics of natality and mortality in a natural population. With the adjustments noted above, these can be derived for the bison populations at kill sites. No claim is made that the results obtained faithfully duplicate reality, only that they are a functional approximation. Certain modes of population analysis such as the "composite" and "time specific" are designed for data such as occur in kill sites. These are actually based on hypothetical populations since this type of census data probably deviates from exact age structures through time. However, the results obtained should still be useful "in about the same way as a mean for a variate" (Kurtén 1953: 48).

Calculations for the life table are simplified by basing them on an initial sample of 1,000. Age is denoted by the symbol x, expressed in units suited to the life span of the species. The symbol dx represents the number of deaths during an interval; qx is the mortality rate, usually expressed per 1,000 (1000 qx); and ex is the life expectancy for an animal of a given age. The symbol lx represents the number of survivors at the beginning of an interval. The life tables for the three bison populations under discussion here are given (Tables 7-9).

The lx values are calculated by the ratio of assigning a value of 1,000 to Group 1, an estimated 32 animals in the Casper Site case. Subtracting the Group 2 lx from that of Group 1 (1,000) gives the dx value for Group 2 and so on. The mortality rate is obtained by the formula:

$$1{,}000 \ qx = \frac{dx}{lx} \cdot 1{,}000$$

The life expectancy is obtained by dividing the number of "person years" left to the survivors by the number of survivors. An Lx value is obtained for each group by the formula:

$$Lx = (lx_n + lx_{n+1} + 1) \div 2$$

The Lx of a particular group is summed with all older groups, and dividing the resultant sum by lx gives the life expectancy.

The survivorship curve also describes the mortality rate in a population. It is obtained by plotting age (x) on an arithmetic scale against survivors (lx) on a logarithmic scale. The survivorship curves are illustrated in Fig. 2.6.

DISCUSSION AND SUMMARY

The bison populations recovered from kill sites

TABLE 2.2 *Life table for animals (Bison bison) from the Glenrock Buffalo Jump.*

Group	x	lx	dx	1,000qx	ex
1	.5	1000	214	214	5.87
2	1.5	786	143	182	6.33
3	2.5	643	100	156	6.47
4	3.5	543	72	133	6.75
5	4.5	471	28	59	6.70
6	5.5	443	14	32	6.09
	6.5	429	15	35	5.27
	7.5	414	28	68	4.45
	8.5	386	29	75	3.73
	9.5	357	28	78	2.99
7	10.5	329	86	261	2.20
	11.5	243	57	235	1.80
	12.5	186	86	462	1.20
	13.5	100	71	710	.80
	13.5+	29	29	1000	.51

TABLE 2.3 *Life table for animals (Bison bison) from the Wardell Buffalo Trap.*

Group	x	lx	dx	1,000qx	ex
1	.4	1000	351	351	4.71
2	1.4	649	70	108	5.98
3	2.4	579	70	121	5.67
4	3.4	509	35	69	5.35
5	4.4	474	70	148	4.92
6	5.4	404	53	131	4.43
	6.4	351	35	99	4.02
	7.4	316	35	111	3.41
	8.4	281	70	249	2.06
	9.4	211	71	337	2.52
	10.4	140	35	250	2.54
	11.4	105	52	495	2.22
	12.4	53	0	0	2.89
	13.4	53	20	377	1.87
	14.4	33	15	455	1.67
	15.4?	18	0	0	1.61
	16.4?	18	18	1000	.56

are amenable to analytic techniques first used in paleontological contexts (e. g. Kurtén 1953, Voorhies 1969). Bison mandibles can be aged and sexed with essentially two measurements and the schedule for molar eruption. From this are

TABLE 2.4 *Life table for animals (Bison antiquus) from the Casper Site.*

Group	x	lx	dx	1,000qx	ex
1	.6	1000	240	240	4.80
2	1.6	760	160	211	5.16
3	2.6	600	100	167	5.40
4	3.6	500	40	80	5.38
5	4.6	460	50	109	4.80
6	5.6	410	10	24	4.32
	6.6	400	20	50	3.42
	7.6	380	40	105	2.57
	8.6	340	100	294	1.81
	9.6	240	80	333	1.35
	10.6	160	120	750	.76
	11.6	40	40	1000	.53

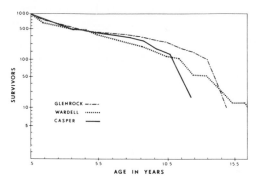

FIGURE 2.6 *Survivorship curves for Glenrock, Wardell, and Casper bison populations.*

determined seasonality and the size and composition of the herds preyed upon, bits of information which are essential to archeological interpretation of the sites. Population dynamics can be a more reliable indicator of numbers of animals utilized than various types of "bone counts". Other aspects of the analysis, such as the reconstruction of survivorship curves are more dependent on estimation and approximation.

Comparable data from other extinct *Bison* kill sites should indicate whether or not the Casper Site population is representative. Assuming that it is, comparison with *Bison bison* kill sites suggests a number of lines of inquiry. Examination of Fig. 2.3 demonstrates that in terms of mandible widths the Casper Site *Bison antiquus* specimens are much larger than specimens of *Bison bison* , which is to be expected. The largest *Bison bison* bulls fall well into the lower end of the Casper Site cows. The Casper Site population demonstrates a greater range of variation, however, for two cows from that site are about as small as the smallest *Bison bison* cows. This larger size is also indicated by measurements of tooth size (Fig. 2.7). Several other populations are included in the figure for comparative purposes.

Several lines of evidence suggest to the writer that the Casper Site *Bison antiquus* population

was under greater stress and selective pressure than the *Bison bison* populations. Greater rates of tooth wear are evident in the Casper Site population which is certainly contra-survival in a grazing animal. At Wardell and Glenrock mature animals averaged 3.3 and 3.2 mm. of molar tooth wear per year, respectively. The Casper Site specimens averaged 4.2 mm. of molar tooth wear per year and ranged as high as 5.6 mm.

A shorter life span is indicated for the Casper Site *Bison antiquus* specimens, probably a result of this wear. The oldest animal at Casper was about 12 years old. The Glenrock and Wardell *Bison bison* specimens were living to at least 14.5 and 16.4 years of age. At these sites the teeth of several animals were worn until only small, unconnected stubs of roots were left in some sockets, and these were probably even older. No animals in the Casper Site sample were surviving in such advanced stages of tooth wear.

The reconstructed Casper Site survivorship curve indicates higher mortality rates than Glenrock, but not as high as Wardell. The latter site was located in an area that was marginal in terms of buffalo carrying capacity (Frison 1973: 1). "Smoothed" curves were obtained for Glenrock and Wardell by adding estimated missing juvenile animals (see Fig. 2.5), and a constant percentage of missing mature bulls. The

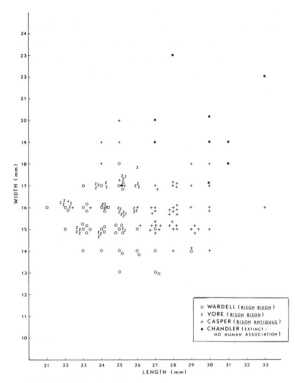

FIGURE 2.7 *M 1 length-width measurements for four bison populations.*

The extremely small cows in the Casper Site population (Fig. 2.3c) and the wide scatter evident in Fig. 2.7 demonstrate increased variability in certain morphological attributes of the Casper Site population. It cannot be said at this time if this is significant in terms of evolutionary stress, but a distinct difference can be seen between the Casper Site scatter and a comparable *Bison bison* population from one level at the Vore Buffalo Jump (Fig. 2.7) (Reher, unpublished data).

The Casper Site population lacks large numbers of expected juvenile animals, a pattern which occurs in most kill sites (Reher 1970:53, 1973: 102). Its widespread occurrence in space and time argues for its significance in interpreting the activity at these sites.

The Casper Site contained more calves than any site yet analyzed by the writer, although this number was only eighteen. The number of cows of breeding age recovered leads one to expect about 32 calves, so close to 50% of the calves may have been removed from the site. In a "smoothed" population, with all age groups containing expected numbers, the calves should number on the order of 50. At the Wardell Buffalo Trap, 57 calves were expected but only two were recovered. Even more striking at the Casper Site was the complete lack of any animals in Group 2 (1.6 years).

Too few young animals or occasional underrepresented age groups in one population could be explained by adverse environmental conditions. Poor preservation of the smaller, more delicate elements has accounted for similar shortages in fossil populations (Kurten 1953: 74, 87). Preservation could be a factor in a few of these sites; in most it is not. Groups 2, 3, and 4 are also often underrepresented.

The behavioral context of a communal kill suggests several possibilities where human activity could have removed the younger animals from the kill sites. Data on bison weights indicate that

descending frequencies of the mature cow age groups were relatively smooth and were what allowed these estimates. At Casper, however, not all mature cow age groups contain the expected descending frequencies. While again suggestive, it cannot be conclusively said whether this uneven age pyramid was a function of environmental stress, sample size, or human activity

Perhaps more convincing are the pathological growths, deformed teeth, and other such problems evident in the Casper Site mandibles (see Chapter 3). These are not quantified for the *Bison bison* populations, but it is the writer's impression after working with several thousand buffalo mandibles that these kinds of malformations occur with much greater frequency in the Casper Site population.

these animals could have been reduced to more easily portable packets with a minimum of field dressing and quartering (Halloran 1960: 212, Novakowski 1965: 176). In some kill situations removal of these animals would have facilitated efficient butchering of the mature animals which produced the largest meat packets.

The main purpose of the fall communal kill was to obtain large packets of meat which could have been processed for winter storage. It also seems reasonable that processing hides for winter clothing would have been important, and that hides from younger animals would have been the most suitable. Wilson (1934: 234) notes that the Hidatsa preferred the skin of a two year-old bull for robes, and also that they wore small calf skins. However, differential treatment of hides does not explain why they could not have been skinned on the site margins and the meat then returned to the regular butchering system. Differential treatment of the meant and bones of young animals was also required. Usage for immediate consumption while the other animals were processed is one possibility. Separate processing areas were not found at some kill sites (e. g. Glenrock). At other sites such as for example, Wardell and Piney Creek (Frison 1967a), processing areas were found but no high frequencies of juveniles were noted.

However, the Hudson-Meng Site (Agenbroad 1973) might represent some sort of processing site, and higher frequencies of juveniles have been noted there (Russel 1973). In fact, when the age group distribution from Hudson-Meng was added to the Casper Site frequency graph it tended to fill in most of the missing segments needed to approximate a normal population.

Population Parameters in Communal Bison Procurement Systems

The above discussion was to outline research developments in monitoring prehistoric bison populations. The following section discusses some of the interrelationships that existed between bison and human population in the Plains ecosystem. If we can test and validate a model of these interrelationships, we should be able to use such data to predict and explain the course of human behavior and of cultural change.

Bison as a critical resource

During frequent periods of the Plains winter, snow and intense cold restrict any subsistence-oriented mobility. In many areas the past winter (1972-1973) serves as an apt example. It is during such periods that the stored meat obtained from the communal bison kills would have become a critical resource in the strictest ecological sense of the word.

Given this climatic condition and the large meat stores, it is likely that bands occupied semi-sedentary base camps in the vicinity of the kill. In such a situation, local game resources can be rapidly depleted. Whether there were in fact such base camps or not, a bad winter or a series of bad winters was enough to deplete game populations on a regional scale. Under such stress the stored meat products became acutely critical, and could have meant the difference between starvation and survival.

During certain periods then, the buffalo exploited in communal kill situations represented the chief limiting factor for the levels of human population attained on the Plains. During such periods, success in a kill operation was mandatory. The aggregated band operating a buffalo jump represented the largest economically cooperative group during the year (Frison 1967a), and population segments of this order were directly relevant to the ecosystematic processes under discussion.

Bison density and distribution

We have no direct measures of bison density under conditions completely suited to archeological comparison, However, data from National Parks and the like should give rough indications of carrying capacities in different types of habitats. Some of these herds are maintained just below the level where they begin to cause environmental "damage"; other densities presumably are somewhat above the prehistoric norm. For instance, the Crow Indian Reservation herd in Montana had to subsist extensively on aspen bark during some winters, and extra water holes had to be established to support the Wind Cave herd in South Dakota (McHugh 1958: 5). A series of densities for *Bison bison* are given in Table 2.5. These range from 648/100 square miles to 3667/100 square miles, but the majority cluster around 1200/100 square miles. Simple densities will not give a complete picture of the availability of animals for communal kills under different conditions. To deal with the "critical numbers" of buffalo necessary to operate a kill (Frison 1973: 6) one must also consider the way in which the animals are distributed across the landscape.

To begin with this varies seasonally, with nursery herds and bachelor herds separated much of the year. Large rutting herds congregate during the late summer and early fall. As noted in the introduction, any subsistence strategy based on buffalo had to be adjusted to these behavioral characteristics. The actual on-the-ground distribution will, of course, also be determined locally by available feed, water, and topography.

The combination of these and other factors served to make the appearance and disappearance of the buffalo highly erratic, Reading Roe (1951: 199) and accounts of Indian hunters such as that of Two Leggings (Nabokov 1967) one realizes that sometimes bison were plentiful and sometimes none could be found for days. Higher densities mean higher probability of occurrence, but several alternative sites had to be scouted before a kill could be undertaken. The distribution and density of bison were much more crucial considerations under the smaller effective search

TABLE 2.5 *Population densities for existing bison herds (from McHugh 1958)*

Herd and location	Density per 100 sq. mi.
Wind Cave National Park, South Dakota	1141.6
Hayden Valley, Yellowstone National Park (summer range)	3666.7
Hayden Valley Yellowstone National Park (winter range)	1222.2
Wichita Mountain Wildlife Refuge, Oklahoma	648.1
Crow Indian Reservation Montana	1318.1

patterns of pre-horse times. Again it can be seen that fluctuations in bison populations had an immediate effect on human behavior.

Predator-prey interaction

In dealing with these ecosystematic variables it is also necessary to consider feedback effects from populations preying on the bison. The first tendency is to be overwhelmed by accounts of uncounted millions of buffalo, and to consider any human action as having little or no significance. This writer believes such a viewpoint is inaccurate. Millions there were, and on the entire Plains the numbers killed may seem negligible, but in considering the local availability of buffalo and subsistence needs of a human aggregation, we are not dealing with the Plains as a whole. Similarly, in terms of predation we are dealing initially with a series of seasonal kills in one specific area. Evidence from various kills indicates that the kill operators could bring in groups from several miles (e. g. The Glenrock Buffalo Jump, Frison 1970: 2), and the figures given above indicate there could easily have been several hundred buffalo in a gathering area. The point is that these human groups were reaching out and removing several hundred cows and calves from the breeding population, and they may have been doing it in adjacent areas during the same season.

The effects of this type of mortality on the population dynamics are immediate and drastic. Data on Shoshonean antelope kills in the Great Basin are not directly comparable, but after communal kills took place there, the antelope populations were unsuitable for another kill for as long as ten years (Steward 1968: 72). At this point the argument is simply that a series of kills may have temporarily reduced bison in an area to below the critical numbers necessary for successful communal hunts, and human population distributions would have had to be adjusted accordingly. Further research is needed to define the topographic scale of this area and the consistency of occupation by a bison population within it. Research is also needed to quantify parameters of population replacement for bison. In-migration may or may not occur; data from McHugh (1958: 2) demonstrate a high rate of population increase under ideal conditions (i.e. no predation and supplemental feeding), but communal predation hy humans had to have an effect of some duration.

Discussion and summary

A series of parameters in the interaction of human and bison populations must be considered if we are to understand Plains prehistory. Stored meat gained from communal kills was oftern necessary for subsistence through the Plains winter, and was one of the chief factors limiting human population levels attained. Frison (1967a, 1970) has demonstrated how characteristics of bison behavior controlled aspects of cooperative human behavior, and we are beginning to understand the characteristics of bison populations which caused other behavioral

adjustments.

Human predation may have at least temporarily made certain areas unsuitable for continued kill operations. Climatic fluctuation or simple "random" movements could also have reduced bison in certain areas below critical numbers.

Climatic deterioration on a large scale (e.g. the Altithermal), may have brought about partial or even nearly complete abandonment of these areas. On the opposite side of the coin, increasing effective moisture and vegetation would have resulted in rapid increases in buffalo populations, and a concomitant rise in human populations. The influx of human groups onto the Plains from all directions in protohistoric times is a probable example. Explaining Plains prehistory requires that we understand this process.

Chapter

3

The CASPER LOCAL FAUNA and its FOSSIL BISON

MICHAEL WILSON
University of Wyoming

Excavations at the Casper Site (48NA304) resulted in the recovery of a large sample of butchered bison skeleta associated with Hell Gap projectile points and other artifacts (see Frison, George C., this volume). Two radiocarbon samples from the bone bed yielded dates of 9,830 ± 350 years B.P. (7,880 B.C.; RL-125, charcoal) and 10,060 ± 170 years B.P. (8,110 B.C.; RL-208, bone). Thus the site is in approximate contemporaneity with the post-fluted point levels at Blackwater No. 1, Clovis, New Mexico; the Midland level and several contiguous levels (including the Hell Gap level) at the Hell Gap Site, Wyoming; the Middle Agate Basin level at the Brewster Site, Wyoming; the bone bed at Plainview, Texas; and other Paleo-Indian bison kills.

Although predominant, the bison bones were not the only faunal remains in the Casper Site bone bed: a sample including eleven animal species (plus the evidence of man) was recovered. All of the faunal remains came from the bone bed

itself, underlying pond and dune deposits noted at the site (see Albanese, John P., this volume). These remains have been designated the Casper Local Fauna.

The fauna includes the following species:

Mollusca

1. *Succinea* sp., cf. *S. stretchiana* or *S. grosvenori*

Aves

2. Woodpecker, cf. *Sphyrapicus* sp. or *Dendrocopos* sp.

Mammalia

3. *Homo sapiens* (indirect evidence)
4. *Lepus townsendii*
5. *Spermophilus* sp., cf. *S. richardsonii*

6. *Spermophilus* sp., cf. *S. tridecemlineatus*
7. *Thomomys* sp., cf. *T. talpoides*
8. *Canis latrans*
9. *Vulpes* sp., cf. *V. vulpes*
10. *Lynx* sp., cf. *L. rufus*
11. *Antilocapra americana*
12. *Bison bison antiquus*

SYSTEMATIC DESCRIPTIONS

PHYLUM MOLLUSCA
　Class GASTROPODA
　　Subclass Pulmonata
　　　Order Stylommatophora
　　　　Family Succineidae

Succinea sp., cf. *S. stretchiana* Bland or *S. grosvenori* Lea

Referred Specimens. NC 2516, 6 specimens (L)[1]; NC 2517, 1 specimen; NC 2518, 2 specimens.

Discussion. Dr. Aurèle La Rocque, Dept. of Geology, Ohio State University noted the resemblance of these snails to *S. stretchiana,* but pointed out that identification of these forms is based

[1]Specimens marked with "(L)" have been identified by Dr. Aurèle La Rocque, Dept. Geology, Ohio State University, Columbus.

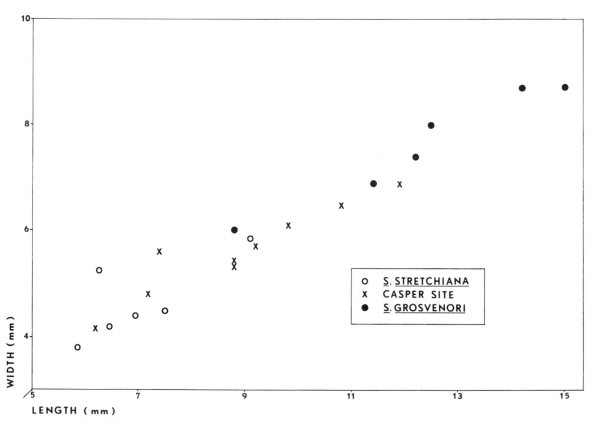

FIGURE 3.1 *Length/width scattergram for three samples of succineid snails. The Casper Site sample is seen to occupy a position more or less intermediate between* Succinea stretchiana *and* S. grosvenori.

upon soft parts; hence the necessity to indicate only similarity to the above species.

Pilsbry (1948: 826) noted that *S. stretchiana* specimens are "nearly uniform in the length of about 6 mm." The specimens from the Casper Local Fauna are much more variable than this, with lengths ranging from 6.2 mm. (3 whorls) to 11.9 mm. (3.5 whorls). The Casper adult specimens possess 3.5 whorls, more than typical *S. stretchiana*. In this sense they resemble *S. grosvenori* Lea; however, most *S. grosvenori* tend to be larger than the Casper specimens.

A biaxial length/width plot (Fig. 3.1) for the three samples shows that *grosvenori* is a larger species than the Casper population but with a very similar trend; while *stretchiana* overlaps the low end of the Casper sample, again with a similar trend. It could well be that the Casper species has relationships with both *stretchiana* and *grosvenori*.

Distribution and Habitat. La Rocque (personal communication to Dr. George C. Frison, 1972) notes that the succineids

> are land snails with a wide range of ecological preferences. Some of them can live in very dry situations so long as they can find cover in the soil or under brush, logs, or stones. Others are semi-aquatic and live near streams and lakes, feeding on beach drift and scavenging on wet sand or mud.

The snails from Casper apparently belong to the *S. ovalis* group which, according to La Rocque (*ibid.*) "prefers rather dry situations". Pilsbry (1948: 826) lists records of modern *S. stretchiana* from western Wyoming and notes that "this is a rather widely spread snail of the Sierra Nevada, but also occurring elsewhere." The species has been collected in Utah in "low marshy land"; however, in distribution and habitat it remains poorly known. Beetle (1961) found the species at 9,500 feet in the Big Horn Mountains in willow on granite.

S. grosvenori is a xeric species found on loess

banks and in alkaline wet spots on the plains (Pilsbry 1948: 822). The only record from Wyoming appears to be that of Beetle (1961: 99) from a locality atop the Big Horn Mountains.

PHYLUM CHORDATA
  Class AVES
    Order Piciformes
      Family Picidae

      Woodpecker, cf. *Sphyrapicus* sp. or *Dendrocopos* sp.

Referred Specimens. NC 2559, left humerus lacking proximal end; broken below level of pneumatic foramen.

Discussion. The specimen closely resembles the sapsuckers (*Sphyrapicus* spp.) and the *Dendrocopos* woodpeckers (Dr. J.R. Jehl, Jr., personal communication, 1973; Dr. H. Howard, personal communication, 1974). Dr. Howard feels that with respect to the development of the ectepicondylar process, the specimen resembles *Dendrocopos* rather than *Sphyrapicus*. However, additional comparison with species of both genera is required.

Distribution and Habitat. Small woodpeckers belonging to the two genera are widespread through the state of Wyoming. *Sphyrapicus varius* is found during the summer among the trees along streams, and in mountain forests; its preferred altitudinal range is from about 7,000 to 9,000 feet. *S. thyroideus* is more scarce in the state, occupying montane aspen groves (McCreary 1937: 60-61). *Dendrocopos villosus* and *D. pubescens* are widespread and abundant: the former in mountain forests, woodlands, and river groves; and the latter in broken or mixed forest, river groves, and orchards (Peterson 1961: 186). Since this was a late summer or fall kill, it is quite possible that migrating woodpeckers of both genera would have been present in the wooded valley of the North Platte River at 5,000 feet.

Class MAMMALIA
Order Primates
Family Hominidae

Homo sapiens L.

Referred Specimens. A large sample of artifacts made by man; no direct skeletal evidence.

Discussion. The artifacts and other evidence for patterned human behavior are considered elsewhere (Frison, George C., this volume).

Distribution and Habitat. A widely ranging omnivore, man by this time seems to have achieved a successful adaptation to a big-game-hunting subsistence pattern, probably with considerable collection of other resources as well. Even at this early period man was distributed across most of North America and southward into South America.

Order Lagomorpha
Family Leporidae

Lepus townsendii Bachman

Referred Specimens. NC 2528, left upper incisor; NC 2519, distal end right tibia; NC 2520, distal end right tibia; NC 2521, left acetabulum; NC 2522, proximal end right femur; NC 2523, left innominate; NC 2524, acromion process left ulna; NC 2525, right calcaneum; NC 2526, left calcaneum; NC 2527, right calcaneum; NC 2529, proximal phalanx.

Discussion. The material clearly belongs to a hare, *Lepus* sp. The large size of several of the elements, and the present distribution of species of *Lepus* strongly suggest *L. townsendii.* The incisor

shows the character of *L. townsendii* given by Hall and Kelson (1959: 281):

> *L. townsendii* has a simple groove on the anterior face of the tooth and *L. californicus,* east of the Rocky Mountains, has a bifurcation, or even trifurcation, of the infold that can readily be seen by examining the occlusal surface of the incisor.

The two innominates differ somewhat in size: inside acetabulum diameters (dorsoventral) are 10.0 and 8.3 mm. This differential is assigned to individual variation in the absence of other evidence for another species at the site. On the basis of minimum numbers of elements, at least two individuals are present.

Distribution and Habitat. *Lepus townsendii* is today found throughout the state of Wyoming as well as in large areas north, east, south, and west of the state (Hall and Kelson, *ibid.*: 281). Cary (1917: 34) lists the species as characteristic of the Transition Zone in Wyoming, a life zone characterized by widespread rather mesic sagebrush stands with abundant understory grasses.

Holocene Record. *Lepus* sp., cf. *L. townsendii* has been recorded from early Holocene deposits at Little Box Elder Cave, Converse Co., Wyoming (Anderson 1968: 11); Horned Owl Cave, Albany Co., Wyoming (Guilday, Hamilton, and Adam, 1967: 98); and Jaguar Cave, Lemhi Co., Idaho (Kurtén and Anderson 1972: 21), dated to 10,370 ± 350 and 11,580 ± 250 years B.P.

Order Rodentia
Family Sciuridae

Spermophilus sp., cf. *S. richardsonii* (Sabine)

Referred Specimens. NC 2530, anterior half of cranium with left and right P^4 - M^3 of a young animal (A)[2] (Fig. 3.2a); NC 2531, right mandible with fragment of M$_3$; NC 2536, fragment of right frontal; NC 2537, atlas vertebra; NC 2532, distal half of left humerus; NC 2533, left humerus; NC 2534, left humerus; NC 2538, left femur; NC 2539, left upper incisor; NC 2540, right radius; NC 2541, left radius; NC 2542, fragment of radius.

Discussion. The characters of P^4 fit those of the subgenus *Spermophilus* as enumerated by Hall and Kelson (1959: 335). The skull is that of a young adult; therefore specific assignment is not definite. At least three individuals are present.

Distribution and Habitat. Spermophilus richardsonii is distributed in a horseshoe-shaped band from the Dakotas northwest to Saskatchewan and Alberta, and down the Rocky Mountain front to Colorado. The species occurs in all but the northeastern one-third of Wyoming, and has been collected in the vicinity of Casper (Poison Spider Creek; *ibid.*: 339). It occurs in both the Upper Sonoran and Transition zones in Wyoming.

[2]Specimens marked with "(A)" have been identified by Dr. Elaine Anderson, The Museum, Idaho State University, Pocatello.

Holocene Record. Spermophilus richardsonii has been reported from possibly early Holocene deposits at Bell Cave, Albany Co., Wyoming (Zeimens and Walker, *in press*); Chimney Rock Animal Trap, Larimer Co., Colorado (Hager 1972: 65); Jaguar Cave, Idaho (Kurtén and Anderson 1972:21); and Moonshiner Cave, Bingham Co., Idaho (Anderson, *in press*). In the first two, deposits from throughout the Holocene are represented; thus the age of individual finds is not completely clear. A date of 11,980 ± 180 radiocarbon years B.P. was obtained from the 4-foot level of Chimney Rock Animal Trap, and a second date of 3,890 ± 105 radiocarbon years B.P. was obtained from the 2-foot level. The age of the Jaguar Cave fauna has already been noted above. Moonshiner Cave contains forms of Late Pleistocene aspect as well as Holocene/modern species.

Spermophilus sp., cf. *S. tridecemlineatus*
(Mitchill)

Referred Specimens. NC 2543, left mandible with P$_4$ - M$_2$; NC 2544, right mandible with P$_4$ - M$_3$ (A) (Fig. 3.2b); NC 2545, left humerus.

Discussion. Small mandibles with hypsodont teeth and nonmolariform P$_4$ identify the subgenus *Ictidomys.* The similarity in size between *S. tridecemlineatus* and *S. spilosoma* is such as to prohibit identification of our material at the specific level. The former species occurs in the area of the site today.

Distribution and Habitat. S. tridecemlineatus is a solitary species preferring "well-drained prairies and areas of short, non-native grass" (Hall and Kelson, *ibid.*: 345). Cary (1917: 25) assigns it in Wyoming to the Upper Sonoran life zone, but its range seems to have more amplitude than this. In Alberta *S. tridecemlineatus pallidus* (the subspecies today found near the Casper Site) also occupies a "sub-humid Transition Zone, in a grass-brush environment" (Soper 1964: 141). *S. spilo-*

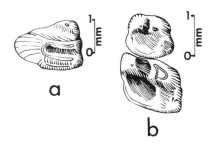

FIGURE 3.2 *Casper Local Fauna sciurids: a.* Spermophilus *sp., cf.* S. richardsonii, *left P^4 (NC 2530); b.* Spermophilus *sp., cf.* S. tridecemlineatus, *right P$_4$ and M$_1$ (NC 2544).*

soma is a species of rather similar habitat; today it is found in extreme southeastern Wyoming.

Holocene Record. *S. tridecemlineatus* has been recorded from Late Pleistocene or Holocene deposits at Little Box Elder Cave, Wyoming; and Bell Cave, Wyoming.

Family Geomyidae

Thomomys sp., cf. *T. talpoides* (Richardson)

Referred Specimens. NC 2550, partial skull with left and right M^1 - M^2 (A); NC 2551, left mandible (A); NC 2552, right mandible (A); NC 2553, left innominate.

Discussion. These specimens in all likelihood pertain to the referred species, *T. talpoides.* However, as critical cranial characters are missing only tentative referral is made. *T. talpoides* is the only species of *Thomomys* found in the state today.

Distribution and Habitat. *Thomomys talpoides* is a burrowing, nocturnal form distributed in a roughly rectangular area from Alberta south to New Mexico and the Dakotas west to Washington. In the montane region there are a great many subspecies endemic to particular valleys and basins, and as a result of this the species is quite variable in size, pelage, and cranial characteristics. Nevertheless, we can generalize and note that the species is most abundant in areas where soils are rich in food plants. Such areas as dense forests, shallow rocky soils, and winter-frozen soils are avoided (Hoffmann and Pattie 1968: 36). In that the plant cover in the stabilized dunes is lower than that to be expected in meadows and scrublands, it is doubtful that pocket gophers were ever particularly numerous at the Casper Site.

Holocene Record. *Thomomys* sp., cf. *T. talpoi-*

des has been recorded from Late Pleistocene deposits at Jaguar Cave, Idaho; and from Late Pleistocene or Holocene deposits at Bell Cave, Wyoming.

Order Carnivora
Family Canidae

Canis latrans Say

Referred Specimens. NC 2555, right dP_4 (A) (Fig. 3.3).

Discussion. This specimen is in excellent condition. The state of resorption of the roots suggests that the tooth was either shed, or was about to be shed at the time of the animal's death. Length, 15.6 mm., width, 6.3 mm. Dr. Elaine Anderson (personal communication to Dr. George C. Frison, 1972) remarks, "I was able to match the deciduous premolar of the coyote with a juvenile jaw of a coyote from...Snake Cave [Idaho]."

Distribution and Habitat. *Canis latrans* today occurs throughout western North America, in many habitat types. Cary (1917: 25 and 34) notes its occurence in both the Upper Sonoran and Transition zones in Wyoming.

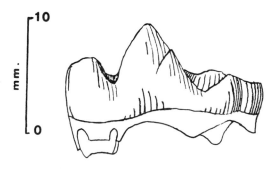

FIGURE 3.3 *Casper Local Fauna* Canis latrans, *right* dP_4, *lingual view (NC 2555).*

Holocene Record. *C. latrans* has been reported from Little Box Elder Cave and Bell Cave, Wyoming; Chimney Rock Animal Trap, Colorado; and Jaguar Cave and Moonshiner Cave in Idaho.

Vulpes sp., cf. *V. vulpes* (L.)

Referred Specimens. NC 2556, left P_4 (A); NC 2557, posterior one-half of right P_4 (A).

Discussion. Both specimens are well preserved. Measurements of NC 2556: length, 8.6 mm., width, 4.0 mm.

Distribution and Habitat. *Vulpes vulpes* (=*V. fulva*) is a wide-ranging omnivore preferring the Canadian Zone forests in Wyoming (Cary 1917: 43). Hall and Kelson (1959: 856) show its range to include the northwestern quarter of Wyoming, some of the southwest, and a portion of the southeastern quarter of the state. They show no records from the Casper area, which lies within Cary's Transition Zone.

Holocene Record. *V. vulpes* has been recorded from all six cave and trap faunas discussed above.

Family Felidae

Lynx sp., cf. *L. rufus* (Schreber)

Referred Specimens. NC 2558, fragment of left P^4 (A).

Discussion. This appears to be a deciduous tooth. Because of its fragmentary nature, measurements are not available.

Distribution and Habitat. The bobcat, *Lynx rufus,* is distributed throughout the continental United States and southern Canada (Hall and Kelson 1959: 970). It is a denizen of "scrub, thickets, and broken country" (*ibid.*) and in Wyoming

prefers the Transition Zone.

Holocene Record. *L. rufus* has been recorded from all the cave and trap faunas discussed above except for Horned Owl Cave, Wyoming.

Family *incertae sedis*

genus and species indeterminate

Referred Specimens. Several coprolites, unnumbered.

Discussion. Several elongate ovoid masses were recovered during excavation and saved because of their color and the presence of small bone fragments. Some were quite reddish in color, in marked contrast to the light red brown to tan matrix. The coprolites, as much as one inch in diameter, contained small bone fragments; some of these were identified as fetal bison (from the kill) and others as probably rodent bone fragments. It is quite likely that these coprolites were produced by coyotes (*Canis latrans*); however, the presence of wolves (*C. lupus*) and domestic dogs (*C. familiaris*) cannot be ruled out.

Order Artiodactyla
Family Antilocapridae

Antilocapra americana Ord

Referred Specimens. NC 2559, ascending ramus of right mandible; NC 2560, proximal phalanx.

Discussion. The ascending ramus shows a coronoid process which is straight and deflected back from the vertical at an angle of about 30° as in *A. americana.* Deer (*Odocoileus* spp.) have coronoid processes that rise vertically and then curve backward. The proximal phalanx is slender in comparison with deer and bighorn sheep (*Ovis canadensis*).

132   *Michael Wilson*

Distribution and Habitat. The pronghorn antelope is found over much of western North America, particularly the drier regions. Pronghorns browse on sage, rabbitbrush, buckbrush, and some grasses. The species occurs throughout Wyoming at lower elevations, being referred by Cary (1917: 24) to the Upper Sonoran and Transition Zones. Pronghorns are quite abundant in the site area today.

Holocene Record. *Antilocapra americana* has been recorded from all six of the cave and trap faunas mentioned above. In addition, antelope bones were reported from the Sister's Hill Site, a Hell Gap and Agate Basin camp site on the east slope of the Big Horn Mountains. The levels have been approximately dated (on the basis of a composite sample) to 9,650 ± 250 years B.P. (I-221: 7,690 B.C.; Agogino and Galloway, 1965). It is likely that this age is only a minimum for the Hell Gap occupation of the site; however, only additional dating analyses will allow a clear appraisal.

Family Bovidae

Bison bison antiquus (Leidy)

Referred Specimens. Skeletal parts of 77 bison, based upon a count of mandibles. Mature male skulls, NC 2323, NC 2326, and NC 2370. Other skulls, 55 in number, include mature and old females, one possible young mature male, immatures possibly of both sexes, and juveniles probably of both sexes. In addition, three fetal individuals are represented, 2 with dentition.

Discussion. One male skull, NC 2326 (Fig. 3.4a), although extremely large, otherwise displays the typical attributes of *Bison "antiquus"* enumerated by Skinner and Kaisen (1947: 178):

Horn-cores moderate in size, length on upper curve seldom exceeding basal circumference or cranial width between horn-cores and orbits, subcircular in cross section, extending from the skull at nearly right angles to the longitudinal axis of the skull; proximally, cores are depressed and swing up on tips with little or no posterior twist; distally, tips tend to be stubby and heavy, seldom rising above the plane of the skull; a superior longitudinal groove is sometimes indicated and is not to be confused with the basal longitudinal grooves common to all mature male bison horn-cores.

Frontals tend to be arched and the cranium broad; orbits tubular; teeth have a suggested tendency to be more complicated than in most *Bison.*

A second male skull (NC 2370) is of average size for *B. "antiquus"* and shows many of its at-

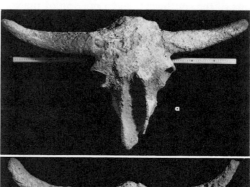

FIGURE 3.4 *Mature male* Bison *skulls from the Casper Site:* a. *NC 2326, a skull closely resembling* B. "antiquus"; b. *NC 2323, a skull resembling* B. "antiquus figginsi" *and* B. bison occidentalis. *Scale: 1 m.*

tributes, including laterally directed horn cores with proximal depression, and relatively broad frontals.

A third male skull has horn cores deflected in a more posteriad direction from the cranium; in doing so, they resemble the cores of *B. "antiquus figginsi"* (= *B. "taylori"*):

> ... horn-cores tend to be longer and a little more posteriorly directed but not approaching *B. (Bison);* cores do not rise far above plane of frontals as in *antiquus* ... (*ibid.:* 181).

This third male skull, NC 2323 (Fig. 3.4b), in fact shows many of the attributes of *B. (Bison)* sp. of Skinner and Kaisen, a problem which will be discussed in more detail below. For the present discussion it is sufficient to note that

a. since *B. antiquus antiquus* (Leidy) and *B. antiquus figginsi* (Hay and Cook) co-exist in the same fauna, they can no longer be considered subspecifically distinct; therefore the latter is subsumed within the former; and

b. the "specific" characters distinguishing *B. bison occidentalis* and *B. antiquus* do not appear worthy of such distinction; therefore the latter is reduced to *B. bison antiquus.*

Distribution and Habitat. Bison bison antiquus has been collected throughout the continental United States west of the Mississippi River (except for the central portions of the Great Basin), in many areas east of the Mississippi and as far southeastward as Florida (Skinner and Kaisen, *ibid.:* 179-183; Robertson 1969), in the western Canadian plains (Russell 1956; Hills *et al,* unpubl. MS), and in the Northwest Territories of Canada (Gordon 1970). It seems to have been a subspecies of considerable ecologic amplitude, although it appears to have been a "southern" form in relation to *B. bison occidentalis.* There is some evidence to suggest that the lower degree of orbital protrusion noted in southern forms is a response to warm-climate conditions and a lowered need for a thick facial hair mat (Guthrie 1966b).

Holocene Record. B. bison antiquus has been recovered from a number of sites in and around Wyoming, although description of the samples has not proceeded very far as yet. A large sample was described recently from the Wasden Site (Owl Cave) in Idaho (Butler 1968a; Butler, Gildersleeve, and Sommers 1971) dated to approximately 7,955 B.P. (Butler 1968a: 8). Bison from the approximately 7,000-year-old Finley Site in southwestern Wyoming were identified tentatively as *B. occidentalis* on the basis of a few metapodials (only one of them complete; and that from a female!) by Schultz and Frankforter (1951). Recently recovered material includes a partial skull much more similar to *B. bison antiquus* (Wilson, *in press*). Bison skulls from the Agate Basin/Brewster Site were identified as *B. antiquus* by Agogino (1972), but on the basis of female skulls. At the latter site, bison occurred in both Folsom and Agate Basin levels. Bison from the Horner Site in northern Wyoming were apparently identified as *B. occidentalis* (Jepsen 1953), but no description of the remains has ever been published. A review of Holocene trends in Wyoming bison populations has been prepared by the present author (Wilson, *in press*).

Conclusions

The Casper Local Fauna is clearly one of modern aspect. There are no extinct species in the fauna, although one phyletically extinct subspecies (*Bison bison antiquus*) is clearly documented. For the most part the species recovered occur in the area today.

The succineid snail, if it is either of the referred species, has not been collected near the site in modern pond areas. However, distributional data on these snails are sparse, and mark a general lack of local interest in such studies. Detailed collecting in the dune sands band which extends northeastward from near Kemmerer, Wyoming to areas northeast of Casper would no doubt yield much previously unrecorded information about species occurrence and habitat tolerances.

As is the case with any archaeological site, the possibility that some of the rodents are intrusive must be considered. However, because the bones all exhibit staining and decalcification directly comparable with that observed in bison bones and bison bone fragments, it is thought that their intrusion into the bone bed was quite soon after the kill episode. Thus, they are temporally similar and may be grouped with the bone bed.

The red fox, *Vulpes vulpes,* apparently did not occur historically in the Casper Site area under natural conditions. Recent trapping, shooting, and poisoning of coyotes (*Canis latrans*) have allowed the fox to move into areas not previously occupied due to competition, including areas not far from Casper. The slight uncertainty of identification in this case prevents us from reaching conclusions about range shifts in the past.

Lynx rufus occurs today in the wooded and brushy river bottoms within one-half mile of the Casper Site. It would not have been unusual for an individual bobcat to be attracted to a bison kill — even though a visit to the kill would have necessitated a brief departure from the preferred cover.

There is, therefore, no evidence as yet in the Casper Local Fauna for a significant climatic or vegetational difference between the period of the kill episode (10,000 years B.P.) and the present. This, of course, tells us nothing about possible Hypsithermal modification, or any other change in the intervening period.

The absence of extinct genera or species at Casper suggests that the Late Pleistocene extinctions were under way; however, the selective nature of a kill episode restricts such speculation. It also suggests that the undated cave faunas including extinct species might well predate the Casper Local Fauna.

IDENTIFICATION AND TAXONOMY OF THE CASPER BISON

The taxonomy of the genus *Bison* and its many species has long been in a state of confusion and controversy; it may well remain that way. As early as 1899 Lucas stated that his goal was

> to assign definite characters to the various species of bison occurring in a fossil condition in North America and to disentangle the complicated synonymy in which they have become involved (1899: 755).

This statement has been echoed by many authors since 1899; and, in fact, it was the goal of even earlier authors. In view of the subjective element which seems to pervade the field of "horn core taxonomy", I shall not echo the statement. Rather, I must make it clear that I have no delusions about the ultimate truth of my views concerning bison taxonomy. As styles in systematics change, so do styles in classification of individual subject groups. Variations over the years in the personal styles of scientists have contributed as much to the justification for revision as has the search for any "truth", or "best fit".

The Casper Sample

The sample of 58 skulls from the Casper Site includes a great many females of all ages, two very large males, and presumably a few juvenile males. Isolated relatively large horn cores are present. A third large male skull was uncovered by amateurs; it disintegrated before archaeologists could treat it with preservative. However, the maxillae (NC 2370) and mandibles were saved, and photographs were taken.

The two large male skulls (NC 2323 and NC 2326) are in a fair state of preservation (Fig. 3.4). There has been exfoliation of the horn cores to some extent, and lesser erosion of the maxillary bodies and occipitals. Both skulls lack nasals as did NC 2370, as a result of the butchering process. NC 2323 is considerably eroded on the right frontal. Nevertheless, enough of the skulls and horn cores are present for us to ascertain that deformation has been minimal. The horn cores show a consistent split-line grain (Tappen 1969; 1971), revealing that the orientation of osteons persists without discontinuities or excessive torsion. The horn cores remain bilaterally symmetrical on the two specimens (Fig. 3.5a,b).

Metric assessment of the two skulls is presented in Table 3.1, along with computed measurements and available direct measurements from NC 2370, and the metric ranges for *Bison* "*anti-*

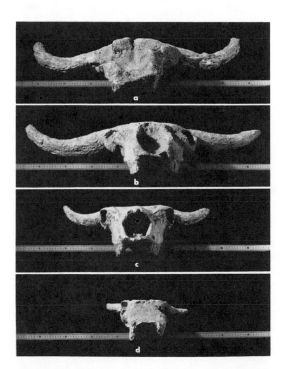

FIGURE 3.5 *Bison skulls from the Casper Site, in anterior aspect: a. mature male, NC 2323; b. mature male, NC 2326; c. mature female, NC 2560; d. 1.6-year-old male (?), NC 2317. Scale: 1 m.*

quus antiquus" (after Skinner and Kaisen 1947: 178). It can be seen from these tables that NC 2323 is an individual of average horn core spread, but with very long, slender, flattened, relatively straight horn cores and a correspondingly narrow cranium. The rostrum is narrow and the skull short; however, measurements involving the premaxillae are suspect in this specimen, as their true extent is hard to estimate. Some of the tip of each is missing. The horn cores are much more compressed than in typical *B.* "*a. antiquus*". Specimen NC 2326 shows a much larger horn core spread, with cores that are long, quite straight, slender, and of average dorso-ventral compression. There is a slight distal twist to the horn cores. The cranium is of average breadth and the rostrum narrow. The skull and cranium are short. Orbital protrusion is as one would expect for *antiquus*.

These individuals have in common the extreme length of their horn cores and the relative straightness of these; the narrow nature of the rostrum; and the apparent shortness of the skulls. Longer premaxillae in NC 2370 may indicate that skulls were in reality of "normal" length. They differ in that NC 2323 has a narrow cranium, while NC 2326 has one of average width for the species; that is to say, of considerable breadth in comparison with other taxa of *Bison*. They also differ in the angle at which the horn cores leave the skull: in NC 2326 the cores depart laterally, extending only 5° away from perpendicular to the longitudinal axis of the skull. This is very characteristic of *antiquus*. In NC 2323 the cores depart with a more posteriad deflection: fully 12° from the perpendicular. In addition, the latter's cores rise in a more posteriad direction and somewhat above the plane of the frontals.

This leaves one with doubts concerning the utility of taxonomic procedures and distinctions proposed to date. If we go solely by the measurement tables in Skinner and Kaisen's monograph (a procedure which I am sure they would brand

TABLE 3.1 *Measurements of Mature Male Bison from the Casper Site (in mm.)*

Standard Measurement	NC 2323		NC 2326		NC 2370	Bison "antiquus antiquus"[2]		
1. Spread of horn cores, tip to tip	870	*880[1]*	980	*1090*	880	816	881	975
2. Greatest spread of cores on outside curve	900	*905*	1010	*1120*				
3. Core length on upper curve, tip to burr	370	*375*	342	*352*		220	281	344
4. Core length on lower curve, tip to burr	420	*425*	405	*415*		280	336	395
5. Length, tip of core to upper base at burr	345	*350*	330	*340*	280	197	245	280
6. Vertical diameter of horn core	80	*85*	88	*90*		90	98	108
7. Circumference of horn core at base	295	*310 +*	303	*310 +*		290	320	358
8. Greatest width at auditory openings			272					
9. Width of condyles	125	*125 +*	135					
10. Depth, occipital crest to upper border of foramen magnum	110	*110 +*	89					
11. Depth, occipital crest to lower border of foramen magnum			120	*120 +*				
12. Transverse diameter of horn core	105		97			92	107	122
13. Width between bases of horn cores	188		190					
14. Width of cranium between horn cores and orbits	296	*296 +*	316		*300*	292	319	357
15. Greatest postorbital width			355			346	353	360
16. Anterior orbital width at notch				*255*				
17. Width of skull at masseteric processes above M[1]	192		190			188	205	218
18. Rostral width at maxillary/premaxillary suture			125					
19. P^2 - M^3, alveolar length	163		173		153			
20. M^1 - M^3, alveolar length	99		105		98.5			
O-P. Overall length, occipital crest to tip of premaxilla	520		575					
F-P. Basilar length, foramen magnum to tip of premaxilla	490		515			520	545	560
O-T. Length, occipital crest to tip of nasals						482	510	527
O-N. Length, occipital crest to nasal-frontal suture					*278*	240	295	350
M-P. Length beyond P^2 to tip of premaxilla	122		130		148			
N-T. Length of nasals								
21. Angle of posterior divergence of horn core	78°		85°		*85°*			
22. Angle of proximal horn core depression	11°		9°		*10°+*			
Index of horn core curvature	122	*121*	123	*122*		128	138	147
Index of horn core compression	76	*81*	91	*93*		83	93	108
Index of horn core proportion	125	*121*	113	*114*		68	88	100
Index of horn core length	125	*127*	108	*111*		66	89	114
Index of tooth row proportion	33		34					
Index of orbital protrusion[3]			89			90		

[1] Numbers in italics represent estimated figures in cases where some erosion or exfoliation has occurred, or where a photograph has been used (NC 2370).

[2] After Skinner and Kaisen (1947: 178) and Guthrie (1966b: 726). Numbers, in order, indicate minimum, average, and maximum.

[3] After Guthrie (1966b).

as inadequate, but one forced by the imprecise nature of some of their non-metric distinctions), the two specimens show their best fit not with *B. antiquus,* but with *B. crassicornis* (now *B. priscus)* — supposedly a member of a different subgenus. If the orbital protrusion effect is shown to be an environmental response of bison in general, rather than a characteristic of given species (and this has yet to be demonstrated), a low degree of protrusion in NC 2326 would not exclude it from *B. crassicornis.* On the basis of the index of horn core proportion neither specimen is *B. "antiquus antiquus"*; and only very doubtfully are they *B. antiquus*:

> Horn-cores moderate in size, length on upper curve seldom exceeding basal circumference or cranial width between horn-cores and orbits (Skinner and Kaisen, *ibid.*: 178).

All three skulls are too big for *B. occidentalis* of Skinner and Kaisen, and NC 2326 is too big even for their *B. "preoccidentalis".*

We are left, then, in a state of indecision if we are to follow the data outlined by Skinner and Kaisen. While their preliminary revision certainly orders a lot of data and allows the identification of individual specimens, it begins to break down as we become familiar with the true range of variation in fossil populations. On the basis of the Skinner and Kaisen revision, we have at Casper

1. two skulls that look like *B. antiquus* is supposed to look; but one which is far too big — yet too small for *B. alleni.* It is metrically very close to *B. crassicornis* but does not fit the non-metric descriptions.
2. a skull that has a *B. occidentalis* cranium, with horn cores drooping like those of *B. "antiquus figginsi",* but small enough in overall spread to fit *B. "antiquus antiquus"* (no measurements are given for *"figginsi"* but it is said that horn cores tend to be longer; however the holotype is crushed). Horn cores of this skull are too large for *B. occi-*

dentalis yet morphologically similar.

It is most problematic that Skinner and Kaisen did not provide in their measurement tables certain key cranial metrics that they themselves observed to be very important in the identification of their "species". Although they show the angle at which the horn cores leave the skull to be of critical importance, and although they provide instructions (*ibid.*: 145) as to how to measure this angle (measurement 21), they do not include this measurement in their own published tables. We are thus left with a non-metric criterion ("horn-cores...posteriorly directed with respect to longitudinal axis of skull") and no idea of the possible range of variation.

The Trend to Synonymy

A good many of the more recent studies of bison have tended toward synonymy of "species" and "subspecies". Although Skinner and Kaisen themselves lumped many forms they did not go far enough to please all students of the subject. Skinner and Kaisen proposed five subgenera of bison for the North American Pleistocene; and these, with their many species, seemed to bespeak more rapid evolution and more inter-group isolation than the temporal and spatial setting warranted.

In 1951 Romer described a large horn core from New England, and noted that *Bison alleni* and *B. crassicornis,* referred to separate subgenera, "are not clearly distinguishable on the basis of Skinner and Kaisen's diagnoses" (1951: 230). On the basis of best fit he referred the specimen to *B. crassicornis.* Hopkins (1951) described additional *B. alleni* from Idaho, and noted that they differed from Skinner and Kaisen's criteria in that their horn cores rose above the plane of the frontals, and they were laterally directed rather than with a slight posteriad deflection. While the former was quite different from the earlier authors' findings, the latter accorded well with their hypothesis that *B. alleni* was ancestral to *B. antiquus.*

Schultz and Frankforter (1946) without stratigraphic or faunal evidence assigned *B. latifrons,* the largest of the North American species, to the Kansan stage of the Pleistocene (fitting their hypothesis that the species of bison were index fossils, the largest being the oldest). Skinner and Kaisen were evidently swayed by this argument and assigned the species (again without evidence) to the "latter part of the early Pleistocene" (1947: 155). However, they suggested that the form had "survived" until the Late Pleistocene in some areas. Later work has shown this picture to be erroneous: all *Bison latifrons* finds to date are Late Pleistocene (primarily Sangamon) in age (Vander Hoof 1942; Hibbard 1955; Hibbard and Taylor 1960; Green 1962; Hibbard 1963; Cheatum and Allen 1963; Hopkins, Bonnichsen and Fortsch 1969; Khan 1970; Lewis 1970; and others). This places *B. latifrons* temporally close to other Late Pleistocene bison taxa.

Dalquest (1957: 350-351) attempted to follow Skinner and Kaisen's criteria in identifying a large horn core from Texas. He found that

...when the descriptions and discussions of *Bison alleni* and *Bison chaneyi* given by Skinner and Kaisen are compared, it is found that almost every alleged character of one form is either contradicted or canceled out by the data concerning the other species. After study, one is left with the impression that the authors consider *B. chaneyi* to have horn cores more depressed proximally, with bases more spread out so that a line connecting their posterior border is posterior to the occipital region, and with horn cores larger and flatter. The first two features can be seen only in a skull possessing the horn cores. Since the holotype of *alleni* is only a horn core, the characters are of no value in separating the type of *alleni* from the other form. In any event, these characters are of the type that are quite variable in all species of *Bison.*

Slaughter (1966: 86-87) experienced difficulty in distinguishing *B. alleni* from *B. chaneyi.*

Wilson (1969: 182-183) suggested synonymy of the two, viewing *chaneyi* as "an extreme variation of *B. alleni,* both morphologically and geographically." This view was also held by Guthrie (1970: 6) who observed that the difference in means between *B. alleni* (= *B. alleni* + *B. chaneyi*) and *B. priscus* (= *B. crassicornis* + *B. preoccidentalis* + *B. alaskensis* + *B. geisti* + *B. priscus*) "are not different enough to give the former 'species' a taxonomic distinction above that of a chronological or geographical subspecies." The synonymy of the four Alaskan forms with the Eurasian *B. priscus* was foreshadowed by Lucas (1899: 761), who synonymized *B. alaskensis* with *B. crassicornis*; Fuller and Bayrock (1965: 57) who synonymized *B. preoccidentalis* with *B. crassicornis*; Wilson (1969: 184) who suggested synonymy of these forms plus *B. alaskensis* and *B. geisti*; and Guthrie's own preliminary summary (1966a).

Harington and Clulow (1973: 735-742) recently obtained radiocarbon dates and stratigraphic evidence suggesting that *B. alaskensis* is considerably older than *B. crassicornis* in the Yukon Territory. The greater size of *B. alaskensis* makes it a good counterpart or antecedent to *B. latifrons.* In biological terms, however, it is unlikely that specific distinction is warranted: very likely *B. alaskensis* and *B. crassicornis* were chronosubspecies in an ongoing lineage. This make it highly probable that *B. latifrons* is merely of subspecific importance as the southern phenotypic counterpart to *B. priscus alaskensis,* and thus can be viewed as *B. priscus latifrons.*

This trend to synonymy has reduced the number of Late Pleistocene precursors to the early Holocene bison of North America to four forms. A similar trend has been under way with the early Holocene forms, and I intend to carry it further in this paper. Originally *B. antiquus* was thought to be a southern species, derived by "retrogressive evolution" from *B. alleni* (although Skinner and Kaisen found no metrically intermediate specimens); while *B. occidentalis* was thought to be a northern species, derived from *B. preoccidentalis* (Skinner and Kaisen 1947).

Lorrain (1968) experienced difficulty in distinguishing *B. occidentalis* from *B. antiquus* for the purpose of identifying an archaeological population from Texas. She concluded,

> ...serious doubts arose concerning the distinctiveness of *Bison antiquus* and *Bison occidentalis.* It seems entirely possible that they are simple varieties of one species (1968: 114).

Butler (1968b) and Wilson (1969) made similar suggestions, with Wilson pointing to the difference between morphospecies (form-species) and biospecies in the fossil record:

> If it could be demonstrated that no mixing occurred, then this would be ample proof that the two morphospecies were, in fact, true biospecies, unable to interbreed. However, this has not been demonstrated. The flat statement by Skinner and Kaisen...that the two "...probably did not interbreed, for no specimens are known that display intermediate characters" is based upon negative proof, and, as such, cannot be accepted without some reservations (1969: 187).

Intermediate-appearing individuals do seem to exist, as evident from the considerable overlap in measurements published in Skinner and Kaisen's own work, and from the morphology of *B. "antiquus figginsi"*, which in fact appears to be characterized as an *antiquus* showing *occidentalis* traits (1947: 181-182).

I further suggested (Wilson 1969: 188) that until something is known concerning the genetic basis for horn-core morphology, we cannot even predict what a truly intermediate individual might look like. Taking a simple case — control at a small number of loci — I pointed out that the offspring of crossed *antiquus* and *occidentalis* phenotypes could favor one or the other parent, rather than display "intermediate" characters. Butler *et al* (1971: 127) criticized my suggestion, contending that "hybridization...is usually quite

rare in the wild among animals". This criticism is quite irrelevant, as I was referring to the crossing of *phenotypes* — not *biospecies*; and in the same article I clearly suggested that

> It may well be that the postglacial *Bison* "species" in reality represented a continuous, polytypic, and perhaps even polyphyletic population (*ibid.*: 189).

Bison *Versus* Bos

Recent work at the generic level has further significance regarding the assessment of specific status for *B. antiquus* and *B. occidentalis.* Stormont, Miller, and Suzuki (1961: 208) concluded on the basis of the common possession of 9 blood-group systems by *Bison bison* and *Bos taurus* that

> The over-all results indicate close taxonomic affinity of the two species. On the basis of the evidence on blood groups and on other observations...further consideration should be given to the proposition that the American buffalo and domestic cattle deserve to be recognized as members of the same genus.

Experiments with the cross-breeding of cattle and bison have been widely successful (Deakin *et al* 1942; Krasinska and Pucek 1967; Zaniewski 1967). F_1 males are sterile, but 100% of the F_1 females are fertile (Krasinska and Pucek 1967: 388).

Early writers describing the problems of crossbreeding cattle and bison noted that the crossing of a buffalo bull with a domestic cow was often fatal to both cow and calf. This they ascribed to factors involving the size of the calf, and the exertion required in delivery. The calf's hump was supposed to be an important factor here. However, the prominent hump is not present in newborn bison — it develops progressively over a period of years. McHugh (1972: 308-309) and Jennings (1973: 15) have pointed out that the problem is in reality an immunological one:

> ...the mother's chemistry regards the hybrid

embryo as an invading foreign protein and tries to reject it by producing excessive amniotic fluid. The excess fluid crowds her heart, causing congestive heart failure (Jennings, *ibid.*).

Successful production of "Cattalo" hybrids to date has been based upon the crossing of domestic bulls and bison cows.

Further evidence of the similarity between *Bison* and *Bos* has recently come to light in the collections of the Department of Anthropology, University of Wyoming. We have the skeleton of a modern 3-day-old *Bison bison* calf exhibiting the characteristic skeletal symptoms of "crooked calf" or "wry calf" disease. This deformity, widely reported in *Bos taurus* (Hart, Guilbert, Wagnon, and Gross 1947; Roubicek, Clark, and Pahnish 1957; Dyer, Cossett, and Roa 1964; Shupe, Binns, James, and Keeler 1967; Shupe, James, Balls, Binns, and Keeler 1967) manifests itself in cleft palate, scoliosis of the spine, arthrogryposis of the limb joints, and other skeletal maladies. Its etiology is complex; like many teratologies, it may have either environmental or genetic causes, and it is virtually impossible to distinguish the two without a good case history involving several animals and controlled conditions. The anomaly has apparently not been recorded before in *Bison bison,* and the skeleton is currently being described for publication elsewhere.

There is evidence that the line ancestral to the modern bison had diverged from *Leptobos* and from early representatives of the genus *Bos* by the Late Pliocene (Kurtén 1968: 183-189; Sahni and Khan 1968). Sahni and Khan considered their bison from the Upper Pliocene Tatrot beds of the Siwalik Hills to represent a new genus, *Probison.* However, their justification for a new genus was that "the difference...is a qualitative one and does not fall within the limit of individual variations" (in comparison with *Bison sivalensis* from the Pinajur beds). Wilson (1972) has suggested that the earlier form be subsumed within the modern genus as *Bison dehmi* (Sahni and Khan)

until valid generic characters are sought and extensive comparisons made. *Probison* may be provisionally retained at the subgeneric level.

The antiquity of this divergence leaves time for the possible (although by no means inevitable) development of a genus *Bison* standing in apposition to *Bos.* It would thus seem that while the synonymy of *Bison* and *Bos* might be warranted in the near future, more descriptive work is needed to back up the highly significant blood-group system evidence.

Whatever the ultimate taxonomic decision in this regard, it is clear that *Bison* and *Bos* as currently understood are close sibling genera. Thus the great degree of specific divergence attributed to *Bison* by past authors becomes even less likely. Can a morphologically conservative genus (in terms of the rate, or degree, of divergence from sibling genera) be made up of wildly adventive species, to the extent that the same Alaskan mucks yield at least three apparently sympatric "species", and the Great Plains, with no physical barriers, yield at least two sympatric "species" and several apparently also sympatric "subspecies"?

I think not. The trends throughout the 1950's, 1960's, and 1970's toward the synonymy of Skinner and Kaisen's many species, and toward the suppression of their subgenera are warranted. These trends should be continued, *if we are seeking biospecies, not morphospecies.* Stratigraphers seeking "index fossils", or at least relative age indicators, may wish to split taxa further than would biologists; thus they may continue the trend started by C. B. Schultz and colleagues in Nebraska. However, we must realize that these chronospecies and chronosubspecies are merely temporal divisions in ongoing lineages — *and their use presupposes definition of those lineages.* In the terms used here, these lineages are the evolving biosubspecies. Taxa are better split at the subspecific level — both chronologically and geographically — among bison.

Some New Combinations

I therefore propose the synonymy of *Bison antiquus* Leidy and *Bison bison occidentalis* (Lucas). Hillerud (1966) attempted this synonymy, but, in the words of Guthrie (1970: 8):

> courts Coon's Dilemma when he says that his *B. antiquus occidentalis* was derived from *B. crassicornis* (= *B. priscus*) while *B. antiquus antiquus* came from the *B. alleni* line.

The resolution of this problem lies in the recognition that *B. alleni* and *B. priscus* are themselves synonymous, and significant only at the subspecific level. This point was touched upon by Guthrie (*ibid.*: 12). It remains a fact that past authors have repeatedly been unable to distinguish *B. alleni* and *B. priscus* adequately (see, for instance, Hay 1913: 183-184; Romer 1951).

The two "species" differ on minor terms regarding the shape and cross-section of the horn cores, as well as the breadth of the cranium and perhaps the angle of horn core divergence — all of these characters quite possibly interrelated through a single cranial allometric function. The degree of orbital protrusion becomes lower in the southern (*B. alleni*) forms, but this too may be related to frontal breadth; or it may be an environmental response of limited taxonomic value, as discussed previously. In addition, the type of *B. alleni* is most inadequate for comparative purposes, as Dalquest (1957) has noted.

I thus consider that *Bison priscus,* the Holarctic steppe-tundra bison, was able to move southward into the continental United States during the late Illinoian glacial or Sangamon interglacial, as suggested by Guthrie (1970: Fig. 2). In response to climatic stresses, *B. priscus* underwent a small amount of geographic differentiation, to the extent that a north-south clinal series (narrow frontals to broad frontals; horn cores deflected posteriad to horn cores less deflected posteriad; protruding orbits to less protruding orbits) existed. Very possibly a lateral constriction of range existed in western Canada, resulting in a slowing of gene flow from one extreme to the other. The result of this climatic adaptation and lessened gene flow was differentiation into two subspecies, *Bison priscus alaskensis* (Rhoads) in the north, and *Bison priscus latifrons* (Harlan) in the south (Fig. 3.6). Specimens from the intermediate area (the western plains of Canada and northwestern plains of the United States) would be expected to show some evidence of intergradation. During the late Sangamon or early Wisconsin some degree of dwarfing occurred in both areas, resulting in the northern *Bison priscus crassicornis* (Richardson) and the southern *Bison priscus alleni* (Marsh).

The Wisconsin glaciation may have caused some slackening in gene flow between northern and southern populations; however, studies by Reeves (1971: 217; 1973) show that coalescence of the continental and Cordilleran ice sheets was a minor event, of brief duration and local extent; and, except perhaps at glacial maxima, of little significance as a barrier to mobile biotic populations. Thus the great ice blockage mapped by Guthrie (1970: Fig. 2) is an exaggeration in keeping with the past scarcity of information from key corridor areas.

Northern and southern populations of bison could have maintained, or easily reestablished gene flow through the Wisconsin. Thus I believe that the populations underwent much the same pressures toward dwarfing, or retrogressive evolution, and gave rise to *B. bison occidentalis* (Lucas) in the north, and *B. bison antiquus* (Leidy) in the south. The subsequent relief of climatic stress with the retreat of the Wisconsin ice allowed freer mixing of populations and more extensive gene flow, with the result that both chronosubspecies contributed to the rise of the modern Plains Bison, *B. bison bison*; while the Wood Bison, *B. bison athabascae,* evolved from a more purely "northern" precursor; hence, *B. bison occidentalis.*

As was the case with the subspecies of *Bison*

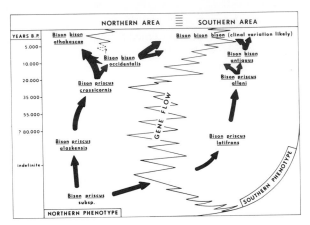

FIGURE 3.6 *Summary chart of relationships among North American fossil and recent bison. Arrows indicate phyletic relationships, and north-south gene flow is assumed.*

priscus, it would be impossible to draw a precise line between *B. bison occidentalis* and *B. bison antiquus* on a map. The two very likely intergraded over a broad area of the northern plains, with the result that *antiquus* and *occidentalis*-like phenotypes could be found in the same population — as at Casper.

Skinner and Kaisen (1947: 163) are quite probably correct in disposing of Figgins' distinction between a southern plains *B. bison bison* and a northern *B. bison septemtrionalis* on the plains in historic (and earlier) times. As they pointed out, Figgins had little control over the temporal provenience of specimens; and the addition of many more "northern" specimens brings the means of the two populations closer together than Figgins was able to demonstrate. However, Skinner and Kaisen were on less secure grounds when they ignored Figgins' observation (1933: 27-28) that in the southern form the tips of the horn cores lie "anterior to plane formed by occipital crest and the upper lip of foramen magnum"; whereas in the northern form the tips lie posterior to such a plane. As we observed earlier, this measurement (angle of posterior divergence) does not appear in

Skinner and Kaisen's measurement tables. Therefore, their own statement that the population means were brought closer together as a result of increased sample size does not have any bearing on the angle of posterior horn core divergence. This character may indeed reflect the persistence of the north-to-south clinal gradient between *B. bison occidentalis* and *B. bison antiquus.* Recent works have tended to assume that clinal variation was essentially lost in the historic plains populations; however, we must remember that Skinner and Kaisen presented measurements of *B. bison bison* from what they considered a single population, from Montana (1947: 163). The homogeneity of such a population has absolutely no bearing on the supposed presence or absence of clinal variation.

Bergmann's Rule

If we accept that there was clinal variation in historic *B. bison bison* and in earlier populations, we must seek reasons for its presence. In general terms, we have considered that climatic variables have been responsible, as with the north-to-south reduction in orbital protrusion.

Butler *et al.* (1971) have made the interesting suggestion that the north-to-south variation in size noted (by them) in paleo-bison, and the range in size noted in the Wasden Site bison sample (*B. bison antiquus*) from Idaho are both the effects of Bergmann's Rule. While I admit that this hypothesis is quite plausible, I do not feel that their evidence supports this suggestion — in fact, I am left wondering if they have any evidence at all.

Bergmann's rule is a generalization postulating that as temperatures decrease from the Equator toward the poles, the body shape of mammals and birds tends to provide a lower ratio of body surface to body weight; that is to say, the surface area is proportionately reduced (Boughey 1968: 115-116).

It would seem, then, that any theory involving the rule should be able to call upon evidence concerning the body surface to weight ratio. With regard to the overall paleo-bison trend, Butler *et al.* do provide some information concerning metapodials:

> ...the median sex lines calculated for the Bonfire Shelter data and for the Wasden data...fall well to the left of the Alaskan median line. In short, the line dividing the sexes varies with the mean size of the metapodials in each population, which seems to vary with latitude.

Notably, the three samples differ considerably in age, through a period apparently critical in the progress of the retrogressive evolution of bison. The Alaskan sample is a mixed one, probably largely Wisconsin in age. The Bonfire Shelter bone bed has been dated to approximately 10,200 years B.P. (Dibble 1968: 33). The Wasden Site is a later bone bed, dating to approximately 7,955 years B.P. (Butler 1968a: 8).

There are a number of problems to be faced here. First of all, I disagree with Lorrain's placement of the male/female median sex line for metacarpals[3] (1968: 87). The tables given by Skinner and Kaisen (1947: 135-137) show a major discontinuity in the width/length ratio between robust female metacarpals and slender male metacarpals at 21.8 . Lorrain's sample shows a very similar, and well-marked discontinuity at a point just below 21.8 – approximately 21.0 . Despite this, she selects a smaller discontinuity at approximately $R = 19.0$. This gives her an unusual recovered population of 4 females and 6 males from Bone Bed 2. Interestingly, her study of metatarsals from the same bone bed and by the same technique yields a sample of 3 females and 1 male.

Most bison populations from archaeological sites (particularly buffalo jumps) contain many more females than males. McHugh (1958: 14-15) discusses this characteristic of the large bison herds, noting that only *bull groups* of one to 12 members contain a preponderance of males among *Bison bison* in Yellowstone Park. *Cow groups* are much larger, and never show a preponderance of males. The highest occurrence of males observed was 44% during the rut; otherwise, it dropped as low as 17%. McHugh noted the cow groups to be more wary and ready to run, a characteristic which would make them more susceptible to and preferable for drives:

> Some bull groups were so obstinate that approach within ten feet and tossing of stones did not move them (*ibid.*: 15).

On this basis, I feel it more likely that the male/female sex line for Bonfire Shelter, Bone Bed 2 metacarpals lies at $R = 21.0$. This places the Bonfire Shelter population between the Alaskan and Wasden Site samples, which gives us a temporal gradient instead of a geographical gradient.

I am also not convinced that sex is the only significant variable governing the size of "mature" metapodials. Another variable which Butler *et al.* could have considered is the postmaturational increase in cross-sectional area of the metapodial after epiphyseal maturity. The cross-sectional area of a long bone continues to adjust to the weight of the animal through the external deposition of periosteal bone tissues in thin layers, and the internal remodelling of the bone by osteoclast action. Zhdanov (1967) found that increased kinetic and/or static loading of tubular bones resulted in their increased perimeter, density, and weight. Zhdanov further noted

> In gymnasts, who went in for sport for a long period of time, a significant thickening of the layer of compact substance and a narrowing of the marrow space in the diaphyses of humerus, ulna, radius and metacarpal bones are observed in comparison with those of a control group (1967: 397).

---

3 "Metacarpals" is preferable to "metacarpi" as used by Skinner and Kaisen (1947) and Butler *et al.* (1971), as the latter is the plural of "metacarpus", which in bison includes the rudimentary separate 5th metacarpal. Inclusion of the latter would change the measurements taken, particularly the anterior-posterior measurement of the proximal end.

Lorrain (1968) and Butler *et al.* (1971) believed that there was "no published data on the fusion rates of long bones in bison" (*ibid.:* 129); thus they chose to use the rates for oxen. Nevertheless, there has been an excellent summary of the epiphyseal fusion rates of the European bison (*Bison bonasus*) widely available for many years (Koch 1935). Koch's paper shows the rate for bison to be much slower than that for the ox given by Lorrain (1968: 87), a finding consistent with the fact that oxen have been selectively bred over many hundreds of years for rapid maturation and weight gain. In bison, the distal epiphyses of the metapodials fuse at the end of the fourth year (2-3 years in oxen) while "bulls grow considerably from the fourth to the sixth, expecially in the apophyses of the vertebral column, the scapula and pelvis" (Koch, *ibid.*: 372). Halloran (1961) and Novakowski (1965) show that bull bison in particular continue to gain weight well after their fourth year. This suggests a need for remodelling of long bone cross-sections (as reflected in minimum shaft diameters) until at least the seventh year, and probably beyond this.

In conclusion, the use of three populations, one of them open to reinterpretation, in an attempt to establish a geographical gradient (when the populations are of three different ages) is clearly inadequate. I see no evidence for Bergmann's rule in this case.

As for the "variation" within the Wasden sample, it seems hardly more than a function of sample size. In support of the existence of an unusual amount of variation the authors can only assert

the metapodials tend to be longer overall than those in the other, presumably fossil, populations, except the 'selected' Alaskan populations; at the same time, there is a considerable overlap in size with the modern bison...(Butler *et al.* 1971: 131).

Elsewhere they note that the Alaskan metapodials measured by Skinner and Kaisen were not identifiable as to species; this seems to be a criticism of the utility of the sample. We have noted, however, that current trends in synonymy have reduced the Alaskan bison of the Wisconsin and earlier periods to a single species (Wilson 1969; Guthrie 1970); therefore, the sample once again becomes at least provisionally useable in the comparative sense at the specific level. Its dispersion is reasonably valid for generalizations concerning *Bison priscus,* and it is not necessarily unusual in extent, even though it is not a random sample. Similarly, the Wasden Site sample shows no disturbing dispersion: it clusters well, and I see no reason to be alarmed by the fact that it overlaps with both earlier and later populations. What could be better for a population temporally intermediate?

Butler *et al.* suggest finally that "the size range of the 8,000 year old Wasden Site bison is a function of the variable temperature conditions prevailing on the Eastern Snake River Plain at the time" (*ibid.:* 133). Yet the sample is from a single kill population. Can a comparative interpopulational trend (Bergmann's rule) be applied in this fashion to a single population at a point in time? Temperatures would have to be changing drastically from year to year for offspring to differ in size from their parents — and even then, we would be comparing individuals of differing maturational stages in the same population. In conclusion, there is absolutely no evidence in Butler's *et al.* study to show that Bergmann's rule is acting in this way at Wasden; nor is there any evidence for variation above and beyond normal sexual and maturational variability.

We are left, then, where we started: only the orbital protrusion and posterior horn core direction clines are even minimally documented. Others, involving width of frontals and posterior twisting of horn core tips, may be related to the first two. Guthrie (1966 b) has suggested a climatic explanation for the orbital protrusion effect.

It is manifestly clear that the problem of clines in bison populations has been badly ignored. Hopefully, workers with site populations will in the future be attentive to possible clinal variations, and will attempt to record relevant data for com-

TABLE 3.2 *Horn-core Angles in Specimens from the Casper Site*

Specimen Number	Sex	Angle of proximal horn core depression	Angle of posterior horn core divergence
NC 2326	Male	9°	85°
NC 2323	Male	11°	78°
NC 2370	Male	10° +	85°
NC 2317	Female ?	5°	80°
NC 2320	Female		68°
NC 2560	Female	11°	72°
NC 2322	Female	c. 10°	66°
NC 2321	Female		72°
NC 2324	Female		77°
NC 2325	Female		70° +
NC 2318	Female ?	c. 0°	73°

parative purposes. For comparative purposes, the horn-core angles of depression and divergence are summarized for several Casper specimens in Table 3.2 .

CASPER SITE FETAL BISON REMAINS

The youngest individual bison from the Casper Site bone bed are unborn fetuses, the remaining bones of which are in several cases very well preserved. The fetal bones were scattered widely over the site (Fig. 3.7), but one definable cluster was noted. The cluster (Fig. 3.8) included both scapulae, several ribs, and a row of vertebrae from the 7th cervical to the 6th thoracic. This appears to have been a butchered unit, although cut marks were not preserved due to the texture of the bone.

Fetal bones are in general easily recognized due to the spongy nature and porous appearance of the periosteal and replacement bone tissue. Periosteal bone tissue is being deposited along the shaft in layers separated by thin cancellous interspaces. The latter rapidly fill with bone tissue once the bones are placed in post-natal stress situations. When the supporting function of the limbs is increased additional osteons appear,

sharply delimited from the surrounding bone tissue. This is a period of intensification of the process of osteonization in the compact bone substance (Zhdanov, 1967: 394). Hafez (1959: 4) observed that "in the shaft of a long bone, while bone is being absorbed to make room for the development of the bony marrow, it is also being added to on its outer surface". This increases the thickness of the compact bone and of the overall shaft, and is clearly related to the weight and con-

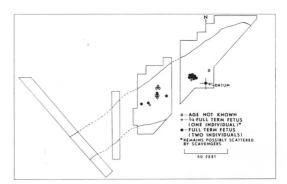

FIGURE 3.7 *Distribution of fetal remains in the Casper Site. Based upon the minimum number of elements, three fetuses (in two age groups) are represented.*

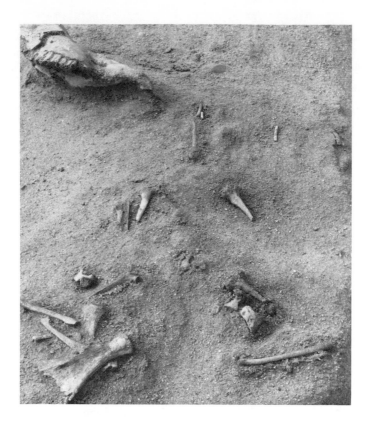

FIGURE 3.8 *Cluster of fetal vertebrae, scapulae, and ribs from a possibly butchered, near full-term individual. The skull in the upper left is that of a 0.6-year-old calf.*

formation of the animal. Smith and Walker (1964: 156) showed that even in aging women,

> ...the diameter of the midshaft periosteum increased as cortical thickness declined. Since the cortical area enlarged, periosteal accretion exceeded endosteal resorption.

Thus the process continues through the life of the mammalian individual, at least partly in response to static and kinetic loading of the long bones.

A minimum-element count of bones suggests the presence of three fetuses in the Casper bone bed, although the wide dispersion of remains suggests that more may have been present. Two of the fetuses are nearly full term, comparing favor-ably with modern newborn and three-day-old modern bison calf skeleta in the University of Wyoming, Department of Anthropology collections. The third fetus is considerably smaller, and seems to be an approximately 7-month-old — 2 months short of parturition.

Vsyakikh (1969: 227-233) reviews the state of knowledge concerning fetal development in domestic animals. While we are saddled with possibly differing development rates as noted before with regard to epiphyseal fusion, it is instructive to note the *order* of development.

In calves of *Bos taurus* the limb bones grow most intensively during the second half of uterine development, with comparatively slight intensity of axial bone growth. After birth this trend begins to reverse, the axial bones growing faster and the peripheral bones slower than before. At the age of about one year in cattle and perhaps later in bison the axial skeleton takes the lead.

The smaller fetal individual from the Casper Site shows comparatively lesser development of the axial skeleton; the first ribs are only 66.7 mm. in length (NC 2470), compared to 96.1 mm. in a modern 3-day-old (no. 91-1.34) and approximately 102.5 in a nearly full-term individual from Casper (NC 2474/NC 2488). However, the peripheral bones of the small fetus have progressed somewhat more in growth, being about 3/4 of the full-term size. The humerus of the small fetus (NC 625) agrees closely in size with that of a 7-month-old modern bison fetus in our collections. The latter is still under preparation and measurements are not available.

Estimates of the gestation period of bison seem to cluster around nine to ten months, 270 to 300 days (McHugh 1958: 31). The gestation period of *Bos taurus* is given by Vsyakikh (1969: 223) as 284 days, or roughly the same as bison.

Stratification in Fetal Bones

A possible aid in the aging of fossil bison fetuses lies in the stratification of periosteum, with thin cancellous interspaces. The presence of the interspaces makes counting of the layers on a cut surface quite easy under moderate magnification. As a preliminary test of the utility of this method I cut oblique and perpendicular sections in the antero-internal portion of the distal end of the humeral diaphysis in several specimens (Fig. 3.9). The sample included three humeri from the Casper Site (one 3/4 full-term and two near full-term), three from the Late Prehistoric Wardell Site in western Wyoming (all of them near full-term), one (newborn) from the Middle Prehistoric Cactus Flower Site in Alberta, one modern 3/4

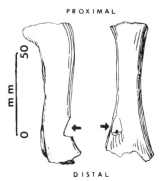

FIGURE 3.9 *Internal and anterior aspects of a fetal bison humeral diaphysis, showing the location of oblique and perpendicular sections. These sections reveal stratification in the periosteum.*

full-term fetus, and one modern 3-day-old newborn. Counts of the periosteal layers revealed a fairly consistent trend for older individuals to show more strata. However, the complicating factors of internal osteoclast action and of occasional periosteal stratum bifurcation could not be assessed adequately in such a small sample. Stratum counts and mid-shaft diameters are summarized in Table 3.3 .

Easily visible layering of periosteal tissue was also observed in midshaft portions of femora, tibiae, metapodials, and radii; in the posterior portion of the nasals; in the frontals; in the mandibular condyle; and in the thin compact bone layer of the ilium. It is hoped that future collection will extend our sample and allow correlation of counts of these sets of strata with the humeral stratum counts already described. Stratification in the periosteal zone of limb bones has been studied in adult animals by Klebanova and Klevezal (1966) and Klevezal and Kleinenberg (1967). These authors noted that the number of layers found in adults did not exceed the maximum

TABLE 3.3 *Stratification and Mid-shaft Measurements of Fetal Humeri*

Site	Specimen No.	Fetal Age	No. of Strata	Min. Ant.-Post. Diameter	Min. Transverse Diameter
Modern	unnumbered	3/4 term (7 mo.)	not counted yet	13.5 mm.	13.0 mm.
Casper Site	NC 625	3/4 term (c. 7 mo.)	11 + partial 12th[1]	13.8	13.8
Wardell Site[2]	Wardell - 2	near full-term	?12 + partial 13th	15.0	14.6
Wardell Site	Wardell - 3	near full-term	?13 + partial 14th	15.1	14.5
Wardell Site	Wardell - 1	near full-term	14 + partial 15th	15.1	14.4
Casper Site	NC 2484	near full-term	13 + partial 14th	18.8	18.7
Casper Site	NC 2124	near full-term	14 + partial 15th	19.2	18.5
Cactus Flower Site[3]	FS 1604 - 1	newborn	15 + partial 16th[4]	20.5	18.0
Modern	91-1.65	3-day-old newborn	15 + partial 16th	19.3	17.1[5]

[1] In each case the partial layer is the surface layer in the process of being deposited. Such layers are generally areally discontinuous in their early stages.

[2] See Frison (1973). Site approximately 900 years old, and is located near Big Piney in southwestern Wyoming.

[3] Specimen loaned by Mr. John Brumley, University of Calgary, Calgary, Alberta. Site is approximately 3,500 years old, and is located in southeastern Alberta.

[4] Specimen appears to have been a newborn, with some osteonization of cancellous interspaces as a result of static and kinetic loading of the limbs. As a result the inner strata are somewhat difficult to discern in comparison with prenatal materials.

[5] This is the deformed specimen already described. Arthrogryposis has markedly affected the lower limbs; however, the humerus appears normal. It is possible that the humerus is abnormally slender, but this cannot be determined at present.

possible age of the species (in years); leading to a suggestion that the number of layers corresponds to the age in years. Presumably the fetal periosteal layers are rapidly obscured during the early post-natal life of the calf, when static and kinetic loads are applied.

Fetal Dentition

A comparison of the mandibular dentitions of near full-term *B. bison antiquus* with full-term (stillborn) and 3-day-old *Bison bison bison* shows the former to display a considerably longer tooth row (Fig. 3.10; Fig. 3.11). This is manifested both in longer teeth and less crowding, particularly of dP_2 against dP_3. In general dP_4 of *B. bison antiquus* shows more openly curved crescents than does that of *B. b. bison*. The modern species thus shows a greater degree of dP_4 molarization, due not only to the increased closure of the crescents, but also to the strengthening and heightening of cross-cristae. The external styles on dP_4 tend to be higher in *B. b. bison*, extending to a level 13.5 mm. below the highest point of the tooth (cusp of second crescent). The corresponding distance in *B. bison antiquus* is 15.0 mm. The dP_2 and dP_3 show tighter closure of fossettes in the modern form than in its predecessor, again with greater development of cross-cristae. In particular, dP_3 in *B. b. bison* shows the development of a bridge between the metaconid and entoconid, completely closing a medial fossette. This fossette is not seen in *B. b. antiquus*, where the metaconid and entoconid remain far apart. This trend in dP_3 resembles the trend in P_4 described by Skinner and Kaisen (1947: 139-140), where expansion of the base of the metaconid and the development of a metastylid result in closure of the fossette in *Bison bison bison*. Measurements of fetal and newborn dentitions are presented in

TABLE 3.4 *Measurements of Fetal and Newborn Bison Mandibles*

Measurement[1]	Specimen: 91-1.2[2] (3-day)	91-2.1 (newborn)	NC 2512 (near	NC 2513 full	NC 2514[3] term)	
1. Total length	175.7	182.1				mm.
2. Total height	81.2					
3. Height at M_1 (unerupted)	34.8	37.8	28.5	28.5		
5. Length of diastema	60.1	c. 56.0				
8. Length of symphyseal surface	20.1	c. 20.0				
9. Height of coronoid process	31.0					
11. Widthe of articular process	31.3					
14. Width of ramus at M_1	15.7	15.6				
16. Width of mandibular condyle	20.7	20.5				
22. Length of tooth row, alveolar, dP_2 - dP_4	59.2	68.1		78.0		
23. Length of dP_2, alveolar	10.3	12.2		12.5		
24. Length of dP_3, alveolar	18.2	20.6		24.6		
25. Width of dP_3, greatest	8.5	9.6		9.5		
26. Length of dP_4, alveolar	34.2	38.3	41.0	42.4	44.0	
27. Width of dP_4, greatest	10.5	11.8	12.2	11.7	10.5	
28. Greatest height of central crescent of dP_4 above anterior lateral style	11.2	13.5	17.0	15.9	15.0	
29. Greatest height of central crescent of dP_4 above posterior lateral style	10.3	12.2	14.1	c. 15.0	15.2	
30. Height of mandible at middle of dP_4	39.3	41.5	38.5	36.6		

[1] Measurements 1-21 (several of these are not applicable to fetal mandibles and are not listed) are after Butler *et al.* (1971: 138). Measurements 22-30 have been added by the present author for the specific purpose of dealing with fetal and newborn calf mandibles.

[2] This is the 3-day-old calf jaw illustrated by Frison and Reher (1970: 50). Unfortunately, this jaw belongs to the deformed individual discussed earlier in the present paper. The mandibles in this individual have, with the rostrum, undergone asymmetric development. Both are shorter than newborn 91-2.1, from the same ranch. Fortunately, the eruption sequence and rate in 91-1.2 does not seem to have been affected.

[3] "91-" specimens are modern, while "NC-" specimens are from the Casper Site.

Table 3.4 .

The extent of eruption is essentially the same in the fossil and modern samples, with dP_2, dP_3, and dP_4 all well up from their alveoli. dP_2 is not yet fully erupted, however; and dP_4 is the most prominent tooth, suggesting eruption in reverse order during the fetal period. M_1 is present as a tooth bud in the modern specimens, with its crown approximately 5 mm. below the level of the alveolus. Unfortunately, M_1 is missing from all three fossil specimens, with the empty socket visible in NC 2513.

Metric Analysis of Selected Bones

A metric analysis of selected fetal bones is pre-

TABLE 3.5 *Measurements of Fetal Bones from the Casper Site*

Bone	Specimen No.	Minimum antero-posterior diameter (mm.)	Minimum transverse diameter (mm.)
Scapula	NC 2486	21.7 (neck)	9.6 (neck)
Scapula	unnumb.	19.7 (neck)	
Scapula	NC 2294	23.2 (neck)	12.1 (neck)
Scapula[1]	NC 2288	17.7 (neck)	8.6 (neck)
Radius	NC 240	13.4	17.6
Radius	NC 2268	12.8	16.6
Femur	NC 32	20.3	20.1
Femur[1]	NC 903	14.5	14.1
Tibia	NC 1288	15.3	18.6
		Length	Width
Sphenoid	NC 2124	30.3	64.2
Nasal[1]	NC 2471	56.3 +	22.0 +

[1] Small fetus (3/4 full-term).

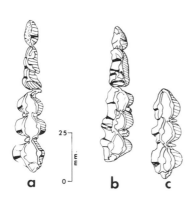

FIGURE 3.10 *Recent and fossil fetal bison dentitions: a. near full-term mandibular dentition of B. bison antiquus, NC 2513; b. mandibular dentition of stillborn B. bison bison, 91-2.1; c. dP4 of near full-term B. bison antiquus, NC 2514.*

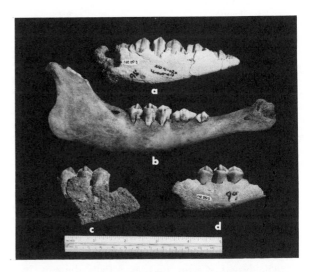

FIGURE 3.11 *Recent and fossil fetal bison dentitions: a. near full-term mandibular dentition of B. bison antiquus, NC 2513; b. mandible of stillborn B. bison bison, 91-2.1; c. dP4 of near full-term B. bison antiquus, NC 2514; d. dP4 of near full-term B. bison antiquus, NC 2512.*

sented in Table 3.5 . Since the epiphyses were
not preserved with the long bones only the mid-
shaft minimum diameters can be given. Mid-
shaft measurements of humeri may be found in
Table 3.3 . Modern and fossil fetal bison limb
bones are compared in Fig. 3.12 and 3.13 .

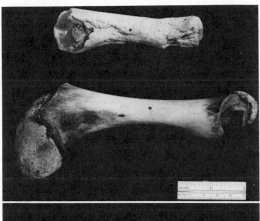

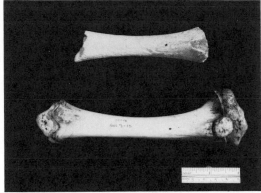

FIGURE 3.13 *Comparison of modern newborn and
fossil fetal bison limb bones. Upper:
left femora, B. bison antiquus (NC 32)
and B. bison bison (91-1.114). Lower:
right tibiae, B. bison antiquus (NC 1288)
and B. bison bison (91-1.100).*

Significance of Casper Site Fetal Remains

The presence of fetal remains at the Casper Site
raises questions about the season of the kill, as
population dynamics studies (Reher, C.A., this
volume) show this to have been an autumn event.
The prime calving season in modern bison at this
latitude is from April 15 to May 31 (McHugh
1958: 30). However, McHugh and many other
authors have noted that occasional calves are
dropped at virtually any season of the year. As
far as population dynamics are concerned, these
out-of-season calves are of little significance, for

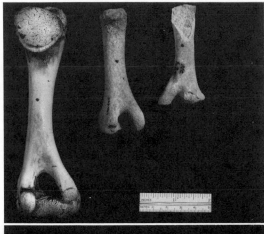

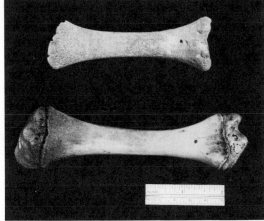

FIGURE 3.12 *Comparison of modern newborn and
fossil fetal bison limb bones. Upper:
right humeri, B. bison bison (91-1.65)
and B. bison subsp. (Wardell Site, c. A.D.
1,000, unnumbered); and left humerus,
B. bison antiquus, 3/4 full-term (NC
625). Lower: left radii, B. bison antiquus (NC 2268) and B. bison bison
(91-1.81).*

many if not all are deleted due to winter stresses they are too young to withstand. Thus subsequent year groups in a kill such as Casper show strong peaks of (n + 0.6)-year-olds with less temporal dispersion. Out-of-season births are also likely to include prematurely born calves and victims of prolonged gestation. Such calves are less likely to survive even under optimum conditions.

Given the relative abundance of mass bison kill sites on the plains it is likely that human predation also resulted in the significant deletion of out-of-season unborn calves. This clearly happened at Casper. Ewers (1955: 128) notes fall to have been in Late Prehistoric and early Historic times the prime hunting season. Consistent seasonality in mass kills would thus have a selective impact on the survival of unseasonal fetuses.

Fetuses at Casper were apparently removed from the uteri of the cows: the one cluster of bones noted above appears to have been a butchered unit, and fetal bones were widely scattered. Fetal material was accessible to scavengers, probably coyotes; a fetal hoof (NC 2469) and one-half of a cervical neural arch (NC 2468) were found in a coprolite.

Ewers (*ibid.*: 126) observed that among the Blackfoot "numerous calves were killed for children's robes and soft skin bags", and that in addition embryos were regularly checked in freshly killed cows to follow the progress of the seasons.

In conclusion there is no evidence from the fetal remains to contradict the evidence from population dynamics studies regarding the season of the kill. In fact, even the small fetal sample from Casper shows great variability in development: one fetus is only 3/4 developed, while the two others are nearly full-term.

AGING OF BISON FROM UPPER DENTITIONS

Several workers have published significant information regarding the aging of bison by various means. Skinner and Kaisen (1947: 143-146) provided a breakdown of bison dentitions into six relative wear categories. Unfortunately, they were unable to correlate these with absolute individual ages of the animals studied, as the latter data were not available. Fuller (1959) investigated the value of horns and teeth as age indicators, this time with some absolute data for individuals up to about 4 years old. He found the incisor-canine group and the styles of the molars to be of particular utility. Wasilewski (1967) determined that incisors wear more quickly in free-living bison than in bison under reserve conditions, a fact which should be considered in future selection of comparative data. Armstrong (1965) and Novakowski (1965) investigated the use of tooth cementum stratification as an aid to aging, with very good results. The former found a significant correlation between lower canine root annuli and age; while the latter found annuli in the roots of premolars and molars to be of utility in aging animals over 4 1/2 years old.

Frison and Reher (1970) on the basis of modern and fossil specimens established an eruption and wear sequence for mandibular teeth from newborn animals to individuals older than ten years. The present effort is an attempt to establish a preliminary wear sequence for *B. bison antiquus* on the basis of upper dentitions from the Casper Site.

The sample available for description is limited by the population structure of the Casper herd. A study of the mandibles (Reher, C.A., this volume) revealed no 1.6-year-olds in a sample of 69 left and 66 right elements (excluding fetal mandibles). In addition, no upper fetal dentitions were available, although 3 mandibles were recovered. Since we are dealing with an extinct subspecies, I have decided to describe only an individual newborn specimen from the modern subspecies to fill the second gap. I prefer at this time not to lump modern and fossil samples together on a larger scale. The 0.6-year-old sample has been augmented through the loan of a superb *B. bison antiquus* calf specimen from the Wasden Site in Idaho. This site is later than Casper (approximately 8,000 years B.P. as opposed to 10,000 years B.P.) but the bison appear morphologically similar. I am grateful to Mr. B. Robert Butler, Idaho State University, for the loan of the specimen.

At the present time we are preparing for comparison material from the Olsen-Chubbuck, Finley, Agate Basin, and other Paleo-Indian sites. Data from these sites will eventually allow us to close the gaps in the present analysis of *B. bison antiquus.*

Given the sampling problem, I remain cognizant of the fact that the age in years assigned to the older specimens to be described must remain tentative.

While the Casper Site sample included individuals of many ages, they were clustered in yearly groups due to the periodicity of the calving peaks and the probable attrition of out-of-season calves. The description will thus follow these groups in an autumn kill situation.

Age Groups

Group I: Newborn or Full-term Fetal. No near full-term fetal or newborn upper dentitions are known from the Casper Site sample. Therefore, a modern 3-day-old skull (no. 91-1.1) was used. This skull, as noted before, is from a deformed animal; however, the eruption sequence seems normal for the lower jaws, and there is no reason to believe it is unusual for the uppers.

In the 3-day-old, DP^2, DP^3, and DP^4 are all in the process of eruption, having cleared their alveoli to a considerable degree. DP^3 is the most fully erupted with its anterior crescent peak (paracone) 14 mm. above the level of the alveolus. The anterior crescent of DP^4 is nearly 12 mm. above the alveolus, but the posterior crescent has just barely cleared the level of it. M^1 is visible in

a large partly open tooth budding alveolus and shows a slight posteromedial deflection. During growth of the skull the posterior end of the tooth swings laterally from this position.

Extremely slight wear is visible on the DP^3 paracone, but it is not enough to break through the enamel. The length of tooth row (DP^2 − DP^4) is 66 mm., which is probably a low figure for the modern subspecies.

Group II: 0.6 Years Old. In animals of the first year there is a fair range of variation in metric attributes and degree of eruption of teeth; nevertheless, a clustering of these attributes is clear.

DP^2 is well into wear, with a sloping planar facet. In some individuals the slope of the facet is from front to rear and in others the reverse. The enclosed fosette in less worn specimens may be a single long, narrow oval area; however, most 0.6-year-olds have progressed beyond this stage and show division on the area into two fossettes, the anterior one being the smaller of the two. DP^2 roots are visible at the alveolus.

The external mid-crown height varies from 10.0 to 13.8 mm. (N = 11; $\overline{X}$ = 12.1).

DP^3 is well into wear. This molariform tooth with two crescents shows an uneven wear surface, with a cross-peak at the middle of each crescent. The tooth is thus bilophodont. The roots are visible at the alveolus. Metric data from DP^3's are summarized in Table 3.6 .

DP^4 is well into wear, with a worn lingual style prominently visible in most specimens. The style was unworn in two specimens of a sample of seventeen teeth. The uneven wear surface is more accentuated in DP^4 than in DP^3, giving this tooth as well a bilophodont appearance. Metric data from DP^4's are summarized in Table 3.7 .

M^1 is almost fully erupted, and is starting to wear. Limited wear is visible on the anterior face of the first crescent cross-loph. There is slight, hard-to-see wear on the posterior face of the same loph. No wear is visible on the posterior crescent,

TABLE 3.6 *Metric Data from 0.6-year-old Upper Dentitions of* B. bison antiquus: *DP³*

Specimen	Side		Alveolar length	Greatest width	Greatest length of wear facet	External mid-crown height
Wasden 80,500	L		22.7 mm.	20.0.mm.	26.1 mm.	14.4 mm.
	R		23.5	20.6	24.9	14.6
Casper NC 1859	L		26.4	20.3	26.9	17.2
	R		25.0	20.7	28.1	16.3
NC 2318	L		24.2	20.4	29.2	15.5
	R	c.	25.0	20.8	29.2	14.4
NC 12	L		24.1	17.9	26.3	15.0
NC 1306	L		23.6	17.3	26.1	14.6
NC 982	R		23.4	18.9	26.9	14.3
NC 1941	R		23.2	18.3	26.5	12.1
NC 1802	L		23.1	17.6	27.6	13.7
	R		22.1	18.6	27.1	14.2
NC 2317	L		22.8	18.7	25.0	13.9
NC 1955	L		22.7	19.8	27.0	15.0
	R		22.4	18.5 +		15.0
NC 1580	R			18.9		
	$\overline{X}$		23.6	19.2	26.9	14.7

TABLE 3.7 *Metric Data from 0.6-year-old Upper Dentitions of* B. bison antiquus: *DP⁴*

Specimen	Side		Alveolar length	Greatest width[1]	Greatest length of wear facet	Height of lingual style	
Wasden 80,500	L		22.2 mm.	24.6 mm.	27.5 mm.	11.3 mm.	(worn)
	R		23.2	24.6	27.5	8.5 +	(worn)
Casper NC 1859	L		25.6	22.9	29.9	12.0	(worn)
	R		24.6	23.1	28.5	11.5 +	(unworn)
NC 1941	R		25.5	23.4	30.1	10.0	(unworn)
NC 1616	L		25.1	24.2	29.8	11.8	(worn)
NC 1955	L	c.	23.0	25.0	29.1	10.1	(worn)
	R	c.	23.9	25.1	29.8	11.0	(worn)
NC 12	L		23.6	21.7	30.8	7.9	(worn)
NC 1306	L		23.0	21.3	29.5	12.6	(worn)
NC 2318	L		23.0		31.2		(worn)
	R				30.4	9.3 +	(worn)
NC 1802	L		22.9	21.3	30.1	10.6	(worn)
	R		22.6	21.8	29.9	10.9 +	(worn)
NC 1580	R		22.3	21.8		9.5	(worn)
NC 2319	L		21.2	22.2	29.1	12.2	(worn)
	R		21.9	21.0 +	28.8 +		(worn)
	$\overline{X}$		23.6	22.9	30.1	10.6	

[1] taken at base of anterior crescent.

TABLE 3.8 *Metric Data from 0.6-year-old Upper Dentitions of* B. bison antiquus: *M¹*

Specimen	Side	Alveolar length	Alveolar width	Crown length	Crown width	Stylar cusp level, style to central valley of crown
Wasden 80,500	L	34.1 mm.	20.0 mm.	36.7 mm.	17.1 mm.	11.7 mm.
	R	36.6	19.8	36.0	17.2	11.7
Casper NC 1802	R	36.5	19.2	36.9	18.2	13.5
NC 1941	R	36.2	18.3	35.9	16.5	19.0
NC 1859	L	35.5	20.0	34.8	16.2	c. 14.0
NC 2317	L	35.0	20.0	34.0	17.6	11.9
	R	34.9	19.2	33.8	16.4	11.6
NC 2318	L	34.8	21.1	36.5	19.9	
	R			34.9	19.2	
NC 1003	R	34.6	19.9	35.0	19.1	14.0
NC 70	R	33.4	17.7	33.5	18.8	13.8
NC 1306	L	33.3		33.5		14.2
NC 12	L	33.2	20.2	33.3	18.8	17.2
NC 1616	R	33.0	19.8	33.3	18.3	16.0
NC 1955	L	32.2	20.5	34.2	19.1	
	R	31.0	21.5	33.3		
$\overline{X}$		34.2	19.8	34.7	18.0	14.05

which is not far above the level of the alveolus. The alveolar margin descends in a posterior direction such that it is closer to the crown in the posterior half of the tooth. A lingual style is barely visible at the level of the alveolus, or is still obscured by bone. The distance from the top of this style to the crown in the valley separating the two crescents was measured, and appears with other metric data in Table 3.8 . This stylar cusp level shows more variation than was expected, which clearly reduces its value as an age indicator in the unworn period. However, measurements of the height of the style once in wear are more useable in that the position of stylar base is quite stable.

The length of tooth row from DP² to M¹ is quite consistent, with a range of 98.4 to 109.6 mm. (N = 8; $\overline{X}$ = 104.3). The longest rows are quite straight, and the shortest ones strongly curved. Variation in the length of the tooth row thus is a function of palatal and maxillary bone growth as well as absolute tooth size. The curvature is most strongly marked in the anterior portion of the tooth row; thus for best consistency palatal width measurements should be taken at the level of M¹.

Group III: 1.6 Years Old. No animals of this age are present in the Casper Site sample.

Group IV: 2.6 Years Old. Two specimens apparently of this age are present in the Casper Site sample, each with essentially complete dentition. One specimen consists of a group of associated teeth freed from their sockets, through deterioration of the maxillary bone (NC 1727).

DP² has been shed, and P² is fully erupted with slight wear on its highest cusps. P² displays a strongly curved enamel corpus with a single wear crescent. DP³ has been shed, and P³ is erupting: however, it remains at a level noticeably below P² and does not show any wear. DP⁴ is a very worn remnant atop erupting P⁴. The roots of DP⁴ are quite variable, in some cases being considerably resorbed as P⁴ moves upward. Metric data are

TABLE 3.9 *Metric Data from 2.6-year-old Upper Dentitions of* B. bison antiquus: *DP*^{4}

Specimen	Side	Crown length	Crown width	Height of lingual style
NC 1727	L	26.6 mm.	19.9 mm.	8.2 mm.
	R	27.4	20.3	7.6
NC 2324	L	26.2		
	R	26.3	21.3	2.9

TABLE 3.10 *Metric Data from 2.6-year-old Upper Dentitions of* B. bison antiquus: *Molars*

Tooth	Specimen	Side	Alveolar length	Alveolar width	Crown length	Crown width	Stylar cusp level, style to central valley of crown
M^1	NC 2324	L	28.1 mm.				
		R	30.7		35.0 mm.	20.8 mm.	
	NC 1727	L	31.6	21.7 mm.	35.2	20.8	8.3 mm.
		R	32.1	21.1	34.9	21.0	8.3
M^2	NC 2324	L					
		R	38.0		40.0	19.9	
	NC 1727	L	36.1	21.0	37.4	19.2	18.9
		R	35.6	22.0	37.0	20.4	19.3
M^3	NC 2324	L					
		R	35.8		34.3		
	NC 1727	L	33.0	21.2	32.4	20.0	22.5
		R	33.4	21.0 +	32.6	21.7	

summarized in Table 3.9 . Molar metric data are in Table 3.10 .

M^1 shows a worn but relatively fresh bilophodont wear surface. A lingual style is visible at the level of the alveolus. The greatest external crown height (of the entire tooth) is approximately 50 mm.

M^2 is bilophodont and in wear, with only slight wear as yet on the posterior face of the posterior cross-loph. A lingual style is present but remains well below the level of the alveolus. The greatest external enamel height is approximately 67.5 mm.

M^3 is erupting, with its anterior loph nearly to the level of the crown of M^2. There is slight or no wear on the highest cusps of the anterior cross-loph. External enamel height is approximately 70.5 mm.

Group V: 3.6 Years Old. From this point on, I am less certain of the ages of the animals described, although I am able to place teeth into relative wear categories. The problem is simply one of sample size: while there are many animals apparently in the 3.6 to 9.6 and higher range, there may be gaps in the sample at specific years. These would be hard to document at this early stage of analysis.

One specimen, NC 1809, has characteristics which show it to be older than the group designated as 2.6 years old. However, the differences are small enough that I do not feel it likely that the animal is more than one year older. In comparison with several older individuals, this specimen is extremely large, particularly in the premolar series. This I suspect to be due to sexual dimor-

TABLE 3.11 *Metric Data from 3.6-year-old Upper Dentitions of* B. bison antiquus: *Molars*

Tooth	Specimen	Side	Alveolar length	Alveolar width	Crown length	Crown width	Style Height
M^1	NC 1809	L	28.8 mm.	25.2 mm.	35.3 mm.	24.5 mm.	27.6 mm.
		R	28.0	25.4	34.4	23.7	
M^2	NC 1809	L	35.6	27.9	41.2	21.3	not worn
		R	36.4	28.0	40.7	23.1	not worn
M^3	NC 1809	L	37.7	25.0	37.0	21.6	not worn
		R	37.7	23.5	36.8	21.3	not worn

phism; perhaps this set of teeth comes from a large male.

P^1 is not present in the sample. P^2 and P^3 are both well into wear, but they retain fresh and prominent cusps. The P^2 fossette is open to the rear of the tooth. The lingual style on M^1 is beginning to wear, and the tooth is losing the prominent cusps noted before as the occlusal surface approaches a more planar condition. M^2 and M^3 are still markedly bilophodont, and both crescents of M^3 are showing wear. The style on M^2 is about 9 mm. below the level of the valley between cross-lophs, and that on M^3 still 14 mm. down.

Protocone heights for the three molars are, M^1: 39.5 mm.; M^2: 59.2 mm.; M^3: 65.8 mm. The roots of M^3 are widely open and only partially formed.

Metric data concerning the molars of NC 1809 appear in Table 3.11.

Group VII: 4.6 Years Old and Over. Above approximate age 3.6 we encounter problems of several kinds relating to tooth wear, and the eruption of teeth can no longer guide us in any way. There is some variation in the initial size of teeth; this will affect size at a given wear stage. It is also probable that different animals wear at slightly different rates: this is especially noticeable in the shape of the wear facets on teeth. Some individuals, for instance, tend to "shear off" their premolars to some extent, developing steeply slanting facets on them. In other individuals the facets are nearly level.

Given these problems, at this time I can only summarize the characters of tentative groups in the Casper Site sample, and hope that future information will add precision to these statements. Assuming no major discontinuities in age classes, the following groups seem to exist:

VI-a, 4.6 years old. P^3 and P^4 still noticeably cusped and cross-ridged. M^2 style not in wear. M^2 and M^3 still strongly bilophodont; wear surface on M^3 still discontinuous, spreading from high cusp areas.

VI-b, 5.6 years old. Premolars flatter on wear surfaces. M^2 and M^3 still bilophodont, but less so. M^2 style not in wear. M^3 fully in wear except for lingual style.

VI-c, 6.6 years old. M^2 style in wear or (rarely) very nearly so. Wear surfaces quite planar except for M^3, which remains bilophodont.

VI-d, 7.6 years old. Wear surfaces essentially flat, with some cross-ridging in M^3. Lingual style on M^3 well visible above alveolus, but not yet in wear.

VI-e, 8.6 years old or more. All styles well into wear. M^1 style reduced, almost completely worn away.

VI-f, 9.6 years old or more. Fossettes of M^1 very small and nearly worn away. M^1 starting to cup out as fossettes cease to retard wear in center of tooth.

M^1 protocone heights from specimens assigned to these tentative groups are summarized in Table 3.12.

TABLE 3.12 *Upper Age Groups of* B. bison antiquus: M^1 *Protocone Heights*

Specimen	Side	Estimated Age	M^1 protocone height
NC 2561	R	4.6	26.8 mm.
NC 1757	R	4.6	30.1
NC 2078	R	5.6	31.0
NC 1808	R	6.6	22.0
NC 1832	L	6.6	25.5
NC 2327	L	6.6	20.1
NC 2560	R	6.6	19.0
NC 2451	R	8.6	16.1
NC 1954	R	9.6 +	9.3
NC 2370	R	9.6 +	9.2

Summary. Although complicated by the absence of key age groups, the upper dentitions from the Casper Site *B. bison antiquus* sample do fall into recognizable groups based upon wear and eruption schedules. The 0.6-year-old age group is easy to recognize and is well represented in the sample. In older individuals problems of variable wear and variable stylar development are undoubtedly soluble, but a larger sample is needed for their resolution.

I heartily encourage workers with samples of upper dentitions of bison to examine them closely in the light of possible individual aging. To date, most studies have been done with mandibles, thought by some to be more precise in terms of eruption and wear schedules. Only through a comprehensive study of upper dentitions may we assess the validity of such an hypothesis.

CRANIAL WIDTH AND SEX OF *BISON BISON ANTIQUUS*

When the project here reported was begun, it was hoped that animals could be accurately assigned to age groups and, as a result, growth curves could be drawn to show the divergence of the sexes in several cranial measurements.

As we saw in the preceding section, it is not at this time possible to be absolutely certain of the age of these bison on the basis of the upper denti-

tions, beyond about 4.6 years. In addition, 1.6-year-olds are absent, leaving a gap at a vitally important stage in sexual dimorphogenesis. Future studies will certainly allow resolution of these sampling problems.

This being the case, the relationship between cranial width and sex is reported here in very preliminary form, it being considered better not to carry the same possible error in age through many plots of cranial measurements. For the purpose of illustration, then, a graph of Skinner and Kaisen's measurement 14 (cranial width between horn cores and orbits) against age is presented (Fig. 3.14).

The Graph

It can be seen from the graph that there is indeed significant sexual dimorphism in cranial breadth. The three large males (NC 2323, NC 2326 and NC 2370) appear at the top of the graph. The rest of the mature sample is arrayed along a single line suggesting that females are represented.

At Casper and Wasden all of the 0.6-year-olds exhibit approximately the same cranial breadth. This was first interpreted as an indication that sexual dimorphogenesis was not yet under way. However, two 0.3 or 0.4-year-olds of *B. bison* ssp. have recently been prepared from the Olsen-Chubbuck Site sample (currently under study by the author).

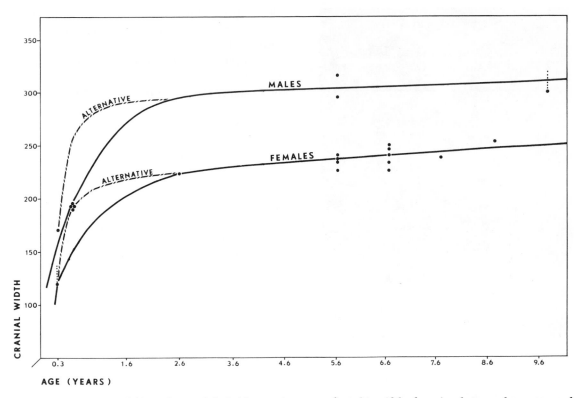

FIGURE 3.14 *Sexual dimorphogenesis in* B. bison antiquus *as reflected in width of cranium between horn cores and orbits. The sample is entirely from the Casper Site with the exception of one 0.6-year-old from the Wasden Site, Idaho, and two 0.3-year-olds from the Olsen-Chubbuck Site. The latter are viewed for the present as* B. bison *subsp.*

They differ considerably in size and give rise to at least three alternative hypotheses:

1. sexual dimorphogenesis was under way by age 0.3 to 0.4 years in *B. bison antiquus*; or
2. the two individuals indicate that young bison born out of season did occasionally survive; or
3. dwarfs were present in the population.

The two Olsen-Chubbuck specimens (Univ. of Colorado colls., nos. 10,958 and 10,895) have their upper and lower dentitions in virtually identical stages of eruption, suggesting that the two bison are of the same age. This makes the second hypothesis extremely unlikely; therefore, the two

may well be of different sexes. At present the sex of the Casper/Wasden specimens is not certain, but they are most likely to be males (Fig. 3.14). Two apparently male 0.6-year-olds (Wasden no. 80,500 and Casper no. NC 2317) are shown in Figure 3.15 .

The upper portion of the growth line for female *B. bison antiquus* generated by these data is reasonably well founded, and probably has at least limited predictive or comparative value for studies at other sites. The line for males is of little use in these terms at present. The addition of data in the critical 1.6 to 4.6-year-old interval will be necessary before the value of the growth lines can be

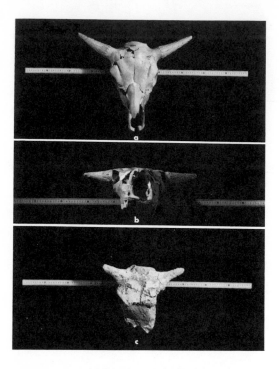

FIGURE 3.15 B. bison antiquus, *0.6-year-olds: a and
b. Wasden Site, Idaho (ISU 80,500);
c. Casper Site, Wyoming (NC 2317).*

upgraded.

Discussion

It is important to note that old females, as cranial width and orbital protrusion increase and horn cores increase in size and rugosity, tend to resemble males of *B. bison bison* (Fig. 3.16). The horn cores of a female *B. bison antiquus* in this area of the subspecies' range show little or no proximal depression, depart from the skull at a moderately posterior angle, rise well above the plane of the frontals, and show a distal twist to the horn core tips (Fig. 3.16, 3.17a). However, the burr at the base of the horn core seldom if ever reaches the rugose state of that in the male; and the degree of frontal midline fusion is a reasonable indicator of the relative maturity of the animal. Metric data from *B. bison antiquus* female crania (over 0.6 years old) are presented in Table 3.13 .

The degree of sexual dimorphism recorded at Casper differs to some extent from that reported by Chandler (1916) for *B. bison antiquus.* However, Chandler's specimens were from California (females) and Oregon (one male in addition to the California male sample). The females described by Chandler resembled the males in most respects except for the possession of slender horn cores. Cranial measurements were otherwise uniformly smaller, but of similar proportions. The Casper Site females display a more "northern" phenotype than the California *antiquus,* which accords with the clinal variation hypothesis proposed earlier in this paper. Thus the Casper females resemble male specimen NC 2323 in horn core characteristics, rather than more typically "southern" *antiquus* NC 2326. This fact serves to reinforce the suggested intermediate nature of the Casper population, which appears to lie *in terms of the males* just on the *antiquus* side of the *B. bison occidentalis/B. bison antiquus* dichotomy.

Of further interest in this regard is a damaged female skull from the Agate Basin Site in eastern Wyoming (Fig. 3.17b,c). Dates on Agate Basin and Folsom point levels from this and other sites suggest an age of as much as 10,000 years for this material. The female skull has been considerably restored and is noticeably asymmetrical in horn-core characteristics, apparently due to problems encountered in restoration. It is nonetheless clear that this female also shows a "northern" phenotypic character in the rise of horn cores above the level of the frontals. Metric data are included in Table 3.13 . The male phenotype at Agate Basin is unknown.

Metric data for 0.3-year-olds from the Olsen-Chubbuck Site and 0.6-year-olds from Casper and Wasden are presented in Table 3.14 .

TABLE 3.13 *Measurements of Female* B. bison antiquus *(in mm.)*

Standard Measurement	NC 2320	NC 2560	NC 2322	NC 2321	NC 2324	NC 2325	NC 2078
1. Spread of horn cores, tip to tip		634	*616*		*530*	*554*	
2. Greatest spread of cores on outside curve		646	*636*		*530*	*554*	
3. Core length on upper curve, tip to burr		190	*220*		*165*	*148*	
4. Core length on lower curve, tip to burr		217	*225*		*180*		
5. Length, tip of core to upper base at burr		185	*200*		*150*	*144*	
6. Vertical diameter of horn core		63.5	*54*			*67*	
7. Circumference of horn core at base		203	*175*				
8. Greatest width at auditory openings	*209*[1]	*227*	*245*	235	*224*	216.5	
9. Width of condyles	115.5	130.3	111.7	132.7	111.8	117.3	
10. Depth, occipital crest to upper border of foramen magnum	98	96.2	83.5	90.6	*60 +*	*105.6*	
11. Depth, occipital crest to lower border of foramen magnum	124.5	129.5	122	120.1	*105 +*	*137.5*	
12. Transverse diameter of horn core		61	*58*	*60*	*50*	58	
13. Width between bases of horn cores	*170 +*	196.5	191.5	191	*166*	164	
14. Width of cranium between horn cores and orbits	227	246	*235*	239	*224*	*235*	
15. Greatest postorbital width	254	283	284	281			
16. Anterior orbital width at notch	199	210.5	221	218		*175 +*	
17. Width of skull at masseteric processes above M[1]	172	170	190	171	*152*	154	
18. Rostral width at maxillary/premaxillary suture	*109*	105	107	*110*		93	
19. P[2] - M[3], alveolar length	160.5	158		156.5	167	158	155.3
20. M[1] - M[3], alveolar length	99	101.5	87.6	103.3	110.5	98	96.9
O-P. Length, occipital crest to tip of premaxilla		*505*	*515 +*				
F-P. Basilar length, foramen magnum to tip of premaxilla		*479*	*482 +*				
O-T. Length, occipital crest to tip of nasals		*413*			*394*		
O-N. Length, occipital crest to nasal-frontal suture	*199*	225	204.5	*240*	*170*	193	
M-P. Length beyond P[2] to tip of premaxilla		*137*					
N-T. Length of nasals		*188*			*224*		
21. Angle of posterior divergence of horn core	*68°*	*72°*	*66°*	72°	*77°*	*70° +*	
22. Angle of proximal horn core depression		11°	*10°*				
Index of horn core curvature		117	*112*		*120*		
Index of horn core compression		104	*95*			*115*	
Index of horn core proportion		*108.5*	*126*				
Index of horn core length		77	*94*		*74*	*63*	
Index of orbital protrusion	89	89	*83*	85			

[1] Numbers in italics represent close estimates in cases of limited damage.

TABLE 3.13 (Cont'd.) *Measurements of Female* B. bison antiquus *(in mm.)*

Standard Measurement	NC 2451	NC 1954	NC 2327	NC 1863	NC 1832	NC 1916	NC 1883
1. Spread of horn cores, tip to tip		660					580
2. Greatest spread of cores on outside curve		670					600
3. Core length on upper curve, tip to burr		206.5					
4. Core length on lower curve, tip to burr		*243*[1]					
5. Length, tip of core to upper base at burr		180					*170*
6. Vertical diameter of horn core		*70*	65				72.9
7. Circumference of horn core at base			204				228
8. Greatest width at auditory openings	230	239	228				238.5
9. Width of condyles		124.5	124				124
10. Depth, occipital crest to upper border of foramen magnum		94.5	102				97.5
11. Depth, occipital crest to lower border of foramen magnum		138.3					131
12. Transverse diameter of horn core		64	62.5				73.6
13. Width between bases of horn cores		218	218				
14. Width of cranium between horn cores and orbits		257	223.9			251	242
15. Greatest postorbital width		308	273				295
16. Anterior orbital width at notch		215	210				215
17. Width of skull at masseteric processes above M^1		167	165	175.3	165.8	184	
18. Rostral width at maxillary/premaxillary suture		110	111	113.9		*120*	
19. P^2 - M^3, alveolar length		147.8	156.5	157.2	146.8		
20. M^1 - M^3, alveolar length	91	93	97	99.4	93.8	*100*	*100*
O-P. Length, occipital crest to tip of premaxilla		525	498			535	555
F-P. Basilar length, foramen magnum to tip of premaxilla		483					502
O-T. Length, occipital crest to tip of nasals			415				445
O-N. Length, occipital crest to nasal-frontal suture		245	215				225
M-P. Length beyond P^2 to tip of premaxilla		142	128	125.3			
N-T. Length of nasals			200				220
21. Angle of posterior divergence of horn core		71°	70°				75°
22. Angle of proximal horn core depression		20°	12°				
Index of horn core curvature		*135*					
Index of horn core compression		*109*	104				99
Index of horn core proportion							
Index of horn core length		81					
Index of orbital protrusion		83	82				82

[1] Numbers in italics represent close estimates in cases of limited damage.

TABLE 3.13 (Cont'd.) *Measurements of Female* B. bison antiquus *(in mm.)*

Standard Measurement	NC 1808	NCU 10	NC 1799	NC 1845	NC 1882	NC 1751	Agate Basin
1. Spread of horn cores, tip to tip					610		675
2. Greatest spread of cores on outside curve					620		685
3. Core length on upper curve, tip to burr							*205*
4. Core length on lower curve, tip to burr					240		*240*
5. Length, tip of core to upper base at burr					180		*190*
6. Vertical diameter of horn core					65.2		*70*
7. Circumference of horn core at base							217
8. Greatest width at auditory openings							*290*
9. Width of condyles	116.5				122.2		
10. Depth, occipital crest to upper border of foramen magnum					95		
11. Depth, occipital crest to lower border of foramen magnum					135		
12. Transverse diameter of horn core					60.2		66
13. Width between bases of horn cores							220
14. Width of cranium between horn cores and orbits							265
15. Greatest postorbital width							
16. Anterior orbital width at notch							
17. Width of skull at masseteric processes above M^1				172	176.8		
18. Rostral width at maxillary/premaxillary suture							
19. P^2 - M^3, alveolar length	169.3	157.5	157.8	159.5	164.2	160	
20. M^1 - M^3, alveolar length	104.9	97.5	95.1	96.1	102.2	99.5	
O-P. Length, occipital crest to tip of premaxilla							
F-P. Basilar length, foramen magnum to tip of premaxilla							
O-T. Length, occipital crest to tip of nasals							
O-N. Length, occipital crest to nasal-frontal suture							*157*
M-P. Length beyond P^2 to tip of premaxilla							
N-T. Length of nasals							
21. Angle of posterior divergence of horn core					*68°*1		75°
22. Angle of proximal horn core depression							0°
Index of horn core curvature					133		*126*
Index of horn core compression					108		*106*
Index of horn core proportion							*94.5*
Index of horn core length							*93*
Index of orbital protrusion							

[1] Numbers in italics represent close estimates in cases of limited damage.

TABLE 3.14 *Measurements of 0.3-year-old* B. bison *subsp. from the Olsen-Chubbuck Site, Colorado; and of 0.6-year-old* B. bison antiquus *from the Casper Site, Wyoming, and the Wasden Site, Idaho (in mm.).*

Measurement	Olsen-Chubbuck Site		Casper Site			Wasden Site
	10,958	10,895	NC 1955	NC 2317	NC 2318	80,500
1. Spread of horn cores, tip to tip		284		*355*[1]	*415*	477
2. Greatest spread of cores on outside curve		284		*355*	*415*	477
3. Core length on upper curve, tip to burr	30	60		*90*	*122*	145
4. Core length on lower curve, tip to burr	27	60		*95*	*125*	155
5. Length, tip of core to upper base at burr	30	60		*88*	*122*	144
6. Vertical diameter of horn core	22.5	31		35	*35*	53.5
7. Circumference of horn core at base	59	102		120	*130*	176
8. Greatest width at auditory openings		145	154	158	155	
9. Width of condyles		93.5			95	
10. Depth, occipital crest to upper border of foramen magnum					62	
11. Depth, occipital crest to lower border of foramen magnum					86	
12. Transverse diameter of horn core	22	33		39	45	56
13. Width between bases of horn cores		141		124	114	*167*
14. Width of cranium between horn cores and orbits	*133* +	170	*182* +	194	195	194.5
15. Greatest postorbital width	*140*	184	*205*	204	*200*	207
16. Anterior orbital width at notch	*114*	137	152	148		147
17. Width of skull at masseteric processes above M[1]	101	110	132	136	136	130.5
18. Rostral width at maxillary/premaxillary suture	61	66	*72*		85	*74.5*
19. dP[2] - M[1], alveolar length	(M[1] not erupted)		*98*	96.8	107	102.5
crown length	(M[1] not erupted)		*97*	96.3	106	100
20. M[1], alveolar length	(M[1] not erupted)		*31.5*		36	35.5
crown length	(M[1] not erupted)		*35*		36	36
O-P. Overall length, occipital crest to tip of premaxilla		350			360	402
F-P. Basilar length, foramen magnum to tip of premaxilla		337			331	
O-T. Length, occipital crest to tip of nasals		280			325	325
O-N. Length, occipital crest to nasal/frontal suture		155		*150*	*153*	*173*
M-P. Length beyond dP[2] to tip of premaxilla	91.5	104.5			83	113
N-T. Length of nasals		125			*172*[2]	152
21. Angle of posterior divergence of horn core		55°		80°	73°	64°
22. Angle of proximal horn core depression		-10°		5°	0°	4°

[1] Numbers in italics are approximate. The estimates are particularly suspect in the case of Casper Site horn cores, where considerable exfoliation has occurred. Estimates on cranial width measurements are usually quite close to the true readings.

[2] There has been some post-mortem deformation here and this reading is probably too high.

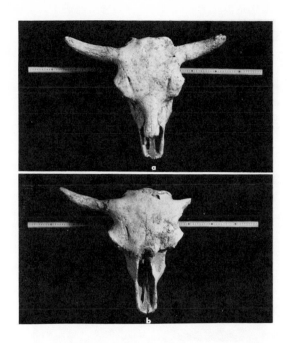

FIGURE 3.16 *Female* B. bison antiquus *skulls from the Casper Site: a. 6.6-year-old (NC 2560), showing constricted nasals; b. 9.6-year-old (or more) (NC 1954), showing increased cranial breadth and orbital protrusion with increased age.*

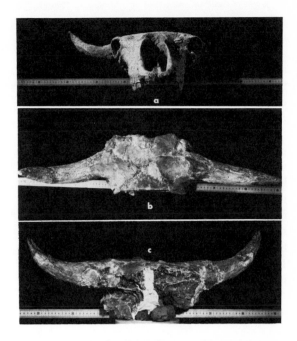

FIGURE 3.17 *Female skulls of* B. bison antiquus: *a. anterior view of 9.6 (or more)-year-old from the Casper Site (NC 1954); b and c. dorsal and anterior views of female from the Agate Basin Site, Wyoming (unnumbered).*

PALEOPATHOLOGY OF THE CASPER SITE BISON

Studies of bison kill populations almost invariably result in the discovery of a few pathological specimens; however, these are seldom recorded in any detail. This is unfortunate, as recent advances in related fields make it possible for us to generate interesting hypotheses about the life style of the bison from their pathologies.

Geist (1971) has suggested that along with ungulate dispersal and speciation goes specialization of combat and display adaptations. Without going into a discussion of the theory, I will suggest that if any sort of change in display and combat is going on, it should be reflected in a change in the location and nature of bone damage. This suggestion was first made to me by Mr. George Zeimens, a colleague at the University of Wyoming, and I feel it to be a very promising one. Detailed analyses of the occurrence of such pathologies are warranted.

In addition, the analysis of genetic anomalies may give us an idea of the selective pressures and degree of inbreeding affecting a given population. Such information may help us determine the extent of gene flow in bison herds of past millenia.

Anomalies of the Dentition

Early in the analysis of mandibles from the Casper Site it was noted that an unusual number of them possessed tooth abnormalities, and that abnormalities of several types were present. Both upper and lower dentitions were affected. The anomalies are listed below together with the nature and extent of their occurrence. This subject certainly will require further study; therefore the present remarks must be considered preliminary.

Shear Mouth. One lower dentition (NC 2320) shows a well developed shear mouth in which the left incisors are quite deeply worn, and the right incisors only slightly worn. The overall wear surface thus slants downward to the left, with the surfaces progressively more worn in that direction. Shear mouth is documented for horses (Colyer 1936) where there is an upper incisor complement; however, its occurrence in bovids, where the lower incisors wear against a premaxillary pad, is far less common.

Congenital Absence of Teeth. No tooth absences were noted in the upper dentition. However, in the mandibular row we have cases of missing P_2 and missing P_3. P_2 is missing from 4 mandibles, 2 lefts (nos. 10 and 14) and 2 rights (nos. 33 and 64). The mandibles cannot be matched into pairs. One such individual (no. 10) shows expansion of the tissue lateral to the root of P_3, causing a swelling along the side of the mandible (Fig. 3.18a). This was apparently due to a food injury (see below) and does not seem to have caused the loss of P_2; no trace of a filled alveolus is visible.

P_3 is missing in one specimen, mandible no. 7 (Fig. 3.18b). In response to this anomaly P_2 has moved posteriad and leans somewhat backward, partially filling the gap.

Improper Eruption of Teeth. A very common anomaly class in the Casper sample (and in other bison samples) is the over-crowding of molars and premolars such that the crown of one cuts into the adjacent crown, often to a distance of one to two millimeters. This is a common anomaly in

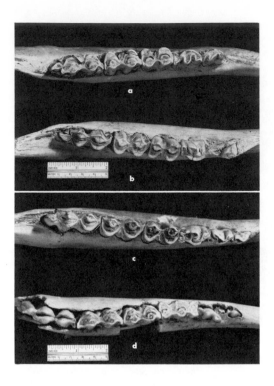

FIGURE 3.18 *Casper Site* Bison *dental anomalies: a. congenital absence of P_2 and lateral swelling (Mand. no. 10); b. congenital absence of P_3 and posteriad deflection of P_2 (Mand. no. 7); c. posteroexternal rotation of P_2 (Mand. no. 103); d. mediad deflection of P_3 (Mand. no. 77).*

ungulates (Colyer 1936: several illustrations) and seems to cause little discomfort to the animal, as chewing and wear show no great asymmetry.

More noticeable is the case of posteroexternal rotation of P_2, such that the tooth slants somewhat outward and backward, with the posterior portion of its crown lateral to the anterior portion of P_3 (Fig. 3.18c). This is a variable trait, which shows up in at least 8 left and 9 right mandibles (including 3 pairs).

One mandible (no. 77) shows rotation of P_3 such that the anterior end of the tooth is deflected medially (Fig. 3.18d). This seems to have been caused by the late retention of a broken deciduous root lateral to the anterior end of the erupting tooth.

A rather frequent and certainly most noteworthy occurrence is the procumbence of M_3 in several specimens. Here, M_3 has roots widely apart from those of M_2; and the tooth inclines forward, often making crown contact with M_2. This abnormal eruption of M_3 is apparently related to other M_3 anomalies to be described below.

Malformed Teeth. One upper dentition (NC 1832) shows bilateral reduction of P^2's to slender, curved, cylindrical pegs. These teeth erupted fully and show wear. There is considerable variation in the development of styles and stylids on $DP\frac{4}{4}$; $M\frac{1}{1}$, $M\frac{2}{2}$, and $M\frac{3}{3}$, particularly in the upper dentition. In one instance (NC 1306) the DP^4 style is extremely slender and flattened rather than cylindrical. Several others are broader than usual and bifurcate, giving rise to one or more accessory stylets. These latter sometimes rival the main style in size.

One otherwise normal M_3 shows no trace of the third loph above the level of the alveolus; it has not yet been X-rayed (Fig. 3.19b). Other M_3's showing the procumbent character noted above have greatly reduced or fully absent third lophs, and these teeth are also abnormally narrow (Figs. 3.20 and 3.21). Another M_3 shows unusually large enamel fossettes (Fig. 3.19a). It is thought, but not certain, that these anomalies are bilateral. A definitely bilateral M^3 anomaly occurs in one skull, where the posterior loph is extremely reduced and its enamel contorted, with development of supernumerary lingual styles. This skull does not seem to match any of the mandibles with malformed M_3's, but this may be a sampling phenomenon. Another M_3 shows unusual robustness in its basal one-third, which is procumbent (Fig. 3.19c). The upper portion of the crown of this tooth developed in the normal orientation and appears normal above the alveolus.

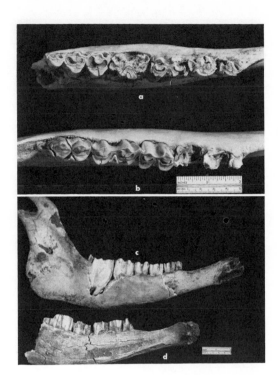

FIGURE 3.19 *Bison bison antiquus mandibles with deformed or unusual M_3's: a. third molar with unusually large fossettes (Mand. no. 33); b. third molar lacking third loph (Mand. no. 1); c. third molar with robust, procumbent base (Mand. no. 109); d. third molar showing uneven wear (Mand. no. 55).*

The occurrence of the apparently linked anomaly for $M\frac{3}{3}$ reduced posterior loph–narrow tooth–procumbent tooth is summarized in Table 3.15 .

If this anomaly is the result of a system of three genes, all of them recessive and autosomal, then the occurrence of recessive homozygotes is higher than one would expect from the progeny of F_1 full heterozygotes (AaBbCc). This would suggest that a certain degree of genetic drift may have occurred to amplify the recessive homozygote frequency. If this hypothesis is valid, gene flow to the Casper population must have been lower than

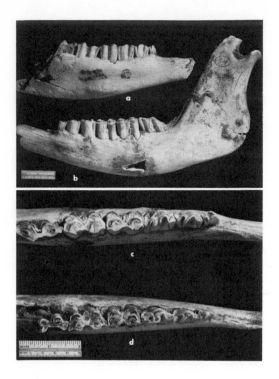

FIGURE 3.20 Bison bison antiquus *mandibles with deformed M₃'s: a and d. left mandible (no. 27) also displaying a small diffuse swelling at the base of M₁; b and c. left mandible (no. 54).*

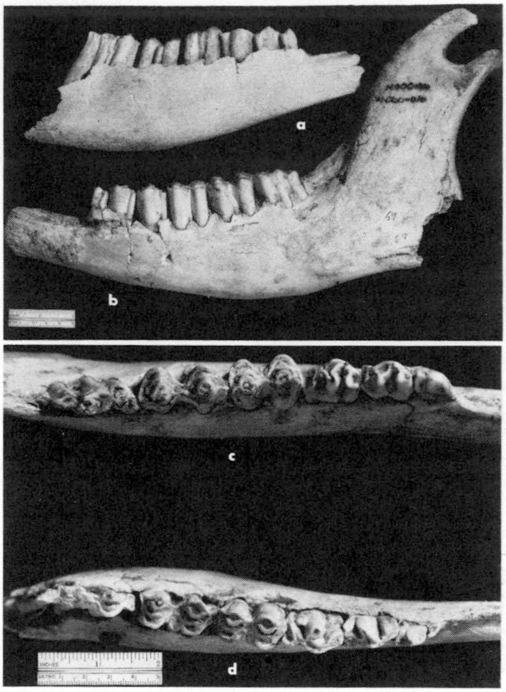

FIGURE 3.21 Bison bison antiquus *mandibles with deformed M₃'s: a and d. right mandible (no. 63) also showing uneven wear; b and c. left mandible (no. 69).*

TABLE 3.15 *Occurrence of Elements of the Third Molar Reduced Third Loph–Narrow Tooth–Procumbent Tooth Anomaly*

Specimen	Side	Reduced Third Loph[1]	Narrow Tooth	Procumbent Tooth
Mandible – 1	R	+	–	–
Mandible – 69	L	–	+	+
Mandible – 63	R	–	+	+
Mandible – 54	L	+	+	+
Mandible – 27	L	+	+	+
Mandible – 68	L	–	–	+
Upper – NC 2322		+[2]	–	–

[1] + = presence of trait (e.g., reduction of third loph).
    – = absence of trait (i.e., normal).
[2] reduced second crescent in upper third molars.

one would expect from freely interacting populations. This would suggest that herds of *B. bison antiquus* in this area of Wyoming—an area geographically marginal to the Plains—were widely scattered, rather than abundant; and that herd populations were rather small. Aboriginal predation on such scattered groups may have resulted in a noticeable Founder's Effect, increasing the frequencies of certain anomalies through genetic drift. I hope to examine the dentitions of populations from several other sites at this time period to test this and related hypotheses.

Cement Hypertrophy. Two upper tooth rows and an isolated M^1 show what appears to be excessive development of cement on the molars, particularly in the area of the lingual style. Several additional individuals show excessive cement infilling of lateral folds on the teeth. The hypertrophic specimens show large hemispherical bulges on the sides of the crowns. These are generally not enamelly (with one possible exception) and have dull, roughened surfaces.

Uneven Tooth Wear. A number of mandibles and maxillae exhibit cases of unusual tooth wear, generally manifested as excessive wear of one tooth or of a portion of one tooth. The extent of occurrence of such wear has not yet been studied in great detail, as comparison with other populations is necessary.

Some examples of uneven wear are illustrated in the accompanying plates. In one specimen (no. 55; Fig. 3.19d) the anterior and medial crescents of M_3 stand above the levels of both M_2 and the posterior loph or crescent of M_3. It has not yet been possible to match this mandible with an upper dentition. Uneven wear is associated with the deformation of M_3 in several specimens; for instance mandible no. 54 (Fig. 3.20b,c) shows a bevelled facet on the posterior half of the tooth. Mandible no. 15 (Fig. 3.22, lower) shows an unusual bevelled facet on the lingual side of the crown of the anterior crescent, giving the crescent a pe-

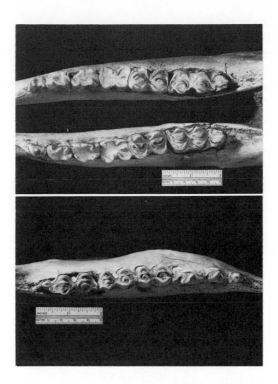

FIGURE 3.22 *Unusual and pathological mandibles of* B. bison antiquus: *upper, pair of mandibles (nos. 47 and 48) showing unusually heavy cement infilling of lateral folds in both M₃'s; lower, left mandible showing lumpy jaw due to internal suppuration (Mand. no. 15).*

culiar "peaked roof" appearance with the peak as the longitudinal axis of the tooth. The second crescent of the tooth is worn normally, with its facets slanting gently to the labial aspect. Mandible no. 63 (Fig. 3.21a,d) displays an unusually high crown on M_1, and somewhat excessive wear on M_2. It is possible that this is the result of malocclusion occasioned by the deformation of M_3, but again the corresponding upper dentition has not been found as yet.

Enamel Hypoplasia. Two individuals (NC 2325 and NC - unnumbered) show marked growth arrests in the development of upper molar crowns. The former, a possible 6.6-year-old, shows the groove of arrest at a level about half the height of the crown on M^2. The latter, a pair of teeth probably 2.6 years old, shows a similar line of arrest at half the height of M^1. Thus the lines of arrest do not correlate with synchronous events. Colyer (1936: 596) relates the anomaly tentatively to malnutrition; but he notes the hereditary nature of the potentiality for the anomaly:

> It seems possible therefore, that where in certain individuals there is a latent hereditary tendency to vary in the direction of defective enamel formation, this tendency may be quickened into activity by some departure from normal environment such as a change producing malnutrition, and hypoplasia may be due to a large extent, and possibly in the majority of cases, to the interaction of endogenous and exogenous causes.

It is thus possible that the hypoplasias are the result of adverse reactions to past drought cycles. The alternative possibility that the hypoplasias are the result of tissue instability brought on by metabolic changes, the result of severe diseases, should also be considered.

Lumpy Jaw. Several mandibles show varying development of bony bosses near the tooth bases. Evidently, these outgrowths are the result of internal suppuration, probably the result of food injury and the injection of viruses, bacilli, or fungi into the mandible. Colyer (1936: 647-649) suggests that

> In animals with long rooted teeth, such as the Bovidae and the Equidae the pus, more especially in the mandible, failing to find an easy exit through the alveolar bone, burrows into the body of the mandible and gives rise to a deep-seated abscess...

An extreme case of this with the swelling lateral to the premolar row appears to have undergone some resorption of bone in the diastema, causing the latter to be abnormally slender. Unfortunately the diastema in this specimen (no. 15) is not complete (Fig. 3.22, lower).

Post-cranial Pathologies

Only four post-cranial pathologies were observed in the Casper sample. Possibly all were the result of minor traumatic injuries.

The most obvious example is a fused first and second phalanx unit (Fig. 3.23). The two phalanges have been ankylosed through the development —probably through localized rheumatoid arthritis —of inflammatory bone tissue which overgrew the joint. The new bone tissue is relatively smooth, with occasional rough outgrowths and vascular foramena. The complete absence of inflammatory tissue at the proximal end of the first phalanx and the distal end of the second phalanx suggests this to have been a very local event, occasioned either through physical injury to the tissue surrounding the bone, or through local infection of the tissue and suppuration in the area of the joint capsule. The pathology closely resembles pedal osteitis of horses, illustrated by Rossdale (1972: 184), although less severe than the latter.

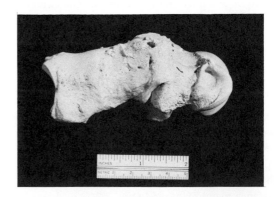

FIGURE 3.23 *Ankylosed first and second phalanges of* B. bison antiquus, *probably a result of traumatically induced rheumatoid arthritis or osteitis (NCU 158).*

Two ribs show pathological development. In one, the curve from shaft to head is unusually broad, having been filled in by thickening of the shaft at the capitulum. The surface of the rib in the area of the capitulum is roughened with several diagonal rugose ridges resembling muscle tendon attachment scars. This may have resulted from physical injury of the bone, although the break, if present, caused little displacement. The second rib shows a swelling in the medial portion of the shaft, evidently the result of a break without displacement. The swelling is somewhat rugose and is filled with normal cancellous tissue.

One metacarpal shows a minor local swelling on the anterior face, possibly the result of a localized impact.

Discussion

Most of the tooth anomalies described above have been noted before in the Pecora, although Colyer (1936: 119, 373) stresses the extreme rarity of such anomalies in wild bovids.

The deformed $M\frac{3}{3}$'s are problematical, however. This type of anomaly (reduced third loph—narrow tooth—procumbent tooth) was not recorded by Colyer (*ibid.*). It seems to be genetic in origin, being certainly not traumatic. If this is the case, the hypothesis concerning the scattering of small herds and lessened gene flow on the periphery of the plains may in fact by valid.

The traumatic injuries described from Casper are minor, and could easily have resulted from stresses sustained during dominance displays, or even from the normal daily stresses encountered by a single animal.

Chapter

4

GEOLOGY of the CASPER
ARCHEOLOGICAL SITE

JOHN ALBANESE
Wyoming Archeological Society

LOCATION AND SETTING

The site is located on the northwest edge of the City of Casper in the northeast quarter of Section 5, Township 33 North, Range 79 West at an elevation of 5240 feet. The eastward flowing North Platte River lies three-quarters of a mile east of the site and occupies a valley that cuts through the upper Cretaceous Steele Shale. The valley is 2 to 2½ miles wide and 140 feet deep. It is bordered by five terraces, the two lowest are Holocene in age and the upper three are Pleistocene in age. The site lies on the northwest side of the valley and is situated 100 feet above the river on the fourth highest terrace (see Fig. 4.1).

Sand dunes partially cover the Pleistocene terraces in the vicinity of the site. These dunes lie on the southwest edge of a large, generally stabilized, parabolic dune field that lies adjacent to and north of the valley of the North Platte

River. The dune field extends from Casper eastward for a distance of 30 miles. The width of the dune field varies from 6 to 18 miles. The trend of the dunes as measured on aerial photographs varies from N 65° E to N 75° E. The resultant direction of the dominant prevailing southwest winds at Casper is N 60°-70° E (U. S. Geological Survey, 1970: 112). Isolated, active elongate, "hairpin" shaped, parabolic dunes are present along the southern margin of the dune field. These features vary from one-quarter to a mile in length and may reach a height of 60 feet (see Fig. 4.2). Longitudinal ridges of sand, stabilized by vegetation, are also present within the parabolic dune areas. These features probably formed by the "halving" of "hairpin" shaped parabolic dunes in the manner described by Smith (1965: 568). Active elongate blowouts are another common feature of the dune field. They generally occur on the windward end of "hairpin"

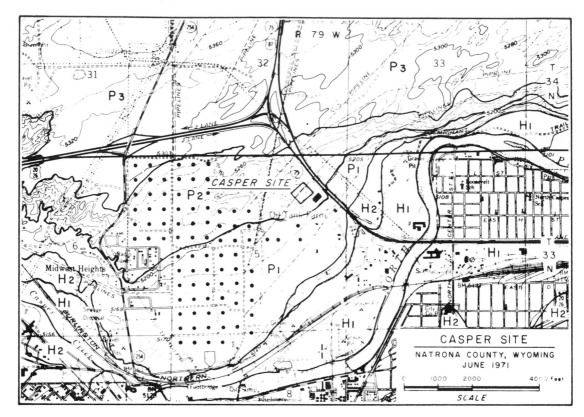

FIGURE 4.1 *Topographic map of Casper Site and vicinity. H_1 and H_2 are Holocene river terraces of the North Platte River. P_1, P_2, and P_3 are Pleistocene river terraces.*

shaped parabolic dunes. The walls of the dune usually surround the blowout on three sides with the windward side open. However in some cases the walls of the dune are poorly developed and an elongate apron or ridge of sand is present on the leeward side of the blowout. The presently active blowouts vary from a few feet to 2,000 feet in length and some attain a depth of 50 feet (see Fig. 1.7). The inner dune walls, parallel to the axis of the blowout, slope at an angle of 33 degrees.

The dimensions of blowout depressions associated with both active and stabilized "hairpin" shaped parabolic dunes were measured on topographic sheets that cover a 92 square mile

area northeast of and adjacent to the Casper Site. Forty eight blowout depressions were noted on the topographic sheets and 10 were checked in the field. Their lengths vary from 3,950 to 510 feet, widths from 1,555 to 80 feet and depths from 10 to 50 feet. The mean average length is 1,565 feet, mean average width is 445 feet and mean depth is 35.18 feet. The length to width ratio was derived for all 48 blowouts. The mean average ratio of length to width is 3.88. the standard deviation is 1.26. The data have a normal distribution (chi-square = 0.5 with one degree of freedom, level of significance greater than 20%). The correlation coefficient between length and width is .85, significant at the .005

FIGURE 4.2 *Aerial photograph of Casper Site and vicinity. Note active parabolic sand dunes and blowouts on windward side of dunes.*

confidence level.

Small perennial intra-dune ponds which vary from 1.4 to 5.5 acres in size, occupy the center of blowout depressions and deflation hollows in bedrock, along the southern margin of the dune field, east of Casper. The ponds vary from 500 to 1,100 feet in length and are one-fourth to a half as wide (see Fig. 4.3, Fig. 1.8). Lakes and ponds are not rare features in dune fields. Keech and Bentall (1971) report 1,640 lakes in the Sand Hills of Nebraska ranging in size from 10 to 2,300 acres. Johnson (1967) describes a parabolic dune field in southern Colorado characterized by large lakes and barren playas.

The climate in the Casper dune field is semi-arid. Precipitation varies from 10 to 14 inches a year. The stabilized dunes support a good growth of grass and sagebrush. The area is classi-fied as a "grama-needlegrass-wheatgrass" grass-land (U. S. Geological Survey, 1970: 90), and is presently utilized by both the livestock industry and the native antelope. Prior utilization by bison is evident from the occasional presence of bison bones in "blowouts" throughout the general area.

The modern dune field near Casper will be used as a model to interpret some of the geologic features present at the archeological site.

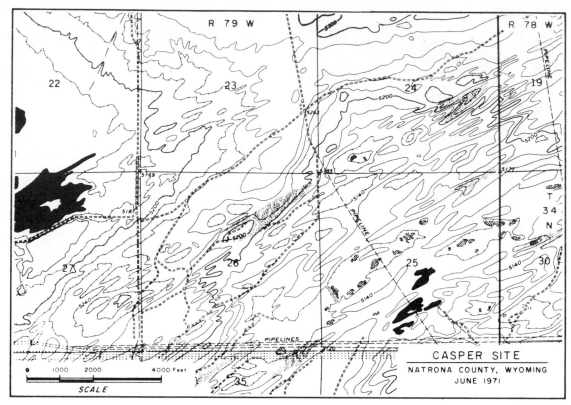

FIGURE 4.3 *Topographic map of dune area three and three quarters miles northeast of the Casper Site. Perennial ponds are marked solid black, intermittent ponds are cross-hatched and active parabolic dunes are stippled'*

SITE GEOLOGY

Methods

The geologic investigation of the site was carried out simultaneously with the archeological excavation during May and June of 1971. An area, 250 x 500 feet in size, was mapped in detail using an alidade and plane table. Two 100 foot long trenches were dug with machinery especially for viewing and sampling the geologic profile. Over 60 lithologic samples were collected and examined under the binocular microscope. Grain size was measured with a micrometer disc eyepiece. Sorting, roundness and sphericity were estimated using the following visual comparators: sorting (Beard and Weyl 1973), roundness (Powers 1953) and sphericity (Rittenhouse 1943).

Stratigraphy

Five post-Cretaceous lithological units were recognized at the site and are shown in Fig. 4.4. The oldest unit is a five foot thick, poorly sorted sandy arkosic gravel of Pleistocene age which rests unconformably upon the upper Cretaceous Steele Shale. The gravel caps the fourth terrace above the North Platte River. Resting on top of the gravel terrace is the remnant of a stabilized sand dune that contained the Hell Gap style

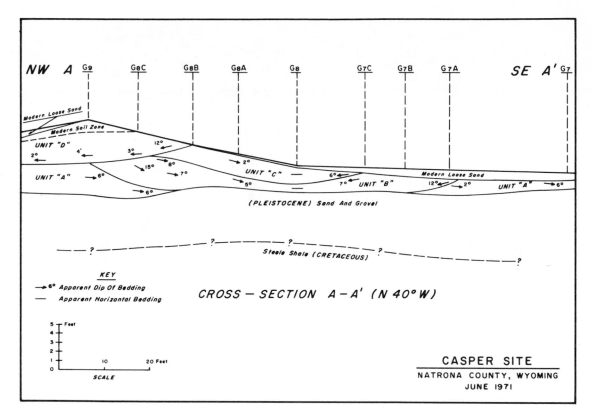

FIGURE 4.4 *Cross-section A-A'. Line of section is shown on Fig. 4.6.*

projectile points, bone tools and 74 specimens of *Bison antiquus* that comprised the bulk of the archeological material recovered at the site. This material was discovered after power machinery had removed most of the dune in clearing ground for the Control Data Corporation industrial plant. Prior to partial removal, the dune was 25 feet high and covered with grass and sagebrush. After the bulldozers had completed their work, a wedge of sand remained which ranged from 0 to 8 feet in height and covered a 200 x 300 foot area. Four lithologic units are present within the dune remnant. These units are herein labeled from oldest to youngest, A, B, C and D. Units A, B and D are unconsolidated eolian sands. Unit C is a lacustrine deposit composed of fine sand and silt.

Pleistocene Gravel

The previously-mentioned, five foot thick Pleistocene gravel is a fluvial deposit. It is semi-consolidated, very poorly sorted and consists of very fine to coarse, calcareous, arkosic sands with included and interbedded, rounded cobbles and pebbles. The cobbles and pebbles range from one to eight inches in length. Approximately 90% of the cobbles and pebbles are Pre-Cambrian rock fragments which consist of granite, granite gneiss, green schist, dark gray diabase and white quartz. The remaining 10% consists of white, crystalline to micritic limestone; tan and white fine grained quartzite and gray chert; all derived from

FIGURE 4.5 *Wind deflated surface of Pleistocene surface (P₂) gravel at the Casper Site.*

Paleozoic formations. White filaments of caliche coat some of the pebbles and cobbles. Bedding is undulating, lenticular and poorly developed. The present terrace surface formed by the top of the gravel bed has been deflated (see Fig. 4.5). The pebbles and cobbles stand out in relief because the fine fractions have been winnowed out.

Unit A

Unit A rests on the terrace surface and varies from 0 to 7.0 feet in thickness (see Fig. 4.6). The sand is light yellow to white in color and thinly bedded. It consists of alternating, slightly undulating sand layers that vary between 0.25 and 2 inches in thickness (see Fig. 4.7) and generally dip 3° to 6° to the southeast, as indicated on Fig. 4.8. Low angle (2° to 3°) cross-bedding is present throughout the unit. The sand is unconsolidated, moderately well sorted, medium grained, rounded to well rounded with sphericity values between .79 and .95. Coarse grains may constitute up to 30% of a given sand

layer. Some layers contain grains that vary between 1.0 and 1.5 millimeters in length. Quartz grains, usually frosted and commonly pitted, are the predominant mineral in the sand, however, accessory minerals may constitute up to 40% of the grains of a given sand layer. White feldspar is the most common accessory and it may constitute between 5% and 25% of a given layer. Other accessories with their varying percentages are pink feldspar, 2% to 5%; green schist, trace to 5%; and chert, 0 to 3%.

Eolian sands nearly identical to Unit A, were noted on the exposed walls of "blowouts" in other stabilized dunes east of Casper. One such example is shown in Fig. 4.9.

Calcareous root "casts" are present in Unit A in the southwestern portion of the site. They average five inches in length and vary between 0.5 and 2 inches in width. The "casts" consist of sand grains cemented together by white, earthy calcium carbonate. They contain a hollow center that averages 1 millimeter in diameter and runs

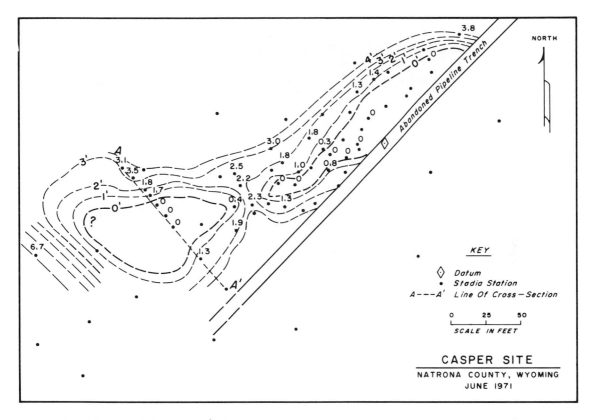

FIGURE 4.6 *Isopach of Unit A ; one foot contours.*

the entire length of the "cast". The hollow center usually contains a long, thin fibrous root. The "root casts" occur in both the vertical and horizontal position. The horizontal "casts" were formerly in the vertical position but were undermined by wind and re-deposited. This same process is currently taking place in some modern blowouts in the Casper area.

Unit B

Unit B contains the archeological material recovered at the site. It varies from 0 to 2.1 feet in thickness (see Fig. 4.10). Unit B was deposited in an elongate, trough-like, hollow depression that had been "scooped" out of Unit A. Unit A is absent along the axis of the depression (see Fig.

4.6) and Unit B rests directly on the Pleistocene gravel. A two foot deep deflation hollow in the Pleistocence gravel surface also coincides with the depression axis (see Fig. 4.11). The configuration of the trough-like, hollow depression is shown on Fig. 4.12 and Fig. 4.13. The depression axis is oriented N 60° E, parallel to the resultant direction of the present prevailing southwesterly winds. The preserved portion of the depression is approximately 305 feet long, 73 feet wide and six feet deep. The bulk of the skeletal remains of the 74 *Bison antiquus* were located two to six inches above the base of Unit B. The bison bones were distributed in the shape of a windrow for a distance of 200 feet along the axis of the depression (see Endpiece). The hollow depression

FIGURE 4.7 *Unit A. Note lenticular bedding and presence of coarse sand lenses in center of photograph.*

in which Unit B was deposited is interpreted to have been the center of a sand blowout. Only a remnant of Unit B is preserved, so it is not possible to determine the original dimensions of the depression. The original depression must have been large enough to hold at least 25 animals, the size of *Bison antiquus*. It also must have been deep enough and with steep enough sides to prevent easy escape. The large, modern blowouts in the Casper area, with depths greater than 35 feet, would satisfy these requirements. The length to width ratio of the trough containing Unit B is 4.18. It may be more than coincidence that this is close to the mean average value (3.88) for the large, modern blowouts near Casper (z test = 0.25, cumulative probability = 0.5986). A further piece of evidence is the presence of lacustrine deposits immediately over-

lying Unit B. The small modern ponds in the Casper dune area are usually contained within blowout depressions. By using all of the above evidence it can be inferred that the ancient blowout at Casper resembled the average modern blowout in the same general area. It was probably between 35 and 50 feet deep, 1,200 to 1,800 feet long and 400 to 500 feet wide.

Unit B generally consists of even, lenticular layers of sand that vary from 0.25 to 6.0 inches in thickness. The strike and dip of the bedding parallels and conforms to the shape of the hollow depression containing the Unit (see Fig. 4.14 and Fig. 4.15). Some bedding is slightly undulating and low angle ($2°$ to $6°$) cross-bedding is present in the southwestern portion of the site. Areas of layered sand may grade laterally into massive sand (see Fig. 1.16).

The sand in Unit B is white, unconsolidated, rounded to well rounded, moderately well sorted with sphericity values ranging from .79 to .95. The sand grains are usually medium to coarse in size. Grain size varies between individual layers. Approximately 10% of the layers contain a preponderance of very coarse, quartz grains that vary between 1.0 and 2.0 millimeters in diameter (see Fig. 4.16). These layers are not restricted to any portion of Unit B. Frosted and pitted quartz grains constitute the bulk of the sand but accessory mineral and rock grains are important constituents and comprise 40% of the sand in some layers. These accessories with varying percentages between individual layers are: white feldspar, 5% to 25%; orange and red feldspar, 3% to 7%; green schist, 0 to 5%; chert, 0 to 3%. Vertical calcareous root "casts" identical to those described in Unit A are sparingly distributed throughout Unit B. One large "cast" at the base of the Unit measured 12 inches in length and 4 inches in diameter.

In addition to the *Bison antiquus*, other faunal skeletal remains were recovered in Unit B. They are Richardson ground squirrel, coyote, jackrabbit, red fox, pronghorn, bobcat and pocket gopher. All of these animals are presently living in the general area of the site. Some of this skeletal material was recovered from what appears to be canine feces. Unit B contained

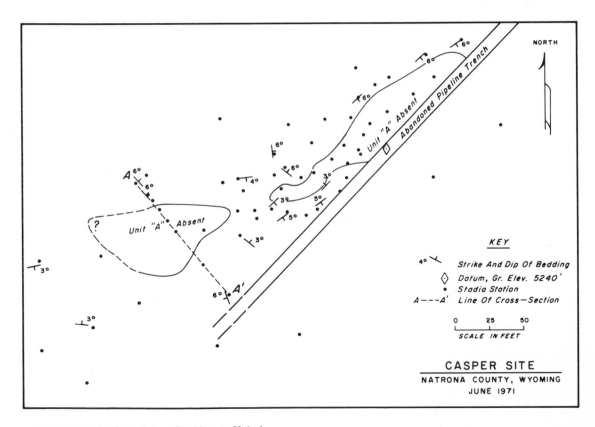

FIGURE 4.8 *Strike and dip of bedding in Unit A.*

FIGURE 4.9 *Bedding in sand similar to that of Unit A. This exposure is present in wall of modern blowout shown in Fig. 1.7, five and one quarter miles northeast of the Casper Site.*

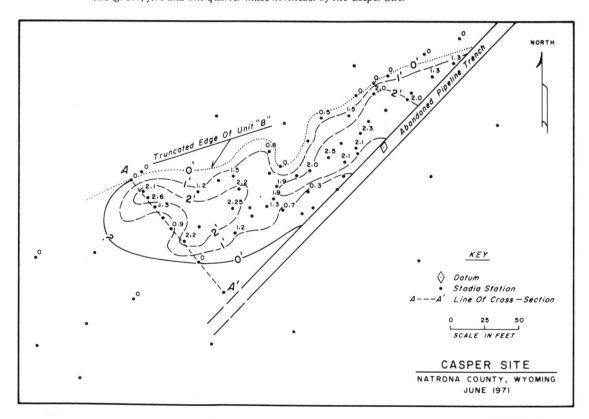

FIGURE 4.10 *Isopach of Unit B; one foot contours.*

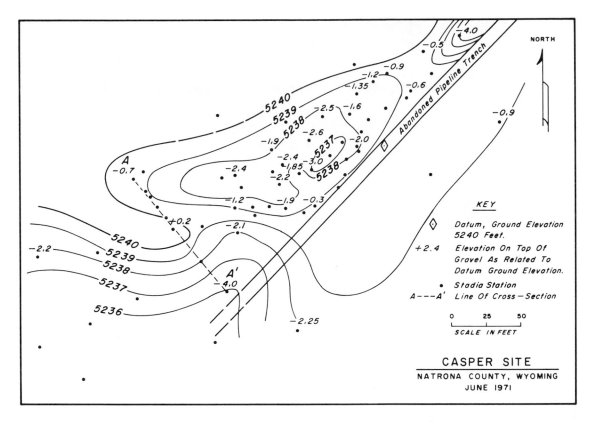

FIGURE 4.11 *Elevations on top of Pleistocene terrace gravel at the Casper Site; one foot contours.*

snails which were identified as *Succinea* sp., cf. *S. stretchiana* Bland by Aurèle La Rocque (personal communication to George Frison 1972). He wrote "these specimens seem to belong to the *S. ovalis* group which prefers rather dry situations."

Samples from all units in the dune remnant were submitted to Arizona State University at Tempe, Arizona for pollen extraction. Unfortunately pollen preservation was poor and did not permit definite conclusions as to the floral history of the dune (see Appendix II).

Two radiocarbon dates were secured from Unit B. A charcoal sample yielded a date of 9,830 ± 350 radiocarbon years (RL-125) and a bison bone yielded a date of 10,060 ± 170 radiocarbon years (RL-208). Thus it would appear that Unit B is

approximately 10,000 years old.

Unit C

Unit C conformably overlies Unit B. Most of Unit C was removed by the bulldozer and as a result its original thickness is unknown. A maximum thickness of 2.1 feet was preserved (Fig. 4.12 and Fig. 4.17) and it consists of 8 to 12 inch thick, massive beds of brown, silty, calcareous sand which grades to sandy silt. The sand is generally fine-grained but medium to coarse fractions are present and in some portions of the Unit may constitute up to 20% of the sample. Silt content varies from 20% to 55%. As was the case in Units A and B, sand grains other than quartz are also present in Unit C. In individual

FIGURE 4.12 *Profile view looking southwest along cross-section A-A'. Dark layers are lacustrine sediments of Unit C which rests on Unit B.*

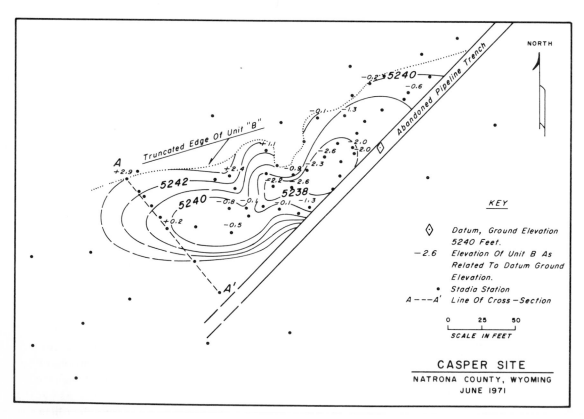

FIGURE 4.13 *Elevations on the base of Unit B; one foot contours.*

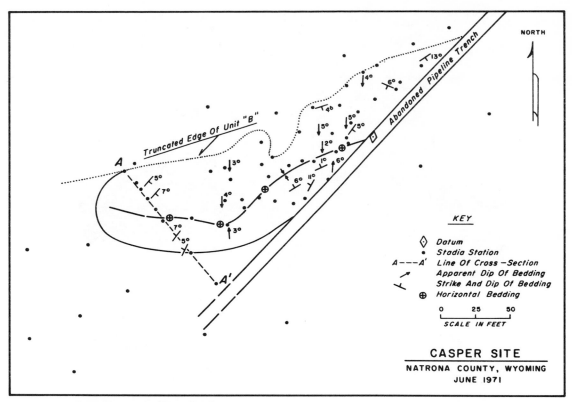

FIGURE 4.14 *Strike and dip of bedding in Unit B.*

samples, feldspar content varies from 13% to 25%, schist from 0 to 5%, chert 0 to 2% and muscovite 0 to trace. Sorting varies from moderately well sorted to poorly sorted. Grass root molds are abundant throughout the Unit and vary between 0.25 and 0.50 millimeters in diameter. The Unit is calcareous and reacts readily with acid. The calcareous cement has an amorphous appearance and is not readily discernible under the microscope. Unit C is interpreted as a lacustrine sediment that accumulated in a pond that formed in the blowout depression after Unit B had been deposited. The silt grains are the "loess particles" that the wind would ordinarily winnow out of the sand and remove from the area. However, these wind-blown silt particles would be

trapped on the surface of a pond and precipitate to the bottom. The same mechanism would trap the sand grains. Sediments very similar to Unit C were noted in modern ponds near Casper, that occupy the centers of blowout depressions. The modern sites of former ponds are grass covered. This would explain the presence of root molds in Unit C.

The fine sediment in Unit C formed a seal which prevented the destruction of underlying Unit B by wind deflation. It is unlikely that an archeological site would have been preserved if a pond had not formed after the event of the bison kill.

FIGURE 4.15 *Massive sands of Unit B overlying Unit A. Pleistocene gravels present in the bottom of the pit.*

FIGURE 4.16 *Unit B overlying Unit A (dark bands). Note coarse lenticular sand layers in Unit B.*

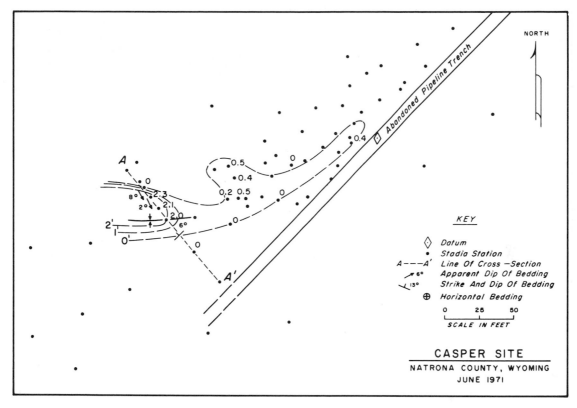

FIGURE 4.17 *Isopach of Unit C; one foot contours.*

Unit D

Unit D is present along the northwest margin of the site area (see Fig. 4.18). This eolian sand deposit has an observed maximum thickness of 3.3 feet. It has a massive appearance with some indistinct broad banding, 6 to 9 inches thick. It dips to the northwest and truncates the underlying A, B and C Units. The sand is unconsolidated and has a light brown appearance. Unit D contains the highest percentage of coarse grains of any unit at the site. Grains that vary between 1 and 2 millimeters in diameter, constituted 40% to 90% of all samples examined. The remaining grains are predominantly medium grained. The sands are frosted, well sorted to moderately sorted and well rounded. Sphericity values range from .79 to .95. Accessory rock grains vary between samples as follows: white feldspar 10% to 15%, pink feldspar 2% to 5%, schist 0 to 5%, and chert 0 to trace.

Wind Velocities - Past and Present

The original source for the eolian sand of the Casper dune field was most probably the fluvial deposits of the North Platte River valley. The time of the original formation of the dune field has not been determined. It most probably occurred during the Pleistocene, as was the case in the Sand Hills of Nebraska (Smith 1964) and the Killpecker dune field of western Wyoming (Moss 1951). The eolian sands at the Casper archeological site are Holocene in age. These

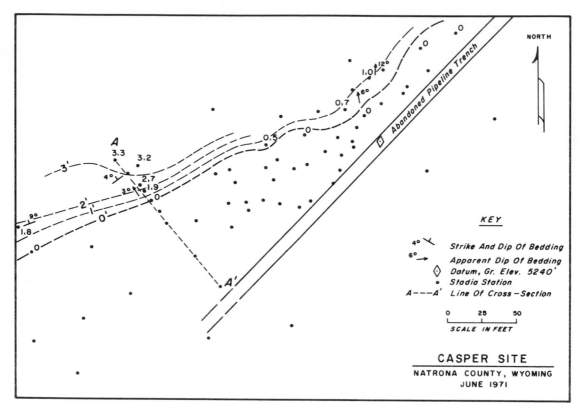

FIGURE 4.18 *Isopach of Unit D; one foot contours.*

sands are characterized by the presence of coarse to very coarse sand grains, some of which even exceed 2 millimeters in diameter. Eolian sands of this size are apparently not common as Allen (1970: 103) reports that wind-blown sands have "a mean size seldom less than 0.20 millimeters and rarely greater than 0.45 millimeters." Gilluly et al. (1968: 319) state that in dune sands "grains 0.3 millimeter to 0.15 millimeter in diameter greatly predominate." Moss (1951) found that eolian sand grains near Eden in western Wyoming varied between 0.125 and 0.270 millimeter. However, Bigarella (1972) in speaking of the distinctive compositional and textural features of sand dunes states "the mean grain size seems to be of little significance."

Glennie (1970: 78-79) describes coarse eolian sands in Libya and the Trucial Coast that contain grains up to 5 millimeters in diameter. He describes a sandstorm in Libya where "most of the sand was seen to move very close to the ground. Grains of about 5 mm diameter, too heavy to be moved by the direct action of the wind were slowly creeping along the surface under the force of impact of saltating grains while grains of 2 mm diameter were rolling continuously over the ground." (Glennie 1970:21).

Bagnold (1954) stated that general field observations indicate that a wind velocity of 5 meters per second (11.2 miles per hour) was necessary to start sand grains moving. Bagnold also developed formulae based on field observations and experimental work that can be used for calculating wind velocity distribution and threshold velocity values for different sized sand grains. Using this information it is possible to make an educated guess as to the magnitude of wind velocities that are necessary to start the movement of large sand grains. The velocity of the wind varies with distance above the ground and ground roughness. It can be calculated that a sand grain 2.0 millimeters in diameter will start to move (fluid threshold) when a wind velocity of approximately 840 centimeters per second (18.57 miles per hour) is present at a height of 10 centimeters (3.94 inches) above the sand surface.

Obviously it takes high wind velocities to move large sand grains. Fortunately or unfortunately depending on your point of view, these conditions are easily met in the Casper area. During the late fall and early winter months of November through February, Casper has one of the highest average wind velocities of any city in the United States. The average wind velocity at Casper during January is 13 miles per hour and winds blow out of the southwest 70% of the time. On the average, only three days in January are free of measurable wind (U. S. Geological Survey, 1970: 112). A not uncommon windy day for this time of the year occurred on December 24, 1972 when winds blew constantly for a twelve hour period, at velocities ranging between 20 and 45 miles per hour with gusts up to 60 miles per hour. The generally flat-lying site area was visited, following one such windy day in January, 1973. Asymmetric sand ripples which averaged 47 inches in width and 1.6 inches in heighth were noted. Sand grains, 1 to 2.5 millimeters in diameter were concentrated at the ripple crests and medium to fine grained sand was concentrated in the troughs. This observation agreed with Bagnold's (1945: 145) statement that " in all cases", the coarse sand grains occur at the crest of the sand ripple.

In summary, the presence of very coarse sand layers in the Holocene eolian units at the Casper Site can be attributed to the high velocity of the wind during deposition. The wind blew as strongly 10,000 years ago as it does at present. The orientation of the blowout depression in which Unit B was deposited also indicates that the wind blew from the same general direction as it does at present.

The different percentages of coarse sand between the eolian units at the site can be explained by the fact that each unit represents a preserved portion of separate dunes. The amount of coarse sand in each preserved remnant would be dependent on what portion of the original dune was preserved, e.g. the crest of a dune contains lesser amounts of coarse sand than the windward side.

CONCLUSIONS

"Parabolic sand dunes form in areas where vegetation is able to establish itself widely over the sand" (Gilluly et al. 1969: 329). They do not form in areas where vegetation is scarce or absent. In fact parabolic dunes can and do form in terperate, wet areas with abundant vegetation, particularly along seacoasts (Flint 1971: 248-249). They "commonly form when the vegetative cover of extensive sand deposits is degraded by man or by increasing aridity" (Butzer 1964: 194). Smith (1965) states in regard to sand blowouts in the Sand Hills of Nebraska, "the climatic conditions under which the blowouts developed probably were not greatly different from those of the very dry years in historic time." "During the drought years of the 1930's, there were many more active moving dunes in the Casper area than there are at the present time. Many of the old blowouts are now grassed over" (oral communication from Bob Barber, local rancher). Therefore we can presume that if a sand blowout was used as an animal trap 10,000 years ago, the Casper area at that time contained a parabolic dune field that was characterized by a fair vegetative covering. It can be further presumed that the ancient blowout at the Casper Site was big enough to serve as a trap for large animals and probably resembled the large modern blowouts, some of which are as deep as 50 feet and as long as 2,000 feet. The lacustrine sediments that formed at the Casper Site subsequent to the bison kill would lead one to conclude that intra-dunal ponds, similar to those of the present, also existed in the same general area 10,000 years ago. The large sand grains recovered at the site along with the orientation of the ancient blowout axis would indicate that the wind blew from the same general direction and as strongly 10,000 years ago as it does at the present time. The vertebrate skeletal remains recovered at the site (except for the *Bison antiquus*) are all modern fauna that presently live in the area.

In summary, it can be concluded that the general biologic, climatic and geologic setting of the Casper area 10.000 years ago was similar to that of the present day.

Chapter

5

COMMENTS on the LITHIC TECHNOLOGY of the CASPER SITE MATERIALS

BRUCE BRADLEY
Southern Methodist University

INTRODUCTION

A limited inventory of lithic artifacts was re-covered in the course of excavation of the Casper Site. It consisted mostly of complete, incomplete, and fragmentary bifaces. Also recovered was a small number of unretouched flakes and four unifacially retouched flakes. This is not a representative sample of a complete manufacture sequence. With the exception of a few pressure flakes there is no manufacture debitage. Any reconstruction of the lithic technology must be inferred with these facts in mind. The following discussion is based entirely upon personal flint-knapping experience and a limited amount of experimental replication.

REPLICATION

In order to replicate the bifaces it is necessary to work from the evidence of the finished implements. When dealing with most bifacially reduced products one sees only the final flake sequences. If one assumes that the most efficient method of manufacture of a desired product is a primary consideration of a flintknapper, then the following description of a lithic reduction sequence is probably the most direct approach to replicating the bifaces recovered from the Casper Site.

RAW MATERIAL

The lithic material selected for the manufacture of the Casper Site artifacts seems to be mostly of southeastern Wyoming origin, with the noted exception of Knife River Flint from which three projectile points and one flake tool were made.

The materials include chalcedonic cherts that are common in the Laramie area, quartzites that are abundant at the Spanish Diggings quarries, and dendritic jaspers that may be found at the Hell Gap quarry sites. Personal experimentation with these materials has convinced me of their general suitability for the manufacture of bifacially thinned implements. From a knowledge of the fracturing qualities of these materials, both thermally altered and in a natural state, and examination of the artifacts I surmise that thermal alteration of the raw material was extensively used prior to the final flaking of the Casper Site bifaces.

PRELIMINARY MODIFICATION

Examination of the finished implements gives no clue whether they were made from cores or flakes. The size and shape of the raw materials that were being exploited suggest that efficient production would have most likely been by using large flakes as blanks. Large flakes can easily be produced by direct percussion with a large hammerstone (3 to 5 pounds). Great control may be gained by having the nodule resting on the ground (Fig. 5.1a) and directly striking a heavy blow a fair distance back from the margin. After several flake removals it is also possible to precondition the shape of a flake during subsequent removals. In this way a primary core and primary flakes are produced (Fig. 5.1b, c).

BIFACIAL PREPARATION

Thinning and Shaping

Once a primary flake-blank has been produced, it is further modified, bifacially, into the intended implement. This work may be divided into four steps of reduction; margin production, thinning-shaping, and margin regularizing-shaping. These steps do not necessarily correspond with

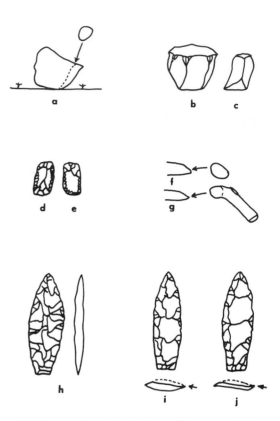

FIGURE 5.1 *Method of primary flake removal (a), primary core (b), and flake (c), bifacial preliminary modification (d, e), margin preparation with hammerstone percussion (f), and antler percussion (g) all selective and non-patterned. Initial biface thinning and shaping (h), and serial percussion thinning on first face (i) and second face (j).*

changes in flaking tools or techniques.

With a flake-blank it is preferable to begin by producing a bifacially flaked margin around the entire perimeter of the flake (Fig. 5.1d, e). This process involves selective, direct freehand percussion with a medium soft, very coarse-grained sandstone pebble. This action not only creates a bifacial margin for subsequent flaking but also gives the knapper an insight into the consistency, strength, weak areas, and inclusions of the material. Bifacial thinning and shaping is then begun. I usually continue using the same hammerstone for at least the initial flaking and sometimes for the entire process. The use of the hammerstone for biface thinning involves careful margin preparation to insure strength of the margin (Fig. 5.1f). This preparation is not difficult to do but must be carefully controlled to produce just the right angle. One of the advantages of using the hammerstone is the ease of making the transition from preparation to flaking. Without a change of tool it is possible to build up a flaking rhythm that improves speed and accuracy. It is not always expedient to do all of the percussion flaking with a hammerstone because much depends upon the material being flaked and the skill and mood of the flintknapper. Some days when I am not working to my maximum proficiency I prefer to do most of the percussion thinning with an antler billet. This method still involves preparation of the margin which may sometimes be done with the antler, by abrasion, but usually involves the use of the stone abrader. As much care must be taken when preparing a margin for antler flaking as for hammerstone flaking, but it usually does not involve as much preparation nor as steep an angle (Fig. 5.1g). Changing from the antler to the stone and back makes it difficult to build up a consistent flaking rhythm.

The bifaces recovered from the Casper Site retain many of the percussion thinning and shaping flake scars. These, of course, represent only the final series of flake removals but show flake removal sequence and spacing. I assume that the initial percussion flaking involved individually selected flake removals. This approach insures the regularity of the margins and thickness (Fig. 5.1h). Once these two characteristics have been achieved it is expedient to begin patterned or serial flake removals. This technique helps retain the regularity and at the same time

makes maximum thinning possible. During the process of percussion thinning it is necessary to space the flake removals uniformly. For this uniformity to be achieved the flintknapper must be able to assess carefully the surface contours, the margin angle and strength, and the striking force. With these variables in mind he can determine the size and shape of his flake removals and thereby overlap them to the extent that he determines necessary to achieve his goal. If this goal is to produce a regular, thin, and flat biface, then spacing is all important.

Once the general shape and regularity is achieved the biface is serially percussion thinned along one margin on one face (Fig. 5.1i). The biface is then turned over and thinned from the other margin on the other face (Fig. 5.1j). Spacing is carefully controlled and many times, the entire length of the point can be thinned with only four or five widely-spaced, slightly-overlapping, expanding, thinning flakes (see e.g. Fig. 1.36a, Fig. 1.36b, Fig. 1.39c, Fig. 1.39g).

After the serial percussion thinning is accomplished, the biface is carefully shaped and the margins regularized and straightened. This step can easily be accomplished either with direct percussion using antler or hammerstone or with selective pressure flaking. Careful examination of the archeological specimens indicates to me that both techniques were employed to varying degrees. Some specimens seem to have been finished entirely with percussion (e.g. Fig. 1.36d, Fig. 1.38f, Fig. 1.40b, Fig. 1.42e, Fig. 1.43b) while others were selectively retouched with pressure (e.g. Fig. 1.35a, Fig. 1.37b, Fig. 1.37d, Fig. 1.38b, Fig. 1.40h) especially at the base of the stem. The term random flaking is commonly used to describe nonpatterned or nonserial flaking; however, I prefer to speak of selective nonpatterned flaking. The term random implies that there is no deliberate choice of the place of flake removal. This is seldom the case in any sort of flintknapping. Usually each flake removal is carefully preconceived. With the Casper Site bifaces one is dealing with a simple margin and facial finishing retouch. Extensive pressure flaking is absent on most of the specimens. Grinding of the stem margins was employed as the finishing technique.

Hafting, Use, and Resharpening

The archeological context from which the specimens were recovered suggests that the bifaces were used as projectile points. Nineteen of the specimens that I examined exhibited impact fractures. An impact fracture is defined by the implement tips being crushed and/or flaked from the tip toward the base (see Fig. 1.39a, Fig. 1.40a, Fig. 1.40e, Fig. 1.40f, Fig. 1.42e, Fig. 1.43c). It is also possible that the implements functioned as knives, although there is no evidence to support this hypothesis. Either as projectile points or as knives they were most likely hafted while in use. Their general morphology and areas of marginal grinding may be used as indicators of which parts of the bifaces were incorporated in the haft. It is possible to infer that the haft or binding was carried up from the base of the biface to the extent of the marginal grinding. This always corresponded with the maximum breadth (Fig. 5.2a) and left the blade of the implement free to function as a projectile point and/or knife, and consequently to be exposed to use damage. Either a split or socket haft could have been used. The tapering stem may indicate that a socket haft was employed. Which style is most efficient with this type of point would be demonstrable by experimentation.

Once damaged the implement could be resharpened without removing it from the haft. If resharpening is done after an impact fracture, the dimensions are altered differentially i.e. the breadth and stem length stay the same while the overall length is reduced. Below is a description of an experiment I did to demonstrate this

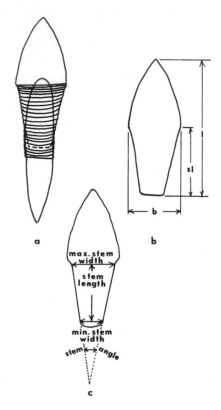

FIGURE 5.2 *Hafted biface, split haft technique (a) and projectile point measurements (b, c).*

observation

Resharpening Experiment

First, I replicated two of the archeological bifaces. I recorded their outlines and measured their stem length, breadth, and overall length (Fig. 5.2b). I then hafted them in a split haft as described above, and impact fractured them by thrusting them against a sandstone block covered with leather. After producing the fractures I recorded their outlines. Then, without removing them from their hafts, I resharpened the tips with selective nonpatterned pressure flaking, the only consideration being to resharpen and straighten the damaged areas and symmetrically to repoint the implements. This procedure was repeated once again with experimental point no. 1(Fig. 5.3) and twice again with experimental point no. 2 (Fig. 5.4). Table 5.1 gives the measurements of their original dimensions and for each stage of resharpening. Because of the disproportional method of resharpening it should be possible to demonstrate a change in morphology for each of these stages. I chose to do this by determining their breadth/length and stem length/length ratios. An increase in these ratios is noted.

Next I applied these findings to the archeological specimens. Only the complete bifaces were included in this sample (n = 19). Table 5.2

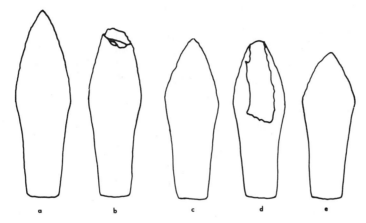

FIGURE 5.3 *Experimental biface No. 1. Primary implement (a), impact fractures (b, d), and resharpened implements (c, e).*

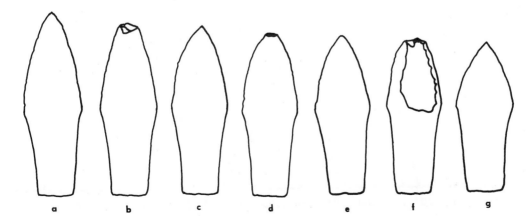

FIGURE 5.4 *Experimental biface No. 2. Primary implement (a), impact fractures (b, d, f) and resharpened implements (c, e, g).*

TABLE 5.1 *Experimental Biface Measurements and Ratios.*

Experimental Point Number	Fig.	l	b	sl	b/l	sl/l
1 Primary implement	5.3a	11.4	3.4	5.9	.30	.52
1 First resharpening	5.3c	9.9	3.4	5.9	.34	.59
1 Second resharpening	5.3e	8.9	3.4	5.9	.38	.66
2 Primary implement	5.4a	8.5	2.3	4.1	.27	.48
2 First resharpening	5.4c	7.9	2.3	4.1	.29	.52
2 Second resharpening	5.4e	7.5	2.3	4.1	.31	.55
2 Third resharpening	5.4g	7.1	2.3	4.1	.32	.58

gives the length, breadth, stem length, breadth/ length and stem length/length calculations. I then added the b/l and sl/l ratios for each specimen and plotted the sum against the number using steps of .05 (Fig. 5.5). A distinctly bimodal curve resulted. By determining which specimen's ratio fell into which I was able to separate the specimens into two groups. By comparing these to the experimental results it is

TABLE 5.2 *Casper Site Biface Measurements and Ratios.*

Fig. No.	l	b	sl	b/l	sl/l
1.35a	13.7	3.3	6.6	.24	.48
1.35b	12.0	2.9	6.0	.24	.50
1.37c	6.8	2.7	3.7	.40	.55
1.39f	8.1	3.3	5.0	.41	.61
1.35d	10.7	3.4	4.5	.32	.42
1.37b	9.6	2.8	5.1	.29	.54
1.39c	9.3	3.8	6.3	.41	.68
1.36a	10.0	3.1	4.6	.31	.46
1.39d	7.0	2.8	3.9	.40	.56
1.39g	7.3	3.1	4.2	.42	.58
1.36b	6.5	2.7	4.0	.41	.62
1.38a	7.5	3.1	4.4	.41	.59
1.35c	5.0	2.6	3.2	.52	.64
1.43b	11.1	2.7	5.1	.24	.46
1.39d	6.5	2.6	3.7	.40	.57
1.39e	5.6	2.8	3.3	.50	.59
1.36c	5.5	2.3	4.1	.42	.75
1.40d	7.3	3.0	5.0	.41	.69
1.40e	7.8	3.3	4.6	.42	.59

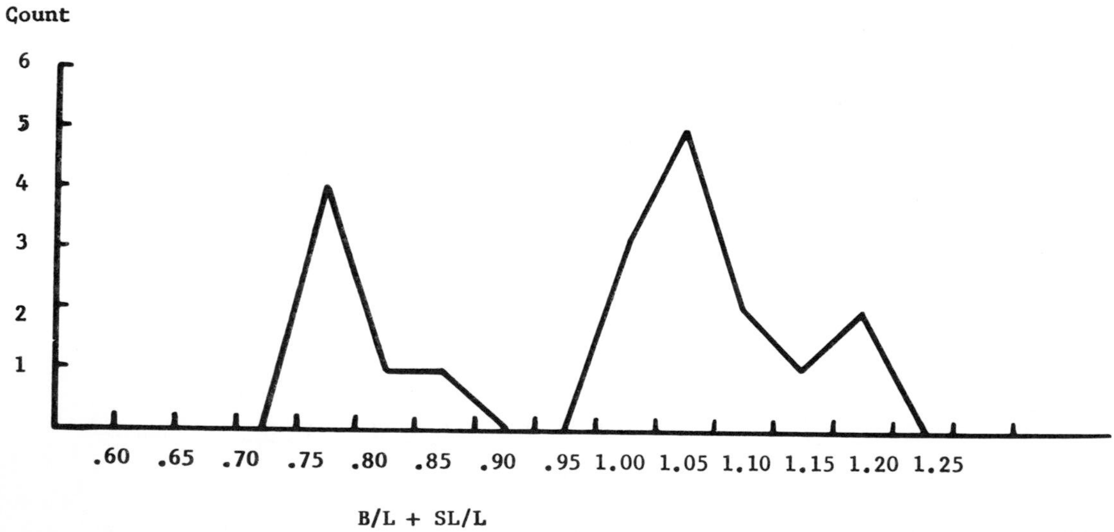

FIGURE 5.5 *Graph demonstrating morphological clustering (n = 19).*

possible to conclude that the specimens in group 1 (b/l + sl/l = .70 to .85) represented the primary implement and that the specimens in group 2 (b/l + sl/l = .95 to 1.15) represented the re-sharpened specimens. Of the nineteen complete specimens, six (32%) were primary implements (Fig. 1.35a, Fig. 1.35b, Fig. 1.35d, Fig. 1.36a, Fig. 1.37b, Fig. 1.43b) and thirteen (68%) were resharpened (Fig. 1.35c, Fig. 1.36b, Fig. 1.36c, Fig. 1.37c, Fig. 1.38a, Fig. 1.38b, Fig. 1.39c, Fig. 1.39d, Fig. 1.39e, Fig. 1.39f, Fig. 1.39g, Fig. 1.40d, Fig. 1.40e) at the time of their final usage.

Breakage

I examined 54 archeological biface specimens. Of these, eleven were unbroken; 30 have at least one break (complete specimens with one break and tip and base fragments) and thirteen have at least two breaks (complete specimens with two breaks and midsection fragments). Thirty-one are blade breaks, twenty are stem breaks, and nineteen are impact fractures. Most of the blade and stem breaks are bend fractures, which can be produced either during manufacture or use. Since there is little evidence of any lithic manufacturing at the Casper Site and the archeological association is with a bison kill and butchering station, I must conclude that all of the breaks were a result of use and not of manufacture.

FLAKE TOOLS

Four unifacially retouched flakes were recovered. Three of them probably were produced in the initial stage of biface manufacture and the fourth was probably a product of primary flake production. Retouch and resharpening could easily have been accomplished with the same tool (s) used to manufacture the bifaces. Several small resharpening flakes fit back onto these tools.

CONCLUSION

The purpose of this article has been to attempt to reconstruct the techniques of lithic modification that were present in the bifacial implements recovered from the Casper Site. These methods included manufacturing, use, breakage, and resharpening.

I have intentionally avoided saying anything about the typology of the artifacts or of making comparisons with materials recovered from other Paleo-Indian sites. I have, however, made some comments about possible explanations of morphological variations of the bifaces within the site.

MORPHOLOGICAL VARIATION in BISON METACARPALS and METATARSALS

JEAN NEWMAN BEDORD
University of Wyoming

INTRODUCTION

This study utilizes two different approaches in analyzing metric measurements of bison meta-carpals and metatarsals. One is the traditional univariate approach which handles each measurement individually and describes the distribution in terms of range, mean, and standard deviation. The other approach can be called multivariate analysis since the simultaneous variation of more than one variable is utilized. The extremes of this approach are factor analysis and multiple regression; the methodology employed here, however, utilizes mostly cross-tabulation and scattergrams. The emphasis is on clustering of groups since the samples are too small to justify the use of either factor analysis or multiple regression.

Both approaches are used to analyze variables involved in describing bison populations from six archeological sites. The major variables include sex, age and species, but other non-quantifiable variables are discussed in the interpretation of results. This information is then used to make cultural and biological inferences.

NATURE AND SOURCES OF DATA

Data used were taken from six archeological sites including the Casper Site; the Olsen-Chubbuck Site (Wheat 1972); the Finley Site (Moss et al. 1951); the Hawken Site (Frison n. d.); the Ruby Site (Frison 1971a); and the Vore Site. The Finley sample is from a probable parabolic sand dune bison trap that was not found during the original investigations and was partially destroyed later by artifact hunters. The Hawken Site, an unpublished trap site excavated by the University of Wyoming in 1972, contained

TABLE 6.1 *Source of Bone Samples and Dates*

Source	Bone Sample Collector	Material Dated	Date	Laboratory
Casper Site	Frison	Charcoal	7880 ± 350 B.C.	RL 125
		Bone	8110 ± 170 B.C.	RL 208
Olsen-Chubbuck Site	Wheat	Bone	8200 ± 500 B.C.	A 744
Finley Site	Frison-1972 Test	No Date		
Hawken Site	Frison	Charcoal	4520 ± 140 B.C.	RL 185
Ruby Site	Frison	Charcoal	A.D. 280 ± 135	GX 1157
Vore Site	Frison	Charcoal	A.D. 1750 ± 90	RL 173

extinct bison and was radiocarbon dated at about 4,500 B. C. The Ruby Site is a Late Archaic bison corral site. The Vore Site is an unpublished Late Prehistoric Period buffalo jump site excavated by the University of Wyoming in 1971 and 1972 (see Table 6.1).

Bone Samples

For five of the sites represented in this study, the sample of bones includes the total number of metacarpals and metatarsals that were recovered, both complete and broken. The exception is the Vore Site from which an extremely large total sample was recovered but only part was utilized because only part of the total sample is curated. Unfortunately, immature specimens were not recovered from the Ruby Site due to poor preservation.

Table 6.2 indicates the sample sizes for mature and immature bison metapodials. These numbers are larger than the totals on any one measurement for a site due to the use of a unique feature on the SPSS (Statistical Package for the Social Sciences) which allows coding for missing data that is automatically excluded from statistical calculations.

Metric Measurements

The specific descriptions of measurements are provided in the next section. Two instruments were used in taking all measurements: a pair of

calipers and an osteometric bone board, both with 1 mm. units. Though instruments with smaller units could have been used, this would have increased error by making distinctions that do not exist. There was wide variation in the condition of the bone, both intrasite and intersite, thereby making very small units useless. This may be a handicap in interpreting smaller measurements with shorter ranges but this problem is inherent in any metric analysis.

Each time a measurement is taken, error is involved due to the instrument, the person handling it, the time of day, the condition of the bone, etc. Rather than set up a mathematical formula to compute error, it has been estimated to be plus or minus 1 mm. This is taken into account in interpreting the data. The amount may be larger than the actual error since the author did all of the measurements using the

TABLE 6.2 *Sites and Sample Sizes*

	Total N	Mature	Immature	Total N	Mature	Immature
		Metacarpals			Metatarsals	
SITE						
Casper	84	65	19	68	50	18
Olsen-Chubbuck	48	37	11	34	25	9
Finley	114	91	23	72	67	5
Hawken	45	33	12	48	38	10
Ruby	36	36	0	28	28	0
Vore (Complete)	102	81	21	64	49	15

same two instruments each time.

All metric data as well as other nonmetric data were placed on computer cards, one card per bone. All of the programs used are in the Statistical Package for the Social Sciences (SPSS).

Explanation of Metric Measurements

This section deals only with the metrical measurements taken on the cannon bones. Other nonmetric data taken included maturity or immaturity of the specimen based on visual observations including fusion or non-fusion of the distal epiphysis, right or left side, part of the bone present, and surface condition.

The first five measurements listed are those used by Lorrain (1968). Her numbering system has been retained to maintain a standard system for the measurements. In addition, several measurements are those used by Butler et al. (1971). His numbering system has not been used because it is arbitarily different from Lorrain's system, yet includes the same measurements. Butler's measurements are indicated where they apparently apply. One of the problems encountered by the writer in utilizing the measurements used by Lorrain and Butler is that there are no precise descriptions for taking the measurements other than a diagram. By giving more explicit instructions and a justification for each measurement, this situation could have been avoided. A justification for Lorrain's measurements is not included as they have been accepted as standardized.

Measurement No. 1 (Lorrain). Length: Maximum length is measured by placing the bone posterior side down on an osteometric bone board with the distal condyles lying flat on the board and the midline parallelling the center slide. The measurement is taken from the highest point on the proximal end (Fig. 6.1). Obviously, this measurement is greatly affected by the surface preservation on these ends;

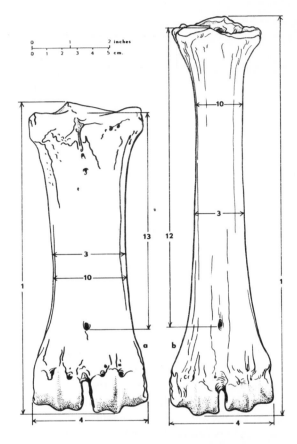

FIGURE 6.1 *Diagram indicating metric measurements: (a) left metacarpal, posterior side. (b) right metatarsal, anterior side. Measurements are described in text.*

therefore, measurements No. 12 and No. 13 (Fig. 6.1) are designed to compensate for this problem.

Measurement No. 2 (Lorrain). Transverse taken using calipers. The base of measurement is the line across the bone which touches the posterolateral muscle attachment and whichever of the two posteromedial muscle attachments protrudes further. Transverse width is taken with the further. Transverse width is taken with the caliper slides at right angles to this line (Fig. 6.2).

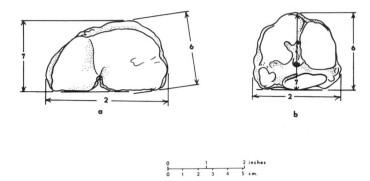

FIGURE 6.2 *Diagram indicating metric measurements: (a) left metacarpal, proximal articular end. (b) right metatarsal, proximal articular end.*

This method is used in preference to Butler's indicated measurement because the two measurements indicated on his diagrams are not the same for metacarpals and metatarsals. The method used here is also more reproducible.

Measurement No. 3 (Lorrain). Transverse width at center of shaft: The measurement is taken with calipers with the bone lying on a flat surface. The distal end is placed flat. The center of the bone was usually judged visually, but frequent checks were made by measuring the distance between the two ends and checking the midpoint (Fig. 6.1).

Measurement No. 4 (Lorrain). Transverse width of the distal end: Using the osteometric bone board, the cannon bone is placed with the distal end flat and the midline perpendicular to the center slide (Fig. 6.1). The greatest width measured in this manner is the correct measurement. This method is used in preference to calipers since it leaves less to individual judgment.

Measurement No. 5 (Lorrain). Anterior-posterior width at center of shaft: This was measured in the same manner as No. 3 with one edge of the calipers flat against the posterior side (Fig. 6.3).

Measurements No. 6 and No. 7 (Butler No. 1).

Anterior-posterior width of proximal end (Fig. 6.2): The measurements originated from that shown by Butler. On the posterior side, the proximal end of a metapodial has three distinct tuberosities. According to Butler's diagram, the medial tuberosity is larger than the center one, so his measurement uses the medial one as the base. However, on almost all of the metacarpals in these samples, the central tuberosity is larger than the medial one. Therefore, measurements were taken from both tuberosities. In practice, metacarpal measurement No. 6 which measured from the medial muscle attachment could not be easily replicated, while measurement No. 7 which uses the line from the central to the lateral tuberosity is easily replicable. Thus measurement No. 6 is a poor measurement for metacarpals and is omitted from the final analysis. For metatarsals, the situation is reversed, so measurement No. 7 is omitted for metatarsals.

Measurement No. 8 (Butler No. 7). Anterior-posterior width of distal end: This measurement was retained for analysis since it completed the set of lateral-medial and anterior-posterior measurements for three points on each bone: proximal end, center of shaft, and distal end. The measurement is taken by placing the specimen in the osteometric bone board so the length certain bones occurs as the animal grows older, particularly in the cannon bones. Measurement No. 9 was taken to test this hypothesis.

Measurement No. 10 (Butler No. 4). Minimum lateral width of shaft: This measurement is taken in the same manner as No. 9 with the calipers rotated 90° then moved to the narrowest point (Fig. 6.1). This measurement was taken to test the same hypothesis as measurement No. 9.

Measurement No. 11. Rotational length: This distance from the center of rotation, medial side, to the proximal articular surface is measured by placing one point of the calipers in the indentation on the condyle, then the other point on the articular surface (Fig. 6.3). The shortest distance, i. e., the lowest point on the articular surface, is the correct reading. This is the effective rotational length, not the greatest length. Therefore, there may be differences here that do not show up in greatest length. Since it has not been used before, the problem is examined in the present study.

Measurement No. 12. Foramen to articular surface length, anterior side: This is measured from the midline foramen on the distal end, anterior side, to the highest point on the articular surface (Fig. 6.1). This does not necessarily parallel the midline. The measurement has been taken because on many bones, particularly the young, the condyles are missing or are in poor condition. The measurement gives another form of length which will be computed as a ratio to greatest length (No. 1). Thus it may be used either alone or as a ratio, depending on its relationship to other variables. Two measurements have been taken, one on the anterior side and one on the posterior side to determine which is "best" for this analysis.

Measurement No. 13. Foramen to articular surface length, posterior side: This is measured the same as No. 12, except from the posterior side and to the lowest point on the articular surface (Fig. 6.1).

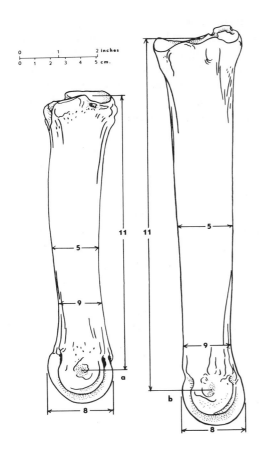

FIGURE 6.3 *Diagram indicating metric measurements: (a) left metacarpal, medial side. (b) right metatarsal, medial side.*

is perpendicular to the center slide and either the lateral or medial side faces up. The measurement is the greatest width of either the condyles or the epiphysis (Fig. 6.3).

Measurement No. 9 (Butler No. 3). Minimum anterior-posterior width of the shaft: This is measured at variable points along the shaft. The narrowest point may be determined visually or by sliding the closed calipers until they cannot be moved in either direction without increasing the width (Fig. 6.3). It has been mentioned (eg. Duffield 1973) that a peculiar thickening of

ANALYSIS OF UNIVARIATE DATA

The complete distribution of metric data for the thirteen measurements discussed in the previous section has been presented for several reasons (Tables 6.3 to 6.15). The format allows better visual comparison between sites, particularly when set up from earliest to latest dates. Other researchers can easily compare their data, particularly along the y axis (value axis). Raw data such as these are not easily summarized by the traditional measures such as mean and standard deviation. Both of these measures are greatly affected by extreme values, especially with relatively small samples. They also do not indicate whether a distribution is unimodal, bimodal, trimodal, or evenly distributed across the range. Mean and standard deviation are measures designed to describe normal (bell-shaped) distribution curves, but a normal distribution is infrequent for these data. Another problem with using mean and standard deviation is that they do not indicate where breaks occur in the distribution. However, since mean and standard deviation have already been included in the literature, they have been included here (Table 6.16) but are not significant to this study. A better summarizing measure would be median (50%ile), with quartiles (25%ile and 75%ile) also indicated; however, the complete distribution is best.

The tables of metric data are further subdivided into mature and immature specimens since inclusion of immature bone with mature would skew the distribution toward the smaller end of the scale, though there is a significant amount of overlapping. The usual method of determining age is relative fusion of epiphyses and only one distal epiphysis (actually two since there are two condyles, but both fuse at the same time) is involved in these bones. According to Koch (1935) this epiphysis fuses at the end of the fourth year in the skeleton of the European bison (*Bison bonasus*). Since comparative data for the American bison *(Bison bison)* are lacking, the time required for this epiphyseal union is assumed to be about the same. This assumption divided the total samples into two groups: mature and immature, depending on whether the epiphysis was fused or unfused. For some measurements, this distinction is critical, i. e., growth in length is stopped when epiphyseal union is complete. However, the width of the shaft continues to enlarge throughout life as the animal gains weight.

Breaks in distributions are very significant in that these indicate possible groupings, in particular, possible male and possible female groups. However, the univariate data provide only hints to these groupings since there are often several breaks that could possibly be used. The traditional method of determining sex on the cannon bones involves the massiveness of the shaft, with the largest shafts labeled "male" specimens and the smaller shafts labeled "female" specimens. Therefore, the distribution should show bimodality with one peak representing males and the other peak representing females. In actuality, such an ideal situation does not exist. For metacarpals, Table 6.5 for measurement No. 3 (transverse width at the center of shaft) shows at least two possible breaks that would allow division into "male" and "female" groups. The Vore Site sample demonstrates no breaks that could be used to differentiate "male" and "female"; the distribution is also trimodal. Therefore, this indicates that either different criteria must be used or that a combination of criteria must be used.

The importance of speciation to the morphological variation shown in the distribution tables cannot be adequately assessed until the critical variable of sex has been resolved. One cannot assume an even split between cows and bulls since this is contrary to what is known of the social organization of bison (McHugh 1958).

TABLE 6.3 *Measurement 1: Greatest Length*

SITE	Casper	Olsen-Chubbuck	Finley	Hawken	Vore	Casper	Olsen-Chubbuck	Finley	Hawken	Ruby	Vore
	Immature Metacarpals					*Mature Metacarpals*					
Value											
177					1						
178		2									
179											
180											
181											
182											
183											
184											
185											
186											
187											
188										1	1
189											3
190	1									2	1
191											
192					1						2
193											1
194										2	2
195					1						6
196											4
197										1	3
198										2	1
199			1							2	4
200						3			1		6
201							1	2	4	4	4
202		1				2		1	2	1	7
203						1				2	5
204						4	1	1	2	3	
205					1	1	1	2	1	3	7
206					1	3	1	2	3	6	4
207							1	2	1		1
208		1					1	3		1	5
209		1			2	1	1	2		1	2
210				1		1	1	2	1		2
211				1		2		2	1		2
212		1				1	2	1			1
213			1	1		6	3	3	1		1
214			1		1	4	3	3	3	1	1
215						6	1	6	1		1
216						4	2	6	1	1	
217						5	4	2			3
218						3	2	4	2		1
219						3	1	2	2		
220						2	1	3	1		
221						2		1			
222						2	4	4	1		
223								3			
224						3	1	4			
225							2	1			
226											
227								1			
228		1					1	3			
229							1				
230								1			

TABLE 6.3 *Continued*

SITE	Casper	Olsen-Chubbuck	Finley	Hawken	Vore	Casper	Olsen-Chubbuck	Finley	Hawken	Ruby	Vore
	Immature Metatarsals					Mature Metatarsals					
Value											
218		1									
219											
220											
221											
222											
223											
224											
225											
226											
227			N								
228			O								
229			N								
230			E								
231											
232											
233											
234											
235											2
236									2		
237											
238					1						
239											2
240										2	1
241	1									2	2
242						1					5
243		1									
244	1								2		1
245										1	2
246										1	3
247							1				2
248							2		1	1	
249					1				2	1	3
250		1		1		2				2	3
251						1			2	1	2
252		1				3			1	1	2
253						3		1	1	2	2
254							1		1		
255						1					2
256						2			3	5	3
257		1				1	1				
258						1		1			1
259				1		2	1	2	2		2
260						1			2		
261					1	3	2	1			5
262						4	2			1	
263							1	3	2	1	1
264						3		2		1	1
265						3	4	2	1	1	
266						3	1		1		
267		1				2		6			
268								2	2		
269						1	2	3	1	1	1
270							2	2			1
271								1	1		
272						1		2			
273								1			

TABLE 6.3 *Continued*

SITE	Casper	Olsen-Chubbuck	Finley	Hawken	Vore	Casper	Olsen-Chubbuck	Finley	Hawken	Ruby	Vore
274						3	1	1			
275						1	2				
276						1	2	3			
277								2			
278								2		1	
279									1		
280							1				
281								2			
282											
283											
284								1			

TABLE 6.4 *Measurement 2: Transverse Width of the Proximal End*

SITE	Casper	Olsen-Chubbuck	Finley	Hawken	Vore	Casper	Olsen-Chubbuck	Finley	Hawken	Ruby	Vore
Value	Immature Metacarpals					Mature Metacarpals					
51					1						
52											
53											
54											
55			1		1						
56	2										1
57				1							
58			1		2						2
59		1			1					1	4
60		1			3						1
61			1							2	7
62	1	4								1	10
63		1							3	5	5
64	1	1			2		1	2	2	3	4
65				3	1		3	3	3		5
66	2		1		1	1	2	3		1	7
67			1	1	2	6	2	5		3	3
68	1	2	1		3	6	4	2			3
69			1	1	1	6	4	2	1		4
70	1				1	5		2	3		5
71			1			15	4	1		2	4
72						7	2	2	1	4	1
73				2		3	1	1	1	1	3
74						4		5	1		3
75						1	1	3	2	1	4
76						1	1		3	1	2
77						1		1	2	1	1
78							1	3		1	
79						1	2	5			
80						1	4	6	2		
81						2	1	7	2		
82								2			
83						2	1	4			
84							1				
85						1	1	1			
86											
87											
88								1			

TABLE 6.4 *Continued*

SITE	Casper	Olsen-Chubbuck	Finley	Hawken	Vore	Casper	Olsen-Chubbuck	Finley	Hawken	Ruby	Vore
	Immature Metatarsals					Mature Metatarsals					
Value											
45				1	1						
46										1	2
47			1	1	4						7
48	3								1	2	1
49		1			1				2	5	6
50	1			1	1				1	2	4
51		3			1				2	3	6
52					3	2		1		2	1
53					1	6	2	3	3	2	3
54	1	1			1	5		3	4	2	1
55	1	1	1	1	2	4	1	3	1		2
56			1	1		6	2	2		1	3
57		2				6	2	2			1
58						3		2	2	1	6
59						2	1	2	4		2
60						3	1	3	2		2
61							2	7	3	2	2
62						2	1	9	1	1	
63						1	4	3	2		
64						4	1	2	1		
65							1	5	1	1	
66								2			
67						1		2			

Depending on the time of year, there were predominantly bull groups and predominantly cow and calf groups as well as mixed groups. Comparison of a bull group with a cow group would be misleading due to sexual dimorphism. If some mature bulls and some mature cows can be assumed to be present in each population, and by comparing the minimum value and the maximum value for each population, then there does exist a slight tendency toward a smaller animal through time, particularly when Casper, Olsen-Chubbuck and Finley are compared with Vore. However, on the basis of the data in this study, all of the populations show considerable overlap with each other.

MULTIVARIATE ANALYSIS

Sex

One of the major problems in accounting for intra-populational variation on a consistent basis has been the inability to assign a bone to either male or female categories. This has been particularly difficult in archaeological contexts in which most of the bone sample consists of disarticulated bones. Thus there has been a need to determine a simple formula for sexing a bone. The traditional method described in an earlier section relies heavily on value judgment to determine the point of separation between males and females.

The problem has been to devise a method of assigning sex so that the element of arbitrariness is held to a minimum. This necessarily involves the use of more than one measurement since single variables do not show this characteristic. Only one measurement (No. 4), comes close to having a bimodal distribution; therefore, this was used as the starting point for analysis. In

TABLE 6.5 *Measurement 3: Lateral-Medial Width at Center of Shaft*

Metacarpals

| | Immature Metacarpals | | | | | Mature Metacarpals | | | | | |
SITE / Value	Casper	Olsen-Chubbuck	Finley	Hawken	Vore	Casper	Olsen-Chubbuck	Finley	Hawken	Ruby	Vore
27			1	2							
28	1				1						
29					1						
30	2				1						
31	2	3			2						
32	2	2			1			1			2
33	2		2		2						
34	5	3		1	2				3		1
35	1	2	2	1						2	7
36	1			2	1	1			2	1	7
37			1				1	3	1	2	9
38			1			2	4	3	4	2	3
39			1		3	2	3	3	2	8	8
40		1			1	9	5	4		1	3
41				1	4	12	2	2	2		4
42	1			2	1	12	5	3	1		6
43			1			12	1	1	2	1	3
44						2	2	6			2
45			2			1		3		2	7
46						2	1	2	1	2	3
47						1	1	2	3		6
48						1		5	2	1	6
49						2	3	10	1	2	1
50						2	4	4	1		2
51							1	9		1	
52						1	2	6	2		
53						1	2	2	1		
54						1	1	2			
55						1					
56							1				

Metatarsals

| | Immature Metatarsals | | | | | Mature Metatarsals | | | | | |
Value	Casper	Olsen-Chubbuck	Finley	Hawken	Vore	Casper	Olsen-Chubbuck	Finley	Hawken	Ruby	Vore
23					1						
24		1			1						
25	3				1						
26	3			1							
27	2		2	2	1						
28	5		1						1		1
29	2	4							3	3	4
30					1		2		3	3	7
31		2			2	1			4	4	3
32		2			3	5	3	3	2	3	7
33	1		1		2	7	2	2	2	5	2
34					1	11	3	7	2	2	6
35				2	2	8	1		1	3	3
36						2		3	3		5
37			1	1		2		4	3		2
38			1					5	6		4
39						2	1	7	1		1
40						2	1	6		1	2
41						5	5	13	1	1	
42							5	6			2
43								2		1	
44											
45								1			
46											
47								1			

TABLE 6.6 *Measurement 4: Transverse Width of Distal End*

SITE	Casper	Olsen-Chubbuck	Finley	Hawken	Vore	Casper	Olsen-Chubbuck	Finley	Hawken	Ruby	Vore
	Immature Metacarpals					Mature Metacarpals					
Value											
60	1										1
61			1							2	3
62	1										4
63					1					1	1
64		2								1	7
65									1	4	5
66		1		1			1		1	3	9
67										5	2
68		2	1				2	3	4	1	5
69				1				2	2	1	1
70						4		4	2	3	4
71			2		1	6	4	3	2	1	3
72		2	1			8	5	1			3
73					2	4	3	2			7
74						9	2	2	1		6
75					1	6	4	1	1		3
76						4	1	1	2	2	9
77						4		1	1	3	3
78						5	1	2	2		2
79			1			1	2	3	3	2	1
80							1	2	1		1
81							2	9	2	2	
82			2			1	2		1		
83						1	1	1			
84			1				2	6	1		
85			2			2	1	8			
86						1		2	2		
87			2			2		2	1		
88								2			
89						1					
90							1				
91						1					
	Immature Metatarsals					Mature Metatarsals					
53					1						
54											
55											
56											4
57	1										1
58									1	2	3
59		1							1	2	5
60								1	1	6	5
61			NONE				1		5	5	5
62	1	1							4	2	2
63		1				2	1	1	2	2	3
64	1	1			2	4		4	1		3
65						2	1	2	1	2	2
66				1		9	1	1	1	1	3
67						5	3	3	1		3
68						10	1	1	1		
69	1	1		1		3	4	2	2	1	2
70						2		1	4		2
71						1	1	3	3	1	5
72		1				2	1	5	2		
73								5	2		
74						1	2	4		1	1
75						2	6	6			

TABLE 6.6 *Continued*

SITE	Casper	Olsen-Chubbuck	Finley	Hawken	Vore	Casper	Olsen-Chubbuck	Finley	Hawken	Ruby	Vore
76						1	2	2			
77							1	3			
78								2			
79					3	1					

TABLE 6.7 *Measurement 5: Anterior-Posterior Width at Center of Shaft*

SITE	Casper	Olsen-Chubbuck	Finley	Hawken	Vore	Casper	Olsen-Chubbuck	Finley	Hawken	Ruby	Vore
	Immature Metacarpals					Mature Metacarpals					
Value											
19					1						
20				1							
21	1	2	1	1	1						
22	3	2			3						
23	3	1	3		3						
24	2			2	2			1	1	3	2
25	4		1	1	4				3	1	18
26	2	3			3	1	1	3	4	9	16
27		2	1	2	3	8	4	7	7	4	5
28		1	3	2		9	6	7	1	3	12
29	1		1			15	9	9	4	5	5
30			1			15	4	2	1	1	10
31						8	1	7	2	1	7
32						1	2	10	1	1	3
33						4	3	7	1	1	1
34						1	4	11			
35						2	1	5	3		
36								1			
37								2			
	Immature Metatarsals					Mature Metatarsals					
22					1						
23											
24			1		1						
25		1	1								
26	3			1							
27	5		1	1	1						1
28	2			1	1						
29	2				4				2	2	2
30	2	4			3				1	1	6
31		1		1	2	1		2	4	5	10
32	1				1	11		4	6	5	9
33		1		2		6	2	7	3	4	3
34		2				10	3	3	3	1	3
35			1		1	7	2	3	2	1	4
36			1	1		2	4	3	3	1	3
37	1					2		6	4	1	4
38						2	2	7	3	1	3
39						1	5	11			1
40						1	5	7			
41							1	1			
42	1					1					

TABLE 6.8 *Measurement 6: Anterior-Posterior Width of Proximal End--Inner Lobe*

SITE	Casper	Olsen-Chubbuck	Finley	Hawken	Vore	Casper	Olsen-Chubbuck	Finley	Hawken	Ruby	Vore
	Immature Metacarpals					Mature Metacarpals					
Value											
28					1						
29			1								
30											
31					1						
32		2			3						4
33			1	1					1	2	4
34			1		1				1	2	3
35	1	2		1	2			2	2	7	6
36	2	2		1	2	3	1	1	3	2	9
37	2	1	1	1	3	5	4	4	2	6	13
38	1	1		1	2	6	6	3	4	1	10
39		1			1	11	3	4		4	6
40	1	1		2	1	13	6	4		3	12
41			1		2	5	1	3	1		2
42						8	1	8	5	2	2
43						1	3	3	3		6
44						2	3	2	3	2	
45						3	1	9	2	1	1
46						2	3	4			
47						1	1	6			
48						1					1
	Immature Metatarsals					Mature Metatarsals					
44					3					2	
45	1										1
46	1		1	2						2	3
47					2				1	1	9
48	1	1			2				2	2	8
49	1			1	1	2			3	1	6
50		1			3	2			2	3	3
51					3	1		2	2	2	1
52		1				1		3	1	1	4
53	1					4	1	5	5	2	1
54	1	3	2	1	1	7	2	2	2	1	2
55		1				7	1	3	2		2
56						7	4	6	1		6
57						3	2	1	3	3	3
58		1				5		5	4		
59						2		4	1		
60						1	3	5			
61						1		4			
62						1		2			
63							3	2			
64							2				
65							1				
66							2				

TABLE 6.9 *Measurement 7: Anterior-Posterior Width of Proximal End--Outer Lobe*

SITE	Casper	Olsen-Chubbuck	Finley	Hawken	Vore	Casper	Olsen-Chubbuck	Finley	Hawken	Ruby	Vore
	Immature Metacarpals					**Mature Metacarpals**					
Value											
31			1		1						
32					1						
33				1							
34			1		2						2
35	1				3						3
36		3	1						1	3	6
37	1	1						1	1	2	6
38	1	2		2	3	1		1	3	6	10
39	1		1	2	2	2		2	1	3	7
40	1	1				3	2	1	4	3	9
41	1				3	19	6	3	2	3	5
42		1			3	11	4	3		1	7
43				1		4	6	4	3	1	9
44	1				1	10	4	2	2	1	6
45			1	1		4	1	5	2		4
46							3	6	6		2
47						1		4	1	1	
48						1	3	5	2		2
49						1	3	7			1
50						3	1	2			
51						1	1	5			
52								3			
	Immature Metatarsals					**Mature Metatarsals**					
45					2					1	
46				1					1	2	6
47		1	1		1				1		5
48				1	3				1	3	6
49		1			5				3	1	8
50	2	1		1	1	3			1	2	2
51		1				2	1	1	4	1	4
52	1	1			1	4	1	2	1	1	4
53	1					5	3	2	1	2	1
54				1		3	5	2	2		4
55		1	2		1	6	4	1	2	3	2
56		2		1		4	2	3	3		2
57				1		4		4	5	1	4
58						5	3	1	1	1	1
59						1	1	4	2		
60						1	2	4			
61						1	2	2			
62						2		5			
63							4				
64							1	1			

TABLE 6.10 *Measurement 8: Anterior-Posterior Width of Distal End*

SITE	Casper	Olsen-Chubbuck	Finley	Hawken	Vore	Casper	Olsen-Chubbuck	Finley	Hawken	Ruby	Vore
		Immature Metacarpals					Mature Metacarpals				
Value											
31										1	1
32											
33										2	4
34				1	1	1				4	10
35	1		1		1				3	9	11
36		3	1	1		1		3	5	6	10
37		3	2			1	3	7	5	2	13
38				2	4	14	2	1	4	1	14
39						16	7	4	2	3	12
40			1			10	9	8	5	2	6
41		1	1			7	2	7	1	2	1
42			2			3	5	5	3		1
43						2	3	11	4		
44			1			2	1	8			
45			2			1	4	2			
46			1			1		2			
47											
48											
49						1					
		Immature Metatarsals					Mature Metatarsals				
33					1	1				1	3
34							1		1	5	6
35									4	9	10
36								1	5	4	6
37	1	1		1	1	1		3	7	2	5
38	1	2		1	1	4	1	8	3	1	4
39				1		11	2	4	3		4
40		2				10	3	9	6	2	9
41		1				11	5	5	4		
42						3	2	9	1	1	1
43						1	6	4	2		1
44						2	1	8			
45						2	2	2			
46	1					1		1			
47							1				

addition, since previous authors had used transverse width at the center of the shaft (No. 3) in determining sex, it was desirable to retain this measurement in some form. Another factor considered was an indicator of length.

Duffield (1973) published a graph on which the transverse width of the distal end was plotted against Ratio 6 (Lorrain 1968: see Table 6.17) for metatarsals, utilizing data from Empel and Roskosz (1963) on European bison of known age and sex from Polish herd books. On this graph the metatarsals separated into two clusters which were male and female mature animals. Females had narrower distal ends and smaller values for Ratio 6, and males had wider distal ends and larger values for Ratio 6. One problem was whether this same pattern held for both metacarpals and metatarsals of fossil bison. A second problem was whether the break between the two clusters varied from site to site. By having six different sites with a time span of approximately ten thousand years, these hypotheses could be tested.

On the chart published by Duffield, eight immature specimens were plotted along with the mature ones. Only one of the four immature

TABLE 6.11 *Measurement 9: Minimum Anterior-Posterior Width of Shaft*

SITE	Casper	Olsen-Chubbuck	Finley	Hawken	Vore	Casper	Olsen-Chubbuck	Finley	Hawken	Ruby	Vore
Value		Immature Metacarpals					Mature Metacarpals				
19					1						
20				1							
21	2	2		1	1						
22	2	2		1	5					1	3
23	4	1	3		2	1			2	3	10
24	1			3	3			2	2	5	15
25	4	3	2	2	3	4	2	3	5	8	15
26	1				5	6	6	5	3	6	14
27		3		2		23	6	6	7	2	14
28	1		2	1		13	9	8	3	4	5
29						9	6	10	3	3	4
30						3	2	15			1
31						1	4	8	2	1	
32						3	1	1	1		
33							1				
		Immature Metatarsals					Mature Metatarsals				
22					1						
23	1			1	1						
24		1	1								1
25	3		1								
26	2			2	3						3
27	6		1	1	3	1		2		7	12
28	2	2		2	4	3		2	5	5	7
29		2	1		1	6		3	8	5	8
30		1		2	1	6	4	9	7	2	7
31	1	3		1		10	3	5	7	1	7
32			2		1	10	9	9	3	2	3
33						5	4	8	2		1
34	1					1	3	11		1	
35						2	2	1			

males fell in the male cluster; the other three males and the four immature females fell into the female cluster or below. Since this is a sample of known age and sex, samples of unknown age and sex must first be separated into mature and immature groups before they can be sexed.

All mature specimens for which transverse width of the distal end (No. 4), transverse width at the center of the shaft (No. 3) and greatest length (No. 1) were available were plotted by site on xy graphs of the same dimensions (using the SPSS program SCATTERGRAM). Transverse width of the distal end was plotted on the y axis and Ratio 6 was plotted on the x axis. The results are shown in Figs. 6.4 to 6.19. Each dot represents a single specimen of a given x and y

value. Multiple specimens having the same x and y values are indicated by numbers. These may or may not represent bones from the same animal. The dimensions on the graphs are different for metacarpals and metatarsals. Each graph shows clustering with a break between the two clusters. These clusters are assumed to represent male and female groups with males above the breaks and females below the breaks. The tightness of each cluster depends on the size of the sample, the relative proportions of male and female bones and the components in the site.

The importance of this last factor is particularly applicable to the multi-component Vore site. Since the specimens included in this sample are a sub-sample of a sample of the entire site, they are

TABLE 6.12 *Measurement 10: Minimum Lateral-Medial Width of Shaft*

Immature Metacarpals

Value	Casper	Olsen-Chubbuck	Finley	Hawken	Vore
26					1
27			1	2	
28	1				1
29					
30	2	1		1	2
31	2	2	2		3
32	2	2	1		1
33	2			2	1
34	7	3		1	1
35		2			
36			1		2
37					
38					1
39					2
40		1			3
41	1			3	1
42			2		1

Mature Metacarpals

Value	Casper	Olsen-Chubbuck	Finley	Hawken	Ruby	Vore
32						2
33				1		1
34				2		1
35				1	2	8
36	1		1	3	1	6
37		1	2	1	3	8
38	1	7	4	3	1	4
39	4		2	2	8	8
40	7	4	2			2
41	12	6	3	1		4
42	11	3	3	2		6
43	14	1	1	1		5
44	2	2	2		2	
45	2	1	1		2	8
46	1		3	2		4
47			3	3	1	5
48	1		3	1	1	4
49	1	3	7	2	1	3
50	3	6			1	
51		2	4	1		
52	1	2	4	1		
53	2	1	1	1		
54			1	2		
55	1					
56		1				

Immature Metatarsals

Value	Casper	Olsen-Chubbuck	Finley	Hawken	Vore
21					1
22					
23					2
24	2	1	1	1	
25	2		1	2	
26	4				1
27	3	1	1		
28	2	3			1
29		2			5
30	1				1
31		2		1	3
32				2	
33	1		2		1
34					
35				1	

Mature Metatarsals

Value	Casper	Olsen-Chubbuck	Finley	Hawken	Ruby	Vore
26						1
27				2	1	3
28				1	2	5
29				4	5	4
30	3	1	2	3		8
31	7	3	3	1	4	5
32	4	2	3	2	3	5
33	11	3	3	1		1
34	7	3	3	2	2	4
35	1	1	5	4		4
36	1		2	7		3
37	2		8			3
38	1	1	5	1	1	2
39	2	3	6		2	
40	4	6	5	1	1	1
41			1			
42		1	1			
43						
44			1			

TABLE 6.13 *Measurement 11: Rotational Length*

SITE	Casper	Olsen-Chubbuck	Finley	Hawken	Vore	Casper	Olsen-Chubbuck	Finley	Hawken	Ruby	Vore
	Immature Metacarpals					Mature Metacarpals					
Value											
153		1			1						
154		1									
155											
156											
157											
158											
159											1
160										1	
161										1	3
162											4
163										1	1
164											
165					1						3
166											
167	1									1	6
168											7
169							1			1	4
170										1	
171						3		2		2	6
172		1				2			2	1	10
173						1		3		3	6
174						1		4		2	4
175						2	1	4	1	4	3
176						3	1	3		5	
177					1	2	2	2	1	1	3
178						1	2	3	2	3	5
179						2	2	2	3	1	3
180		2				1	3	3	2	1	4
181		1				4	2	2	1		
182					2	2	4	2	1		2
183						4	1	6		2	1
184			1	2		9	2	5	3		2
185					1	6		5	3		3
186						2	4	3		1	
187						5	2	2			
188						2		5	1		
189						1	2	2	1		
190						1	1	2			
191						1		2			
192						1	3	2			
193						2	1	2			
194							1	2			
195								1			
196								1			
197											
198		1				1					
	Immature Metatarsals					Mature Metatarsals					
185		1									
186											
187											
188											
189											
190											
191											
192											
193											

TABLE 6.13 *Continued*

SITE	Casper	Olsen-Chubbuck	Finley	Hawken	Vore	Casper	Olsen-Chubbuck	Finley	Hawken	Ruby	Vore
194											
195											1
196											
197	1										
198									1		
199											1
200									1		
201											1
202					1						2
203											
204	1									1	2
205						1				2	3
206										1	3
207										1	1
208											1
209			NONE		1				1		1
210	1	1									1
211							1		3		2
212									1	3	3
213						2			2		2
214				1		2	1			1	3
215						2			2	3	1
216						2		3	2	1	2
217				1		1		1	2		4
218		2				5	1	1	1	1	3
219		1				2		1		1	3
220								1	2	1	2
221					1	1		1		2	1
222						4	1	2			1
223						5	4	4	7		2
224						2	2	1		3	
225						2		1			1
226						1	2	2			1
227		1				3		6			
228						1	1	2		1	
229						2	2	3			
230						1	1	4			
231							2	3			1
232								3			
233						1		2			
234						1		1	1	1	
235						2	3	1			
236						1		1			
237							1	2			

TABLE 6.14 *Measurement 12: Foramen to Articular Surface Length--Anterior Side*

SIDE	Casper	Olsen-Chubbuck	Finley	Hawken	Vore		Casper	Olsen-Chubbuck	Finley	Hawken	Ruby	Vore
	Immature Metacarpals						Mature Metacarpals					
Value												
124					1							
125												
126												
127												
128												
129					1							
130					1							
131												
132		2										
133					1							
134			1									
135												
136												1
137												
138	2	3										1
139	1											
140				1	2							
141											3	1
142			1								1	1
143			1		2							3
144											3	3
145	2						1		1			4
146					1							3
147											1	2
148	1				2		2				2	4
149	2			1	1							7
150	1	1			1		2			2	1	6
151					3		1			4	5	4
152				1			4			2	3	9
153	1						5	1		4	1	7
154			1				3		3	1	1	4
155	1				2		1	1	3		1	4
156			1		1		2	2	3	3	3	3
157				3			4	2	1	1	3	2
158				1			4	1	3			3
159					1		3	2	3	3	2	3
160		1	1				1	3	4	1		
161		1					5	3	6	3	2	
162	1	1					3	2	2		1	
163							3	2	4	2		2
164							5	5	6	1		2
165							3	2	1			1
166							3	1	3	1		1
167							1	1	1			
168		2					4	3	2			
169							2	1	2			
170								1	3			
171												
172												
173								1				
174												
175								1				
	Immature Metatarsals						Mature Metatarsals					
154					1							
155												
156												

TABLE 6.14 *Continued*

SITE	Casper	Olsen-Chubbuck	Finley	Hawken	Vore	Casper	Olsen-Chubbuck	Finley	Hawken	Ruby	Vore
157					1						
158											
159											
160											
161											
162											
163		1									
164											
165											
166											
167											
168					1						
169											
170	1										
171				1							
172					1						2
173	1				1				1		1
174	1				1				1	2	1
175						1				1	
176										1	
177			2		1					1	2
178									1		2
179	1				1						2
180						1					1
181					1	1			2	1	5
182				1	1	2				1	1
183					1						5
184				1		1					1
185								1	1		4
186		1		1	1				1	2	2
187		1		1	1				3	3	1
188			1		1	2	1	1	3	3	2
189		1		1		4	1	2	2	1	3
190		1				2		2	1	1	4
191		1				3		2	2		4
192				1	1	1		1	2	1	1
193							1		2	2	2
194	1	1				7	2	4	1		
195			1			5	2	6		2	
196			1			3	1	5		1	
197							2	4			1
198					1	4	3	2	2	1	
199							2	1	1		
200		1				3	2				
201								2		1	1
202						1	1	1			
203		1				1		4	2		
204								1	1		
205						1	2	1			
206							1	1			
207						1	2	5		1	
208									1		
209								2			
210											
211							1				

TABLE 6.15 *Measurement 13: Foramen to Articular Surface Length--Posterior Side*

SITE	Casper	Olsen-Chubbuck	Finley	Hawken	Vore	Casper	Olsen-Chubbuck	Finley	Hawken	Ruby	Vore
Value			Immature Metacarpals					Mature Metacarpals			
121					1						
122											
123											
124											
125											
126											
127											
128											
129					2						
130											1
131											
132					1						2
133		2			1						
134		2	1								1
135										1	
136										1	
137				1							1
138	1			1	1					3	2
139						1				3	5
140		1		1	1					3	
141											3
142			1		1	1	1	1	1	1	6
143									1		9
144	1		1			1			2	1	3
145				1	2	5		1	2	2	6
146					3	1	2	2	3	4	6
147	2				2	2	1		4	3	11
148	1				1	3		2		2	4
149	1		1				1	4	2		6
150			1	1	1	2	5	2	2	3	4
151				3	1	3	2		1	2	2
152					1	4	3	4	1	3	1
153		1	1			4	4	2	2	1	1
154	1					4	2	5		1	1
155		1				5	2	1	2		1
156	1	1				9		5	1		2
157			2			3	6	5			1
158				1		4	2	6	2		1
159						2	3	4			1
160					1	3			1		
161						2	1	2	1		
162						1	1	1			
163		1				1	1	1			
164		1						1			
165						1		1			
166											
167											
168			Immature Metatarsals					Mature Metatarsals			
160					1						
161											
162					1						
163											
164											
165											
166											
167											

TABLE 6.15 *Continued*

SITE	Casper	Olsen-Chubbuck	Finley	Hawken	Vore	Casper	Olsen-Chubbuck	Finley	Hawken	Ruby	Vore
168											
169											
170		1									
171											
172											
173	1				1						
174											2
175				1	1				1		
176	1								1		1
177										1	
178										1	
179	1				2						2
180			1								2
181					1					1	2
182					1	1			1	1	
183	1					1					3
184											4
185					1	1				1	2
186	1	1				2	1		1		3
187									1		3
188						2			2		2
189				3	2	2		1		1	5
190						1	1	2	4	2	1
191		1			1	3	1	1	3	2	4
192						2		1		1	3
193		1		1		2		3	2	1	2
194		1		1	1	1	2	2	3	1	1
195					1	1		5	1	2	1
196						2		3			1
197			1			4	1	1	1		
198		1				3	1	2	1		1
199					1	3	2		1	2	
200			1			1	2	4			1
201						2	1	2	3	3	1
202						5	2			1	
203	1					2			1		
204							1	2	1	1	1
205		1				1	4	1			
206						1		3			
207						1		1	1		
208							1	2	1		
209								2			
210	1						1	3			
211											
212											
213											
214						1	1				

TABLE 6.16 *Means and Standard Deviations for Metric Measurements*

SITE	Casper	Olsen-Chubbuck	Finley	Hawken	Ruby	Vore
			Immature Metacarpals			
Measurement 1:						
Mean	190.0	202.1	208.7	211.3	—	200.9
Standard Deviation	0.0	18.3	8.4	1.5	—	12.1
Measurement 2:						
Mean	63.5	63.0	64.4	66.8	—	63.0
Standard Deviation	5.2	3.0	5.7	5.2	--	5.3
Measurement 3:						
Mean	33.1	33.5	37.3	35.6	—	35.7
Standard Deviation	3.1	2.7	5.5	5.7	—	4.7
Measurement 4:						
Mean	61.0	67.7	78.0	67.5	—	71.0
Standard Deviation	1.4	3.4	8.4	2.1	—	4.7
Measurement 5:						
Mean	24.1	24.5	25.9	24.9	—	24.1
Standard Deviation	2.1	2.7	3.0	2.9	--	2.2
Measurement 6:						
Mean	37.0	36.0	34.8	37.0	---	37.7
Standard Deviation	1.6	2.7	4.5	2.6	—	3.6
Measurement 7:						
Mean	39.1	37.9	37.0	39.3	—	37.9
Standard Deviation	2.9	2.0	5.3	3.9	—	3.8
Measurement 8:						
Mean	35.0	37.1	40.8	36.5	—	36.9
Standard Deviation	0.0	1.8	3.8	1.9	—	1.7
Measurement 9:						
Mean	23.7	24.1	25.0	24.3	--	23.6
Standard Deviation	1.9	2.4	2.2	2.5	--	2.0
Measurement 10:						
Mean	32.9	33.5	34.2	34.3	—	34.8
Standard Deviation	2.8	2.8	6.3	5.4	—	4.8
Measurement 11:						
Mean	167.0	174.0	184.0	184.0	—	174.0
Standard Deviation	0.0	16.0	0.0	0.0	---	12.5
Measurement 12:						
Mean	147.6	149.7	151.0	150.6	---	145.0
Standard Deviation	7.2	14.5	11.6	7.3	--	9.8
Measurement 13:						
Mean	147.9	146.5	148.2	146.8	---	142.4
Standard Deviation	5.6	12.9	7.9	7.2	—	9.5
			Mature Metacarpals			
Measurement 1:						
Mean	213.4	215.7	215.7	209.6	202.1	202.1
Standard Deviation	6.5	6.8	7.1	7.0	6.3	7.1
Measurement 2:						
Mean	71.7	73.3	75.1	71.4	67.6	66.2
Standard Deviation	4.3	6.0	6.4	6.0	5.5	5.2
Measurement 3:						
Mean	43.0	44.0	46.3	42.5	41.2	41.0
Standard Deviation	3.9	5.6	5.2	6.0	4.8	4.8
Measurement 4:						
Mean	75.5	76.3	78.8	75.4	69.8	69.8
Standard Deviation	4.9	5.6	6.3	6.5	6.0	5.3
Measurement 5:						
Mean	29.6	29.9	31.2	28.5	27.4	27.5
Standard Deviation	2.0	2.5	3.1	3.2	2.3	2.4

TABLE 6.16 *Continued*

SITE	Casper	Olsen-Chubbuck	Finley	Hawken	Ruby	Vore
Measurement 6:						
Mean	40.4	40.7	42.1	39.7	37.6	37.8
Standard Deviation	2.8	3.2	3.5	3.7	3.2	3.2
Measurement 7:						
Mean	42.8	44.2	46.0	42.6	39.4	40.4
Standard Deviation	2.8	3.2	3.9	3.6	2.7	3.4
Measurement 8:						
Mean	39.7	40.9	41.1	38.7	36.1	36.7
Standard Deviation	2.1	2.7	2.7	2.6	2.4	2.2
Measurement 9:						
Mean	27.6	28.1	28.6	26.8	25.8	25.4
Standard Deviation	1.7	1.9	2.0	2.3	2.1	1.8
Measurement 10:						
Mean	43.0	43.6	45.9	42.0	40.8	40.7
Standard Deviation	3.8	5.6	5.2	6.1	4.6	4.7
Measurement 11:						
Mean	182.5	183.4	183.9	179.0	174.2	172.3
Standard Deviation	6.0	5.8	6.1	5.1	5.8	6.4
Measurement 12:						
Mean	159.0	162.8	161.3	156.2	151.6	151.4
Standard Deviation	6.0	5.1	5.1	4.8	6.2	6.0
Measurement 13:						
Mean	153.5	154.8	154.6	150.0	145.7	145.4
Standard Deviation	5.5	4.9	5.2	5.4	5.4	5.6
Immature Metatarsals						
Measurement 1:						
Mean	242.5	247.8	––	254.5	—	249.3
Standard Deviation	2.1	16.7	––	6.4	—	11.5
Measurement 2:						
Mean	50.5	53.1	52.7	50.6	—	50.4
Standard Deviation	3.2	3.0	4.9	4.8	—	3.2
Measurement 3:						
Mean	27.4	29.6	31.4	31.4	—	30.5
Standard Deviation	2.0	2.4	5.6	4.6	—	3.9
Measurement 4:						
Mean	63.0	64.8	––	67.5	—	60.3
Standard Deviation	5.0	4.8	––	2.1	—	6.4
Measurement 5:						
Mean	28.5	30.8	29.4	30.6	––	29.1
Standard Deviation	2.7	2.8	5.7	3.7	––	3.1
Measurement 6:						
Mean	49.2	53.1	51.3	48.8	—	48.5
Standard Deviation	3.7	3.1	4.6	3.8	—	3.0
Measurement 7:						
Mean	51.2	52.0	52.3	51.8	—	48.8
Standard Deviation	1.5	3.4	4.6	4.5	—	2.6
Measurement 8:						
Mean	40.3	39.0	––	38.0	—	36.0
Standard Deviation	4.0	1.6	—	1.0	—	2.6
Measurement 9:						
Mean	27.1	20.0	28.0	27.8	––	27.1
Standard Deviation	2.5	2.2	3.8	2.4	––	2.5

TABLE 6.16 *Continued*

SITE	Casper	Olsen-Chubbuck	Finley	Hawken	Ruby	Vore
Measurement 10:						
Mean	26.8	28.3	28.4	29.1	—	28.1
Standard Deviation	2.3	2.1	4.3	4.4	—	3.4
Measurement 11:						
Mean	203.7	212.8	—	215.0	—	210.7
Standard Deviation	6.5	14.7	—	2.1	—	9.6
Measurement 12:						
Mean	178.0	189.2	186.2	184.6	—	178.5
Standard Deviation	9.5	11.4	10.7	6.8	—	12.1
Measurement 13:						
Mean	184.5	192.5	192.3	188.2	—	182.2
Standard Deviation	13.3	11.0	10.8	6.8	—	11.4
Mature Metatarsals						
Measurement 1:						
Mean	261.2	258.7	268.8	256.7	253.6	250.6
Standard Deviation	7.9	4.4	7.0	10.3	9.4	8.6
Measurement 2:						
Mean	57.2	58.7	60.2	56.7	52.3	52.6
Standard Deviation	3.8	4.4	4.1	4.9	4.4	4.6
Measurement 3:						
Mean	38.2	37.0	38.7	34.0	33.0	33.8
Standard Deviation	3.0	4.4	3.4	3.7	3.6	3.6
Measurement 4:						
Mean	68.5	70.8	71.4	65.9	62.4	63.2
Standard Deviation	4.1	4.6	4.7	4.7	4.0	4.9
Measurement 5:						
Mean	34.3	37.2	36.6	33.7	32.5	32.9
Standard Deviation	2.4	2.6	2.9	2.8	2.4	2.9
Measurement 6:						
Mean	55.2	59.4	57.0	53.3	50.4	50.4
Standard Deviation	3.0	4.3	3.5	3.6	4.0	3.7
Measurement 7:						
Mean	55.2	57.7	57.5	53.4	51.1	50.6
Standard Deviation	3.2	4.3	3.4	3.8	3.9	3.6
Measurement 8:						
Mean	40.3	41.4	40.9	38.2	35.8	36.9
Standard Deviation	2.2	2.8	2.5	2.4	2.2	2.5
Measurement 9:						
Mean	31.0	32.2	31.8	29.8	28.8	28.8
Standard Deviation	1.8	1.5	1.8	1.6	1.9	2.0
Measurement 10:						
Mean	33.9	36.0	36.2	32.9	32.0	31.9
Standard Deviation	3.0	3.9	3.3	3.5	4.0	3.5
Measurement 11:						
Mean	222.4	226.2	226.9	216.4	216.1	213.0
Standard Deviation	6.8	6.7	5.7	7.6	7.9	7.7
Measurement 12:						
Mean	193.0	198.4	197.9	190.8	187.5	184.9
Standard Deviation	6.7	6.1	6.1	8.2	8.5	6.5
Measurement 13:						
Mean	196.0	200.2	199.6	193.2	192.3	187.6
Standard Deviation	6.9	7.0	6.3	8.0	7.9	6.6

TABLE 6.17 *Formulas for Derived Ratios*

Ratio 1 = $\dfrac{\text{Anterior-Posterior Width at Center of Shaft}}{\text{Minimum Anterior-Posterior Width of Shaft}}$

Ratio 2 = $\dfrac{\text{Transverse Width at Center of Shaft}}{\text{Minimum Lateral-Medial Width of Shaft}}$

Ratio 3 = $\dfrac{\text{Greatest Length}}{\text{Rotational Length}}$

Ratio 4 = $\dfrac{\text{Greatest Length}}{\text{Foramen to Articular Surface Length--Anterior Side}}$

Ratio 5 = $\dfrac{\text{Greatest Length}}{\text{Foramen to Articular Surface Length--Posterior Side}}$

Ratio 6* = $\dfrac{\text{Transverse Width at Center of Shaft}}{\text{Greatest Length}} \times 100$

*Lorrain (1968)

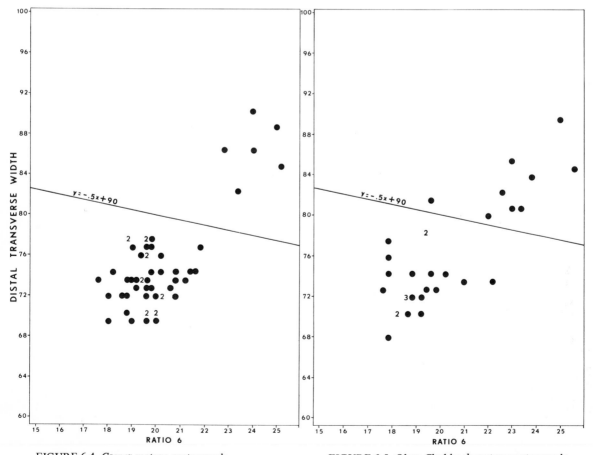

FIGURE 6.4 *Casper mature metacarpals.*   FIGURE 6.5 *Olsen-Chubbuck mature metacarpals.*

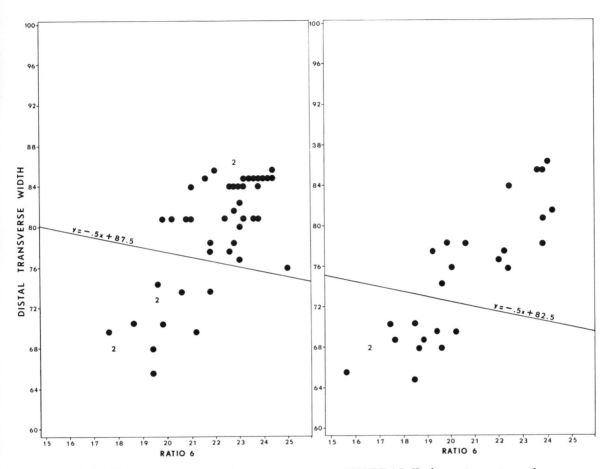

FIGURE 6.6 *Finley mature metacarpals.*   FIGURE 6.7 *Hawken mature metacarpals.*

from different levels in the site and two different years of excavation. The first year the levels were arbitrary,whereas the second year they were cultural. At this point, there is no reliable correlation between the arbitary and the cultural levels. Therefore, since the middle levels (5 and 6) could be reasonably expected to overlap, they were placed on a separate graph and then the top levels (1 to 4) and the bottom levels (7 and lower) were compared to each other. This immediately clarified the problem. When the entire site was plotted on a single graph, there was little clustering when compared with the graphs of the other sites; when the top and the bottom were

plotted on separate graphs, there was distinct clustering with the break between clusters falling at a lower point on the top (or more recent) segment. This suggests that different populations are represented, even though present dating of the site suggests a total time span of several hundred years (Frison, personal communication). Thus ideally, for purposes of sexing, the bones in each component should only be compared with each other. In practice, the size of the sample became too small to determine where the break between clusters occurred, so for comparative purposes the top segment is used as the modern sample.

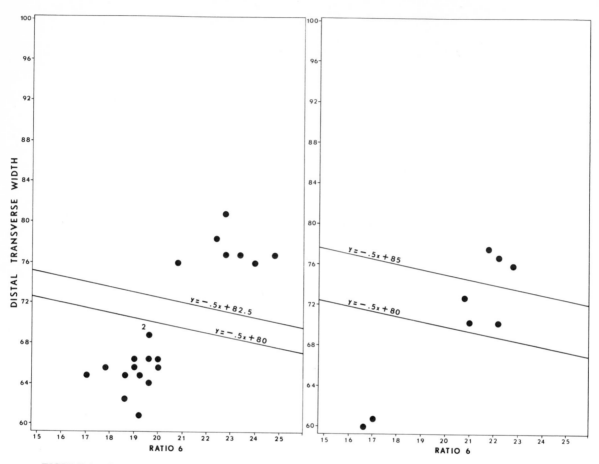

FIGURE 6.8 *Ruby mature metacarpals.*

FIGURE 6.9 *Vore mature metacarpals, levels 7 and lower.*

The second site for which component became important is the Finley site because it possibly has two components. However, since the bone was removed from uncontrolled excavation, evidence of stratigraphy no longer existed. The existence of two components within the site might account for the fact that the clustering is not as tight for this site as for the other sites. In addition, the Finley bone was in the poorest condition of any of the bone measured. The same situation existed for the Hawken site with three components which may represent three consecutive years of use. Part of the sample of

bone was also recovered from uncontrolled excavation. However, this site shows distinct clustering between males and females so the three levels probably represent the same local population, rather than different populations as is the case with Vore and possibly Finley. The other three sites are single component sites. On a theoretical level, clustering or lack of clustering may prove to be quite important as an indication of whether a site contains more than one bison population.

For the scattergrams produced by SPSS, Pearson's correlation coefficient *r* has been

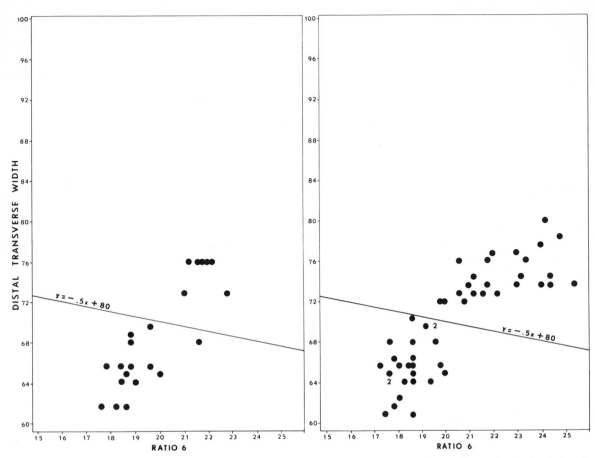

FIGURE 6.10 *Vore mature metacarpals, levels 5 and 6.*   FIGURE 6.11 *Vore mature metacarpals, levels 1 to 4.*

calculated. This correlation coefficient is an indicator of the amount of spread about the linear least squares equation (Blalock 1960: 286). The value ranges from −1 to 1 with −1 indicating a perfect negative relationship and 1 indicating a perfect positive relationship. A value of 0 would indicate either total randomness or a nonlinear relationship. As noted in Table 6.18, the values of r for these graphs are comparatively high, and all are significant at the usual .05 level. The slopes of the linear least squares equations are also given. For the metacarpals, the slopes are clustered about 2 and for the metatarsals, the slopes are clustered about 3, with the greatest

variation away from these two points in the smallest samples. Though the least squares equations and r are consistent, the problem lies in defining the break between the two clusters in each graph that are interpreted to be male and female. To do this, the line that is perpendicular to the least squares linear equation and that passes through the break between clusters was calculated and plotted on the scattergrams. The point-slope form of a linear equation, $y - y_1 = m (x - x_1)$ where (x_1, y_1) represent a given point on the line, was used. The theorem that two lines are perpendicular if and only if $m_1 m_2 = -1$, where

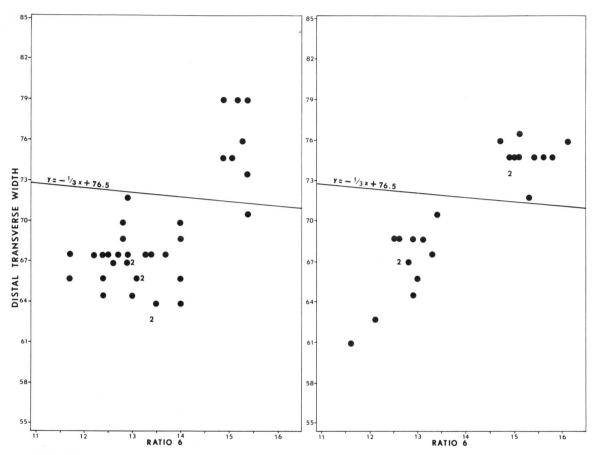

FIGURE 6.12 *Casper mature metatarsals.*   FIGURE 6.13 *Olsen-Chubbuck mature metatarsals.*

m_1 and m_2 represent the slopes of the two lines (Goodman 1963: 21), was used to determine the slope ($-1/m$) of the perpendicular line, where m is the slope given by the program SCATTERGRAM. When the perpendicular slopes are calculated using this formula, they cluster around the value of $-.5$ for the metacarpals and $-.33....$ for the metatarsals. For computational and graphing ease, these values were used in the point-slope equation; linear equations for each site were then determined and placed in the standard $y = mx + b$ form where b represents the y-intercept. These equations were drawn on the graphs; they are also given

in tabular form in Table 6.18.

The element of arbitariness is not completely eliminated by this technique since the researcher determines the point through which the perpendicular line will pass. This point is determined at least partially for graphing ease. However, since the slope of the perpendicular line does not vary greatly, i.e. for graphing there is little difference in slope between .4, .5 and .6, particularly for small graphs, the two slopes determined for metacarpals and metatarsals may be accepted as given with only the y-intercept varying between sites. For the computer, this equation was interpreted in the following

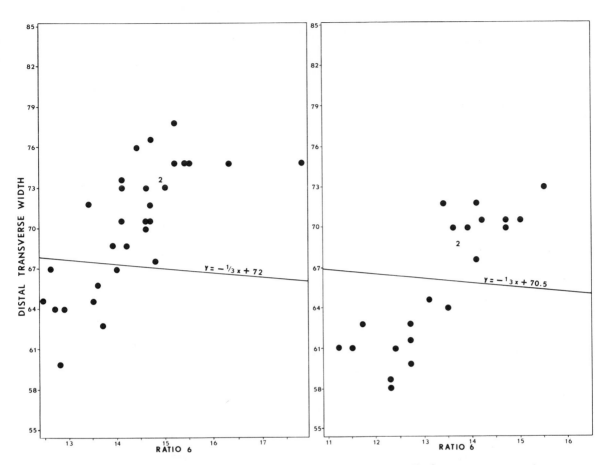

FIGURE 6.14 *Finley mature metatarsals.*   FIGURE 6.15 *Hawken mature metatarsals.*

manner for metacarpals:

IF (Measurement No. 4 is greater than $-1/2$ (Ratio 6) + y-intercept for that site) Sex= Male

IF (Measurement No. 4 is less than $-1/2$ (Ratio 6) + y-intercept for that site) Sex = Female

IF (Measurement No. 4 equals $-1/2$ (Ratio 6) + y-intercept for that site) Sex = Indeterminate

The same procedure was used for the metatarsals except $-1/3$ was used instead of $-1/2$. The results of using these linear equations are tabulated in Table 6.19.   The relative proportion of males and females in percent and absolute numbers for

each side and each bone are included. The true population proportions are probably between the values derived. In this table the ratio of males to females varies greatly. In the case of the Casper site, there is supporting evidence in the form of skulls (Wilson, this volume). Three skulls have been positively identified as male as well as a possible fourth. While exact corroboration is an unusual situation, what is important is that the number of males determined by this technique did not differ greatly from the number of males determined by analysis of the skulls. The minimum number of individual animals per site are given in Table 6.20 with the total number broken

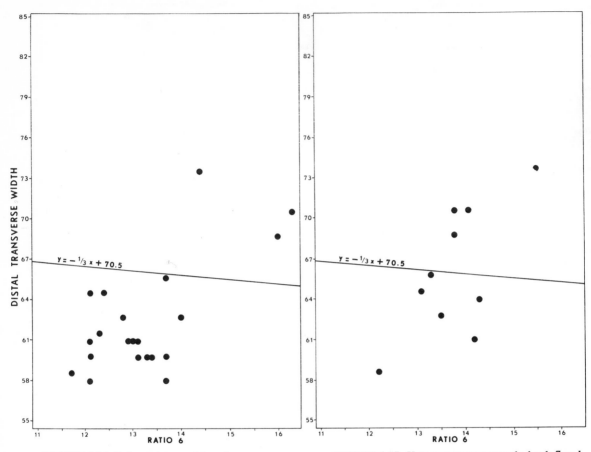

FIGURE 6.16 *Ruby mature metatarsals.*

FIGURE 6.17 *Vore mature metatarsals, levels 7 and lower.*

down into males, females and immatures.

In interpreting the scattergrams, it should be kept in mind that a minimum number of bones is necessary to be able to determine the clusters of males and females. In looking at Table 6.18, the lower number for good separation appears to be twenty. For example, the bottom levels of Vore contain only eight metacarpals (Figure 6.9); when these are plotted on an xy graph, two separations occur, either one of which is equally probable based on such a limited sample. In this case, a larger sample can be obtained and is needed to determine which separation is valid.

A second situation occurs in the case of the Ruby metacarpals where the separation between the two groups is quite wide. Two equations have been derived, either one of which may be used to separate males and females. To determine which is the "true" separation would require a larger sample which is unavailable; therefore, use of either equation is equally valid.

Another problem lies in the area of sexing immature animals. The technique described does not work for this category except in a very limited way because most of the immature bones fall in the female cluster and below. If an

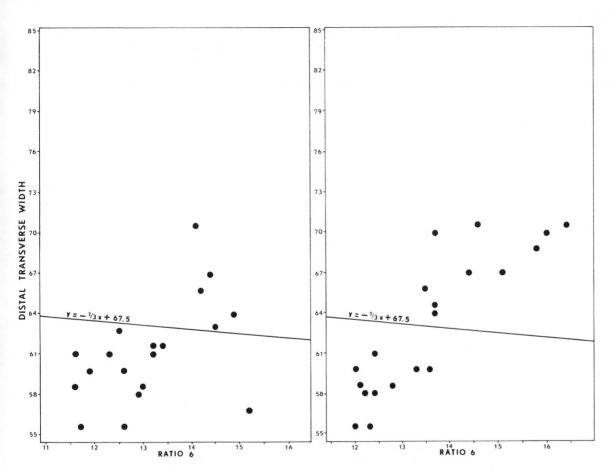

FIGURE 6.18 *Vore mature metatarsals, levels 5 and 6.*

FIGURE 6.19 *Vore mature metatarsals, levels 1 to 4.*

immature bone falls into the male cluster for a given site, then it is probably an immature male; but if the bone falls into the female cluster, it may be either male or female.

Age

The usual grouping in this paper has been between mature and immature animals since the number of immature animals is quite small for each site and the immature bones have as a rule been in poorer condition and less complete. This division has been based entirely on whether the distal epiphysis has been fused or not; thus

maturity has been a relative term. The original coding forms had two divisions within the mature and immature categories. For the immature, the category was sub-divided into "calf" and "immature"; separation was entirely subjective, with the smaller bones both in mass and length being labeled "calves" and any other immature bones being labeled "immatures". Since a dividing line could not be established that would be consistent for all six sites, such a division was not satisfactory. The same was true in the mature category, where a sub-division was labeled "young mature" which included bones in which the epiphyseal union was not yet entirely complete, and which

TABLE 6.18 *Derived Statistics for Male-Female Separation*

Site	Correlation (Pearson's r)	Significance	Slope (m)	$-1/m$	No. of Plotted Values	Linear Equation*
			Mature Metacarpals			
Casper	.76	10^{-5}	2.20	.45	55	$y = -1/2x + 90$
Olsen-Chubbuck	.81	10^{-5}	1.93	.52	33	$y = -1/2x + 90$
Finley	.76	10^{-5}	2.36	.42	48	$y = -1/2x + 87.5$
Hawken	.87	10^{-5}	2.20	.45	27	$y = -1/2x + 82.5$
Ruby	.86	10^{-5}	2.40	.42	22	$y = -1/2x + 82.5$ or $y = -1/2x + 80$
Vore (Levels lower than 6)	.94	2.4×10^{-4}	2.70	.37	8	$y = -1/2x + 85$ or $y = -1/2x + 80$
Vore (Levels 5 and 6)	.86	10^{-5}	2.65	.38	22	$y = -1/2x + 80$
Vore (Levels 0 to 4)	.86	10^{-5}	1.87	.53	50	$y = -1/2x + 80$
			Mature Metatarsals			
Casper	.70	10^{-5}	2.83	.35	38	$y = -1/3x + 76.5$
Olsen-Chubbuck	.92	10^{-5}	3.10	.32	25	$y = -1/3x + 76.5$
Finley	.74	10^{-5}	3.05	.33	32	$y = -1/3x + 72$
Hawken	.86	10^{-5}	3.67	.27	23	$y = -1/3x + 70.5$
Ruby	.65	6.6×10^{-4}	2.31	.43	21	$y = -1/3x + 70.5$
Vore (Levels lower than 6)	.66	1.8×10^{-2}	3.68	.27	10	$y = -1/3x + 70.5$
Vore (Levels 5 and 6)	.48	2.0×10^{-2}	1.61	.62	19	$y = -1/3x + 67.5$
Vore (Levels 0 to 4)	.87	10^{-5}	3.27	.31	20	$y = -1/3x + 67.5$

*In the linear equations, y = Transverse Width of the Distal End and x = Ratio 6 (Lorrain 1968).

TABLE 6.19 *Male-Female Distributions and Percentages by Site*

Site	Category	Total N (100%)	Males N	%	Females N	%	Total N (100%)	Males N	%	Females N	%
			Mature Metacarpals					**Mature Metatarsals**			
Casper	All	55	6	11%	49	89%	38	7	18%	31	82%
	Left Side	21	2	10%	19	90%	18	3	17%	15	83%
	Right Side	34	4	12%	30	88%	20	4	20%	16	80%
Olsen-Chubbuck	All	33	10	30%	23	70%	25	12	48%	13	52%
	Left Side	15	6	40%	9	60%	10	6	60%	4	40%
	Right Side	18	4	22%	14	78%	15	6	40%	9	60%
Finley	All	48	35	73%	13	27%	32	23	72%	9	28%
	Left Side	24	16	67%	8	33%	14	10	71%	4	29%
	Right Side	24	19	79%	5	21%	18	13	72%	5	28%
Hawken	All	27	15	56%	12	44%	23	12	52%	11	48%
	Left Side	17	9	53%	8	47%	10	6	60%	4	40%
	Right Side	10	6	60%	4	40%	13	6	46%	7	54%
Ruby	All	22	7	32%	15	68%	21	4	19%	17	81%
	Left Side	11	3	27%	8	73%	12	2	17%	10	83%
	Right Side	11	4	36%	7	64%	9	2	22%	7	78%
Vore (Levels 0 to 4)	All	50	25	50%	25	50%	20	10	50%	10	50%
	Left Side	22	13	59%	9	41%	11	5	46%	6	55%
	Right Side	28	12	43%	16	57%	9	5	56%	4	44%

TABLE 6.20 *Minimum Number of Individual Animals Per Site*

Site	Male	Female	Immature	Total
Casper	4	30	12	46
Olsen-Chubbuck	6	14	6	26
Finley	19	8	11	38
Hawken	9	8	7	24
Ruby	4	10	0	14
Vore (Levels 0 to 4)	13	16	10	39

Note: Male and female groupings are based on the linear equation derived for each site.

possibly indicated animals that were slightly younger than most of the mature animals. Again, this was entirely subjective and proved to be an unsatisfactory division, particularly since less than 5% of either metacarpals or metatarsals fell into the "young mature" category.

Two ratios were calculated for the metapodial data to remedy this problem, hereafter referred to as Ratio 1 and Ratio 2 (see Table 6.17 for formulas). Ratio 2 proved to be entirely unsatisfactory since the difference between the transverse width at the center of shaft (Measurement No. 3) and the minimum transverse width of the shaft (Measurement No. 10) proved to be too small to be reliable, particularly when the error of measurement was taken into account. For mature metacarpals, this meant that 73% of the total sample had values of 1.00 and 98% of the sample had values less than or equal to 1.05. For mature metatarsals, the results were not quite as bad in that only 17% had values of 1.00, 54% had values less than or equal to 1.05 and 76% had values less than or equal to 1.07. However, when these results are compared with the results of calculating Ratio 1, given in Table 6.21, the limited value of Ratio 2 is evident, particularly since both were designed to measure the same phenomenon.

Several authors, including Duffield (1973) have referred to a phenomenon in which the posterior face of the shaft when viewed from the side is bowed in some specimens. Whether this was pathological or the result of captivity was

unknown; there is no solid evidence on a population basis. The results for the six populations used in this study are given in Table 6.21. The lowest possible value is 1.00 which would indicate both measurements are the same, i.e. no bowing has occurred. The highest value is 1.24 for metacarpals and 1.27 for metatarsals. For the animals at this end of the range, the anterior-posterior width of the center of the shaft is about 25% larger than the shaft minimum. According to Wilson (this volume), this is caused by the deposition of additional bone along the shaft as the animal grows older and puts on additional weight. It is very possible that this trend is accentuated in the case of older bulls, and that there is a different gradient for bulls and cows. However, this question remains unanswered until data on a complete population of known age and sex are available. In interpreting the data, the individual values should not be used to indicate that one bone represents an older individual than another bone, except in the extreme ends of the continuum. In particular, adjacent values should be presumed to be equivalent, since each measurement contains error of measurement and both have small values, thus making the error greater proportionally than on a large measurement such as length. The bone available from an eleven year old cow gives a value of 1.13 for the metacarpals and 1.11 for the metatarsals. The known immature modern samples have values of 1.00 to 1.05 for both metacarpals and metatarsals. Without additional data from animals of known age and sex, the usefulness of this ratio is extremely limited. This author finds it useful only to the extent that those animals with a value of 1.00 to 1.10 for Ratio 1 are probably younger than those animals with a value of 1.20 or greater. Those with values between 1.10 and 1.20 could fall into either category. This statement is supported by the fact that none of the immature cannon bones have a value for Ratio 1 over 1.15. For immature metacarpals, 67% have a value of 1.00 and 93%

TABLE 6.21 *Ratio 1: Anterior-Posterior Width at Center of Shaft/Minimum Anterior-Posterior Width of Shaft*

Immature Metacarpals / **Mature Metacarpals**

Value	Casper	Olsen-Chubbuck	Finley	Hawken	Vore	Casper M*	Casper F*	Olsen-Chubbuck M	Olsen-Chubbuck F	Finley M	Finley F	Hawken M	Hawken F	Ruby M	Ruby F	Vore M†	Vore F†
1.00	11	7	4	7	12		5	1	4	2	2	3	2	1	2	1	7
1.01																	
1.02																	
1.03						1	4	1		2				1		1	
1.04	3	4		1	6		13		8		2	3	6	2	6	5	9
1.05	1				1												
1.06										1							
1.07			1				9	1	4	7	1	2		1		1	
1.08				1			4		3		2		3		3	1	3
1.09					1	2						1	1		1	1	
1.10						2		5		4						1	
1.11							9		2				1		1	6	
1.12			1				1		2	2						3	1
1.13										4	1	2					5
1.14						1		2		3		2		1		1	
1.15							2					1				2	
1,16										2					1	1	
1.17										2							
1.18																	
1.19							1			1							
1.20										1							
1.21										2							
1.22							1										
1.23																	
1.24																1	

Immature Metatarsals / **Mature Metatarsals**

Value	Casper	Olsen-Chubbuck	Finley	Hawken	Vore	Casper M*	Casper F*	Olsen-Chubbuck M	Olsen-Chubbuck F	Finley M	Finley F	Hawken M	Hawken F	Ruby M	Ruby F	Vore M†	Vore F†
1.00	5	2	3	2	2		1										
1.01																	
1.02																	
1.03	1	1			1		2		2				1				
1.04	4	1			3								1				
1.05																	
1.06				1			5		1	1	1						
1.07	2	2			2		1				2		5		2		2
1.08	1			1	1												
1.09	1		1	1	1	2	4		1		2			1		1	
1.10		2		1			13				3	1	2			1	
1.11				1	3				1						1		1
1.12	1				1	1				1	1						
1.13			1				1		3	1	1				3		
1.14		1		1	1	1	1				1		2		3		
1.15						1		1	1		1				3	1	3
1.16							1	2	2		2		1		2		
1.17							1	1	1		1				1		
1.18							2	5	1								1
1.19							1				3	1			1		3
1.20							1		1	1	1						
1.21							2		2						1		
1.22	1					1	3			1							
1.23							2				1						
1.24																1	
1.25								1		1							
1.26								1									
1.27																	1

*Male (M) and female (F) groups are separated on the basis of the linear equation derived for each site.
†The sample from Vore in this table is from levels 1 to 4.

have a value for Ratio 1 less than or equal to 1.05. For immature metatarsals, 28% have a value of 1.00 and 63% have a value less than or equal to 1.07.

Given more data, particularly from known populations, this index may be useful in determining relative ages beyond the mature-immature division. But given the present state of knowledge, it is of extremely limited value and must be used carefully. In particular, the relationship between the measurements on the metacarpals and the metatarsals of the same animal needs to be explored. For Ratio 1, 70% of the mature metacarpals fall in the category 1.00 to 1.10, whereas only 38% of the mature metatarsals fall in the same category. However, 15% of the metatarsals fall in the 1.20 and over category, but only 3% of the metacarpals . While the percent of specimens in the "younger" age category would be expected to be larger than the percent in the "older" category by the dynamics of catastrophic death (Voorhies 1969), the size of the discrepancy between the two bones suggests that there are different breaking points in the distributions. For example, perhaps the "younger" category for metacarpals should remain the same, but the "older" category defined as values greater than or equal to 1.15; for metatarsals, the "younger" category could be defined as 1.00 to 1.15, with the "older" category remaining the same. This would make the discrepancy smaller since 70% of the mature metacarpals would fall in the "younger" category and 64% of the metatarsals; 10% of the mature metacarpals would fall in the "older" category and 15% of the metatarsals.

Other Derived Ratios

Ratios 3, 4 and 5 were calculated from the formulas given in Table 6.17. The primary purpose for deriving these indices was to find predictors of length (greatest length) since this is one of the most common measurements taken for com-

parison between population samples and one of the measurements prone to error due to loss of surface on the ends. In addition, the condyles are often missing in immature animals. Since length is one of the measurements used in assigning sex using the technique developed in this paper, finding accurate predictors in the case of missing bone becomes more critical. The results are summarized in Table 6.22. The entire distribution is not presented since only the central portion is important in this study.

Of the three derived ratios, Ratio 4 seems to be the best predictor based on consistency since the median value for all four groups is either 1.34 or 1.35. However, there is enough variation present

TABLE 6.22 *Statistical Values for Derived Values*

Values	Mature	Immature	Mature	Immature
	Metacarpals		**Metatarsals**	
	Ratio 3			
Range: Minimum	1.12	1.14	1.11	1.15
Maximum	1.22	1.18	1.24	1.19
25%ile	1.16	1.15	1.17	1.16
Median (50%ile)	1.17	1.16	1.18	1.18
75%ile	1.18	1.16	1.19	1.18
Number of Values (All Sites)	287	19	194	13
	Ratio 4			
Range: Minimum	1.27	1.30	1.27	1.30
Maximum	1.43	1.39	1.43	1.39
25%ile	1.32	1.34	1.34	1.32
Median (50%ile)	1.34	1.35	1.35	1.34
75%ile	1.35	1.36	1.37	1.37
Number of Values (All Sites)	278	19	205	13
	Ratio 5			
Range: Minimum	1.33	1.33	1.26	1.28
Maximum	1.47	1.43	1.39	1.38
25%ile	1.37	1.34	1.32	1.30
Median (50%ile)	1.39	1.39	1.34	1.32
75%ile	1.41	1.40	1.35	1.34
Number of Values (All Sites)	279	18	196	13

to make use of this constant questionable because the range is .16 for both mature metatarsals and mature metacarpals. The samples of immature cannon bones are so small that values other than the median are of little use. Variation in these ratios is apparently not due to site (time) or sex. Males and females fall equally into the lower and upper ranges, and the range of variation is approximately the same for all the sites. Controlling for excellent accuracy of measurement does not affect the median value, although it does narrow the range for some sites by .01 to .02. Therefore, in situations where a possible error of ± 15 mm. would be acceptable and measurement No. 12 is available, use of 1.34 or 1.35 as a multiplicative constant would give an estimate of maximum length where this is totally missing. In situations where this size of error is not acceptable, this technique will not be useful.

Speciation

According to published data on speciation based on mature male skulls (Skinner and Kaisen 1947; Guthrie 1970; Lorrain 1968), three species would possibly be found in the Northwestern Plains over the time period considered: *Bison bison, Bison antiquus, and Bison occidentalis.* The data from the cannon bones do not support the existence of more than one species during this time period. The univariate data show that there is a general trend for the measurements to get smaller, but that all overlap without distinct breaks. More importantly, the linear equations of the lines separating male and female groups all parallel each other for a particular bone (since the slopes are the same), but the y-intercept gets smaller through time indicating that for all three measurements concerned with assigning sex, the trend is toward a smaller animal. Therefore, this represents a chronocline in which there is no distinct break between populations, but there is a trend toward a smaller animal with the modern bison being the end result. In the

other direction, the fossil bison of Skinner and Kaisen are distinctly larger animals than the bison in this study. Therefore, when discussing bison evolution during this ten thousand year time span, the variation caused by sex, age and individual morphological variation within a population is greater than the variation caused by speciational evolution; the emphasis should be on the individual population, not on assigning a specific title.

NONQUANTIFIABLE VARIABLES

An important nonquantifiable factor in morphological variation is nutrition. This part of the Great Plains is particularly prone to droughts since the difference of a few inches in rainfall is far more critical than in areas where the rainfall is higher. Much of the nutritional variation may be due to varying nutritional conditions during the period of gestation and first year of growth. The variation at Vore in the different levels may very well be due to population movements in this area during periods of relative wetness and dryness and consequent vegetational changes.

Another nonquantifiable factor not examined in this study is bone pathologies. When a bone pathology was present, it was noted on the data cards, particularly when it affected a measurement. The total number was comparatively low, with the most common phenomenon being arthritic lipping on either the distal or the proximal ends. The other pathologies consist of lumps of various sizes on the bone shaft; the bone with the largest lump (Ruby) had a deep indentation in the center of it.

ARCHAEOLOGICAL INFERENCES

This study has dealt with a specific cultural phenomena: prehistoric bison kills. These kills were not the result of accidents or natural disasters, but resulted from deliberate actions by man to provide food for himself and the members of his cultural group. Consequently, information determined from the bison bone can be used to make cultural inferences about the human populations hunting these animals. The techniques developed in this paper are intended to provide practical tools for archaeologists in interpreting a site.

In the field many single cannon bones can be sexed by taking three measurements: transverse width of the distal end (No. 4), transverse width at the center of shaft (No. 3) and length (No. 1). For sites within the past ten thousand years, if the bone measurements fall below the line defined for the Vore Site, the bone is probably female or if the bone measurements fall above the line defined for Casper, Olsen-Chubbuck and Finley, then the bone is probably male. Specifically for metacarpals, if measurement No. 4 is greater than $(90 - 1/2 [\text{Ratio } 6])$, then the bone is probably male, and if measurement No. 4 is less than $(80 - 1/2 [\text{Ratio } 6])$. then the bone is probably female. For metatarsals, the corresponding divisions would be as follows: if measurement No. 4 is greater than $(76.5 - 1/3 [\text{Ratio } 6])$, then the bone is probably male and if measurement No. 4 is less than $(67.5 - 1/3 [\text{Ratio } 6])$, the bone is probably female. For those falling between these two lines, the entire population should be plotted to determine where the break occurs between males and females.

Once sex ratios are determined for the entire population, different hypotheses may be formulated. Examination of Table 6.20 which gives minimum herd composition for the sites in this project shows striking differences in sex ratios. The Casper herd is primarily cows and immature animals, while the Finley herd is primarily composed of bulls. Only Vore and Hawken have an approximately equal bull and cow ratio, while Olsen-Chubbuck and Ruby have more cows than bulls, though not to the degree found in Casper. This difference in sex ratios suggests a number of

different hypotheses.

First, it suggests that prehistoric man exercised little control over the composition of the herd taken in a bison kill, though cows and immature animals might have been preferred as food. Nonetheless, any meat was food and enabled a cultural group to survive. The most important factor was probably whether a herd was in a position to stampede into the kill site, not the actual herd composition. Another hypothesis is that there was great variation in the composition of herds, particularly small herds, which changed from day to day. This is supported by the relatively small sizes of the minimum number of individual animals per site (Table 6.20). Ruby has only fourteen individuals as the minimum number while the largest minimum is in the Casper site with forty-six individuals. With the exception of the Casper females, there are less than twenty specimens per site in each of the three categories of male, female and immature animals. These numbers are quite small when compared with the millions of animals that lived on the Great Plains until the extermination period in the 1800s. Still another hypothesis is that herd composition may be a subtle indicator of the time of the year that the kill occurred. All of the sites are seasonal fall kills, but the actual herd composition may be different in September than in November. However, confirmation of this interpretation would require additional biological evidence to determine the time of year independently of the skeletal material.

The number of immature animals present in a site reflects herd compositon, but only to a limited extent. Other factors must be taken into consideration when comparing the number of immature bones to the number of mature specimens. The Ruby Site contained no immature bones; this is probably because the bone was in relatively poor condition and none of the immature cannon bones were preserved. The Vore Site bone was very well preserved so the number of immature bones is

probably proportionally correct. Immature
bone is less likely to survive poor preservation
conditions since it is smaller and the condyles
unfused, thereby often disintegrating before and
during excavation; this frequently gives a
skewed distribution to the site sample.

Determination of the sex and relative age of a
bone is useful in other ways when interpreting a
site. It is quite useful when analyzing butchering practices to know whether the animal was
a bull or a cow since this may have affected the
way the animal was handled. Sex and age may
also be important in analyzing bone distributions
within a site since smaller cows and immature
animals were easier to process than large and
mature animals. Bulls and cows may also have
been utilized differently for hides, bone tools,
ceremonial objects (i.e. skulls), food, etc.

The role of component within a site has been
mentioned in an earlier section, but cannot be
underestimated in its bearing on determining
whether the same local populations or different
populations are involved in a site. In multi-
component sites, perhaps bison bone can be used
to determine whether different components are
in fact present and where the point of separation
occurs.

Chapter

CONCLUDING SUMMARY

7

GEORGE C. FRISON
University of Wyoming

The Casper Archeological Site is an approximately 10,000 year old, communally-operated bison trapping, killing, and butchering station which can be associated with the Hell Gap cultural complex. The trap was formed naturally by the trough of a parabolic sand dune and apparently was utilized without modification. The feasibility of this kind of trapping operation has been tested with behavioral studies of modern, free-ranging bison herds, and found positive, always assuming, of course, that the behavior of the extinct variants of bison was similar to that of the modern one.

Parabolic sand dunes are common to the same sand dune area today. They are formed in areas of sand anchored by vegetation, and there is apparently a delicate balance between environmental conditions that allow sand transport on the one hand and stabilize the area by vegetation on the other. All evidence recovered from the site strongly suggests that environmental conditions in the site area were about the same at the time of the bison kill as they are at present. All of the remaining fauna that was recovered in the site still inhabits the area today with the exception of the extinct bison.

Bison studies have come into their own only within the last decade even though bison kill sites seem to be the most frequent and obvious of the major archeological manifestations on the high plains. In the future, a proportionately larger share of our archeological interpretations will probably have to come from these kinds of sites. Underlying the methodology presently employed for bison studies is an assumption that knowledge gathered from studies of bison populations will provide a basis for deriving knowledge of what the economically dependent human populations were doing. The communal kill sites offer optimum means for such population studies because they provide sufficient samples in good contexts from what may be assumed as single animal populations. If the sample is large enough, the age of individual animals (or more exactly, individual animal cohorts--cohorts being a term now much in vogue with demographers) in a catastrophically killed population can be determined by tooth eruption and wear. With this age determination made, the time of year in which any population kill was made can be extrapolated; assuming, of course, that the time of year of calving has remained constant. The age and sex structure of a bison population can be determined within limits through metric and morphological analysis of the skeletal remains, and study of the skeletal remains can also indicate something of the carcass-handling techniques used after the kill was made.

Geological identification of the features used for handling, trapping, and killing the animals, along with behavioral tests of modern bison herds, can give some idea of the human activities which must have been associated with communal animal procurement operations. In addition, replicative experimentation in methods of production and subsequent use of chipped stone projectile points and tools provides a hypothetical reconstruction of additional human activity. Thus the Casper Site and others like it provide the basis for a number of hypotheses about economic and technological aspects of the human cultural systems involved.

In addition communal kill sites offer a basis for a number of specialized sudies. Butchering after a communal kill required a maximization of effort on the part of the entire human group in order to prevent loss of the products of the kill. This known situation should provide the optimum opportunity for studies of tool use with functional tools in known tasks. Bone butchering tool assemblages recognized in certain sites allow study of a heretofore

unrecognized class of tools and this knowledge prevents incorrect assignment of functions performed by bone tools to other classes of tools. The communal kill site also offers an optimum arena for studies in projectile point and tool typologies. Large samples are obtained which can be regarded as functional for specific activities, and ranges of variation in objects produced by a single human group for a specific purpose can be observed and studied. Such a study at the Casper Site suggests that projectile point typology, though it must be used cautiously, is still a useful indicator of cultural affiliation.

Within the biological discipline, the finer trends of bison evolution are not yet well understood, and the number of current hypotheses is almost as great as the number of investigators (see e. g. Guthrie 1970). It is, however, generally accepted that the extinct animals were larger than the present form and it is known that these larger animals had measurably larger bones. It has thus been hypothesized that bone measurements should indicate whether the animal remains are from modern or extinct varieties. To test this hypotheses, metacarpals, metatarsals, and astragali from a number of sites, covering a wide range of time and including the Casper Site, were measured and the results evaluated. These indicate that in general, the older sites containing extinct animals tend to produce bones larger than the recent sites containing the modern form, but there is a large area of overlap and there are disturbing multimodal distributions that cannot be readily explained. These kind of measurements will undoubtedly become the basis for further biological studies of bison but better controls over the age and sex of the specimens will have to be developed. Evidence from a large number of bison kill sites now suggests a gradual size diminution of the species and furthermore that the endpoint of this trend in size was reached somewhere between 6,500 and 3,000 years ago. Recently recovered evidence suggests an acceleration of this diminution during the Altithermal interval, and additional data are being sought.

The tooth anomalies observed among the Casper Site bison are also poorly understood at this time. The third molar deformity appears to be at least partly genetic in origin and could have been the result of inbreeding because of geographic isolation. If so, we need to know the conditions that brought about the isolation, that is, whether they were climatic or otherwise. Comparisons with bison populations from other Paleo-Indian kill sites are needed to determine if the conditions at the Casper Site were unique or common to other areas as well. Such information may eventually offer some clue to the cause of the gradual disappearance of the large extinct bison, in favor of a smaller descendent form. A working hypothesis at this time is that the Casper Site bison were part of an isolated and inbred population. In any case, the reasons for the phyletic extinction are not simple explained, and probably include such generalized factors as changing climatic conditions that may have produced an ecology unfavorable to the continuation of that variant of the species.

Geological expertise is becoming more and more indispensable to bison studies. The geological interpretation of the Casper Site was more straightforward than at most kill sites, but even at this site an archeologist alone would have been in serious trouble. Correct identification of the geological features essential to the operation of bison jumps, traps and corrals is absolutely necessary before meaningful archeological interpretations can be made. Unfortunately, too few archeologists are well enough trained to reconstruct paleo-landforms properly from the sites which now demonstrate mere remnants of the original topography. A bone level high in the bank of an arroyo may represent a kill accomplished by driving animals into what was in Paleo-Indian times a trap

formed by a knickpoint at the bottom of the arroyo. It might otherwise represent a jump over a terrace escarpment; or it might even be the remnant of a corral on what was at one time an advantageous location on a flood plain or terrace. All of these situations have been encountered in the archeological record and each would have required a different set of animal handling techniques during operation. The archeological interpretation of each is different, and proper identification of each feature is predicated on sophisticated geological expertise.

The techniques for aging animals, defining population structures, and writing morphological description are borrowed directly from paleontology. Other concepts are taken freely from biology and animal ecology. Pollen studies at the Casper Site were largely non-productive, due to poor pollen preservation but this does not negate the value of pollen studies in other contexts. In summary, a strong and well integrated interdisciplinary effort is required to make bison studies provide meaningful interpretations of past human cultural systems. The next problem will be to find the archeologist talented enough to synthesize the findings of all these experts into a meaningful whole.

Appendix

I

VOLUMES of
BISON ASTRAGALI

GEORGE ZEIMENS and SANDY ZEIMENS
University of Wyoming

The use of the astragalus as an indicator of relative animal size and consequently a species indicator was proposed by Sellards nearly two decades ago. The astragali are usually better preserved than other bones of the animal carcass and thereby offer the best means for intersite comparisons. One method of measurement is to compute the volume of the bone by calculating its desplacement in liquid. Sellards' results (1955: 338) indicated a significant size difference between modern and extinct bison.

The astragali at two different levels at Bonfire Shelter were also measured by volume (Lorrain 1968) with similar results. Those from the recent levels were smaller than those of the extinct animals from the earlier levels. It was decided to measure the astragali from the University of Wyoming collections. A sample was measured also from the Olsen-Chubbuck Site. Lacking a good sample from the Ruby

Site, a sample was added from the Glenrock Buffalo Jump (Frison 1970), a Late Prehistoric Period site. A sample was also included from a recent test at the Agate Basin Site but it is not regarded as large enough to be entirely valid. Site samples and volume measurements are given in Table A I.1.

Volume measurements for the astragali were obtained by water displacement. Each specimen was made water resistant by boiling in paraffin for 30 to 45 minutes which resulted in removal of air from the bone which was necessary to keep the specimen from floating when placed in water. After the specimens had cooled, the volume of each was calculated by the amount of water displaced when immersed in a 500 milliliter graduated cylinder. Measurements were recorded to the nearest 5 milliliters.

Measurements of astragali and the results are presented in Tables A I.1 and AI.2. These

TABLE AI.1 *Volume Measurements for Astragali*

Volume CC.	Casper	Agate Basin	Olsen-Chubbuck	Finley	Hawken	Vore	Glenrock
50							2
55						1	6
60						3	10
65				1		3	24
70				1		9	31
75	1				4	8	19
80	1	2	1	1	3	9	10
85	2		2	2	1	6	2
90	2		4	1	5	4	7
95	5		8	2	1	4	3
100	10		5	3	1	3	4
105	9	1	6	5	4	1	1
110	9	2	9	2	3	3	3
115	5		2	5	6		
120	5		5	3	2		
125	3		2	2	3		
130	1			2			
135				4			
140	1			5			
145	2		1				
150			1				
155	1						
Totals	57	5	46	37	35	54	122

TABLE AI.2 *Astragali Statistics*

Site	N	Mean	Standard Deviation
Casper	57	108.40	11.45
Agate Basin	5	97.00	14.00
Olsen-Chubbuck	46	105.76	19.90
Finley	37	115.13	17.38
Hawken	35	98.85	17.73
Vore	54	80.83	13.31
Glenrock	122	72.99	12.45

analysis of this nature can provide meaningful statements concerning relative sizes of animals of the same age group from one site to another.

indicate that the means of the samples from sites containing modern bison are well below 100 cc. A word of caution from these kinds of results needs to be mentioned. The largest astragalus recorded is from the Casper Site from which only threekknown males were recorded. The sample from the Finley Site contained what is apparently a large numer of males so that a simple computation of means of the two site samples suggests that the Finley Site animals were larger than those at the Casper Site. This is an erroneous picture of the relative sizes of different sex and age groups within the two populations. It is obvious from this that age and sex of the bones measured must first be known before an

Appendix II

POLLEN REPORT on the CASPER SITE

JANE BEISWENGER
University of Wyoming

Collections of sediment for pollen analysis were taken from the following locations at the Casper Site: (A) an area of undisturbed surface of the stabilized sand dune, (B) 0-5 cm. and 5-10 cm. below the undisturbed surface of the stabilized sand dune (Fig. 4.4, Unit "D"), (C) the pond sediment at seven levels (Fig. 4.4, Unit "C"), (D) dune sand below the earthmover cut (Fig. 4.4, Unit "B"). This sandy unit contained the archeological materials and bison remains. (E) the laminated sand into which the old parabolic dune was cut (Fig. 4.4, Unit "A"), and (F) the top 15 cm. of the Pleistocene sand and gravel terrace. The pollen samples were prepared by vigorously treating them with the following chemicals: HCl, HF, HNO_3, KOH and Acetolysis Mixture (9 parts Acetic Anhydride: 1 part H_2SO_4).

The only samples with sufficient pollen to make percentage counts were the surface sample and the sample taken 0-5 cm. below the surface. Plants showing the highest pollen percentages were *Pinus* (surface, 61%; 0-5 cm., 56%), *Artemisia* (surface and 0-5 cm., 14%. Pollen grains of *Picea, Juniperus, Pseudotsuga, Abies, Populus, Alnus,* Gramineae, Cyperaceae, *Ephedra,* Compositae, cf. Cruciferae, and Leguminosae were recorded in amounts less then 3%.

As mentioned above, other samples did not contain enough pollen for a percentage determination, however, Table A II. 1 does give the numbers and kinds of grains seen in each sample counted. The number of slides prepared and examined for each sample is given in the explanation of the table.

Grains that were probably *Pterocarya* were noted in the laminated sand sample No. 1. This could indicate that this sample contained some redeposited tertiary material This sample also had a higher content of Juglandaceae, spores and

TABLE A II.1 *Casper Site Pollen Analysis. Pollen Number Given for Samples Counted. Percentages Given for Surface Sample and 0-5 cm. Sample.*

Pollen Types	Surface Number Counted	Surface Percent	0-5 cm. (Unit "D") Number Counted	0-5 cm. (Unit "D") Percent	Dune Sand (Unit "B")	Pond (Unit "C") No. 1	Pond (Unit "C") No. 3	Pond (Unit "C") No. 5	Pond (Unit "C") No. 7	Pond Total	Laminated Sand (Unit "A") No. 1	Laminated Sand (Unit "A") No. 2
Pinus (Pine)	228.5	61.3	201.5	56.4	1.5	1	3	3	9	16	25	1
Picea (Spruce)	5	1.3	4	1.1	1							
Juniperus (Juniper)	5	1.3	2	0.6	4		1			1	1	
Pseudotsuga (Douglas Fir)			8	2.2			1			1	3	
Abies (Fir)			1	0.3								
Populus (Populus)	7	1.9	5	1.4	3	1	1		6	8	5	
Betula (Birch)							2			2		
Carya (Hickory)									1	1		
cf. *Pterocarya*											3	
Juglandaceae (Walnut family)											12	
Alnus (Alder)	1	0.3			1							
Artemisia (Sage)	51	13.7	49	13.7	7	2	7		3	12	8	
Chenopodiaceae (Goosefoot fam.)	44	11.8	51	14.3			1			1		
Gramineae (Grass fam.)	1	0.3			1							
Cyperaceae (Sedge fam.)	2	0.5	3	0.8								
Ephedra (Jointfir)	1	0.3	3	0.8								
Compositae (Composite fam.)	7	1.9	10	2.8								
cf. Cruciferae (Mustard fam.)	1	0.3	6	1.7								
Leguminosae (Pulse fam.)			1	0.3								
Rosaceae (Rose fam.)									1?	1		
cf. *Brasenia* (Water-shield)									1	1		
Monocots											3	
Unidentified triporate grains					5							
Trilete spores	3	0.8	1	0.3	1		1		1	2	24	1
Monolete spores									1	1		
Unknown	6	1.6	4	1.1	4		5		4	9	16	
Unidentifiable	10	2.7	8	2.2	10		5		3	8	11	
Totals	372.5	100.0	357.5	100.0	34.5	4	27	3	30	69	111	2

The number of slides prepared and analyzed for each sample is as follows:

Surface	2	Laminated Sand (Unit "A"	
0-5 cm. (Unit "D")	6	No. 1	6
Dune sand (Unit "B")	2	No. 2	1
Pond (Unit "C")			
No. 1	2		
No. 3	7		
No. 5	4		
No. 7	8		

unknown grains than the other samples.

Unfortunately, the Casper Site pollen samples did not contain enough material to make definite statements concerning the vegetational history of the area.

REFERENCES

Agenbroad, Larry D.
  1973 The Hudson-Meng Paleo-Indian Bison Kill,
        Northwestern Nebraska: An Analysis After
        Two Seasons. *Paper presented at the 38th
        annual meeting of the Society for American
        Archeology,* San Francisco.
Agogino, George A.
  1961 A New Point Type from Hell Gap Valley,
        Eastern Wyoming. *American Antiquity* **26:**
        558-560, Salt Lake City.
  1972 Excavations at a Paleo-Indian Site (Brewster)
        in Moss Agate Arroyo, Eastern Wyoming.
        *National Geographic Society Research
        Reports, 1955-1960:* 1-6. Washington D. C.
Agogino, George A. and W. O. Frankforter
  1960 A Paleo-Indian Bison Kill in Northwestern
        Iowa. *American Antiquity* **25:** 414-415,
        Salt Lake City.
Agogino, George A and Eugene Galloway
  1965 The Sister's Hill Site: A Hell Gap Site in
        North Central Wyoming. *Plains Anthropologist*
        10: 190-195, Lincoln.

Albanese, John
  1970 Geology of the Glenrock Site Area, Wyoming.
        In *The Glenrock Buffalo Jump, 48CO304,* by
        George C. Frison. Plains Anthropologist
        Memoir 7, Appendix III. Lawrence.
  1971 Geology of the Ruby Site Area, Wyoming,
        48CA302. *American Antiquity* **36:** 91-95.
        Salt Lake City.
Allen, John R.
  1970 *Physical Processes of Sedimentation.*
        American Elsevier, New York.
Anderson, Elaine
  1968 Fauna of the Little Box Elder Cave, Converse
        County, Wyoming. The Carnivora. *University
        of Colorado Studies, Series in Earth Sciences*
        6: 1-59. Boulder.
  in press A Survey of the Late Pleistocene and
        Holocene Mammal Fauna of Wyoming. In
        *Applied Geology and Archeology: the
        Holocene History of Wyoming,* by Michael
        Wilson (ed.). Geological Survey of Wyoming,
        Laramie.

Armstrong, G.
    1965   Tooth Cementum of Bovidae with Special
            Reference to its use in Age Determination.
            Science in Alaska, 1965: Proceedings
            Sixteenth Alaskan Science Conference,
            College, Alaska: 29-30.
Bagnold, R. A.
    1954   *The Physics of Blown Sand and Desert Dunes.*
            Methuen and Co., London.
Bass, William M.
    1970   Excavations of a Paleo-Indian Site at Agate
            Basin, Wyoming. *National Geographic
            Society Research Reports, 1961-1962*: 21-25.
            Washington D. C.
Beard, D. C. and P. K. Weyl
    1973   Influence of Texture on Porosity and
            Permeability of Unconsolidated Sand.
            *American Association Petroleum
            Geologists Bulletin 57*: 349-369.
Becker, Clarence F. and John D. Alyea
    1964a   Precipitation Probabilities in Wyoming.
            *University of Wyoming, Agricultural
            Experiment Station Bulletin 416.* Laramie.
    1964b   Temperature Probabilities in Wyoming.
            *University of Wyoming, Agricultural
            Experiment Station Bulletin 415.* Laramie.
Beetle, Dorothy E.
    1961   Mollusca of the Big Horn Mountains.
            Nautilus 74: 95-102.
Bigarella, Joao Jose
    1972   Eolian Environments: Their Characteristics,
            Recognition and Importance. *Society
            Economic Paleontologists and Mineralogists,
            Special Publication 16*: 12-62.
Blalock, Hubert M. Jr.
    1960   *Social Statistics.* McGraw-Hill, New York.
Bordes, Francois
    1961   *Typologie du Paleolithique Ancien et Moyen.*
            Publications de L'Institut de L'Universite de
            Bordeaux, Memoire 1, Bordeaux.
Boughey, Arthur S.
    1968   *Ecology of Populations.* Macmillan and Co.,
            New York.
Butler, B. Robert
    1968a   An Introduction to Archaeological
            Investigations in the Pioneer Basin Locality of
            Eastern Idaho. *Tebiwa* 11: 1-30, Pocatello.
    1968b   *A Guide to Understanding Idaho Archaeology.*
            Second Edition (Revised). Special Publication,
            Idaho State University Museum, Pocatello.

Butler, B. Robert, Helen Gildersleeve and John Sommers
    1971   The Wasden Site Bison: Sources of
            Morphological Variation. In *Aboriginal Man
            and Environments on the Plateau of North-
            west America*: 126-152, by Stryd, Arnoud H.
            and Rachel A. Smith Eds. Archaeological
            Association, University of Calgary, Calgary,
            Alberta.
Butzer, Karl W.
    1964   *Environment and Archaeology.* Aldine,
            Chicago.
Cary, Merritt
    1917   *Life Zone Investigations in Wyoming.* North
            American Fauna, No. 42, U. S. D. A. Bureau
            of Biological Survey, Washington, D. C.
Chandler, A. C.
    1916   A Study of the Skull and Dentition of *Bison
            antiquus* Leidy, with Special Reference to
            Material from the Pacific Coast. *University of
            California Publications, Bulletin of the
            Department of Geology, 9*: 121-135.
Cheatum, E. P. and Don Allen
    1963   An Ecological Comparison of the Ben Franklin
            and Clear Creek Local Molluscan Faunas in
            Texas. *Journal of the Graduate Research
            Center* 31: 174-179.
Colyer, Sir Frank
    1936   *Variations and Diseases of the Teeth of
            Animals.* John Bale, Sons and Danielsson,
            Ltd., London.
Dalquest, W. W.
    1957   First Record of *Bison alleni* from a Late
            Pleistocene Deposit in Texas. *Texas Journal
            of Science* 9: 346-354.
Dart, Raymond A.
    1957   *The Osteodontokeratic Culture of*
            Australopithecus prometheus. Transvaal
            Museum Memoir 10.
Deakin, A. G., W. Muir, A. G. Smith and A. S. MacLellan
    1942   *Hybridization of Domestic Cattle and Buffalo
            (*Bison americanus*).* Progress Report of the
            Wainwright Experiment 1935-41. Experi-
            mental Farms Service, Department of
            Agriculture, Dominion of Canada. 10 p.
            Mimeographed.
Deetz, James
    1968   Hunters in Archeological Perspective. In *Man
            The Hunter,* ed. by Richard B. Lee and Irven
            DeVore: 281-285. Aldine, Chicago.
Deevey, E. S.
    1947   Life Tables for Natural Populations of
            Animals. *Quarterly Review of Biology* 22:
            283-314. Baltimore.

Dibble, David S.
  1968 The Archaeology. In *Bonfire Shelter: A Stratified Bison Kill Site, Val Verde County, Texas,* by Dibble, David S. and Dessamae Lorrain. Texas Memorial Museum, Miscellaneous Paper No. 1: 9-76. Austin.

Dibble, David S. and Dessamae Lorrain
  1968 *Bonfire Shelter: A Stratified Bison Kill Site, Val Verde County, Texas.* Texas Memorial Museum, Miscellaneous Papers No. 1, Austin.

Dodge, Richard I.
  1877 *The Plains of the Great West.* G. P. Putnam's Sons, New York.

Duffield, Lathel F.
  1973 Aging and Sexing of the Post-Cranial Skeleton of Bison. *Plains Anthropologist* **18**: 132-139.

Dyer, I. A., W. A. Cossett, Jr., and R. R. Roa
  1964 Manganese Deficiency in the Etiology of Deformed Calves. *Bioscience* **14**: 31-32.

Eiseley, L. C.
  1946 The Fire Drive and the Extinction of the Terminal Pleistocene Fauna. *American Anthropologist* **48**: 54-59.

Empel, Wojciech and Tadeusz Roskosz
  1963 Das Skellett der Gliedmassen des Wisents, *Bison bonasus*. *Acta Theriologica* **7**: 259-297.

Ewers, John C.
  1955 *The Horse in Blackfoot Indian Culture.* Bureau of American Ethnology Bulletin 159. Washington D. C.

Figgins, J. D.
  1933 The Bison of the Western Area of the Mississippi Basin. *Proceedings of the Colorado Museum of Natural History* **12**: 16-33. Denver.

Flannery, Kent C.
  1968 Archeological Systems Theory and Early Mesoamerica. In *Anthropological Archeology in the Americas.* By Betty Meggers (ed.). Publication of the Anthropological Society of Washington: 67-87. Washington D. C.

Flint, Richard Foster
  1971 *Glacial and Quaternary Geology.* John Wiley, New York.

Forbis, Richard G.
  1968 Fletcher: A Paleo-Indian Site in Alberta. *American Antiquity* **33**: 1-10. Salt Lake City.

Frison, George C.
  1967a The Piney Creek Sites, Wyoming. *University of Wyoming Publications* **33**: 1-92. Laramie.

  1967b *Archaeological Evidence of the Crow Indians in Northern Wyoming: A Study of a Late Prehistoric Period Buffalo Economy.* MS, Ph.D. Dissertation, University of Michigan, Ann Arbor.

  1968 A Functional Analysis of Certain Chipped Stone Tools. *American Antiquity* **33**: 149-155. Salt Lake City.

  1970 *The Glenrock Buffalo Jump, 48CO304.* Plains Anthropologist Memoir 7, Lawrence.

  1971a The Bison Pound in Northwestern Plains Prehistory. *American Antiquity* **36**: 77-91. Salt Lake City.

  1971b Shoshonean Antelope Procurement in the Upper Green River Basin, Wyoming. *Plains Anthropologist* **16**: 258-284. Lawrence.

  1973 *The Wardell Buffalo Trap 48SU301: Communal Procurement in the Upper Green River Basin, Wyoming.* Anthropological Papers, No. 48. University of Michigan, Ann Arbor.

  n. d. The Hawken Site: A Paleo-Indian Bison Kill in the Wyoming Black Hills.

Frison, George C. and Charles A. Reher
  1970 Age Determination of Buffalo by Tooth Eruption and Wear. In *The Glenrock Buffalo Jump, 48CO304.* By George C. Frison. Plains Anthropologist Memoir 7, Appendix I. Lawrence.

Fuller, W. A.
  1959 The Horns and Teeth as Indicators of Age in Bison. *Jour. Wildlife Management* **23**: 342-344.

Fuller, W. A. and L. A. Bayrock
  1965 Late Pleistocene Mammals from Central Alberta, Canada. In *Vertebrate Paleontology in Alberta.* Conference Report at the University of Alberta, Edmonton, Alberta, August 29-September 3, 1963: 53-63. Edmonton, Alberta.
  in Alberta, Conference Report at the University of Alberta, Edmonton, Alberta, August 29-September 3, 1963: 53-63. Edmonton, Alberta.

Geist, Valerius
  1971 The Relation of Social Evolution and Dispersal in Ungulates During the Pleistocene, With Emphasis on the Old World Deer and the Genus *Bison*. *Quaternary Research* **1**: 283-315.

Gilluly, James, Aaron C. Waters and A. O. Woodford
  1968 *Principles of Geology.* W. H. Freeman, San Francisco.

Glennie, K. W.
1970 *Desert Sedimentary Environments.* Elsevier, Amsterdam.

Goodman, A. W.
1963 *Analytical Geometry and the Calculus.* The Macmillan Company, New York.

Gordon, Bryan C.
1970 Bison Antiquus from the Northwest Territories. *Arctic* 23: 132-133.

Green, Morton
1962 Comments on the Geologic Age of *Bison latifrons. Journal of Paleontology* 36: 557-559.

Guilday, John E., H. W. Hamilton and E. K. Adam
1967 Animal Remains from Horned Owl Cave, Albany County, Wyoming. University of Wyoming, *Contributions to Geology* 6: 97-99. Laramie, Wyoming.

Gunnerson, Dolores A.
1972 Man and Bison on the Plains in the Proto-historic Period. *Plains Anthropologist* 17: 1-10.

Guthrie, R. D.
1966a Bison Horn Cores--Character Choice and Systematics. *Journal of Paleontology* 40: 738-740.
1966b Pelage of Fossil Bison--A New Osteological Index. *Journal of Mammalogy* 47: 725-727.
1970 Bison Evolution and Zoogeography in North America During the Pleistocene. *Quarterly Review of Biology* 45: 1-15.

Hack, John T.
1941 Dunes of the Western Navajo Country. *Geographic Review* 31: 240-263.

Hafez, E. S. E.
1959 Skeletal Development in Ralation to Muscle Differential Development. Proceedings, Annual Meeting of the Western Section, *American Society of Animal Production* 10: 1-5. Tucson, Arizona.

Hager, Michael W.
1972 A Late Wisconsin-Recent Vertebrate Fauna From the Chimney Rock Animal Trap, Larimer County, Colorado. University of Wyoming, *Contributions to Geology* 11: 63-71. Laramie, Wyoming.

Hall, E. Raymond and Keith R. Kelson
1959 *The Mammals of North America.* Two Volumes. Ronald Press Company, New York.

Halloran, A. F.
1960 American Bison Weights and Measurements from the Wichita Mountains Wildlife Refuge. *Proceedings of the Oklahoma Academy of Science* 41: 212-218.

Harington, C. R. and F. V. Clulow
1973 Pleistocene Mammals from Gold Run Creek, Yukon Territory. *Canadian Journal of Earth Sciences* 10: 697-759.

Hart, G. H., H. R. Guilbert, K. A. Wagnon and H. Gross
1947 "Acorn Calves" A Nonhereditary Congenital Deformity Due to Maternal Nutritional Deficiency. *California Agricultural Experiment Station Bulletin 699.*

Hay, O.P.
1913 The Extinct Bisons of North America; With Description of One New Species, *Bison regius. Proceedings of the United States National Museum* 46: 161-200.

Haynes, C. Vance Jr. and Donald C. Grey
1965 The Sister's Hill Site and its Bearing on the Wyoming Postglacial Alluvial Chronology. *Plains Anthropologist* 10: 196-211.

Hester, James
1967 The Agency of Man in Animal Extinctions. In *Pleistocene Extinctions.* By Martin, Paul S. and H. E. Wright Jr. (eds.): 169-192. Yale University Press.

Hibbard, C. W.
1955 The Jinglebob Interglacial (Sangamon?) Fauna from Kansas and its Climatic Significance. University of Michigan, *Contributions to the Museum of Paleontology* 12: 179-288.
1963 A Late Illinoian Fauna from Kansas and its Climatic Significance. *Michigan Academy of Science, Arts and Letters Papers* 48: 187-221.

Hibbard, C. W. and D. W. Taylor
1960 Two Late Pleistocene Faunas from South-western Kansas. *Contributions of the Paleontology Museum of the University of Michigan* 16: 1-223.

Hillerud, John M.
1966 *The Duffield Site and its Fossil Bison, Alberta, Canada.* Master's Thesis, Department of Geology, University of Nebraska, Lincoln Nebraska.

Hills, L. V., Michael Wilson, John Chambers and Bill Wishart
MS *Bison antiquus* from Gravels at Calgary, Alberta. Manuscript in Preparation.

Hoffmann, R. S. and D. L. Pattie
1968 *A Guide to Montana Mammals: Identification, Habitat, Distribution, and Abundance.* University of Montana, Missoula.

Hopkins, Marie L.
1951 *Bison (Gigantobison) latifrons* and *Bison (Simobison) alleni* in Southeastern Idaho. *Journal of Mammalogy* 32: 192-197.

Hopkins, Marie L., Robson Bonnichsen and David Fortsch
1969 The Stratigraphic Position and Faunal Associates of *Bison (Gigantobison) latifrons* in Southeastern Idaho, a Progress Report. *Tebiwa* 12: 1-8. Pocatello, Idaho.

Irwin-Williams, Cynthia, Henry Irwin, George Agogino and C. Vance Haynes
1973 Hell Gap: Paleo-Indian Occupation on the High Plains. *Plains Anthropologist* 18: 40-53.

Jennings, Dana Close
1973 Do Buffalo Hold Human Health Secrets? *Buffalo!* 1: 12-15. Rapid City, South Dakota.

Jepsen, Glen L.
1953 Ancient Buffalo Hunters of Northwestern Wyoming. *Southwestern Lore* 19: 19-25. Boulder, Colorado.

Johnson, Ross B.
1967 The Great Sand Dunes of Southern Colorado. *U. S. Geological Survey Professional Paper 575-C*: C-177 to C-183.

Jones, Charles J.
1899 *Buffalo Jones' Forty Years of Adventure,* by Col. Henry Inman (ed.). London.

Keech, C. F. and Ray Bentall
1971 *Dunes on the Plains-The Sand Hills Region of Nebraska.* Conservation and Survey Division, The University of Nebraska, Lincoln.

Keiss, Robert E.
1969 Comparison of Eruption-Wear Patterns and Cementum Annuli as Age Criteria in Elk. *Journal of Wildlife Management* 33: 175-180.

Khan, Ehsunallah
1970 *Biostratigraphy and Paleontology of a Sangamon Deposit at Fort Qu'Appelle, Saskatchewan.* National Museums of Canada, Publications in Palaeontology, 5.

Kivett, Marvin F.
1962 *Logan Creek Complex.* Paper Presented At 20th Plains Anthropological Conference, Lincoln, Nebraska.

Klebanova, E. A. and G. A. Klevezal
1966 Stratification of the Periosteal Zone of Tubular Bones in Limbs as a Criterion for Age Determination in Mammals. *Zoologicheskii Zhurnal* 45: 406-413.

Klevezal, G. A. and S. E. Kleinenberg
1967 *Age Determination of Mammals from Annual Layers in Teeth and Bones.* Academy of Sciences, U. S. S. R. Translated 1969 from Russian for the Department of the Interior and the National Science Foundation. U. S. Department of Commerce, Clearinghouse for Federal Scientific and Technical Information, Springfield, Virginia.

Koch, Walter
1935 The Age Order of Epiphyseal Union in the Skeleton of the European Bison (*Bos bonasus* L.). *Anatomical Record* 61: 371-376.

Krasinska, M. and Z. Pucek
1967 The State of Studies on Hybridization of European Bison and Domestic Cattle. *Acta Theriologica* 12: 385-389.

Kurten, Bjorn
1953 On the Variation and Population Dynamics of Fossil and Recent Mammal Populations. *Acta Zoologica Fennica* 76: 1-122.
1964 Population Structure in Paleoecology. *Approaches to Paleoecology,* by John Imbrie and Norman Newell (eds.). John Wiley & Sons, New York.
1968 *Pleistocene Mammals of Europe.* Aldine, Chicago.

Kurten, Bjorn, and Elaine Anderson
1972 The Sediments and Fauna of Jaguar Cave: II-The Fauna. *Tebiwa* 15: 21-45.

Laws, R. M.
1952 A New Method of Age Determination for Mammals. *Nature* 169: 972-973.

Lee, Richard B. and Irven DeVore
1968 *Man the Hunter.* Aldine, Chicago.

Leopold, Luna B. and John P Miller
1954 *A Postglacial Chronology for Some Alluvial Valleys in Wyoming.* U. S. Geological Survey, Water Supply Paper 1261.

Lewis, G. Edward
1970 New Discoveries of Pleistocene Bison and Peccaries in Colorado. *U. S. Geological Survey Professional Paper 700-B*: 137-140.

Lorrain, Dessamae
1968 Analysis of the Bison Bones from Bonfire Shelter. In *Bonfire Shelter: A Stratified Bison Kill Site, Val Verde County, Texas.* By Dibble, David S. and Dessamae Lorrain. Texas Memorial Museum, Miscellaneous Paper 1: 77-132.

Low, W. A. and I. McT. Cowan
1963 Age Determination of Deer by Annular Structure of Dental Cementum. *Journal of Wildlife Management* 27: 466-471.

Lucas, F. A.
1899 The Fossil Bison of North America. *Proceedings of the United States National Museum* 21: 755-771.

McCreary, Otto
1937 *Wyoming Bird Life.* Burgess Publishing Co., Minneapolis.

McHugh Tom
1958 Social Behavior of the American Buffalo (*Bison bison bison*). *Zoologica* 43: 1-40.
1972 *The Time of the Buffalo.* A. A. Knopf, New York

Mann, C. John
1968 Geology of Archaeological Site 48SH312, Wyoming. *Plains Anthropologist* 13: 40-45.

Moss, John H. in collaboration with Kirk Bryan, G William Holmes, Linton Satterthwaite Jr., Henry P Hansen, C. Bertrand Schultz, W. D. Frankforter
1951 *Early Man in the Eden Valley.* University of Pennsylvania Museum, Museum Monographs No. 6. Philadelphia.

Mulloy, William T.
1959 The James Allen Site near Laramie, Wyoming. *American Antiquity* 25: 112-116.

Nabokov, Peter
1967 *Two Leggings, The Making of a Crow Warrior.* New York.

Nimmo, Barry W.
1971 Population Dynamics of a Wyoming Pronghorn Cohort from the Eden-Farson Site, 48SW304. *Plains Anthropologist* 16: 285-288.

Novakowski, N. S.
1965 Cemental Deposition as an Age Criterion in Bison, and the Relation of Incisor Wear, Eye-Lens Weight, and Dressed Bison Carcass Weight to Age. *Canadian Journal of Zoology* 43: 173-178.

Odum, Eugene P.
1971 *Fundamentals of Ecology (Third Edition).* W. B. Saunders Co., Philadelphia.

Oliver, Symmes C.
1962 Ecology and Cultural Continuity as Contributing Factors in the Social Organization of the Plains Indians. *University of California Publications in American Archaeology and Ethnology* 48: 1-90.

Peterson, Roger Tory
1961 *A Field Guide to Western Birds. Second Edition.* Houghton Mifflin Co., Boston.

Pettipas, Leo
1970 Early Man in Manitoba. In *Ten Thousand Years, Archaeology in Manitoba.* By Walter M. Hlady (ed.), Manitoba Archaeological Society. D. W. Friesen & Sons, Altona, Manitoba.

Pilsbry, Henry A.
1948 *Land Mollusca of North America (North of Mexico).* Academy of Natural Sciences of Philadelphia, Monographs 3(vol 2, part 2).

Powers, M. C.
1953 A New Roundness Scale for Sedimentary Particles. *Journal of Sedimentary Petrology* 23: 117-119.

Reeves, Brian O. K.
1971 On the Coalescence of the Laurentide and Cordilleran Ice Sheets in the Western Interior of North America with Particular Reference to the Southern Alberta Area. In *Aboriginal Man and Environments on the Plateau of Northwest America:* 205-228. By Stryd, Arnoud H. and Rachel S. Smith (eds.). University of Calgary, Archaeological Association, Calgary, Alberta.
1973 The Nature and Age of the Contact Between the Laurentide and Cordilleran Ice Sheets in the Western Interior of North America. *Arctic and Alpine Research* 5: 1-16. Boulder, Colorado.

Reher, Charles A.
1970 Population Dynamics of the Glenrock *Bison bison* Population. In *The Glenrock Buffalo Jump, 48CO304.* By George C. Frison. Plains Anthropologist Memoir 7, Appendix II.
1973 The Wardell *Bison bison* Sample: Population Dynamics and Archaeological Interpretation. In *The Wardell Buffalo Trap 48 SU 301: Communal Procurement in the Upper Green River Basin, Wyoming.* By George C. Frison. University of Michigan, Anthropological Papers No. 48, Appendix II. Ann Arbor.

Rittenhouse, G.
 1943 A Visual Method of Estimating Two-
dimensional Sphericity. *Journal Sedimentary
Petrology* **13**: 79-81.
Roberts, Frank H. H.
 1935 A Folsom Complex: Preliminary Report on
Investigations at the Lindenmeier Site in
Northern Colorado. *Smithsonian
Miscellaneous Collections* **94**: 1-35.
 1936 Additional Information on the Folsom
Complex. *Smithsonian Miscellaneous
Collections* **95**: 1-38.
 1943 A New Site. *American Antiquity* **8**: 100.
Robertson, Jesse H.
 1969 Fossil *Bison* from Florida. *Plaster Jacket* **12**
Roe, Frank Gilbert
 1951 *The North American Buffalo.* University of
Toronto Press.
Romer, Alfred S.
 1951 *Bison crassicornis* in the Late Pleistocene of
New England. *Journal of Mammalogy* **32**:
230-231.
Rossdale, P. D.
 1972 *The Horse, From Conception to Maturity.*
California Thoroughbred Breeders
Association, Arcadia; and Deseret News Press,
Salt Lake City, Utah.
Roubicek, C. F., R. T. Clark, and O. F. Pahnish
 1957 *Range Cattle Production. 7. Genetics of
Cattle.* Arizona Agricultural Experiment
Station Report 149.
Russel, Kathleen D.
 1973 An Analysis of the Bison Dentition, Hudson-
Meng Site, Nebraska. *Paper Presented at the
83rd Annual Meeting of the Nebraska
Academy of Science.* Lincoln.
Russell, Loris S.
 1956 Additional Occurrences of Fossil Horse
Remains in Western Canada. *National
Museum of Canada, Annual Report for
1954-1955:* 153-154.
Sahni, M. R. and E. Khan
 1968 *Probison dehmi* n. g. n. sp., A Recent Find
of an Upper Siwalik Bovid. *Mitteilungen der
Bayer. Staatssammlung fur Palaontologie und
Histor. Geologie* 7: 247-251.
Sauer, Carl O.
 1944 A Geographical Sketch of Early Man in
America. *Geographical Review* **34**: 529-573.
Scheffer, V. B.
 1950 Growth Layers on the Teeth of Pinnipedia as
an Indication of Age. *Science* **112**: 309-311.

Schultz, C. Bertrand
 1935 Paleontological Evidence of the Antiquity
of the Scottsbluff Bison Quarry and its
Associated Artifacts. *American Anthropologist, New Series* **3**: 521-524.
 1943 Some Artifact Sites of Early Man in the
Great Plains and Adjacent Areas. *American
Antiquity* **8**: 242-249.
Schultz, C. Bertrand and W. D. Frankforter
 1946 The Geologic History of the Bison in the
Great Plains (A Preliminary Report). *Bulletin
of the University of Nebraska State Museum*
3: 1-10.
 1951 A Preliminary Report on the Bison Remains
from the Finley Site (Eden Bison Quarry).
In *Early Man in the Eden Valley.* By John
H. Moss. University of Pennsylvania Museum,
Museum Monographs **6**: 119-124.
Sellards, E. H.
 1955 Fossil Bison and Associated Artifacts from
Milnesand, New Mexico. *American Antiquity*
20: 336-344.
Sellards, E. H., Glen L. Evans, and Grayson E. Meade
 1947 Fossil Bison and Associated Artifacts from
Plainview, Texas, with Description of
Artifacts by Alex D. Krieger. *Bulletin of
Geological Society of America* **58**: 927-954.
Shay, C. Thomas
 1971 *The Itasca Bison Kill Site, an Ecological
Analysis.* Minnesota Historical Society,
Prehistoric Archaeology Series Publication.
Shupe, James L., Wayne Binns, Lynn F. James and
Richard F. Keeler
 1967 Lupine, a Cause of the Crooked Calf Disease.
*Journal of the American Veterinary Medical
Association* **151**: 198-203.
Shupe, James L., Lynn F. James, L. D. Balls, Wayne
Binns, and R. F. Keeler
 1967 A Probable Hereditary Skeletal Deformity in
Hereford Cattle. *Journal of Heredity* **58**: 311-
313.
Skinner, M. F. and O. C. Kaisen
 1947 The Fossil *Bison* of Alaska and a Preliminary
Revision of the Genus. *Bulletin of the
American Museum of Natural History* **89**:
123-256.
Slaughter, Bob H.
 1966 The Moore Pit Local Fauna: Pleistocene of
Texas. *Journal of Paleontology* **40**: 78-91.

Smith, H. T. U.
 1965 Dune Morphology and Chronology in Central and Western Nebraska. *Journal Geology* **73:** 557-577.

Smith, R. W. Jr., and R. R. Walker
 1964 Femoral Expansion in Aging Women: Implications for Osteoporosis and Fractures. *Science* **145:** 156-157.

Soper, J. Dewey
 1964 *The Mammals of Alberta.* Alberta Department of Industry and Development, Edmonton.

Steward, Julian H.
 1968 The Great Basin Shoshonean Indians: An Example of a Family Level of Sociocultural Integration. In *Man and Adaptation.* By Yehudi Cohen (ed.): 68-81. Aldine.

Stewart, O. C.
 1956 Fire as the First Great Force Employed by Man. In *Man's Role in Changing the Face of the Earth.* By William Thomas Jr. (ed.): 115 133. University of Chicago Press.

Stormont, C., W. J. Miller, and Y. Suzuki
 1961 Blood Groups and the Taxonomic Status of of American Buffalo and Domestic Cattle. *Evolution* **15:** 196-208.

Tappen, N. C.
 1969 The Relationship of Weathering Cracks to Split-line Orientation in Bone. *American Journal of Physical Anthropology* **31:** 191-198.
 1971 Two Orientational Features of Compact Bone as Predictors of Split-line Patterns. *American Journal of Physical Anthropology* **35:** 129-140.

United States Geological Survey
 1970 *The National Atlas of the United States of America.* Department of the Interior, Washington D. C.

Vander Hoof, V. L.
 1942 A Skull of a *Bison latifrons* from the Pleistocene of Northern California. *University of California Publications, Bulletin of the Department of Geological Sciences* **27:** 1-24.

Voorhies, M. R.
 1969 *Taphonomy and Population Dynamics of an Early Pliocene Vertebrate Fauna, Knox County, Nebraska.* University of Wyoming, Contributions to Geology, Special Paper No. 1. Laramie, Wyoming.

Vsyakikh, A. S.
 1969 *Principles of Livestock Breeding (Teoreticheskie osnovy plemennogo dela).* Izdatel'stvo "Kolos", Moskva 1964. Translated from Russian, 1969, Israel Program for Scientific Translations, Jerusalem.

Wasilewski, W.
 1967 Differences in the Wear of Incisors in the European Bison Living Under Natural and Reserve Conditions. *Acta Theriologica* **12:** 459-462.

Wendorf, Fred, and James J. Hester
 1962 Early Man's Utilization of the Great Plains Environment. *American Antiquity* **28:** 159-171.

Wheat, Joe Ben
 1971 Lifeways of Early Man in North America. *Arctic Anthropology* **8:** 22-31. Madison, Wisconsin.
 1972 *The Olsen-Chubbuck Site: A Paleo-Indian Bison Kill.* Society for American Archaeology, Memoir No. 26.

Wilson, G. L.
 1934 The Horse and Dog in Hidatsa Culture. *American Museum of Natural History, Anthropological Papers* **15:** 125-311.

Wilson, Michael
 1969 Problems in the Speciation of American Fossil Bison. In *Post-Pleistocene Man and his Environment on the Northern Plains.* By Forbis, R. G., L. B. Davis, O. A. Christensen and G. Fedirchuk (eds.). Proceedings of the 1st Annual Paleoenvironmental Workshop of the University of Calgary Archaeological Association: 178-179. Calgary, Alberta.
 1972 Review: Biostratigraphy and Palaeontology of a Sangamon Deposit at Fort Qu'Appelle, Saskatchewan, by Ehsunallah Khan. In University of Wyoming, *Contributions to Geology* **11:** 87-92.
 in press History of the Bison in Wyoming, with Particular Reference to Early Holocene Forms. In *Applied Geology and Archaeology: The Holocene History of Wyoming.* By Michael Wilson (ed.). Geological Survey of Wyoming, Laramie, Wyoming.

Witkind, Max
 n. d. *An Archaeological Interpretation of the Roberts Buffalo Jump Site, Larimer County, Colorado.* Master's Thesis 1971, Department of Anthropology, Colorado State University, Fort Collins, Colorado.

Wormington, H. M., and Richard G. Forbis
    1965 *An Introduction to the Archaeology of
          Alberta, Canada.* Proceedings No. 11,
          Denver Museum of Natural History. Denver.
Zaniewski, Leon
    1967 Observations on the Cross-Breeding the
          European Bison with Domestic Cattle of the
          Polish Red Breed. *Acta Theriologica* **12:** 481-
          486.
Zawasky, Peter
    1971 Age Analysis of Roberts Site Bison Remains
          by Dentition Analysis. *Student Anthro-
          pologist* **3:** 125-129. Boulder, Colorado.
Zeimens, George, and Danny N. Walker
    in press Bell Cave, Wyoming: Preliminary
          Archaeological and Paleontological
          Investigations. In *Applied Geology and
          Archaeology: The Holocene History of
          Wyoming.* By Michael Wilson (ed.).
          Geological Survey of Wyoming, Laramie,
          Wyoming.
Zhdanov, D. A.
    1967 Functional-Morphological Principles of
          Skeletal Formation. *VIIe Congres Inter-
          national des Sciences Anthropologiques et
          Ethnologiques* **II:** 393-399. Moscow.

Author Index

Subject Index

A
B
C
D
E
F
G
H
I